Commercial Awareness for Lawyers

English/Welsh Edition

First Edition

Commercial Awareness for Lawyers

English/Welsh Edition

First Edition

Andrew Todd, LLB (Hons), Dp Law, MBA
Solicitor, Glasgow

Iain Sim, LLB (Hons), DLP, NP
Solicitor; Company Director; and Visiting Lecturer at the University of Strathclyde

SWEET & MAXWELL

First Edition   2019

Published in 2019 by Thomson Reuters, trading as Sweet & Maxwell. Registered in England & Wales, Company No.1679046.
Registered Office and address for service: 5 Canada Square, Canary Wharf, London, E14 5AQ.

For further information on our products and services, visit *www.sweetandmaxwell.co.uk*

Typeset by Letterpart Limited, Caterham on the Hill, Surrey, CR3 5XL.

Printed and bound in Great Britain by CPI Group (UK) Ltd, Croydon, CR0 4YY.

No natural forests were destroyed to make this product: only farmed timber was used and re-planted.

A CIP catalogue record of this book is available from the British Library.

ISBN: 978-0-414-07155-1

Thomson Reuters, the Thomson Reuters Logo and Sweet & Maxwell ® are trademarks of Thomson Reuters.

Crown copyright material is reproduced with the permission of the Controller of HMSO and the Queen's Printer for Scotland.

TABLE OF CONTENTS

CONTENTS

CONTENTS

CONTENTS

CONTENTS

Appendices

TABLE OF CASES

Introduction

WHAT IS COMMERCIAL AWARENESS?

Job adverts want you to show it. Interviewers ask you about it. Employers expect you to have it—but what is commercial awareness?

Finding a single (or simple) definition is difficult. To misquote Justice Stewart: "Commercial awareness is like pornography—you know it when you see it". But do we? When lawyers are described as being "commercially aware" what are we *actually* describing?

Ask one person and they'll tell you that commercial awareness is about acting professionally. Commercial awareness is knowing and following the standards required to work as a lawyer. Are you honest? Are you discreet? Do you put your client's interests ahead of your own?

Ask a second person and they'll tell you that commercial awareness is about knowing you act for clients. Lawyers don't write academic essays. When lawyer give legal advice, it has real consequences. Clients will divorce spouses, cut people from wills, buy a home, change their business or even face jail based on what lawyers tell them. Commercial awareness means understanding that what you do has consequences and you must reflect those consequences in the advice you give.

Ask a third person, and they'll tell you that commercial awareness has nothing to do with being a lawyer or acting for clients. Instead, they'll say it refers to the general knowledge and skills required of business people: finance, strategy, operations, marketing and HR, for example. Can you read a set of financial accounts? Do you know the difference between profit, cash, capital and debts? Can you manage people? You're not just a lawyer, you're also a business person.

Who is correct? What is commercial awareness? Is it the first person who believe that commercial awareness is about lawyers? Is it the second, who believes it's about clients? Or is it the third, who believes it's about business? We believe commercial awareness is a combination of all three: it's about knowing you are a *lawyer* who acts for *clients* as part of a *business*. You cannot separate them.

Let's assume a client phones you and asks for advice. What happens? First, you'll need a phone. And, unless you're using a mobile, you'll need an office with a phone line. And that office will need lights because you don't answer calls in the dark. And you'll need a computer because clients expect a letter or email to follow a call. And you'll need money to pay for all of this—your office, your computer, electricity, a phoneline and, perhaps, most importantly, your salary. You'll need all of these things before you even pick up the phone.

When you answer, you need to be professional. You're a lawyer. You must be honest, discreet and independent. You must follow professional standards—and you've not yet asked why this client has phoned you.

And then your client tells you that they are looking for someone who can help them with a contract to purchase a business or write a will or sell a house or a thousand other tasks that they believe only you, a lawyer, can do.

And you don't talk about conveyancing, intestacy or tort. You ask them questions. You want to know more about the business they want to buy so that you can help them decide what the contract should cover. You show empathy and compassion when discussing their family and how a will can protect them. You try and help them understand the consequences of what you say. You're showing that you are commercial. That you are a *lawyer* acting for *clients* as part of a *business* and that you have commercial awareness.

HOW DO YOU DEVELOP COMMERCIAL AWARENESS?

How do you get there from here? How do students, trainees and new lawyers develop the knowledge and skills they need to demonstrate commercial awareness?

It's not easy. Think about driving. You can't drive a car unless you know the Highway Code—you need to know what signs to obey and what side of the road to drive on. But, once on the road, what happens if someone runs out between parked cars in front of you? Will the Highway Code show you how to perform an emergency stop? It might provide the knowledge of what to do–press the clutch, then the brake—but you need to turn that knowledge into action.

Commercial awareness for lawyers is no different. You need to turn knowledge into action. You can read this book and tell everyone you know how to negotiate (Ch.9) but, until you sit down with another lawyer and argue successfully to change a contract in favour of your client you're not actually negotiating. That's why in each chapter is a 'How To...' guide to various commercial awareness topics. We'll try, as best we can, to show you how lawyers turn knowledge into actionand we'll share the practical steps you can follow too.

WHAT TOPICS DO YOU NEED TO KNOW TO BECOME COMMERCIALLY AWARE?

There is no right answer to this. Commercial awareness is a combination of professional, client and business knowledge and skills. But that combination is different for everyone depending on what stage they are at and what work they will do. As a trainee lawyer, you may not need to understand your firm's business accounts, as a partner, you may deal with finance and cash every day. As a litigator, you'll rarely negotiate a contract, as a conveyancer, you'll always be negotiating contracts. As a family lawyer, you'll deal with clients with very personal issues–divorces, illness, bereavement. However, as a banking lawyer, you'll deal with commercial issue—sometimes just as personal, but often the clients will be more dispassionate about what they are doing. Commercial awareness will mean different things to you depending on what you do.

That's why we've tried to cover a range of skills you may need and why we've selected the most useful 'commercial awareness' topics for you to know and practice. Some will address professionalism, others will examine clients and how you give advice, while others will cover general business knowledge and skills. Very roughly, as there is a lot of crossover within topics, if you want to know more about being a lawyer then start with Chs 1 and 3. If you want to know more about acting for clients then read Ch.2. And if you want to know more about business skills such as marketing then read chapter 5, operations is discussed in section 2 and finance has its own section at the end of the book.

However, if you think we've missed anything or covered something in too much detail—or not enough—do let us know. Future editions can be tailored to cover the commercial awareness topics you want as a lawyer acting for clients as part of a business.

YOUR FUTURE CAREER

Commercial awareness is at the heart of every modern, successful business. If a business doesn't listen to its customers (or clients), it won't make money. If a business doesn't make money, it won't last. Just look at some of the high-profile failures on the high street in the last few years. Blockbuster once had thousands of stores, worldwide, renting and selling videos, DVDs and Blu-ray discs. In the UK, today, it has none. Blockbuster failed to understand that its customers no longer rented films from physical stores; the internet had changed everything.

As a lawyer, the pace of change may be slower. There's been no legal equivalent of a Netflix yet, but it's still there. Firms have collapsed, others have merged. The UK legal market is almost unrecognisable from a decade ago. Client demands have changed and you (and your firm) need to change with them.

Modern firms know this. A 2013 study of nineteen global firms, by Kings College, listed commercial awareness as one of the top three attributes they expect future lawyers to show. Law firms want lawyers who know what it means to be a professional, and someone who understands what clients want and need. You cannot expect clients to just walk through your door or email you out of the blue. And. If law firms don't change, if they don't recruit lawyers who are 'commercial', they'll be as relevant as Blockbuster. That's why job adverts want you to show commercial awareness; interviewers ask you about it and employers expect you to have it.

NEXT STEPS

It takes time to become commercially aware. No one can drive a car the first time they sit in the driving seat, no matter how many times they've read the Highway Code. You need to practice, and learn, and practice again (and again) until it becomes second nature.

Commercial awareness is no different. It's a continuous process as you learn to meet clients, negotiate, provide tailored advice, work efficiently, and work smartly to make a profit. It may sound complicated, but you won't know what you're capable of until you start. And, just like a new driver, while you may have a few bumps and scrapes along the way, in the end, practicing your commercial awareness will help you become a modern lawyer who understands your clients, your business and your profession. This is just the start.

THE SRA HANDBOOK

All laws and regulations are intended to be accurate as at 1 February 2019. However, on 14 June 2018 the Solicitor's Regulation Authority (SRA) published a response to its consultation on a new SRA Handbook—which included a draft of the revised Handbook.

The new Handbook is intended to be simpler and easier-to-understand. It sets out principles, codes and rules for solicitors and law firms, and at 130 pages it is more than 300 pages shorter than the current Handbook.

The SRA intends that that the new Handbook will come into force in 2019, after we finished writing this book but before this book is published. In order to provide you with an up to date guide to professional standards, we have based this book on the new Handbook as set out in its 14 June 2018 draft.

Iain Sim and Andrew Todd
27 February 2019

PART 1

BECOMING A LAWYER

CHAPTER 1

Becoming a lawyer

INTRODUCTION

It's Monday. It's your first day. You're nervous: you don't know what to expect as you walk into your new office. You're a trainee lawyer—but what does that mean? 1–1

Lawyers are involved in everything from buying homes, writing wills, helping 1–2 companies grow and expand, prosecuting and defending people accused of crimes, to even advising governments on how to behave. We work everywhere: law firms, private businesses, charities, public sector, in court rooms and, as you have seen these last few years, as academics in universities. We advise, strategise, problem solve, write, advocate, negotiate—the list is endless. But what does it mean in practice to be a lawyer? And how does it differ from being a student?

If you're a student just starting your legal practice course (LPC), the answer to this question may be a mystery. You have books and essays, but you've never dealt with clients, courts or fielded calls from other solicitors. You don't yet know what it means to practice law rather than study it. Working as a lawyer means taking your knowledge and using your skill and judgment to *act* on behalf of clients. It means working in a business and using that knowledge to make money.

You have technical knowledge, but you also need practical skills to use that knowledge on behalf of your clients. While you can read every book in the world about hairdressing, that doesn't mean you can pick up a pair of scissors and start cutting. You could read the Highway Code, but that doesn't mean you can take the wheel and drive. Or you can read every volume of Halsbury's Law of England, but that doesn't mean you know what to say to a client when they arrive at your office. You need to act. You need to become a lawyer who acts for clients as part of a business. And, in this first section, we'll show you why it's important that you know what a lawyer is and what a lawyer does because that's what your clients expect you to be—a lawyer.

Outcomes

This chapter introduces ideas we'll examine in-depth elsewhere in the book. We 1–3 kick-off with what happens as you start as a trainee. What are the big differences and changes you need to know from studying law at university? We examine how the reputation of the legal profession (and that of your firm) can shape client's perceptions of you. We then look at how you can mould your own reputation to help build your career. By the end of this chapter you'll know the difference between law students, trainees and lawyers.

YOUR CAREER: FROM STUDENT TO LAWYER

Student to trainee

1–4　　The difference between studying law and practising is the same as that between reading a book about swimming and jumping in the sea. Reading books and writing essays are useless without practice. You learn to be a solicitor through doing, and your traineeship is your chance to practice, practice and practice some more. You won't write essays. You'll rarely engage in legal debate. Instead you need to speak to clients and other solicitors about more mundane matters. What happens with the keys to the house you're selling? How do you get to court and where should you sit? When you study law, you don't need to open files and manage a mountain of paperwork. Nor do you need to choose between twenty emails arriving at the same time and decide which one to answer first. You can't learn all this in a library or a lecture hall. You won't even find the answers in a book; not even this one. You can only do it in an office, at your desk, surrounded by people who have done it before.

1–5　　As a trainee, you have a public persona. Whether as an individual, a member of your firm, or as a member of the legal profession, you're expected to live up to the professional standards all lawyers must follow. Your firm will expect you to be an ambassador, and your reputation amongst your colleagues, the profession, clients and the general public will grow. Your traineeship is your first chance to show that you have the skills, experience and judgment to become a great lawyer.

It's also your chance to make mistakes, which is something experienced lawyers should say more. No one is perfect. Mistakes do happen, particularly when you're starting out. Your traineeship gives you an opportunity to gain confidence, improve your existing skills and gain lots of new skills. You will not be the first to make a mistake, nor the last. When it happens, tell your colleagues—they'll have made exactly the same mistakes and they'll know how to fix it.

Trainee to lawyer

1–6　　As a lawyer you will start to build your reputation. If you work in a particular area of the country or in some areas of law you tend to find that peers working in the same field quickly come to know you. The profession is small: people know who you are and, if they deal with you, they will quickly form an opinion about you. There may be over 140,000 lawyers in England & Wales but, within that there'll be a few thousand in Leeds, and maybe only a few hundred who specialise in family law. As a family lawyer in Leeds you'll soon know the rest. London is the same. The City is small and those who specialise in Corporate Finance soon know those in other firms competing for the same clients.

When you start as a trainee you do have some protection. Any mistakes are assumed to be a result of inexperience. As a solicitor this protection evaporates quickly. You're expected to know and follow the professional standards expected of a lawyer and you're expected to justify your firm's reputation—and indeed your own. Other lawyers might gossip about you with colleagues and exchange stories about what you're like to deal with. Are you pleasant? A pedant? Can you be trusted in a courtroom, or on the other side of a boardroom table? All of these things create your reputation and—like your shadow—follow you for the rest of your career.

What is the difference between a lawyer and a solicitor?

In this book we'll refer to you as a lawyer. A lawyer has a wider meaning than solicitor. It refers to anyone who practices law. This includes solicitors but also includes barristers, legal executives and the judiciary.   1–7

A solicitor is a qualified legal advisor who carries out specific legal activities. Those activities are the administration of oaths, advocacy, conveyancing, litigation, acting as a notary and probate.

There are four routes to becoming a solicitor:

- as a *law graduate* with a degree in law, Legal Practice Course (LPC), training contract and Professional Skills Course;
- as a *non-law graduate* with a degree in any subject, Common Professional Examination or Graduate Diploma in Law. Legal Practice Course, training contract and Professional Skills Course;
- as a *legal executive* via the Chartered Institute of Legal Executive; or
- as a *foreign lawyer* under The Qualified Lawyers Transfer Scheme for lawyers transferring from another jurisdiction.

A barrister is not a solicitor. A barrister is regulated by the Bar Standards Board which sets the standards of behaviour expected from barristers and can take action where it needs to if those standards aren't being met. Most of you will start as solicitors, as you will work for a law firm. As your career develops, however, you can go on to train as a barrister or become a judge or academic. In other words, you may not always be a solicitor, but you'll always remain a lawyer. For that reason, we'll refer to you as a lawyer unless the context specifically requires us to refer to you as a solicitor.

YOUR CAREER: APPLYING FOR TRAINEESHIPS

It's all well and good to talk about your future career as a top notch lawyer, a razor sharp barrister, a fair and just judge, or a leading academic, but that career has to start with a first step: you need a traineeship. This book is not a guide to finding a traineeship. For that, we recommend you start with the Law Society and the traineeship sections on your university's website. However, we do have a number of general tips to help you.   1–8

Start early

If you want to work for one of the larger commercial firms, you need to get involved in their summer programmes. Firms recruit most of their trainees from these programmes. If you want to increase your chances of working for them, you   1–9 need to know not just the dates for traineeship applications (by which time many of the posts could be filled) but also the dates for summer programmes.

Look widely

1–10   Commercial firms and public sector traineeships are advertised early, and widely. Many high street firms, however, only advertise with the Law Society (if indeed at all). They may also decide to take a trainee at the last minute, when they know they'll definitely need one. If you're looking for a traineeship, you should be proactive. Don't just send a generic CV and covering letter. You should do your research and tell your target firms why you want to work for them. No one wants to feel as if they have received the job seeker equivalent of "you'll do".

Research

1–11   This chapter (and Ch.5) should help you to research firms so that you know what to look for. Ideally, you should speak to someone who works for the firm but, if that's not possible, use the web, legal directories like Legal 500 and Chambers, local newspapers and any relevant contacts to garner useful intelligence.

Attend law fairs

1–12   Law fairs are the perfect opportunity to speak to people who work in firms, to find out first-hand what they're like. Those who attend law fairs on behalf of firms are keen to talk to you, so don't be shy in asking questions. Good questions to ask might include:

- "How would you describe a typical traineeship at [your firm]?"
- "How would you describe [your firm?]"
- (And, because people like to talk about themselves) "What is your typical day like at [the firm]?"

Be specific

1–13   Tailor your application to each firm you approach. Why are you interested in that firm? Is it because of the type of work it does? Is it because of its name? Maybe it offers opportunities to work in particular offices (whether locally, nationally or internationally)? Tell them why you want to work for them. Firms are interested in students who are interested in them. You have to demonstrate that interest by customising your application.

> "I want to work for [your firm] because I want to pursue a career in civil litigation and [your firm] is ranked as a number one firm in this area. I want the opportunity to work on cases such as [list example you've found in your research]."

Or:

"I want to work for [your firm] because I want to help families and small businesses in Dorset. I was born and raised in Weymouth and I want to build my career here by helping the local community."

Be yourself

Different firms look for different types of people. Some look for legal brains, others for outgoing charmers. You can't be something you're not, nor do you want to spend your traineeship acting. Be yourself during interviews. Some firms will want you, some will not but, if you're yourself, you'll find a firm that suits you best.

1–14

YOUR CAREER OPTIONS

You'll take on different roles as your career develops. What follows are a summary of the roles that you would be expected to follow (along with roles required by the Solicitors Regulation Authority (SRA)), assuming you tread the traditional path of trainee to partner. We then cover some other roles that don't follow the traditional path.

1–15

Traditional roles

Trainee solicitor

You begin your career as a trainee. A trainee lawyer is someone who's learning to become a lawyer and has to meet professional standards, before they qualify as an:

1–16

Assistant solicitor (or newly qualified lawyer (NQ))

This is a junior lawyer. You start to gain more client contact and get to tackle increasingly complex work. You will often work with a senior lawyer, who will supervise you.

1–17

Associate

Typically this is a junior lawyer with more than three years post-qualifying experience. They have assumed more responsibility and are starting to be the main day-to-day point of contact for clients.

1–18

Senior Associate

This is a senior lawyer, with strong technical knowledge and experience. They enjoy significant client contact and even have some management responsibility for supervising a team of junior lawyers, on behalf of a partner, dealing with fees and some firm administration.

1–19

Partner

1–20 Historically, this is someone who owns a share of the firm. A partner is responsible for bringing in new business and keeping existing clients happy. They may do less legal work, so they can concentrate on management, finance and client relationships. They are, though, experts in their area of law and take charge of the most complex work. A partner actually might not own a share of the firm. This is a so-called 'salaried partner' —a solicitor who, as far as the outside world is concerned, has the authority to bind his/her firm and make decisions on its behalf but, in reality, has no ownership interest in the firm (and is not entitled to share in its profits). A salaried partner is paid a salary, which is subject to National Insurance contributions (just like any other employee).

A partner might also take on a number of different roles. These include:

Managing partner

1–21 This is 'The Boss'. Your managing partner is elected by his/her fellow partners, to provide strategic direction and to take charge of the management decisions relating to finance, marketing, Human Resources, IT, operations and other business functions. Your managing partner may work with a board of partners to help with specific parts of the business, e.g. some firms may have an IT partner or human resources partner to deal with these functions.

Senior partner

1–22 This has two elements. Your firm may view its senior partner as an ambassador. He or she is the firm's public face and is expected to play an important role in dealing with clients, contacts and the press. In some firms, a senior partner will have another role, too. He or she will chair partner meetings and act as the link between ordinary partners and the board (like a union rep). This is more common in larger firms, where partners may not wish to raise matters directly with the managing partner or board.

Other options

1–23 A number of new roles have been created over the last 30 years. These reflect modern business practices and the need to offer alternative careers for those that don't want to become partners.

Directors

1–24 This is a role that sits above senior associate, but below that of a partner. A director shares many powers and responsibilities with partners, but are paid a salary instead of a share of the profits. In return for being paid a fixed salary (rather than an uncertain share of profits), a director is unlikely to have voting rights and may be excluded from partnership discussions. They tend to have lower targets than a partner (in terms of fees billed and new clients won).

Of counsel

This is similar to a director, and is a designation preferred by some London (and global) firms. The name 'of counsel' originated in the US and referred to someone who was not an associate or a partner of a law firm.

1–25

Professional support lawyer/knowledge lawyer (PSL)

This is a lawyer who specialises in knowledge, legal documents and processes. It is an internal role to help provide lawyers with current information, documents and processes. PSLs are heavily involved in training, IT and (as knowledge specialists) providing support to solicitors on complex legal questions.

1–26

Legal engineer

This is similar to a PSL. However, instead of specialising in knowledge, they specialise in reviewing legal processes and devising new, cost efficient ways of working. A legal engineer often has strong IT skills.

1–27

Legal project manager

This is a lawyer who manages projects involving large numbers of people, documents and jurisdictions. They make sure that different teams are working effectively by ensuring that everyone knows what they need to do (and when they need to do it). They don't tend to work directly on transactions themselves; they just ensure the teams that do are managed well. We examine project management in Ch.16 (how to be a project manager).

1–28

Non-lawyer roles

Along with the roles a lawyer may take, there are many other roles and teams needed by law firms in order to be effective businesses. These include:

1–29

Business development

This is a person (or team) who assists with the work required to win new clients or manage a relationship with clients.

1–30

Facilities

This team manages the physical things required by a firm, whether it's paper in the print room, a desk in a boardroom, or the office itself. Facilities also deal with health and safety and may manage the people required to ensure offices work perfectly e.g. receptionists, cleaners or print-room assistants.

1–31

Finance

1–32   This team deals with all the cash coming into and out of your firm. It manages client accounts and assists the managing partner, cashroom partner and board with financial information and budgeting.

Human resources (HR)

1–33   This team deals with pensions, recruitment, pay, grievances and all aspects of managing employees. It may also assist with training (though this may be a separate department in larger firms).

IT

1–34   A firm cannot operate without an IT system. Larger firms have their own IT staff, while smaller firms usually need to outsource this to specialist companies that can provide 24-hour support.

Legal secretaries/PAs/typists

1–35   These are people who act as typists or administrative assistance for one or more lawyers. Many have specialist skills and are as comfortable reading and understanding legal documents as any solicitor.

Librarians

1–36   Law firms still have libraries, but the traditional idea of a librarian sitting among dusty books is no more. The majority of legal knowledge is contained in digital libraries and online resources (such as Westlaw or Lexis Nexis). A good librarian ensures that a firm has access to the latest legal journals, textbooks and online sources along with helping with any legal research that is required.

Marketing

1–37   This is a person (or team) who assists with organising events for clients, brochures, online materials and anything that a client might see or hear (see Ch.6 (Clients and You) for more on marketing).

Paralegals/legal analysts

1–38   This is a person who is not a lawyer but is qualified (through education or training) to perform legal work that requires knowledge of law and procedure. Paralegals usually specialise in a single area of law. For example, many conveyancing firms use paralegals to deal with settlements, or to deal with repetitive work. Baker McKenzie has established an office in Belfast and uses paralegals/legal analysts to assist with volume work. In July 2018 it announced it was to add over 150 new roles alongside the 300 currently working in Northern Ireland.[1]

Regulatory roles

Alongside the roles identified above there are two important roles required by the SRA. These are the roles of Compliance Officers for Legal Practice (COLP) and for Finance and Administration (COFA).

1–39

Compliance Officer for Legal Practice (COLP)

This is a role required by the SRA and was introduced on 1 January 2013. The COLP is a lawyer at your firm tasked with ensuring your firm's systems and procedures comply with (i) all regulatory obligations as set out in the SRA Handbook or under the terms & conditions it is authorised to follow; and (ii) all relevant legislation, regulations and rules that apply to the firm, its managers, or employees.

1–40

Along with ensuring compliance, the COLP is responsible for reporting any failures to comply any obligation or relevant law. In short, the COLP is both an enforcer and a reporter.

Compliance Officer for Finance and Administration (COFA)

This was introduced by the SRA on 1 January 2013 to deal specifically with financial compliance. Unlike the COLP, the COFA doesn't need to be a lawyer as long as they are:

1–41

- an employee or manager of the practice
- of sufficient seniority and in a position of sufficient responsibility to fulfill the role
- approved by the SRA for that role; and
- have consented to undertake the role.

The COFA is tasked with ensuring your firm takes all reasonable steps to comply with the SRA's accounts rules. And, just like the COLP, it must report any failures to comply to the SRA.

A COLP and COFA can be the same person. This is particularly useful for smaller firms where it may not be possible to separate the roles to different people.

---

[1] Julian O'Neill, "Baker McKenzie law firm creates 150 jobs in Belfast", *BBC News*, *https://www.bbc.co.uk/news/uk-northern-ireland-44714858* [Accessed 3 January 2019].

YOUR CAREER: BUILDING YOUR REPUTATION

1–42   When you start as a trainee or a lawyer you sit at a desk in front of a computer, with a phone, a filing tray and a new pad of paper and you think, 'Finally, I'm a lawyer!' But what does that mean? The first thing it means is that the general public treats you as a lawyer. Don't think of yourself as a trainee or be under the illusion that being a trainee makes you any less a lawyer. The general public won't make that distinction. You're not just a trainee; to your clients you're a trainee *lawyer*. And their idea of a lawyer will be based on three things.

Professional standards

1–43   If you hire a trainee plumber you expect them to fix your toilet. If you get a junior doctor you expect them to cure you if you're unwell. You may give them some leeway because you know they have less experience than a fully qualified plumber or doctor, but you still expect them to know one end of a pipe (or leg) from another.

In exactly the same way, your clients expect you to be of a certain standard. If they walk into an office in London or Newcastle, Carlisle or Norfolk, they expect someone who's honest, trustworthy and discreet. They expect a lawyer who puts clients' interests ahead of their own. In other words, they expect you to be professional. As a trainee, on your first day, you automatically share in the reputation (built on professional standards) that all lawyers in fact share.

The reputation of your firm

1–44   The second thing you may notice is that your firm has a reputation, and that reputation applies to you. As a trainee, no one knows who you are. You haven't done anything yet. You haven't spoken to a client or emailed a contact. You've only just arrived. But, while you may be an unknown, your firm is not.

Law firms come in all shapes and sizes. A firm can be large (500+ lawyers), medium (40+ lawyers) or small (2–40 lawyers). You can even choose to work for yourself, as a "sole practitioner". Large law firms with offices in London include Clifford Chance, DLA Piper and Eversheds Sutherland. They each have hundreds of partners, more than a thousand lawyers and offices right around the world. National firms (including the traditional large UK firms) include Shoosmiths, Womble Bond Dickinson, Ince & Co and others. They also include regional heavyweights like Hugh James in Cardiff, Brabners in Liverpool, Ashfords in Exeter and Ward Hadaway in Newcastle. Smaller firms include specialists and local firms too many to highlight.

Law firms also vary by type. Not all firms cover the same areas of law. They have a large variety of practice areas. They might cover traditional areas like corporate, real estate, banking, trusts and estates, insolvency, immigration, employment, environmental, IP/IT, insurance, intellectual property, criminal, or tax. Alternatively, they might specialise in a limited number of areas (or even just one, if it's boutique).

A firm's size is no indicator of how many areas it covers. A two-partner firm in Chester could provide advice about buying and selling homes, wills and trusts, family law, partnership law, litigation, commercial law, powers of attorney, statutory declarations, and executries. It covers a full range of services for individuals, families and businesses. In contrast, a firm like Slater & Gordon with c30 partners specialises predominately in one area, namely consumer law, particularly personal injury. It has a number of departments, but these are divided according to the type of accident, injuries sustained and the location or circumstances.

Regardless of a firm's size or the work it does, all firms have a reputation. A reputation based on what they do, what they say about themselves and what others say about them.

Personal reputation

Along with your reputation as a lawyer and your reputation gained as an employee of your firm, you have your personal reputation. On day one this will not extend further than your office. Partners will have read your CV, interviewed you, and have an impression about you (what you say about yourself and what they believe you can do). As you walk round the office and start working, people then judge you. Are you fast? Are you accurate? Do you ask smart questions? Do you produce good work? How do you treat people? Your personal reputation evolves (for good or bad) every day until it becomes known alongside your firm (and the profession). Together they make you a lawyer.

1–45

YOUR REPUTATION: PROFESSIONAL STANDARDS

Law Society

As a trainee you start with a certain reputation, because every trainee must meet basic professional standards. These include academic standards. After all, you need to sit and pass professional exams. You need to complete your LPC before you can start working for a law firm. You need to complete your traineeship and then be admitted as a lawyer. But why do we have standards?

1–46

In 1823, several prominent attorneys formed 'The London Law Institution'. Its aim was to raise the profession's reputation by setting standards of good practice. It also enforced these standards by disciplining those who did not meet them. The London Law Institution became the Law Society, on 2 June 1825. To be exact, it became "The Society of Attorneys, Solicitors, Proctors and others not being Barristers, practising in the Courts of Law and Equity of the United Kingdom". Not that anyone used this lengthy name. People called it 'the Law Society' and, in 1903, this became its official name.

Since 29 January 2007, the Law Society's original role of setting standards was separated into an independent body—the Solicitors Regulation Authority, which acts as an independent regulator of solicitors. The SRA was formed in January 2007 by the Legal Services Act 2007. It now sets the principles and codes of conduct which solicitors and law firms in England & Wales must follow in order to provide legal services.

On 6 October 2011, the SRA introduced a new outcomes focused regulation. This was a break from the past. Previously, the Law Society has set prescriptive rules. You will do something, or you won't do something. It was a tick box approach to regulation. Either you had done something, or you had not. There was little discretion to observing the rules. An outcome focussed regulation doesn't focus on a particular action instead it focuses on the outcome of the action. Instead of checking whether solicitors or law firms were complying with rules, it could check they had met the outcomes required. An example of the difference might help.

Under rules-based regulation, you would have a rule which said that every law firm must have a complaints process in place and provide clients with a copy. If you didn't provide a copy of it to your client, then you'd failed to meet professional standards even if you're client knew how to complain. Under an outcomes focused regulation, provided the client knows that they have the right to complain it doesn't matter whether there is a policy in place or not (though it may be good practice to have one!). Instead, a conversation could meet this outcome if the client was told about their right to complain when you speak to them for the first time. It's the outcome that matters—the client knows how to complain—not the process—the client has been given a copy of the policy.

We will examine professional standards in more detail in Ch.3.

Other standards

1–47　　Regulation has increased and, as a profession, we work in many different areas, both geographically and business-wise. Being a lawyer doesn't exempt you from following the same rules as everyone else and, depending on what you do, you may also need to comply with rules of the Financial Conduct Authority, competition authorities and other regulators. For example, perhaps the most challenging of the new regulations has been the anti-money laundering regulations. These require firms to put in place systems and controls to prevent (and detect) money laundering. These include systems to confirm the identity of clients and to assess the risk that they may be involved in money laundering.

Complying with the anti-money laundering regulations can be incredibly time consuming, particularly when dealing with individuals who don't have a lot of paperwork. For example, many spouses have their utility bills in the name of one spouse only, so many do not have their own proof of address. You might complain that the regulations are more appropriate for banks, which after all deal with transfers of money every minute of every day. Yet, you need to follow them, nonetheless.

Along with regulators there's another group that imposes standards on the profession—your clients. Your clients demand that you work in a certain way. This could be as simple as the demanding client who wants you to "always pick up the phone when I call, I won't speak to your receptionist", to formal service level agreements which set out targets for you to follow, such as all calls returned the same day or emails acknowledged within two hours. Some clients will even dictate who you may work for so that you don't work for rivals or act for anyone who might raise a court action against them. Client demands can take all forms. We know of one prominent supermarket that requires all of its solicitors to write in plain English. If they don't, they refuse to pay. Another expects its lawyers to work one day a year in their stores so that they understand its business better.

YOUR REPUTATION: YOUR FIRM

All law firms have a reputation. It might be for a particular type of work (for example, Allen & Overy for global corporate work or Bircham Dyson Bell for public sector). This reputation doesn't mean that this is everything that they do. Each of these firms does more. It simply means it's the first thing that may come to mind when you hear its name.   **1–48**

Reputation may apply to an area as well as a skill. A firm may be known as one of the leading firms in a town, city or region. This doesn't mean that they're the best, there are many other good firms in those areas, it just means that those are the first names you may think of when you think of a particular area. Again, you share in this reputation.

On day one at Bircham Dyson Bell, for example, because of its public sector reputation, your clients will assume you know how councils operate. If your firm is good at something, you're assumed to be good at it, too.

Measuring reputation

Legal directories

For larger firms, reputation can be measured. In the UK there are legal directories that rank firms based on quality of service and the reputation of their teams and partners. The two best known directories are *The Legal 500* and *Chambers and Partners*. Both employ researchers to review and rank firms. The research results are published annually. If you check a firm like BDP Pitmans you find, for example, that it's praised for its work with local government. The website of *The Legal 500* says: **1–49**

> "Bircham Dyson Bell's [author's note – who merged to become BDB Pitman] public law team is lead by David Mundy and Matthew Smith and is noted as 'strong in its specialist areas'. It counts local authorities such as Slough Borough Council, Three Rivers District Council and Bristol Council and the National Audit Office among its clients and covers areas ranging from regulations and health care to the environment."[2]

These directories are the 'who's who' of the legal sector, across the UK. They have dedicated sections covering each region and area of expertise. They're compiled from interviews with firms and associated organisations.

---

[2] See: *http://www.legal500.com/firms/2695-bdb-pitmans/2106-london-ec2v-england* [Accessed 28 June 2019].

Awards

1–50   Winning (or even just being nominated) for an award is an achievement. A law firm can use an award to promote itself and you frequently see winners mention the awards in their adverts and PR. Each of the main legal press titles holds their own awards ceremonies. *The Lawyer*, *Legal Week* and *Legal Business* each are considered to be important awards to win. In 2018, *The Lawyer* named Pinsent Masons the Law Firm of the Year, for example. At the other end of the scale, local business networks, chambers of commerce and local press all provide opportunities for firms to win awards and promote themselves within their local communities.

Other

1–51   For many firms, their reputation is based on word of mouth. What do people say about them? This is particularly true for high street firms and local firms, which draw clients from a local community.

Clients talk. People recommend one lawyer over another. You want clients to be happy with their service, so they recommend you to others. Conversely, if clients complain then this can quickly build a negative picture of a firm that is best avoided. What you want is for clients to talk like this:

> "[Firm Y] are quick with their advice and don't sit on the fence, which is unusual in a lawyer." (Testimonial posted on website for a national law firm).

Or:

> "I had heard all the horror stories about lawyers charging you for every phone call, letter and email that is sent on your behalf, but I was quoted a figure and that turned out to be the figure charged. This was even with me contacting [them] about nearly everything to do with both the sale and purchase (and a few other things as well), and not once was I made to feel that I was bothering them, and every question I had was met with a clear understandable answer. Thank you." (Testimonial posted on website for a high street firm).

Or:

> "[Firm X] has been my lawyer since 1999. I have got off with all trials that [they have] acted for me in. Most recently I was charged with assault to severe injury and permanent disfigurement and I was found not guilty by a unanimous verdict of the jury. [They] seem to always be a step ahead of the rest." (Testimonial posted on website for a law firm specialising in legal aid cases).

Benefits

1–52   In the USA, the career resource *Vault.com* has created an annual 'Law 100' ranking. This uses the reviews of 17,000 lawyers, who rank firms on a scale of one to 10, according to their perceptions of a firm's "prestige". Respondents are not allowed to rank their own firms and are asked to comment only on those firms with which they're familiar. The ranking provides valuable information about firms and their clients, and the way that reputation links them. For example, the Californian firm, Cooleys, is described by peers as entrepreneurial, tech savvy and a leader in its area. From this you can guess that its clients include Facebook and eBay (which themselves are entrepreneurial, tech savvy and leaders in their fields).

A good reputation reinforces why existing clients instruct you and helps persuade new clients to come to you. When Andrew was looking for a firm to help with a large house-building project involving more than 2,000 homes, he used legal directories and other sources to help identify which firms he would invite to bid for that work.

How do law firms develop a reputation?

Let's imagine you meet a client for the first time. You're charming and smart.   **1–53**
They're impressed. Within 10 minutes you've worked out what they need and you've helped them decide on a course of action. The next day you write to them with your engagement letter. It's a masterpiece of plain English. It's simple, straight to the point and explains clearly what your client should do next. There's only one problem. You have spelled their name wrong. Instead of being their 'hero', who knows all the answers, suddenly, you're inattentive. And what does that say about your firm?

It doesn't matter what directories say, what awards you win, or word of mouth, sometimes the most important element of any firm's reputation is actually you.

YOUR CAREER: OTHER OPTIONS

It's worth remembering that not all lawyers work for law firms. Some work for   **1–54**
businesses, the public sector or in universities. However, even though a large number of the profession works in-house, as a trainee you're more likely to be working for a law firm. Most trainees start with law firms, before changing direction after they qualify into areas such as:

Working in private practice

If you work for a law firm you might work for a billion-pound business with   **1–55**
offices all around the world, like Clifford Chance. You might work for a single partner on a high street in Devon. Both are law firms, but both are different and with different challenges. In general, we can divide firms into different types:

Magic Circle

This is the name given to five firms that once were the five biggest firms in   **1–56**
London (and are still top 10, today). These are Allen & Overy, Clifford Chance, Freshfields Bruckhaus Deringer, Linklaters and Slaughter and May. These are global firms with offices around the world. They specialise in the biggest corporate and financial deals (such as the £12.5 billion sale of mobile operator EE to BT). They don't do wills.

Silver Circle

1–57   These are the next largest firms in London. These include Herbert Smith Freehills, Ashurst, Berwin Leighton Paisner, King & Wood Mallesons, Macfarlanes and Travers Smith.

Global firms

1–58   These include Magic Circle and Silver Circle firms, but also include firms that have global offices. Some, like DLA Piper, are larger than the Magic Circle firms. Again these firms specialise in massive deals, but they may also have regional offices so as to work in the Midlands, Manchester and Leeds. They may share some deals and clients with national firms.

National firms

1–59   These are firms with offices throughout the UK. Examples include DWF, TNT and Shoosmiths. They typically work on UK deals that don't require a foreign office. They tend to be strong in regional cities like Liverpool, Manchester, Leeds, Birmingham or Newcastle.

Scottish firms

1–60   This is exactly what it says: a firm from Scotland such as Brodies, Burness Paull or Shepherd & Wedderburn (but can also refer to smaller firms based there too). These are firms that dominate in Scotland and that may have a London or regional office. They work on the largest Scottish deals, act for wealthy individuals and act for medium to large companies.

High street firms

1–61   Again, this is intuitive. These are firms that traditionally would have an office on the high street (in larger towns and cities across England & Wales), but might just deal with individuals, families and small companies.

Rural firms

1–62   Rural firms traditionally would have an office in smaller towns, in more remote areas. They may be the only firm in town and will cover a wide geographic area, and deal with individuals, families and small companies. They are also usually familiar with agriculture law and practice.

Legal aid firms

1–63   A legal aid firm is one that deals predominately with clients using legal aid.

Working for a business

If you work for a business, you're an in-house lawyer. Typically, you're referred to as 'legal counsel'. Senior in-house lawyers are typically referred to a 'legal directors' or 'general counsel'. The general counsel is usually the most senior lawyer and has a position advising the board of directors (and may be part of the management team). As a lawyer for a company, the company will be your only client. Your role will include giving business and legal advice, drafting and reviewing contracts, negotiating deals, developing opportunities, helping the business avoid risk, working on investor relations and managing outside law firms that perform legal work for the business. The size of any particular in-house department varies greatly. Some companies may only have one lawyer. Lloyds Banking Group, on the other hand, has over 400 lawyers in its group legal team. Some of those lawyers will specialise by working for specific departments within the bank. **1–64**

Working for local or central government: civil

There are lawyers at every level of government: local and UK. At local government level you're exposed to a wider variety of work than in the UK Government, where you're more likely to support a particular department. Depending on the department, you might draft legislation, review contracts that the government intends to enter into, and draft, research, provide advice on and enforce laws, rules and regulations. **1–65**

Working for local or central government: criminal

One of the largest legal teams you can join is the Crown Prosecution Service. As a crown prosecutor, you prosecute criminal cases that have been investigated by the police and other investigative organisations in England and Wales. **1–66**

Working as an academic

Lawyers in academia teach, research and publish books and articles on legal issues. They also spend time on administration that may involve tasks such as designing exam questions and answers (and getting these validated through the relevant committees) or dealing with student applications. Typically, an academic will start their career by undertaking a masters or a PhD. This may in turn lead to a teaching fellowship with a focus on lecturing, research or a mix of both. **1–67**

Working as a judge

An extremely small percentage of lawyers work as judges or tribunal members. Lawyers typically don't have the necessary experience and skill to become a judge until many years into their professional careers. **1–68**

Other options

1–69   A number of new roles have evolved. These include: professional support roles (as discussed above), legal engineering (which we'll discuss in a later chapter), legal project management (as we also discuss later) and specialist business development roles. Again, these tend to be for lawyers who have worked for a few years and gained the skill and knowledge to understand the legal topics they're dealing with, alongside wider business issues.

YOUR REPUTATION: PERSONAL REPUTATION

1–70   We're back at day one. You're sitting at your desk and you're wondering what will happen next. You may have worked for a law firm as part of a summer placement, but let's assume that this is your first time in a law office.

As a trainee you start with a reputation informed by your CV, application and interview. That is quickly cast aside as people get to know you. In your first week, the people you work with will ask each other "what's he like?" and "what do you make of her?" You're judged not just on the quality of the documents, emails and letters you write, but also on your appearance, your manner and your personality—that's just human nature. You may be the best lawyer in the world, but if you pick your nose at your desk, your colleagues will talk.

Be yourself

1–71   As you meet clients and talk to other lawyers, you develop a reputation that extends beyond the walls of your office. We look closely at how you develop a professional reputation in Ch.2 (clients and you). Networking, PR and social media can all help you grow your reputation. As a trainee, however, your first step is to show clients and external lawyers that you're a true professional. There are a number of tips you can follow to help you demonstrate this.

Firstly, remember that as soon as you open your mouth people start forming judgments. You shouldn't try to be someone you're not. Use your personality. You're not a robot. You don't need to be a particular type of person to be a lawyer. Some lawyers are serious, but many are not. Clients (and other lawyers) respond to you as a person, not as a character you play. Be open—be honest. That doesn't mean that you should tell inappropriate jokes, or gossip like you would if you were out with your friends. Showing a personality doesn't mean you need to be an extrovert. Some clients want a Rottweiler. Others want an egghead, with your nose buried in books. Showing your personality—whatever it is—allows clients to choose the lawyer they want. If you're not comfortable snarling, don't pretend to be an attack dog. You don't need to be a lawyer and an actor.

Avoid sharp practice

1–72   Don't get us wrong, showing your personality doesn't mean you should be liked. You're not paid to be liked. Rather, you should aim to be respected. If clients don't respect you, they won't trust you, and they won't use you. If other lawyers don't respect you, they may be downright suspicious of you. Being respected in a business context is about treating people fairly. It means avoiding sharp practice—i.e. pushing the boundaries of what is legal or acceptable. If you promise to do something, do it. If you can't do something, don't promise to do it, and then say you've changed your mind or, worse, say nothing.

Follow professional standards

We've come full circle. As a trainee you must follow the same professional standards as other lawyers. Not every situation that you encounter can be foreseen. This is especially true when you start, when every day brings new tasks and challenges. Fundamental principles, however, are always present for guidance. If you know that you have to be honest, you then know you can't act for a client who wants to plead 'not guilty' when they tell you they have, in fact, committed the crime. If you know that you owe a duty to your fellow lawyers, you then know that you should not mislead them. If you know that you must maintain confidentiality, you know that you shouldn't divulge information about your clients. **1–73**

SUMMARY

This chapter has introduced ideas that we examine more closely in later chapters. **1–74**
Firstly, professional standards are an essential part of becoming a lawyer. It's those standards that help define how lawyers act. It's your actions, along with your knowledge, that make you a lawyer. Those standards also define how clients view you. We look at clients more closely in the next chapter.

Second, your actions are shaped by the firm you join. When you start as a trainee you don't get to choose your reputation to wrap around you like a coat or jacket. Clients, fellow lawyers and others choose it for you based on your firm's action. We'll examine firms more closely in Ch.4 (Law firms) and Ch.5 (Law firms and clients).

Finally, as your career develops, your actions alone will come to define you so that clients will come to you not just because you're a lawyer, or work for a particular firm, but because they want to use you and you alone. We'll examine how you can build your reputation in Ch.6 (Clients and you).

CHAPTER 2

Clients

INTRODUCTION

It's Tuesday. You're at your desk. The phone rings. It's reception. A client wants to speak to a lawyer in your team. Your colleagues are in meetings and you're the only one available to speak to the client. What do you do?   **2–1**

    The first time you meet or talk to a client can be nerve-wracking. You don't   **2–2**
know what they might ask. You're scared you won't know the answer. You don't
want to look stupid. These thoughts are normal. We've all thought that before our
first meeting. We *still* think like that when we meet new clients. It's human nature
to worry about the unknown. The same applies to phone calls. It could be a
current client, it could be a new client, it could be about something you're dealing
with or it could be something new. A ringing phone brings the fear of the
unknown just as much as a surprise meeting.

    That's why preparation is key. The more you know in advance about clients
and the problems they face the easier it becomes to deal with them. But what do
you need to know? We believe you need to know three things:

One—technical knowledge

You know the area of law that applies to your client. You know the ins and outs of   **2–3**
the Companies Act 2006 and you can help your client if, for example, they're
looking to set up a new company.

Two—commercial knowledge

You can talk confidently about the issues that matter to your client. If your client   **2–4**
is looking to buy a home, you can talk about the local housing market. Are prices
rising? Do they need to move quickly to secure the home they want?

Three—personal knowledge

You know what your clients want from you as their lawyer. Some clients want to   **2–5**
be consulted on every clause. Others expect you to highlight "the important ones"
i.e. they want you to use your judgment. At the other end of the scale, do you
know if they prefer emails to letters? Do they like small talk? Some clients like to

chat for a few minutes, whereas others want to get straight down to business. You even need to know if they prefer tea or coffee (a client will remember if you get this wrong).

Knowledge in action

2–6   Technical and commercial knowledge can be taught. As a trainee, you already have years of technical knowledge behind you from university. You may know more about an area of law than your partner who, after all, hasn't spent the last few years studying the latest developments. Take confidence from that. You may also have a good commercial knowledge from following the news, working part time or simply being engaged in current events. In short, you're book smart. But book smart is only part of the story. Anyone can make a cup of tea (you just leave a tea bag in hot water). The real skill is making tea for someone else. You need to judge the strength of the tea; you need to know how much milk and sugar to add. You need to turn your knowledge of how to make tea into a cup that someone will drink.

Law is exactly the same. You need to take your knowledge and turn it into advice that your client will understand and can follow. You tailor it based on your personal knowledge of your client. And, if you don't have experience, you do the same thing you would do if making a cup of tea; you ask them questions.

This chapter aims to help you understand who clients are and what they want from lawyers. We examine different types of clients and summarise some of the business and personal knowledge you need when dealing with them. While this summary won't be true for everyone (every client is different, just as every person is different) it will give you a head start.

Outcomes

2–7   By the end of this chapter you'll know the difference between different types of clients. We'll look at characteristics they share, and the types of people, businesses and other groups who may instruct you.

WHO ARE YOUR CLIENTS?

Introduction

2–8   *You are in a meeting room. You've introduced yourself to a prospective client. You've talked about the weather and it's time to discuss why they're here.*

2–9   When you meet a client you need to find out why they want to speak to you. Do they want to move to a new house? Are they in trouble with the police? Do they run a business and need help with it? Secondly, you need to talk about what you can do to help. If they're buying a house, do they need help submitting an offer, or with a mortgage, or both? Finally, if instructed, you need to turn your words into action. If they're buying a house you need to draft the contract, order searches, check the title, assist with the mortgage, and complete the purchase.

These are the actions you must take after your meeting. Your meeting may only last 30 minutes, but the actions required might take weeks (or even months).

As a trainee, you feel most comfortable talking about the actions you plan to take. These are based on your technical knowledge. For example, you know how to draft a claim form. You can talk for hours about alternative dispute resolution. However, clients don't want to know what you know. Your client won't wake up and think, "I'd really love to know the difference between mediation and litigation". Instead, they're thinking, "someone owes me money, when will I get it back?".

Talking about cases and statutes is fine as a student. You're an academic, after all. You're learning, testing and challenging the law. You're expected (and indeed encouraged) to talk about laws and how they apply in your jurisdiction. As a lawyer, talking about the law can be too technical a conversation for your clients.

You know how to write a 10,000-word essay and debate it with your professors, but if you use that many words to explain it to your client, you'll traumatise them. Many clients don't want legal debate. They want to know that you can fix a problem; they leave the "how you will do it" to you.

This doesn't mean that explanations are irrelevant. Some clients may want to know what your plan is, but that doesn't mean you need to share your knowledge in detail. The best lawyers know what their clients want. They know when to speak to them, and in a way they understand. They know what to ask so that they get all the relevant information they need. This is what we mean when we talk about client skills, and this is different for each client.

Before we look at different types of clients, it's worth stating upfront that clients are just like you. They're not mythical beasts and they're not superhuman. They're no different to your mum, your dad, your brothers, sisters and your best friends. You can deal with people wanting to move home, who want advice when they're made redundant, or who want to divorce but be sure they have access to their children. Alternatively, you can act for companies. That doesn't mean you're not dealing with people too. While your file may say you're acting for Vodafone, a company cannot give you instructions. Companies don't talk, write, email or text. You still deal with people: employees, directors and owners. And, because you're dealing with people, there are certain things you can assume about them when you ask questions.

Individuals—civil

Most people don't speak to lawyers regularly. If they think of a lawyer, they probably think of someone they've seen on TV. They think of wigs, gowns and gavels (even though they're not used in UK court rooms). They probably know that lawyers have professional standards but might not be able to define them beyond the basic idea that:

2–10

- "they always tell the truth";
- "they can't tell anyone anything you tell them"; and
- "they'll fight for you"

Most importantly, they probably never deal with a lawyer other than at the significant moments in their life. Think about your own life: when have you met a lawyer outside of university or work experience? It may be when a grandparent died and your parents dealt with the estate. Perhaps you have been called as a witness and attended court? Or it may have been when your parents moved house (or you bought your first flat)? All of these are red-letter moments. For individuals, lawyers are associated with major life events. These events, when they do happen, can also be years apart.

This means three things when you meet them:

Individuals don't know much about the law

2–11 Many clients have no experience of distributing an estate, attending court or selling a house. However, they assume you do and that you can guide them through it.

You need to hold their hand

2–12 Don't assume that an individual understands everything you tell them. When a mechanic starts talking about fuel pressure when you take a car to the garage do you tell them you don't understand, or do you nod your head to pretend that you do? Many clients will nod their heads when you talk. Keep your advice simple and check that they do—in fact—understand. If they don't, your client can become dissatisfied (and you may never know it).

Whatever they ask you to do is important to them

2–13 Most individuals have a good reason to seek you out. No matter how small the task they ask you to do, you should treat them as if it's important. You might have a five-day hearing the following week, but if a client asks you about a simple will, it might be that, due to a recent illness, they're worried about care costs and protecting their family. It's important to them, and you should always treat client requests with the respect they deserve.

Individuals—criminal

2–14 If you're dealing with a client accused of a crime, you might not meet them in your office. Instead, you may have to visit a prison or a police cell. You can be called at short notice. Many firms operate an on-call service, outside normal office hours. You could get a call at 2 am asking you to attend a police station to act for someone who has just been arrested. If so, not only will you have the pressure of picking up their case at short notice, you also have to get to know your client as best you can in a short time (and in a highly pressured situation).

You also might have police officers in attendance. You want to try and find time to speak to your new client privately so that you can work out the best course of action. You can't panic. Your client is depending on you to help them, so you must appear to be in control of the situation.

One major difference between civil and criminal clients is that you have to tell people news they don't want to hear. For example, David (a newly qualified lawyer we know) was asked to go to a local police station to defend a man who'd admitted assaulting a bouncer with a flare. When David met the client he was told the man's wife was pregnant. The baby was due to be born a week later. The man asked David if he'd be released to see the birth. David had to tell him the bad news. A flare was equivalent to a firearm and, because of previous convictions, he would unlikely be released before his sentencing, and any sentence would be at least six years. David was called every name under the sun. It wasn't his fault. He told his client what would happen to him. However, clients facing bad news can 'shoot the messenger'.

Individuals—families

Many families use the same firm. Parents recommend lawyers to their children. Your firm is seen as the 'family lawyer'. The same tips apply to families as to individuals, but one other factor to consider is that the family may have a relationship with other lawyers in your firm. You're not the first lawyer they've dealt with. It might be unfair, but automatically you're compared with the senior partner who has just retired (and who had dealt with them for 30 years). They assume you know who they are, that you're familiar with all of their files (including that time twenty years ago one of them got a speeding ticket) and they might be offended if you don't know them as well as your senior colleagues do.

    When meeting a family for the first time ask colleagues if there's anything you should know, as they can provide all the background information that can help you know what the client wants and how to deal with them.

2–15

Individuals—high net worth

Wealthy individuals often need more specialist advice. Family issues may be more complex, as estates are larger and powers of attorney and trusts are required to protect assets for children (and grandchildren). Often, you'll provide advice alongside an accountant, or an independent financial advisor. They also tend to expect a hands-on approach from their lawyer. They're used, and expect, the best service.

2–16

Businesses—types of people

There are three types of people you may deal with:

2–17

- owners—the people who own the business;
- directors—the people who run the business (they may also be owners); and
- employees—the people who work for the business.

Businesses—types of work

Any business needs two types of work:

2–18

Operations

2–19 Basically, this is what a business does (its purpose). WHSmith, for instance, sells newspapers, magazines and books. Part of its operational business deals with everything required to sell newspapers, magazines and books. This includes paying suppliers and landlords for premises; preparing advertising and marketing for customers; employing staff; and buying equipment like automated tills that intone loudly that you have an "unexpected item in the bagging area".

Management

2–20 In order to run effectively, a business needs a management tier. WHSmith has about 15,000 employees. It needs HR staff to deal with things like training, dealing with problems, salaries, managing pensions and generally making sure that they're in the shops every day of every week, to help customers. Most large businesses require legal advice just to manage them, before they do anything to make money.

Owners and directors

2–21 You tend to deal directly with the owners or directors of small businesses. As businesses get bigger, the directors and owners take less of a hands-on role and you're more likely to deal with its employees. Just like any individual, an owner or director tends to seek you out when something important has happened. Equally, just like a family, the business may have a long relationship with your firm. Even if they're a new client, they're likely to have used lawyers before. It's worth checking with them what they like and what they don't. There is a reason why they have moved firms.

When taking instructions there are two things worth considering:

Instructions

2–22 You need to be sure you're taking instructions from the right person. This can be tricky with small companies, as they might be managed by one person and yet owned by a number of people. Many family businesses have one family member who runs it, with the others being shareholders only. Most of the time the person who gives you instructions has authority, but there may also be times when you need the approval of a board of directors or shareholders. Always check.

Mistaken identity

2–23 Some small business owners don't distinguish between themselves and their company (or companies). It's up to you to make sure that you don't do anything that you shouldn't. Sometimes this may involve reminding your client that the company has its own identity and that you need to ensure that any corporate governance is followed. This could mean that you need to see (or draft) shareholder resolutions or board minutes to confirm actions.

Employees

The larger the business the more likely you are to deal with employees (rather than an owner or director). It may be obvious from their job title what an employee does. You may also be able to deduce their seniority. For example, the title 'HR Manager' tells you what part of the business that person is in (and also their seniority). To state the obvious, they work in HR and they're a manager, so unlikely to be a senior figure. They probably report to someone more senior, whether in HR or on the board of directors.

It's worth checking with a colleague to confirm the position, so that you understand what that person expects of you. A title can only tell you so much. Each person will have a different way of working and expect different things from a lawyer. Andrew once acted for a developer. The main contact was a senior employee who had dealt with many lawyers. Before acting for him, Andrew asked his partner if there was anything he should know. The partner said:

> "Yes. He travels all the time and uses his phone for emails. He hates typing on it so try and write any emails so they can be answered 'yes' or 'no'. If you send him a long email don't expect him to answer it. Phone him instead."

Employees normally report to a boss e.g. an HR director. It's worth knowing the lie of the land, as you may need to change how you provide them with advice. Andrew's client, for example, reported to a board of directors. The board also wanted to know if there were any legal issues that they should be aware of. Andrew would prepare two reports for the client. One was a full report setting out the issues they needed to deal with. The second was a summary that his client could use as part of the board's papers, rather than having to summarise Andrew's advice.

Large businesses and public limited companies (Plcs)

Large businesses require a lot of legal work. BP operates in more than 80 countries around the world. It has almost 85,000 employees (more than twice the population of Lichtenstein). It has a turnover of £360 billion (equivalent to South Africa). And, if you run out of petrol, it has over 15,000 petrol stations to help you fill up.

How do you provide advice to a company bigger than a country? Most global companies act through divisions and subsidiaries, and also tend to be split geographically. If your firm acts for BP it may just act for its offshore oil and gas industry in the UK. Alternatively, it might just provide employment advice. The people you deal with usually are employees and the same advice as dealing with any business applies.

Some firms act for BP across the world. At the start of 2015, there were rumours that BP and Shell might merge. If they did, lawyers would need to do due diligence on each company and deal with the merger documents. This would be a global task. Hundreds of thousands of documents would need to be reviewed. Tens of thousands of documents would be needed to make the merger work in the 80 countries within which BP operates. Only the largest law firms have the people, offices, skills and knowledge to lead a project like this. If you work for them, you might feel like a small cog in a big wheel. Remember that your contact might feel the same—they're one employee out of 85,000, after all. In these situations, you're not expected to know everything. How could you? Instead, try and obtain clear instructions from your partner or a senior lawyer involved as to your role.

The difference between a private company and a public company

2–26   Along with size, there is another important legal distinction between companies. They can be private companies or public companies. While there are many differences between private and public companies (derived from statute and practice) the general rule is that any company that is not a public company is a private company.

What is a public company? Broadly speaking this is a company that has offered its shares to the public, usually through a recognised stock exchange. To do so, it must satisfy the conditions for listing. A public company uses a recognised stock exchange, so it can raise money by its offering shares to the public. This also enables shareholders to buy and sell their shares easily. In return for this benefit (and also to protect investors) public companies are subject to considerably more stringent controls than private companies. Many UK Plcs are, however, not listed on a stock exchange, so the owners should carefully consider whether they're happy to comply with these extra burdens, or whether they should consider re-registering as a private company.

As a lawyer to a Plc you need to be aware of the regulations that might apply. For example, information has to be announced to the exchange before the rest of the world. Breaching these rules, even inadvertently, can have big consequences. Before starting some work, Andrew requires all law firms to confirm they will keep an insider information list to confirm all the individuals who have access to information which may need to be announced to the stock market first. This list helps ensure information is contained before it can be formally announced.

Financial institutions

2–27   A financial institution is a business that conducts financial transactions (for example, a bank). Banks typically take two forms. Commercial banks (like Lloyds Banking Group and Barclays Bank) provide savings accounts to individuals and businesses. They provide loans, such as mortgages. They deal in the daily transfer and use of money. You see their names on the high street.

You won't find the second type of banks—investment banks—on the high street. These include Goldman Sachs, Morgan Stanley, Merrill Lynch and Deutsche Bank. They don't offer mortgages or personal loans. Instead they specialise in complex financial transactions. They typically act for companies and governments, either providing advice on transactions, mergers and acquisitions, or arranging (and sometimes providing) finance for these transactions.

Most banks appoint law firms via a formal tender. Firms are asked to bid to provide certain work (for example, securitisation for loans up to £100 million) and the best bids are accepted. Bids contain a number of conditions and may include detailed instructions from the bank about how it'll instruct your firm. For example, it may say that instructions can only be in writing from certain people. As a lawyer you need to be aware of these sorts of instructions.

A bank may be one of your firm's most prestigious clients. You won't deal with them alone. Partners, senior associates and other lawyers are also likely to be doing work for this sort of client (and know its procedures). Again, you should speak to them and ask how they deal with their contacts at the bank; they're best placed to know how such clients operate and what they like from their lawyers.

Other financial institutions include:

Insurance companies

Insurance companies don't just sell insurance. They also invest their customer's money into the stock market and other investments.

2–28

Private equity firms

A private equity firm is an investment company that raises money to invest in businesses in order to increase their value. Companies such as Blackstone or Terra Firma buy out financially struggling companies and turn them around through involvement in management and restructuring. If successful, the private equity firm will look to sell the now healthy business to another company through a merger or sale or raise money on the stock market by listing the shares on the stock exchange.

2–29

Stockbrokers

These are companies that help individuals and companies invest in the stock market by buying and selling shares.

2–30

There's cross over between commercial banks, investment banks, private equity firms and insurance companies. Different parts of the same bank may have different functions. The Royal Bank of Scotland, for example, is a commercial bank, but it also had a part of its business that functioned as an investment bank. It also provided insurance through Direct Line (now spun-off). Following the 2008 recession, and it's bail out by the UK Government, it is now refocusing on being a pure commercial bank again.

2–31

Every part of a bank has different objectives, and the people who work there view their role in different ways. A commercial banker may value building a long-term relationship with a client. An investment banker may only see a short-term gain. Understanding your client can help you work out what you need to do.

Local authorities and public sector bodies

Local authorities

England has 353 councils. Councils vary in size and geographic coverage but most deliver services, including: education, social work, roads and transport, economic development, housing, the environment, libraries, waste management,

2–32

arts, culture and sport. It also has its own operational issues to deal with. It can employ thousands of staff. It owns hundreds of properties and large tranches of land. All of these matters need to be managed, along with its duty to deliver services to local people. Their official powers and responsibilities are governed by statute. Some services reflect mandatory responsibilities. For example, councils must provide education for five to sixteen-year olds. They must also provide fire services and social work services. Some are discretionary, like encouraging economic development. Others, in turn, are regulatory (in order to comply with legislation)—these include trading standards, environmental health, licensing for alcohol and licensing for gambling.

A council governs every authority. A council consists of elected members (councillors) elected directly by local residents, normally every four years. A leader heads up the council. Usually they are the leader of the largest single political grouping in the council. However, not all powers require a decision of the council. Traditionally, a council delegates many of its powers to committees, subcommittees and council officers.

Depending on a local authority's size, the people you deal with may be from an in-house legal team or may be a manager or director of a department. Whoever you deal with, however, take care to ensure that any action is intra vires (that is to say, lawful). Usually this means that the decision you're implementing was taken the correct way by the full council, a committee, sub-committee or officer (as appropriate).

A practical aspect of dealing with local authorities is that you may need to provide advice around any committee or sub-committee's schedule. For example, if you're providing legal advice on a licensing matter, you need to know when the licensing authority meets (and from that extract the date it requires papers to be produced, so that members can review them). A practical tip is that you should always check timescales and make diary entries for all the important dates.

Public bodies

2–33   A public body is an organisation that delivers a public service but is not a government department or local authority. Public bodies come in a variety of shapes and sizes and cover areas like health, social care, economic investment, arts, culture and more. Notable ones include the DVLA, HM Courts & Tribunal Services, HM Prison Service, the Health & Safety Executive and Network Rail among many others. Just like local authorities, public bodies' official powers and responsibilities are governed by statute or statutory instrument. When you act for public bodies you should check not only what legal advice it needs but also how it *should* operate.

SUMMARY

2–34   The examples in this chapter are general. Everybody's different. The people you deal with each have their own personality and expectations. However, if you know what they want from a lawyer then you're well on the way to providing them with the right advice. It may seem daunting to deal with all these different types of clients. In practice you tend to deal with just a few. If you work for a big firm, you rarely act for an individual. If you act for a rural firm, you're unlikely to act for a bank. Firms, based on their location and the type of work they do, work for different types of clients.

CHAPTER 3

Lawyers

INTRODUCTION

You meet the client. They've agreed a deal to buy a business and, to save money,   **3–1**
they've also agreed that your firm will act for both them and the seller. What do
you do?

This is an example that highlights the need for you to think not just about the   **3–2**
legal advice that you give, but also how you conduct yourself. As a lawyer you
have a duty to your client, but that isn't the only duty you have. You also have a
duty to other lawyers, to the court and to the general public to maintain
professional standards. These include: trust and integrity; independence; acting in
the best interests of your client (which doesn't mean blindly doing what they
ask); avoiding conflicts of interest; observing confidentiality and maintaining a
relationship with the courts. How do you balance all of these interests? In
practice, if you understand how professional standards are set and followed, it
becomes a natural process. Professional standards are your guide as to how to act.

In this chapter we look at how lawyers are regulated in three ways by the
Solicitors Regulation Authority (SRA) via (i) seven fundamental principles;(ii)
by the Code of Conduct for Individuals and, (iii) by the Code of Conduct for Law
Firms. When you start working for clients, the principles and the codes help you
decide how to act. And, if a client tries to make you act in a way which might
breach your professional standards, such as in a conflict of interest as in our
example above, they help you decide how to respond in a way which shows
you're a trusted professional.

Outcome

By the end of this chapter you'll understand the seven principles and the two   **3–3**
codes of conduct set out by the SRA.

PROFESSIONAL STANDARDS

What is a 'professional'?

3–4   You may have heard the phrase 'the professions'. Traditionally, these were regarded as including architecture, the clergy, engineering, law and medicine (though the list has expanded as modern jobs have evolved). These professions had a different status to other jobs because they had requirements that set them apart. These were:

- a specialised training or education;
- a statutory qualification;
- formal apprenticeship;
- code of ethics;
- regulatory oversight by the government (or self-regulating); and
- membership of a professional body in order to practice.

We can see from this how you are considered to be a professional.

In order to become a lawyer, you must have complied with the SRA Training Regulations; passed the Legal Practice Course (LPC); completed the Professional Skills Course (PSC) modules and electives and passed the PSC Financial and Business Skills exam before completing your traineeship and been admitted as a lawyer. I.e. in order to become a 'professional' lawyer you must have completed your specialised education, obtained your statutory qualification, then completed your apprenticeship or traineeship, been admitted to the Law Society and be regulated by the SRA and follow its ethical code.

And it is this need to follow an ethical code that helps sets you apart from other professions or other roles. You are not just a business person, you are a lawyer. And clients will therefore expect certain things from you.

Why should you follow professional standards?

3–5   No matter where you work, whether London, Newcastle, Carlisle or Norfolk, your clients will know that you are someone who's honest, trustworthy and discreet. They know that you will put clients' interests ahead of your own. And, most of all, they will know that you are someone who understand 'the law' and can help them when they have legal problems. The standards are your passport to client's trusting you.

Remember, you are not the first nor will you be the last person to become a lawyer. You are joining a profession that is centuries old. And, on day one of your traineeship you benefit from the professional standard required to educate you; to train you and show you how to act.

How do you show that you're 'professional'?

3–6   Clients expect you to be professional. As we saw in Ch.1 (Becoming a lawyer), this is built on the reputation that lawyers have developed over centuries.

Originally professional standards were summed up the case of *Re G Mayor Cooke*[1]. It stated that professional misconduct was an act by a lawyer which was "dishonourable to him as a man and dishonourable to his profession" i.e. your professional standard was to act 'honourably'.

The problem with this approach was that it led to subjective judgements. If the only requirement was to act 'honourably' then it was up to each lawyer to justify his or her actions when accused of misconduct. Despite this lack of objective guidance, it was not until 1960 that the Law Society published A Guide to the Professional Conduct and Etiquette of Solicitors and another 47 years before it was updated on 1 July 2007 by the Law Society's Code of Conduct.

The Guide and Code represented a break from subjective tradition. They contained mandatory rules that all lawyers had to follow. No longer were you required to judge your actions as 'honourable', with all the subjective judgement calls that could involve, instead you were required to follow set rules. This made judgements calls simpler. Either you had complied with a rule or you hadn't. But many of the rules were criticised. They were thought to be too detailed and rigid. They didn't reflect how lawyers worked and they were not considered flexible enough to understand the differences in practice between a an executory for a high street firm with one partner and a £3 billion merger involving different jurisdictions at a global firm with 1,000 partners. Instead, either you complied with the rules or you didn't. No excuses.

This need to offer lawyers flexibility led to the introduction of a new system of regulation on 6 October 2011 with the SRA's publication of an outcomes-focused regulation code. Rather than enforcing rigid rules, the code would focus instead on the outcome's clients should expect of a lawyer. So long as set outcomes were achieved, then lawyers had the flexibility to decide themselves how to achieve it.

Today, in order to show that you're 'professional' you must understand (and follow) professional standards.

What are the professional standards for a lawyer?

You need to comply with *seven principles* and *two codes of conduct*, set out within the SRA Handbook.[2] There are seven principles and two codes of conduct: one for solicitors and one for law firms. 3–7

PRINCIPLES

Lawyers are important. As we saw in Ch.2 (Clients), you are involved in the biggest events of your clients' lives. You'll help clients buy their first home, you'll deal with the death of parents and grandparents, you can help them when they marry, you'll be involved if they divorce, you'll protect children, you'll save innocent people accused of crime, you'll ensure that those who plead guilty are 3–8

---

[1] 5 T.L.R. 407.

[2] On 14 June 2018 the SRA published a response to its consultation on a new SRA Handbook—which included a draft of the revised Handbook. The SRA has submitted the handbook to the Legal Services Board for approval and intends, as at the time of writing this chapter, that that the new Handbook will come into force in mid 2019. We have based this book on the new Handbook as set out in its 14th June 2018 draft.

treated fairly, you'll help businesses grow, you'll help people make fortunes (and protect them if deals turn sour), you'll stand in court and throughout it all you're expected to show you're a professional and justify the trust they place in you.

What are the principles?

3–9   There are seven principles and these are designed to set out how you should act, not just to your clients but also to the court, the public and to others in the legal profession. You must act:

- in a way that upholds the constitutional principle of the rule of law, and the proper administration of justice;
- in a way that upholds public trust and confidence in the solicitors' profession and in legal services provided by authorised persons;
- with independence;
- with honesty;
- with integrity;
- in a way that encourages equality, diversity and inclusion;
- in the best interests of each client.

We'll examine each in more detail

Upholds the constitutional principle of the rule of law, and the proper administration of justice

3–10   The rule of law is a principle that means politicians govern within their powers, that the law applies equally to all and that the law is certain. In his 2010 book, 'The Rule of Law', Lord Bingham[3] identified the core principle of the rule of law as being:

- The law must be accessible, clear & predictable.
- Questions of legal rights should be resolved by the law and not the exercise of discretion.
- The law should apply equally to all, except where objective differences justify differentiation.
- Ministers must act within their powers and not exceed their limits.
- The law must afford adequate protection of fundamental human rights.
- The law should provide access to justice, especially where people cannot resolve inter-personal disputes themselves.
- Courts and tribunal processes should be fair.
- The state should comply with international law.

---

[3] Bingham, Tom; *The Rule of Law*; (London: Allen Lane, 2010).

Upholds public trust and confidence in the solicitors' profession

It is damaging to all lawyers when one case of abuse of any kind surfaces. Good reputations are hard to win but easily lost. In an age when so many institutions have been rocked by scandal, lawyers cannot take public support for granted.

    3–11

While public trust in lawyers has remained high with a 2017 Ipsos MORI Veracity Index showing 54% of respondents saying they trusted lawyers to tell the truth and 81% said they trusted judges,[4] there are challenges. Whether a national newspaper branding Supreme Court judges 'enemies of the people' or the perennial image of 'fat cat' lawyers despite years of cuts to the legal aid budget and to the justice system. It's important that lawyers and firms show that they abide by professional standards and that the principles are more than just words as we'll show with our examples below.

Independence

Your client expects you to provide advice free of external influences. This includes, for example, any influence from your firm. Your firm might want to benefit from the fees associated with a five-week hearing in the Supreme Court. However, if you know that your client wants to avoid confrontation, mediation may be a better option for them and you have to advise them accordingly.

    3–12

Honesty

You must always act honestly and with integrity. This means you must not knowingly lie to anyone (whether clients, other lawyers or the court). You must behave in a way that demonstrates that you have personal integrity and are fit to carry out the duties of a lawyer.

    3–13

Lying can take a number of forms. At one extreme a lawyer who told his client that they were divorced and then forged a divorce certificate, clearly lied. However, not all lies are so flagrant. Let's say your client phones you at 3pm to ask if you've sent out a contract. You'd forgotten all about it. You can either tell them the truth, or you can tell them that it's "in typing" and that it will be sent later that day (after you write it!). What do you do? It's just a little white lie, isn't it?

Acting honestly also means that you shouldn't act recklessly. It would be reckless to tell your client that a contract has been sent out because you think a colleague has sent it. You could check and find out for certain. While, you may not have intended to mislead your client, that's what you've done by failing to check. It is vital that you always try and act honestly, even if that means admitting your faults.

---

[4] Reported in the Law Society Gazette available from *https://www.lawgazette.co.uk/news/trust-in-lawyers-edges-up-but-profession-still-lags-ordinary-man-in-the-street/5063936.article* [Accessed 2 February 2019].

Integrity

3–14   It's the same with acting with integrity. You'll deal with other lawyers every day. They might be on the other side of a transaction, you might face them in court, but you mustn't forget that they're bound by the same professional standards and should be treated in the same way you would wish to be treated. It can be hard to remember this, particularly in court when (in the heat of the moment) you view everything as 'them v us'. It doesn't matter how hard you fight; you must treat other lawyers with integrity. This means that you stand by the 'promises' or undertakings you make and you don't knowingly (or recklessly) mislead them. It also means that you don't speak to their clients directly, without their permission. Once a client instructs a lawyer, he or she is their spokesperson and you're not showing them respect if you try and circumvent them.

Encouraging equality, diversity and inclusion

3–15   As well as being the law, not only must you not discriminate against anyone based on race, sex, marital status, disability, sexuality, religion, belief or age you should encourage equality, diversity and inclusion. This could be in your behaviour towards clients and colleagues, but it could also form part of your behaviour on behalf of clients as, whether drafting employment policies, undertaking litigation or dealing in criminal cases involving discrimination, you will be expected to show the same qualities. This can be difficult. It could lead you into difficult areas where you have to decide how to balance the client's point of view with their right to access to justice, representation and the next principle.

Act in the best interests of the client

3–16   Acting in the best interest of the client doesn't mean blindly following a client's instructions. It may seem in their best interests (and sometimes the path of least resistance) to just do as your asked. However, if a client asks you to argue discrimination in an employment tribunal when you know that they're inventing it to leverage more money, you need to tell them that you can't do that, and that it would be in their best interests to avoid any arguments that could involve them (and you) lying to a court. While, not every example will be as extreme as this, you shouldn't be afraid of uncomfortable conversations and having to tell your clients that they be better taking a different action.

What happens if the principles conflict?

3–17   The principles may overlap, and they may come into conflict. In our example, it is possible to act with honesty and integrity when dealing with a conflict of interest. You client's may approve the conflict, your firm may take all steps to preserve confidentiality through information barriers between teams but do all these steps absolve you of your need to act with independence? Is your firm truly independent knowing that in acting for both parties it will benefit from two fees, rather than one. And, is it going to be entirely open with the clients if it the team acting for the buyer discovers a 'fault' caused the team acting for the seller? Will the firm want both clients to know it may have made a mistake?

The SRA has confirmed that if principles conflict, those which safeguard the wider public interest (such as the rule of law, and public confidence in a trustworthy solicitors' profession and a safe and effective market for regulated legal services) take precedence over an individual client's interests. Accordingly, the public interest in ensuring you, as a lawyer, are considered to be independent, may outweigh your interest to act for your two clients, even with their consent.

How do you evaluate the principles?

Balancing the principles can be difficult for trainees and new lawyers, because you may not know your client's best interests as you may not deal directly with them. You might be asked to work on a task within a transaction. You don't have the whole picture of what's happening and why. You may have a supervisor or colleague giving you instructions. You assume it must be okay, otherwise they wouldn't have told you to do it. **3–18**

A good example is page swapping. This is the practice of swapping a page in a signed document, to change a word or phrase. Usually this happens if someone spots a mistake. Perhaps there is a typo and, rather than have the entire document re-signed, it seems easier just to swap the page with a corrected version. Let's say your partner tells you to do it because it'll take a week to get everyone to sign it again and it'll annoy the client to ask them to sign it. So far, this seems entirely trivial. However, what happens if your client changes firm and has a copy of the original document that they then refer to in a court action? That document is lodged with a court and questions are raised as to why their version is different from the version you sent. Have you acted in a way that upholds public trust?

Ultimately, your reputation and professionalism are more important than being your client (or colleagues) unthinking mouthpiece. You're a lawyer and you know that you have standards. You have a reputation and a career that will last far longer than your relationship with any client. It's too important to risk for anyone. If you're ever in doubt, then speak to colleagues or the Law Society and ask for help.

CODE OF CONDUCT FOR INDIVIDUALS

You are responsible for complying with the code. Not your firm, not your supervisor or partner. You. **3–19**

There are eight requirements set out in the code. You should know what they are and the requirements set out within them. Together, they help expand on the seven principles. We have set them out in full below with some additional comments.

First requirement—maintaining trust and acting fairly

1.	You do not unfairly discriminate by allowing your personal views to affect your professional relationships and the way in which you provide your services.

2.	You do not abuse your position by taking unfair advantage of clients or others.
3.	You perform all undertakings given by you, and do so within an agreed timescale or if no timescale has been agreed then within a reasonable amount of time.
4.	You do not mislead or attempt to mislead your clients, the court or others, either by your own acts or omissions or allowing or being complicit in the acts or omissions of others (including your client).

This is self-explanatory. You must not discriminate, you must not abuse your position, you must perform all undertakings and you must not mislead anyone.

Second requirement—dispute resolution and proceedings before courts, tribunals and inquiries

1.	You do not misuse or tamper with evidence or attempt to do so.
2.	You do not seek to influence the substance of evidence, including generating false evidence or persuading witnesses to change their evidence.
3.	You do not provide or offer to provide any benefit to witnesses dependent upon the nature of their evidence or the outcome of the case.
4.	You only make assertions or put forward statements, representations or submissions to the court or others which are properly arguable.
5.	You do not place yourself in contempt of court, and you comply with court orders which place obligations on you.
6.	You do not waste the court's time.
7.	You draw the court's attention to relevant cases and statutory provisions, or procedural irregularities of which you are aware, and which are likely to have a material effect on the outcome of the proceedings.

3–20   Courts operate on the basis that they have the full facts needed to reach a fair judgment. Witnesses need to give honest statements (as far as they can remember) and lawyers need to provide information and legal arguments that cover everything a court needs to know. This means you don't hide evidence from your opponents (or the court) just because it doesn't support your case. Nor do you do anything that might affect the information a court receives from witnesses.

This requirement can conflict with the principle to act in the best interests of your client. You may think that it's in your client's best interests that a witness statement is not shared with the crown. However, if the court finds out, your actions will be far more damaging to your client than if you had made a disclosure. Now, you're not only dealing with evidence that supports the case against your client, you're viewed unfavourably (and potentially in breach of professional standards) because you tried to hide it.

Third requirement—service and competence

1.	You only act for clients on instructions from the client, or from someone properly authorised to provide instructions on their behalf. If you have reason to suspect that the instructions do not represent your client's wishes, you do not act unless you have satisfied yourself that they do. However, in circumstances where you have legal authority to act notwithstanding that it is not possible to

obtain or ascertain the instructions of your client, then you are subject to the overriding obligation to protect your client's best interests.

2. You ensure that the service you provide to clients is competent and delivered in a timely manner.

3. You maintain your competence to carry out your role and keep your professional knowledge and skills up to date.

4. You consider and take account of your client's attributes, needs and circumstances.

5. Where you supervise or manage others providing legal services:
   (a) you remain accountable for the work carried out through them; and
   (b) you effectively supervise work being done for clients.

6. You ensure that the individuals you manage are competent to carry out their role, and keep their professional knowledge and skills, as well as understanding of their legal, ethical and regulatory obligations, up to date.

Think about how we talk about legal work. We take 'instructions' from clients. **3–21** We give 'advice'. We're our client's 'legal agent'. You give clients options, you tell them about risks, you may even recommend a particular course of action, but, ultimately, you need a client to tell you what to do. You can't stand up in court and say your client is guilty without speaking to them first. Equally, you won't draft a contract without knowing what your client wants it to say or do.

For some clients this may involve issuing instructions about everything. Let's say you're asked to draft a lease for a client who wants to lease a property to Starbucks. Your client may want to know what every clause says as they've never leased a property before. They need to know what the process involves and how it'll affect them. Another client, a big property company like Land Securities, knows exactly what leases say and may only need to know that the rent will increase every five years. Different clients require different approaches. The ultimate goal is the same; you need to have your client's instructions before you can do anything. Knowing how to take instructions is a skill that you develop as you deal with clients. At all stages it's also important that you record your instructions. Then, if you're ever asked to justify an action you have an email, letter or file note to cover it.

Linda Moir, Senior Claims Technician for RSA Professional & Financial Risks Claims, sets out three useful tips to follow to ensure lawyers have a record of instructions[5]:

"A brief handwritten note is good; a detailed typed one is better—outline the advice given."

And:

"Ideally, issue a letter [*authors note—or email*] to the client to confirm the advice given —not only that advice was provided, but exactly what was said . . . Make sure the file tells as full a story as possible of the transaction, including clear notes of discussions with clients and of any instructions provided. Remember: memories fade, file notes do not."

[5] L. Moir, "Magic bullets" (14 December 2015), The Journal of the Law Society of Scotland, *Journalonline.co.uk*, *http://www.journalonline.co.uk/Magazine/60-12/1021099.aspx* [Accessed 29 January 2019].

While it's useful to know how a court will look at your files,

> "be aware that in any dispute as to what was said, a court will generally assume that the client—for whom the transaction is probably more significant—is likely to have a clearer recollection than the lawyer, for whom it was only one of many similar transactions in a career. The client file is the single best weapon available to those who seek to defend the claim."

You should ensure that you have proper instructions and keep a clear and accurate record of it in your client file.

3–22   The other side of taking instructions is confirming that you can act. You are not expected to say yes to every client who asks you to act for them. You are only expected to act if you have the knowledge and skill to represent them.

Former US Vice President, Donald Rumsfeld, once spoke of the 'known knowns', 'known unknowns' and the 'unknown unknowns'. What he was trying to say was that there are some things you don't know that you don't know, and that these are the most dangerous of all. How can you avoid something completely unexpected? The 'unknown unknowns' can be a problem for lawyers. You may think you know an area of law, like contract law. Let's say you're asked by a client to draft a £2 million contract between a construction company and a plant hire company, to hire JCB diggers. The plant hire company is to be paid monthly for the next two years. You draft this and, six months later, your client comes in and tells you that they've just received a demand for the remaining £1.5 million because they'd not paid last month's payment on time. It's only then, after asking a colleague, that you find that there's an Act of Parliament that deals with this issue. If you don't follow set instructions, they have the power to demand instant payment. You didn't know about this law. You didn't even suspect such a law existed. You have an 'unknown unknown'. Situations as extreme as this are uncommon, but it's easy to stray into territory where you think you know everything. That's why you need to be careful to avoid "dabbling" and only give advice on the areas you're comfortable with. Not everyone is a polymath. This doesn't mean that you can't research new areas. Many lawyers are generalists who know a wide number of areas. However, as the number of laws increase, it's harder to keep up to date with everything.

Along with the knowledge to advise on a particular area, you should also have the time to deal with it. If you have all the time in the world, you can advise on anything. You would have the time to research the answer and check that there are no unknowns. You'll rarely have time, though, to do everything as thoroughly as you might like. A client may phone you at 5pm and need an answer by 9am the next day. A client may be due in court in two hours and you've only just spoken to them. You need to act fast and that means you need to be comfortable with what you're doing, so that you can give the client the best advice in the circumstances.

We know that this standard can be intimidating. You may think that if you fail, your partner or colleagues will think less of you. They won't. They've all been in the same position. They know what it's like and they'd all much rather you asked for help than if you tried (and failed) to do something they asked. Trust us, if you find yourself in a situation where you're unsure what to do, ask for help.

Fourth requirement—client money and assets

> 1. You properly account to clients for any financial benefit you receive as a result of their instructions, except where they have agreed otherwise.
> 2. You safeguard money and assets entrusted to you by clients and others.
> 3. You do not personally hold client money save as permitted under regulation 10.2(b)(vii) of the Authorisation of Individuals Regulations, unless you work in an authorised body, or in an organisation of a kind prescribed under this rule on any terms that may be prescribed accordingly.

As trainees and new lawyers you will not be expected to know every requirement of the SRA accounts rules. Instead, we recommend that you become familiar with the processes required by your firm (which is required to follow the Code of Conduct for Firms and the SRA Rules). If they don't automatically offer training with their systems and processes, then ask for it as early as you can.

3–23

We will though offer one tip. Never send money to a bank account without phoning the person who sent you the account details first. You should check the phone number independently to make sure it is genuine too. We know of one national firm that receives 20 phishing requests a week. Don't get caught out by sending money to a fraudster.

Fifth requirement—referrals, introductions and separate businesses

> 1. In respect of any referral of a client by you to another person, or of any third party who introduces business to you or with whom you share your fees, you ensure that:
>   (a) clients are informed of any financial or other interest which you or your business or employer has in referring the client to another person or which an introducer has in referring the client to you;
>   (b) clients are informed of any fee-sharing arrangement that is relevant to their matter;
>   (c) the agreement is in writing;
>   (d) you do not receive payments relating to a referral or make payments to an introducer in respect of clients who are the subject of criminal proceedings; and
>   (e) any client referred by an introducer has not been acquired in a way which would breach the SRA's regulatory arrangements if the person acquiring the client were regulated by the SRA.
> 2. Where it appears to the SRA that you have made or received a referral fee, the payment will be treated as a referral fee unless you show that the payment was not made as such.
> 3. You only:
>   (a) refer, recommend or introduce a client to a separate business; or
>   (b) divide, or allow to be divided, a client's matter between you and a separate business;
>   where the client has given informed consent to your doing so.
>
> **Other business requirements**
> 4. You must not be a manager, employee, member or interest holder of a business that:
>   (a) has a name which includes the word "solicitors"; or
>   (b) describes its work in a way that suggests it is a solicitors' firm;
>   unless it is an authorised body.

5. If you are a solicitor who holds a practising certificate, an REL or RFL, you must complete and deliver to the SRA an annual return in the prescribed form.
6. If you are a solicitor or REL practising in a non-commercial body, you must ensure that the body takes out and maintains indemnity insurance that provides adequate and appropriate cover in respect of the services that you provide.

3–24 If your client asks you to do something that you have a personal interest in, you must tell them. This lets the client decide if they want to use you. A good example is if a client asks you to recommend a mortgage broker or financial advisor. You might receive a fee for referring clients to other service providers. If so (and assuming the fee is legitimate) you need to tell your client so they can consider whether that fee might influence your opinion and obtain their consent.

Sixth requirement—conflict, confidentiality and disclosure

Conflict of interests
1. You do not act if there is an own-interest conflict or a significant risk of such a conflict.
2. You do not act in relation to a matter or particular aspect of it if you have a conflict of interest or a significant risk of such a conflict in relation to that matter or aspect of it, unless:
    (a) the clients have a substantially common interest in relation to the matter or the aspect of it, as appropriate; or
    (b) the clients are competing for the same objective, and the conditions below are met, namely that:
        (i) all the clients have given informed consent, given or evidenced in writing, to you acting;
        (ii) where appropriate, you put in place effective safeguards to protect your clients' confidential information; and
        (iii) you are satisfied it is reasonable for you to act for all the clients.

Confidentiality and disclosure
3. You keep the affairs of current and former clients confidential unless disclosure is required or permitted by law or the client consents.
4. Where you are acting for a client on a matter, you make the client aware of all information material to the matter of which you have knowledge, except when:
    (a) the disclosure of the information is prohibited by legal restrictions imposed in the interests of national security or the prevention of crime;
    (b) your client gives informed consent, given or evidenced in writing, to the information not being disclosed to them;
    (c) you have reason to believe that serious physical or mental injury will be caused to your client or another if the information is disclosed; or
    (d) the information is contained in a privileged document that you have knowledge of only because it has been mistakenly disclosed.
5. You do not act for a client in a matter where that client has an interest adverse to the interest of another current or former client of you or your business or employer, for whom you or your business or employer holds confidential information which is material to that matter, unless:
    (a) effective measures have been taken which result in there being no real risk of disclosure of the confidential information; or
    (b) the current or former client whose information your business or employer holds has given informed consent, given or evidenced in writing, to you acting, including to any measures taken to protect their information.

Lawyers can't, in general, work for two or more clients who have conflicting **3–25**
interests. A good test is to ask whether, if both clients were sitting in front of you,
you would give them the same advice. If not, you have a potential conflict of
interest and you must inform the clients before you can act further, for either
party. In some circumstances you can continue to act provided you have told
them about the conflict, and they agree that you can continue. However, just
because you have consent doesn't mean that you avoid all conflict. If something
then unfolds and the clients are unable to agree, you may still need to withdraw
from acting for one (or both).

In some cases, you might not have a legal conflict but rather a commercial
conflict. Some retailer clients, for instance, won't want you to work for a
competitor, to obviate the risk that the information they share with you might be
passed to that competitor. Many large companies stop their lawyers acting for
anyone who sues them. That's why, in London, some law firms specialise in
banking litigation because the Magic Circle (and indeed other global firms) are
prevented by their clients from taking on banks.

Clients expect you to keep their secrets. Whatever they tell you should not be **3–26**
repeated (unless a court orders you to, or they intend to commit a crime). It can
be hard to keep secrets. Sometimes you want to talk about your work to friends,
flat mates, relatives and colleagues. You might be acting in an exciting court case,
or on transactions that are making front page (or back page). When Andrew
started as a trainee, he worked for a famous football club. However, he couldn't
tell anyone about it even though he knew the inside track on a number of big
sporting stories. Even one slip can destroy your reputation.

Take the case of Christopher Gossage, a lawyer with Russells. He told his
wife's best friend that one of his clients (an author, Robert Galbraith) was, in fact,
JK Rowling. This best friend revealed all on Twitter and soon the whole word
knew. Gossage said he believed he was speaking "in confidence to someone he
trusted implicitly"[6] but the lesson here is that you shouldn't share confidential
information with anyone. The rules don't have an exception for people you trust
implicitly.

Seventh requirement—cooperation and accountability

1. You keep up to date with and follow the law and regulation governing the way you work.
2. You are able to justify your decisions and actions in order to demonstrate compliance with your obligations under the SRA's regulatory arrangements.
3. You cooperate with the SRA, other regulators, ombudsmen, and those bodies with a role overseeing and supervising the delivery of, or investigating concerns in relation to, legal services.
4. You respond promptly to the SRA and:
    (a) provide full and accurate explanations, information and documents in response to any request or requirement; and
    (b) ensure that relevant information which is held by you, or by third parties carrying out functions on your behalf which are critical to the delivery of your legal services, is available for inspection by the SRA.

---

[6] Quoted in M. Kennedy, "Lawyer who uncovered JK Rowling's Robert Galbraith alter ego fined £1,000" (31 December 2013), *Guardian.com, http://www.theguardian.com/books/2013/dec/31/ lawyer-uncovered-jk-rowling-robert-galbraith-fined-cuckoos-calling* [Accessed 21 January 2019].

5.   You do not attempt to prevent anyone from providing information to the SRA or any other body exercising regulatory, supervisory, investigatory or prosecutory functions in the public interest.

6.   You notify the SRA promptly if:

    (a)   you are subject to any criminal charge, conviction or caution, subject to the Rehabilitation of Offenders Act 1974;

    (b)   a relevant insolvency event occurs in relation to you; or

    (c)   if you become aware:

        (i)   of any material changes to information previously provided to the SRA, by you or on your behalf, about you or your practice, including any change to information recorded in the register; and

        (ii)   that information provided to the SRA, by you or on your behalf, about you or your practice is or may be false, misleading, incomplete or inaccurate.

7.   You ensure that a prompt report is made to the SRA, or another approved regulator, as appropriate, of any serious breach of their regulatory arrangements by any person regulated by them (including you) of which you are aware. If requested to do so by the SRA you investigate whether there have been any serious breaches that should be reported to the SRA.

8.   You act promptly to take any remedial action requested by the SRA.

9.   You are honest and open with clients if things go wrong, and if a client suffers loss or harm as a result you put matters right (if possible) and explain fully and promptly what has happened and the likely impact. If requested to do so by the SRA you investigate whether anyone may have a claim against you, provide the SRA with a report on the outcome of your investigation, and notify relevant persons that they may have such a claim, accordingly.

10.   Any obligation under this section or otherwise to notify, or provide information to, the SRA will be satisfied if you provide information to your firm's COLP or COFA, as and where appropriate, on the understanding that they will do so.

3–27   You don't stop learning as soon as you become a lawyer. The law is always evolving. New laws are created. Judges make decisions casting old law in fresh light. You need to keep up to date in order to provide your clients with the best and current advice.

    If you work for a large firm, you're probably covered by a formal training programme, administered in-house by a training team or by professional support lawyers. This programme probably includes regular update meetings (where your team shares knowledge), seminars and workshops from colleagues (or external presenters) and skills workshops that are appropriate to the different stages of your career (for example, financial skills training when you start as a qualified solicitor, so you understand fees and billing).

    This doesn't mean, though, that you should forget everything we covered at the start of this chapter. Just because your firm has a training regime, it doesn't follow that it's going to be right for you. After all, we've already said that other people formulating your goals can lead to undesirable goals being set.

    You're in charge of your own career. While your firm might think you should have 10 hours of training on the topic of legal privilege, you're best placed to know whether that time would be better spent learning how to draft commercial contracts. Think about your diploma in legal practice. Some courses are compulsory; some you choose. Which courses did you learn more from? We hope you'll say the ones you selected yourself. Even if you have a training programme designed and delivered by your firm, you should still carry out the process of goal setting and pick the right goals for you and your career. Once you've identified what you need, speak to your Personal Support Lawyer (PSL) (or training partner) so they can help you.

Eighth requirement—when you are providing services to the public or a section of the public

Client identification

1. You identify who you are acting for in relation to any matter.

Complaints handling

2. You ensure that, as appropriate in the circumstances, you either establish and maintain, or participate in, a procedure for handling complaints in relation to the legal services you provide.
3. You ensure that clients are informed in writing at the time of engagement about:
   (a) their right to complain to you about your services and your charges;
   (b) how a complaint can be made and to whom; and
   (c) any right they have to make a complaint to the Legal Ombudsman and when they can make any such complaint.
4. You ensure that when clients have made a complaint to you, if this has not been resolved to the client's satisfaction within eight weeks following the making of a complaint they are informed, in writing:
   (a) of any right they have to complain to the Legal Ombudsman, the time frame for doing so and full details of how to contact the Legal Ombudsman; and
   (b) if a complaint has been brought and your complaints procedure has been exhausted:
      (i) that you cannot settle the complaint;
      (ii) of the name and website address of an alternative dispute resolution (ADR) approved body which would be competent to deal with the complaint; and
      (iii) whether you agree to use the scheme operated by that body.
5. You ensure that complaints are dealt with promptly, fairly, and free of charge.

Client information and publicity

6. You give clients information in a way they can understand. You ensure they are in a position to make informed decisions about the services they need, how their matter will be handled and the options available to them.
7. You ensure that clients receive the best possible information about how their matter will be priced and, both at the time of engagement and when appropriate as their matter progresses, about the likely overall cost of the matter and any costs incurred.
8. You ensure that any publicity in relation to your practice is accurate and not misleading, including that relating to your charges and the circumstances in which interest is payable by or to clients.
9. You do not make unsolicited approaches to members of the public, with the exception of current or former clients, in order to advertise legal services provided by you, or your business or employer.
10. You ensure that clients understand whether and how the services you provide are regulated. This includes:
    (a) explaining which activities will be carried out by you, as an authorised person;

> (b) explaining which services provided by you, your business or employer, and any separate business are regulated by an approved regulator; and
> (c) ensuring that you do not represent any business or employer which is not authorised by the SRA, including any separate business, as being regulated by the SRA.
> 11. You ensure that clients understand the regulatory protections available to them.

3–28   Your firm should have known your client (based on anti-money laundering regulations) and a complaints procedure in place. You should confirm how these operate and the actions you are required to take. For example, you should be required to confirm your client's identity when acting for someone new. Equally, you should inform your client in writing of how they can complain every time you start a new transaction.

We will examine the publicity guidelines in Ch.6 (Clients and you).

CODE OF CONDUCT FOR FIRMS

3–29   The Code of Conduct for Firms sets out the standards and controls that must be followed by all managers of a firm (all partners, members, directors or sole principals). Each is jointly and severally responsible for compliance with the code. The SRA may also take action against employees working within the firm for any breaches for which they are responsible. A failure or breach may be serious either in isolation or because it comprises a persistent or concerning pattern of behaviour.

The code of conduct complements and expands on the code for individuals. For example, while the code for individuals requires you to promote diversity, the code for firms includes specific requirements to publish workforce diversity data as part of the profession's push for greater inclusivity.

For the latest version of the code of conduct see the SRA's website.[7]

OTHER STANDARDS

3–30   As we discussed in Ch.1 (becoming a lawyer), regulation has increased and, as a profession, we work in many different areas, both geographically and business-wise. Being a lawyer doesn't exempt you from following the same rules as everyone else and, depending on what you do, you may also need to comply with rules of the Financial Conduct Authority, competition authorities and other regulators. To those we would also mention:

---

[7] https://www.sra.org.uk/.

UK Finance (formerly known as Council of Mortgage Lenders (CML))

UK Finance is the main trade body representing UK mortgage lenders. It includes banks, building societies, and other lenders who, together, account for around 95% of the nation's residential lending. All lawyers involved in residential lending should be aware of the UK Finance Mortgage Lenders' Handbook. It provides comprehensive instructions for lawyers and licensed conveyancers acting on behalf of lenders in conveyancing transactions. The Handbook covers general instructions that apply to all lenders, and specific instructions from specific lenders. If you're acting for Lloyd's Banking Group, you should check the Handbook to find out what general instructions apply and if the bank has any specific instructions you need to follow.

3–31

Client requirements under contract law

Individual clients may require you to adopt standards, too. Large companies, for example, may have a service level agreement that contains targets, such as returning calls the same day or acknowledging emails within two hours. At the other end of the spectrum, a client may ask you only to phone them in the afternoon. However, whatever they ask you to do you must comply with the professional standards set by the Law Society. If a client asks you to do something that would cause you to breach the standards, you should refuse, explain why and, if they persist, withdraw from acting for them.

3–32

WHAT TO DO WHEN YOU FIND YOURSELF IN A DIFFICULT POSITION

Remember, professional standards are like the Highway Code. They'll tell you what to do and how to behave, but it's up to you, ultimately, to comply. The Highway Code tells you how to drive on a motorway, but it's up to you to work out how to drive on the M25 at 5pm, in a three-mile tailback, with impatient cars darting from lane to lane. The professional standards are no different. They may tell you not to act in a conflict of interest scenario, but what happens when a client who has used your firm for 30 years asks you to act for both him and his wife in a "simple transaction", and gets angry when you say you can't? Life can't be lived by paper rules. You'll have times when you don't know what to do. In those situations, you can turn to:

3–33

- colleagues;
- friends;
- the Law Society; or
- LawCare.

Colleagues and friends

3–34   If you find yourself in a difficult position you should always tell your colleagues. This is easier in larger firms, as there are more people to speak to who can give you an independent view. You may even wish to speak to your client relations partner; he or she will be keen to help, to deal with any issues as soon as possible. You may be nervous about talking to others. You want to appear as if you know what you're doing. It's hard to admit you've made a mistake. That's only natural. What you'll find, though, is that your colleagues will have been in the same sort of position themselves. They'll know how you're feeling, they'll have a good idea what to do next, and they won't look down on you for bringing it up. In fact, they'll be pleased that you've raised it and that you haven't tried to hide it.

        If you work in a smaller firm it can be a bit harder to speak to colleagues. If so, speak to your friends in other firms. You must abide by confidentiality rules, but you can still speak to them generally. "A problem shared is a problem halved" is a cliché, because it's true. If you need independent advice, you can speak to the Law Society.

Practice Advice Service at the Law Society

3–35   If you have a query relating to lawyer rules or are looking for guidance, you can call the Law Society's team of lawyers on the Practice Advice Service on 020 7320 5675. The Law Society helpline provides confidential support and advice.

        In addition to the main Practice Advice line, the Law Society also runs two other helplines:

- Lawyerline—this provides advice to lawyers on client care issues and how to deal with complaints.
- Pastoral Care—the Law Society can help refer lawyers needing professional or personal support to appropriate organisations offering legal advice and emotional support, such as LawCare below.

LawCare

3–36   If you're dealing with a difficult situation, you may be stressed or depressed. You may feel you're relying on alcohol or drugs to help you cope. If so, you can speak to LawCare, a specialist charity that deals with lawyers who are experiencing personal issues. LawCare can be contacted by email or, anonymously, by phone via its helpline 0800 279 6888.

SUMMARY

3–37   As your career develops from trainee through lawyer to, perhaps, becoming a partner, your professional reputation goes with you. That reputation is built on professional standards and it's up to you to live up to those standards. It may not be easy but if you know what they are (and who to turn to when you need help) you'll go a long way to showing clients and colleagues that you are a professional lawyer.

CHAPTER 4

Law firms[1]

INTRODUCTION

It's Wednesday. You have a meeting at another law firm, just one street away. You walk into its reception and you notice that it's very different from your office. It looks like Starbucks; your reception looks like a bus station waiting room. Behind it, you see lawyers sitting in a plush, open plan office space. Your office is filled with small rooms.

4–1

Even the name is different. They're called 'Lawyers4U'. Your firm is named after its eighteenth-century founding partners. How can two firms that work in almost the same place, for the same people, and do essentially the same work, be so different?

Everyone knows what a lawyers' office should look like. It's wood-panelled. There's a big desk, surrounded by books on statutes and cases. It's old, traditional and timeless. Or is it? the reality is that you probably will not see an office like this in 2019. When you start, you might work for a wide variety of firms. You can work in a high street firm in Derby or Slough, working for individuals, families or small businesses. You can work for a criminal law practice beside a local magistrate court, with clients drawn from police cells and accused of crimes they 'absolutely didn't do'. You can work for estate agencies/legal firms, which operate across England and specialise in residential conveyancing. You can work for national firms with large city centre offices, and clients drawn from the public sector and household name businesses. You may even work for global firms on multi-national deals involving FTSE 100 companies.

4–2

That's not all, as we learned in Ch.1 (Becoming a lawyer), a large number of lawyers works in-house in the public and private sectors and, for them, giving advice is only part of their role. They work directly for (and often as part of) a board of directors or, in the public sector, as part of a management team for a local authority. They're business people as much as they're lawyers.

And that's just in England. You can work around the world. If you go to London, you could join an international firm and work in offices from Singapore to New York. You have more opportunities than ever before. When you look out the window of your office you might be looking at Albert Square in Manchester, Canary Wharf or the Empire State Building. Yet, to most people, there's only one type of law firm, and it has a large desk, a small library and a wood-panelled

---

[1] We refer to the history of Dundas & Wilson and Slaughter & May throughout this chapter. We are indebted to Burns D; *Dundas & Wilson CS: The First 200 Years*; (Dundas & Wilson) and Dennet L; *Slaughter & May A Century in the City*; (Granta Editions) for historic information about both firms.

office. That's where your friends and family imagine you work. Yet, there are hundreds of different types of law firms. This chapter and the next examine how these firms differ and why.

Outcomes

4–3   In the last ten years, law firms have undergone big changes. These changes continue to shape both what they do and how they do it. This chapter shows you how changes have led law firms to alter the way in which they work, from simple things (like changing their name, or the location of an office) to more complicated matters (like the way the firm is structured to deal with client matters). We illustrate these types of decision by tracing the history of a single firm, to demonstrate how client demand helped it grow from two partners to national firm to one of the largest firms in the world.

DIFFERENCES BETWEEN LAW FIRMS

4–4   Each year the legal press publishes comprehensive lists of the UK's biggest and most powerful law firms. You can find these in *The Lawyer*, *Legal Week* and *Legal Business*. The lists measure and rank firms based on the number of partners they have; the number of lawyers and staff they employ; the profits they make; and their turnover for the previous year. The lists tell you which firms make the most money; which have the most staff; and how they compare year on year. Are firms increasing in size? Are profits rising? How much are partners paid?

In the last eight years many of the biggest names in the UK legal market (that had been around for centuries) have disappeared. Cobbetts, Halliwells and Heller Ehrman. Globally, Kings Wood Malleson and Dewey & Leboeuf are no more. The last 10 years have seen unprecedented change.

Other changes are less obvious. Many firms have changed their internal structures so that their management improved. Instead of being run by a partnership (with all partners having an equal say in management) today it's more common to find firms run by a management team, led by one person (a managing partner or chief executive) who makes most of the decisions.

These changes are inevitable and are part of the reason why firms that you might think should be identical are, in fact, radically different. Each firm has responded to change in a unique way. The decisions made over the life of a firm result in the firm you see today. We can demonstrate this best by examining the decisions made by one firm over the last 250 years. Our case study is Dundas & Wilson, originally Scotland's biggest law firm before it became a national firm, and then a global one, first as part of Anderson Legal before, in 2014, it merged with CMS Cameron McKenna Nabarro, the sixth largest law firm in the world. In the following section we'll use its history to examine wider issues and choices for all UK firms.

THE HISTORY OF A LAW FIRM: DUNDAS & WILSON & CMS CAMERON MCKENNA OLSWANG (CMS)

Dundas & Wilson was founded in Edinburgh in 1759 and joined CMS in May 2014. Over 250 years it grew from just one partner to having over 1,500 partners globally, in the early 2000s. It led the way in changing how law firms operate by introducing specialist partners, new technology and new processes. It's an excellent example to show the choices that law firms can make when responding to change, whether it's choosing an office, choosing a name, selecting partners, making difficult business decisions (like making people redundant), expanding nationally and then globally, or deciding on a growth strategy.   4–5

Choosing an office

In 1759, if you were walking along Chamber Street in Edinburgh you wouldn't see the National Museum of Scotland, as you would today. Instead you'd pass the Duke of Douglas gardens and the new law office of David Erskine, the founder of Dundas & Wilson. You might wonder why Erskine would choose to open his office in Chamber Street. The reasons were simple—and the principles are still followed today. Erskine worked in Chamber Street because it was a few minutes' walk from the civil and criminal courts at Parliament House. He wanted an office that was convenient, close to court and which was easy for clients to visit.   4–6

It was no different in the City of London. Slaughter & May's first office was at 18 Austin Friars, close to their former firm of Ashurst Morris Crisp, who worked with them for the same clients. Those clients could then easily speak to partners at both firms.

We still see lawyers choosing offices that lie near courts, or near clients and contacts, whether it's the global firms with offices in the City, or national firms opening offices in the most prestigious offices like Pinsent Masons and DWF in Spinningfields in Manchester.

Lawyers need clients, and one of the main ways in which they win business from clients is to have offices that are conveniently sited. So, while Slaughter & May originally opened an office next to their former firm to be near shared clients, decades later firms as big as Clifford Chance moved their headquarters to Canary Wharf when the banks relocated their London headquarters to the Docklands to continue to be near them too.

Choosing a type of business

You may have decided on an office, but what type of business do you plan to run? Will you work on your own as a sole practitioner, will you work in a partnership, or will you work as a company (or other corporate entity)?   4–7

Erskine was a sole practitioner, just like many lawyers are today. At its simplest, being a sole practitioner means exactly that; you're on your own. You own and you run your business. You do everything. You open your office, collect the mail, fix computers, deal with finances, and sort out the admin, answer phones, make the tea and then, once that's all done, carve out the time to carry out the legal work that your clients instruct. Sole practitioners rarely are completely alone. They often employ a secretary or receptionist to staff the office. They may employ a bookkeeper to deal with client funds and finances. They may even have legally trained employees like paralegals, trainees or lawyers who work for them. A sole practitioner is someone who owns 100% of their own business, and that business can range in size from one person to hundreds of people.

Erskine was a good lawyer. He acted for lots of wealthy clients, building a successful legal business before dying in Naples (of gout) in 1791. His will shows that he died a wealthy man. It also shows he left behind 16 children, some illegitimate, and many called David too-including one daughter (!). He was rich, and one of the key advantages of being a sole practitioner is that you keep everything you make. You don't share profits with anyone else. If you're successful, then you alone enjoy the fruits of that success.

However, working as a sole practitioner was easier then, than it is for lawyers today. Sole practitioners need to comply with more and more regulations from the SRA and others. They need to deal with strict financial controls. They may need staff to help them, as they have less time each day to generate fees. It can be a constant balancing act between how much time they spend working for clients and how much time they need to spend running their business. Sole practitioners need to be a combination of lawyer, businessperson, IT engineer, accountant, marketing expert and more, all of which takes time.

For Erskine, running a business was easier. There were fewer regulations. He didn't need to undertake ID checks to comply with anti-money laundering regulations. Nor did he need to ensure his email server was maintained. One of the biggest advantages Erskine had over modern lawyers was that there was actually less law to follow. The 20th century saw the volume of laws expand hugely, requiring lawyers to specialise in different areas just so that they could become experts in a particular area. Today, many lawyers prefer to work in a partnership, so they can cover more areas of law for clients.

The pros and cons of partnership

4-8   This is the traditional business vehicle, where two or more lawyers go into business together. Although Erskine was a sole practitioner, he didn't work alone. He had an apprentice, James Robertson, who took control of the firm when Erskine died. Unlike Erskine, Robertson decided that he needed a partner to help him run the business. He approached William Wilson and, when Robertson died, Wilson became partners with James Dundas. The firm changed its name to Wilson & Dundas, and then Dundas & Wilson (though no one knows why, or exactly when, they swapped around).

From Erskine, Robertson, Wilson and Dundas we can identify two trends. Firstly, lawyers opened offices where they could source (and then carry out) business. Secondly, some lawyers worked out that it was easier to work together than alone. However, unlike the directors and members of a limited liability partnership (LLP), which we'll cover shortly, partners in a partnership can be held personally liable for the firm's debts. In other words, every partner is responsible for everything the partnership makes and everything it loses.

For William Wilson, this meant that if he made a profit of £100, he would need to share £50 with James Dundas (though in practice, as we see later, they would have agreed a way to divide profits rather than rely on a simple split). However, if James Dundas ran up a debt of £1,000 then William Wilson would need to pay £500 of that debt. What's more, if James Dundas couldn't afford to pay his share of the debt, then William Wilson would need to pay on his behalf; while both shared in the profits, either partner could be 100% responsible for the debts.

This is why partners in a partnership tend to have a unique bond. They need to trust each other, because they're entrusting something precious to each of their partners, namely their bank balance.

Most partnerships will enter into a partnership agreement. Others will rely on trust. William Slaughter and William May were said to have never signed a partnership agreement. There is no record any contract between them

This bond between partners also meant something else. If you potentially could face a huge bill because of something your partner has done, you probably want a say in every decision that he or she makes. If every decision could affect you adversely, wouldn't you want to know about it?

So why join a partnership?

The main benefit of being in a partnership is that you can do more. As the 20th century dawned, law libraries grew so big they could no longer be contained on a bookshelf. The big question for many firms was whether lawyers could still do everything. Could every partner cover every area of law?   4–9

Choose a specialism

At the start of the 20th century, Dundas & Wilson had 10 partners. It was one of the largest firms in Scotland. It had an office in Edinburgh beside its main client, the Royal Bank of Scotland. Partners of the firm even sat on the bank's board. It was a success, but one partner knew it had to change to face the challenges the 20th century would bring.   4–10

John Richardson was a specialist in banking, agriculture and trusts, and one of the smartest lawyers in the country. The UK Government even had to introduce legislation to try and stop some of his tax schemes as he regularly out-thought the treasury.

Yet, he knew that Dundas & Wilson had to change. In 1911, Richardson called a meeting of his partners and he demanded that each should choose an area of law that would be their speciality. He didn't want partners who were "jack of all trades". He wanted partners who would be experts in just one area. He knew that increased regulation (and a burgeoning volume of law) meant that clients needed lawyers who could give in-depth advice.

He also realised that by specialising in particular areas, the firm would become more than just a collection of individuals. It would be a genuine team that would require its partners to work together. It was this decision, faced not just in Dundas & Wilson but in firms across the UK, that led to the modern careers of banking, corporate, criminal, property and litigation. For Slaughter & May, this change led to the creation of separate departments, with the first being Conveyancing, set up to deal with the volume of regeneration work required after the Second World

War. The partners realised it would be more efficient for one partner to deal with all conveyancing than for each partner to deal with it separately for clients.

This choice also led to greater innovation. As it became more efficient to specialise, it also became more efficient to ensure all records and admin were centralised too. Slaughter & May even took the unusual step of asking a business efficiency firm to review all their processes in the 1950s to find ways to save time and costs.

Your career

4–11   Think about your own career. As a trainee you normally work in a number of different areas of law. Depending on the firm you join, that might include a formal six-month rotation of seats in particular departments. Alternatively, you may just work for a number of partners with different interests over the course of your traineeship. When you qualify, you need to specialise. This could be in one area. In larger firms, for example, this could involve narrow specialisms. By way of illustration, you might not just work in banking but—instead—work on just one particular financial product. It can be that detailed.

In smaller firms you may carry out a wider range of work. On the high street you could deal with conveyancing and corporate work, but it's unlikely you also would do court work too. The days of one person carrying out all the legal work required by any client that walks through their door largely are gone—with one notable exception.

Slaughter & May still expect their lawyers to adopt a multi-disciplinary approach. Steve Cooke, Slaughter & May's senior partner explained their approach in 2017:

"It goes hand in hand with the client relationship focus. Rather than having a massive team, you have one person who does a number of different things, and is their contact person. It means you have to work a lot harder because you are covering a bigger waterfront than our competitors.

On the other hand, the benefits of this are focused toward the sort of law that we do, which is trying to find new ways of doing things. And our lawyers are much, much more likely to come up with new ways of doing things because they are less likely to be pigeonholed into one specific discipline and they will see the potential for ideas cross-fertilizing from one area to another."[2]

Choose a second office (and a third and a fourth...)

4–12   Between 1980 and 2000, Clifford Chance grew from 12 partners to over 500 partners worldwide. Expansion was vital if firms wanted to complete globally. Dundas & Wilson was ambitious and it opened an office in London in the late 1990s and, in 1997, joined Arthur Andersen's legal network of over 3,000 lawyers. Within two years, revenue shot up by 20%. New partners at the firm would be sent to Andersen's international training centre in Chicago as part of

---

[2] David J Parnell, *"Steve Cooke of Slaughter and May: 'Strong Culture Means That Money is Not The Only Factor'"*, Forbes.com, *https://www.forbes.com/sites/davidparnell/2017/04/18/steve-cooke-slaughter-and-may-strong-culture-money-not-only-factor/#5efe9d5c19f9* [Accessed 8 December 2018].

their induction. Every morning they would be woken up by an alarm clock programmed to play Tina Turner's 'Simply The Best'. The firm was growing bigger and bigger.

How could firms increase in size so rapidly in just 20 years? They were responding to client demands. As national companies like BP and British Airways dropped the 'British' and evolved into multinationals, law firms expanded to match their clients. The opening of trade borders made it easier for companies to move beyond geographic boundaries and become global businesses. Law firms followed. However, even on this larger scale, firms still followed the same instincts they'd always used. Instead of opening an office in the City to be near clients, firms were opening in Frankfurt and Hong Kong, in order to capture global clients on the world's biggest stock exchanges.

Growth presented new problems, however. The biggest problem was cash. In order to expand, firms needed money. They needed to pay for more staff, new offices and new equipment. These are costs that any firm needs to pay before they open their doors and start charging fees to clients. Partners had to decide how much they were willing to invest. However, they also had to rely on their partners to 'cough up' if things went wrong. Allied to that was the question of trusts—as the number of partners increased, could you trust all your partners, all the time?

Choose your partners wisely

In 2000, Dundas & Wilson was one of the leading firms in Andersen Legal, a   **4–13** network of firms linked to global accountants Arthur Andersen, with responsibility for developing the network worldwide. Though the network was a success, trouble was brewing. In 2001, Arthur Anderson was implicated in a massive fraud at the US energy company Enron. Despite being one of the five biggest accounting firms in the world, in just one year it was gone (along with its legal network). One of the reasons it collapsed so quickly was because it was a partnership.

With over 700 partners, partnerships in accounting had grown so big it was actually no longer possible for one partner to trust all their fellow partners. Indeed, with such a large number (and such a geographical spread) it was likely that they had never met most of their partners.

When Enron collapsed, Anderson faced huge financial claims. It also suffered fatal damage to its reputation. Even though its revenue was nearly $10 billion in 2002, it couldn't survive. One of the effects of Anderson's collapse was that regulators worldwide realised that partnerships were no longer suitable for big global businesses. If one claim could lead to a $10 billion business ceasing to trade, then a replacement would be required to help stop potential losses. Limited Liability Partnerships (LLP) were born.

In 2004, Dundas & Wilson became one of the first firms in Scotland to convert from a partnership to an LLP. The move meant that most partners could limit the losses they would need to contribute to, and it would protect non-negligent partners if the firm faced a claim. In return for this new protection, the firm would publish accounts and release more information publicly than a traditional partnership.

An ordinary partnership doesn't need to publish its accounts with any outside body (such as the Companies House). The only people who know how well or how badly a firm is doing are the partners themselves, their accountant, their bank and HMRC. An LLP has to be more open, however, and publish accounts that then are publicly available (via Companies House). The reorganisation meant that Dundas & Wilson was able to successfully relaunch itself as a UK firm. The firm's turnover rose 12%, in 2001/02, to £38 million. By 2004/05 it had grown another 17.1%, to £44.5 million. Its partners regularly were paid over £250,000.

In spite of the new LLP structure, big law firms still faced problems. They had become bloated and developed bad habits.

Choose unemployment?

4–14   In 2008, a property crash that started in the USA then spread worldwide. Banks became nervous and businesses stopped doing deals. The UK Government had to inject billions of pounds into the economy in order to keep the banks afloat. For the large commercial firms, it was like a tap had been switched off. The banks stopped lending, clients stopped deals and no one bought or sold property. The recession was as swift as it was unexpected. One month, offices were busy with lawyers regularly working late and on weekends; the next month everyone was leaving at 5pm because they had nothing to do.

Law firms had to react. The first thing to happen was a series of redundancies. Firms simply didn't need all of the lawyers they employed. While having a speciality is good (because lawyers became experts and expertise sells), if you specialise in an area that has no work, then redundancy swiftly follows. There were no property deals and no banking deals. Couples put divorce on hold because they couldn't sell the house they shared. Lawyers lost their jobs because their firms no longer had any work to give them.

Allen & Overy was the world's fifth-largest law firm in 2008. In December that year it kicked off its restructure with a comprehensive review of its global business, and announced a slew of measures in February 2009. This included a global reduction in its partner headcount by 9%, a proposed 9% cut in the number of associates and other fee earners, a 9% reduction in support staff and pay freezes across the board.

On 1 May 2009, the firm (which has 31 offices worldwide and approximately 5,500 staff) reached the end of its redundancy programme. It resulted in the laying off of around 450 members of staff. The figure comprised 200 associates, 200 support staff, plus a further 47 equity partners. Half of the cuts centred on its London headquarters. An undisclosed number of voluntary redundancies also were agreed.

Choose fixed fees

4–15   Clients had less money and were less willing to pay big fees (or fees that were not agreed in advance). They started to demand fixed fees. Instead of paying, for example, £100 or £200 per hour, clients would tell firms that they could have £5,000, and not a penny more. Firms had to become smarter. They needed the right people. They needed the cheapest resource to carry out work so they could make a profit on that £5,000. They needed paralegals, IT and project management skills. This is where the great divide started. Innovation, IT and training all cost money and money is the one thing most firms don't have (certainly not in 2008).

Choose the right skills

Let's imagine a typical high street in any large town. On it you'll find a betting shop, a chemists, a café, an off-licence and, probably on the side streets leading off the high street, one or more law firms. All are 'high street' firms. Some specialise in conveyancing, others in criminal law or immigration, but most covering a bit of everything. These firms are a mix of sole practitioners and small groups of partners (with one who predominantly specialises in court work, one who deals with conveyancing and one who specialises in family law).

4–16

The property partner might bring in £100 an hour, the family law partner slightly more. The court partner however might only earn £653 (in 2015) for a two-day trial in the Crown Court. Excluding time taken to prepare, to meet your client and to attend plea or case management hearings (which are all covered by the same fee) then even just the two days at court is £41 per hour for 16 hours.

When business is tough, when a recession means individuals have less money to spend, and when government cuts reduce legal aid contributions, what kind of conversations are the partners having in high street firms? Will the property partner and family law partner share their income with a court partner, who may bring in pennies when they bring in pounds? These and other difficult conversations have been taking place across the UK.

Choose a merger, takeovers or alternative business structures

The need to make money and reduce costs meant some firms closed. Dewey & Lebeouf globally and Halliwells in the UK were among the highest profile firms to become insolvent. For a number of firms, merging was the solution to reducing costs. Two firms working together offered many benefits. Sometimes the growth brought about by merging opened up new areas of work. Some clients might have wanted larger teams and more back up, and a merger was one way of addressing these concerns before the client left for a rival. The merger also would save costs due to economies of scale (i.e. paying less for goods and supplies, reduced office space and redundancies to obviate duplication).

4–17

Finally, a demand for alternative business structures (ABSs) grew. ABSs, as we see later in this chapter, permits non-lawyers to invest in a law firm. Lawyers don't have a monopoly on good ideas. Can you imagine a law firm run by Richard Branson or James Dyson? The problem with ABSs is that non-lawyers don't share your professional standards. They don't owe duties to courts, clients, society or fellow solicitors. Can you imagine Tesco accepting a legal aid case for £15 per hour when they could have a lawyer working on a property transaction for ten times that amount?

Choose...the future

In the future. we believe that there will be three types of successful firms:

4–18

International

4–19 These are firms like Slaughter & May, DLA Piper or CMS or Dentons, servicing clients who need advice from London to Sydney and from Beijing to New York.

Niche

4–20 These are firms that offer the best service in a particular area, like Schillings for media law, or Brabners for sports law.

Volume

4–21 These are firms like insurance specialists Slater & Gordon, who charge little per transaction and make profits from running thousands of files at once.

The challenge presented by this future will affect the high street, criminal practices and national firms alike. Will people walk into a high street firm when there is no high street? If legal advice is a phone call away do you need an office on the high street? As for Dundas & Wilson, would it need an office in London if its clients work in Europe? Remember the first thing Erskine did? He opened an office where he could find work. How do lawyers find work? They get work from clients. For Dundas & Wilson, in 2014, those clients were large public limited companies (Plcs), FTSE 100 companies and global businesses. What did their clients tell them after 2008? They said they wanted firms with offices in Singapore, New York and Australia. The wanted more than Dundas & Wilson then could offer.

Merge or die

4–22 Dundas & Wilson merged with CMS on 1 May 2014. One year later, Caryn Penley (former Managing Partner of Dundas & Wilson), was quoted (19 May 2015) praising the success of the merger:

> "I'm from the legacy Dundas & Wilson side and from my perspective I think it has gone really well. From a Dundas & Wilson perspective, we had a lot of good clients, but we weren't the right size and we didn't have the reach to service our clients in the way we really wanted to. The combination has allowed us to do that. There are a number of examples where, historically, CMS and Dundas & Wilson would have had contact with similar clients. But the combination has meant we have got more work, have been able to service those clients in a way that those two separate firms could not have done before. For me that really underpins the success."[3]

THE FUTURE

4–23 Law firms have not fully recovered from the recession. Financial results have certainly improved, with many firms reporting healthy profits. However, the attitude and approach of firms has changed because clients have changed. The

---

[3] Caryn Penley quoted in: *http://www.scottishlegal.com/2015/05/19/cms-enters-organic-growth-following-scottish-acquisition/* [Accessed 17 April 2019].

pressure to reduce fees, to provide better services and to truly understand clients' needs has meant that firms cannot be complacent. Firms cannot assume that their business will stay the same. They need to provide better service; tailored fees and they need to train lawyers who understand what clients want (and who can truly deliver).

That's why law firms look different—they're responding to what they think their clients want. It's clients who help shape what law firms will look like and what they offer. However, clients are not the only factor in the future of law firms. There are a number of other trends that we can identify. These are: technology, gender diversity, outsourcing and finance.

Technology

There are firms that send letters rather than emails. There are firms with sophisticated case management systems that automate many common tasks. There are others still working from a paper file. No two firms are the same.

4-24

Technology is changing law firms but it doesn't change every law firm at the same pace, because technology requires money and commitment. It requires money because new systems (like case management software) require upfront investment. The benefits of the system are then spread across future work (with costs reduced by lawyers working faster and smarter). If you can't afford the software to begin with, then saving money in the future is just a pipedream. Costs need to fall before all law firms can join the pioneers who invest first. Equally, firms need commitment from staff to use the new technology. We know of one firm that introduced an internal messaging system, yet no one used it. Staff still sent emails to each other. The messaging system was abandoned. For any new system to work it must be used, and that requires training. This takes time, and—yes—even more money.

However, the benefits are clear, as this report from DWF suggests:

> "[We use] optical character recognition technology to scan intercepted mail coming into the firm and route it directly into live matters on the firm's document management system…It scans 10,000 items of mail per day to London alone, which translates into a reduction in on-site storage from twelve to five linear metres per fee earner and reduces the cost of floor space—creating flexibility for fee earners and supporting DWF's environmental values.
>
> Building on this, we have implemented printing software that enables fee-earners to print office-specific headed notepaper from an app, regardless of location. This reduces the cost of printing and transporting headed paper to all locations and ensures there is minimal wastage. Clients also have access to the mobile print solutions, and a supported cloud solution enables them to print securely in any DWF office.
>
> Across the business, we have implemented matter-specific scanning, which enables fee-earners to access client documents securely, regardless of their location, and delivers cost and time savings to clients, as work is turned around more efficiently. It also enables our people to work more flexibly—whether on the move, working from home or hot-desking at a client's office—which can deliver benefits to our employees and allows our business to deliver a more responsive service for clients.

In addition, reducing commuting time and allowing employees greater flexibility to work remotely can improve work-life balance, improve stress levels and increase productivity."[4]

It also creates a challenge from clients. While technology can speed up processes, it also increases expectations. Perhaps it's not a surprise, then, that some firms still send letters if they know it means they won't have to deal instantly with responses. Technology also requires money and staff buy-in. This is why, over 10 years after the recession, many firms don't look (or act) radically differently than the way they did in 2007. However, the need for change is still growing, not just because of client demand, but also because of the way that the profession is becoming more diverse.

Gender diversity

4-25   Historically, people from diverse backgrounds have been underrepresented in the legal profession. Even today, the law school population (as well as the legal profession) does not reflect society.

For a number of years Andrew has delivered a lecture to post graduate law students. In it, he asks the students to describe what they imagine when he asks them to think of a lawyer. Nine times out of 10 they describe an old white man. He then asks them to look around the lecture hall and ask themselves what they saw. Young women as most classes would be 70% female.

And, if you look at any photo of an admission ceremony for new solicitors for the last five years, you'll see mostly women. Around 70% of all new solicitors are female. For the first time, the Law Society reported in June 2018 that the profession has more female than male solicitors.[5] This is a major development. However, the feminisation of the legal profession presents two big challenges. Firstly, although junior lawyers are mostly female, senior lawyers are not. Partners certainly are not, with less than 30% of partners being female.

This means that male lawyers (typically aged 40 and over) have to adjust to managing a team of female solicitors with career aims and aspirations that they might not share. Quite simply, that male team leader might not understand the challenges that a female lawyer faces. Men design law firms for men. They may expect long hours that are incompatible with family life. Outside the office, even business development activities might deter female solicitors:

> "Another barrier, that was specific to women in the profession, involved the nature of the work being centred around the traditional 'male' lifestyle/work pattern and not flexible enough to either accommodate 'female' responsibilities or recognise and reward different inputs. i.e. the extensive networking and client entertainment that is required within the profession is typically centred on evening events/activities,

---

[4] W. Lawrence and R. Hodkinson, "The technological edge" (16 November 2015), The Journal of the Law Society of Scotland, p.24. Available at *http://www.journalonline.co.uk/Magazine/ 60-11/ 1020978.aspx* [Accessed 17 May 2019].
[5] Law Society of England & Wales, *https://www.lawsociety.org.uk/news/press-releases/historic-shift-as-women-outnumber-men-practising-as-solicitors/* [Accessed 17 May 2019]

making it very difficult for female solicitors who have families to attend/engage in this, certainly with the frequency required to progress their careers within some firms."[6]

Carolyn Fairburn (Director General of the Confederation of British Industry (CBI)) flagged this issue:

"I've never been a fan of the business dinner. A lot of women aren't. They'd rather go home to their families in the evening. Why not have more early evening events like a panel discussion, a nice glass of wine or two and then everyone off home by 7.30? Maybe the business dinner is a vestige of old business life."[7]

The CBI has taken a lead by phasing out all business dinners it organises, except for its annual dinner.

While, we're generalising that family life is a concern for female solicitors. We recognise it's also a concern for male solicitors. However, there's a need for firms to recognise that maternity leave and part-time working are more prevalent among female employees than male. This means that firms need to develop ways of working which are compatible with a family life. This includes encouraging home working, part-time working and a better work life balance. This brings us back to technology. Home working requires firms to have IT systems that allow people to work from home as easily as if they were in the office. It needs electronic files so that people don't need access to filing cabinets and desk drawers. It requires many small changes that, again, cost money. However, unlike the technology trend, this time the need to spend cannot be ignored. If the majority of solicitors are female, then firms will need to make these changes or they'll lose talented staff.

Outsourcing

London is home to the biggest law firms in the UK. Many global firms like Clifford Chance have traditionally had an office in London only. The problem with London is that rents are high, salaries need to match, and fees need to be even higher to make a profit. In recent years, because of the pressure on fees that we've discussed, the biggest firms have had to look at alternative ways to save money. One solution was to move work offshore. In 2007, Clifford Chance launched a Knowledge Centre in New Delhi, to carry out paralegal work and offer support to the firm globally.

4–26

This offshoring trend also led to firms looking closer to home to save money as the difference in costs between an office in London and one in Bristol, Leeds or Belfast was considerable. Perhaps not as much as moving work to India, but, having work closer to home meant access to more staff trained in the UK and more staff working in the same time zone as the London offices.

---

[6] E. Wilson Smith, Perceptions and Impacts of Working Patterns Within the Legal Profession in Scotland (research for the Law Society of Scotland, May 2015), p.29. Available at *https://www. lawscot.org.uk/media/519915/Work-patterns-final-.pdf* [Accessed 17 May 2019].
[7] J. Armitage, "Black-tie business dinners should make way for more female-friendly events, says CBI chief" (23 November 2015), *Independent.co.uk*, *http://www.independent.co.uk/news/business/ news/black-tie-business-dinners-should-make-way-for-more-female-friendly-events-says-cbi-chief- a6744456.html* [Accessed 19 April 2016].

In 2011, Herbert Smith Freehills launched an office in Belfast to offer support services to the firm, focusing mainly on reviewing and analysing large volumes of documents, investigations and due diligence.

It employs over 200 people. More and more firms are using offshoring and nearshoring to provide legal advice—and this is a trend that will only increase in subsequent years as lawyers increasingly use their project management skills (see Ch.14 (How to manage teams and projects)) to identify ways to improve legal work and provide it cheaper and faster.

Finance

4–27 New technology, better processes and managing workloads all require money. The partnership structure has meant that law firms have been reluctant to invest as partners become personally responsible. Although LLPs have helped, many firms are reluctant to invest because, in practice, while the LLP structure may protect individual partners, a bank lending money may still seek personal guarantees, no matter what the LLP agreement may say.

That's why there has been a push to widen the number of people who can invest in law firms. Large companies, entrepreneurs or investment funds have money to invest in businesses looking to expand. However, until recently, they were banned from doing so as only solicitors could own law firms. This has changed with the introduction of ABSs. ABSs allow non-lawyers to invest and become partners in law firms.

Alternative business structures

4–28 In England and Wales, ABSs were introduced by the Legal Services Act 2007, which came into force between 2008 and 2011. Applications to become an ABS are overseen by the Solicitors Regulation Authority (SRA), which is responsible for judging applications for issuing licences. The first ABS licence was granted in April 2012, and by the end of 2018 it had nearly 800. Many have gone to existing law firms that want to add a non-lawyer to their partnership or to niche new outfits in areas like personal injury. For example, among the firms licenced was Lawbridge Solicitors in Kent, a sole practitioner who wanted to add a non-lawyer partner as its practice manager (in this case, his wife).

Other new ABSs are established law firms. Irwin Mitchell was ahead of the pack. It was the first top-50 firm to make the transformation. Since then firms such as Gateley, and Weightmans, have followed suit.

However, the rise of ABSs has not been easy. Among the first licences granted was a licence to Co-Op Law, part of the Co-Operative Group. In 2012 it announced that it had plans to recruit 3,000 lawyers by 2017, to challenge high street firms across the UK. However, despite the backing of a major business it has only about 400 staff (about 100 more than when it started). In April 2015 it announced a loss of approximately £5 million in the first six months of the financial year, and had only edged into the black in the second half (to post a £50,000 profit). In late 2015 there was a high profile failure of an ABS firm. Parabis Law, a personal injury firm, went into administration in November 2015. In 2012, it became the first private equity-backed ABS to be licensed by the SRA, and was seen as one of the forerunners of the new legal landscape. Three years later and with debts of over £70 million, it became insolvent and the business was sold and split between seven firms.

SUMMARY

In this chapter you've considered the difficult choices one firm made as it grew from a sole practitioner to a global law firm. You've seen how change affects all businesses and that responding to change is the key to success. Firms that don't change simply don't survive.

    4–29

Imagine you could start a law firm from scratch. Imagine you could ignore 250 years of history and build a new law firm. What choices would you make today? How would you respond to the challenges of technology, diversity and investment?

In the next chapter we look at how clients choose law firms and how your firm can react to what your clients want. In other words, we take a look at what happens before a client even walks through the door, picks up the phone or emails you with a new instruction. Why did your client choose your firm on the second day of your traineeship?

BACKGROUND INFORMATION: A GUIDE TO SOLE TRADERS, PARTNERSHIPS, LLPS AND LIMITED COMPANIES

Sole traders

The basics

The sole trader is the most basic business vehicle that there is. It's also one of the most popular. Sole traders are at the forefront of business growth in the UK, with almost 200,000 start-ups in 2014, according to the UK Government's business population statistics.[8] At the start of 2014 there were 5.2 million private sector businesses (330,000 more than in the previous year). Of those 330,000 new businesses, 197,000 were sole traders, according to the report. In the Scottish legal market, there are more than 600 sole practitioners.

    4–30

The term 'sole trader' (or sole proprietor) describes any business that is owned and controlled by just one person. In other words, if you decide to be a sole trader you'll trade in your own right. This is the case even if you employ workers. For example, if the owner of a 24/7 store employs an assistant, the owner is still regarded legally as a sole trader.

As a sole trader you're flying solo. You've to manage every aspect of your firm: advertising for new clients, creating a marketing plan (using your knowledge of clients from Chs 2 and 5), cash flow and financial management,

---

[8] See: *https://www.gov.uk/government/statistics/business-population-estimates-2014* (26 November 2014) [Accessed 17 April 2019].

client relationships (including issuing your business terms), client files, hiring staff, delegating to staff, compliance with Law Society rules, and so on.

Business planning

4–31   Business planning is critically important for sole traders. See Chs 5 and 6 for advice on marketing, and Chs 18, 19 and 20 for a guide to accounts and basic financial awareness. It's worth making sure that you avail yourself of the support offered by the Business Gateway organisation. You can access their website at *www.bgateway.com*.

Formation

4–32   There aren't any special rules if you want to be a sole trader. It's easy to get started. You don't need to go through Companies House and there's no formal paperwork to fill in. The only thing you must do is to notify HMRC that you're trading as a self-employed person, because that has tax implications (as we'll see).

Business name

4–33   One consideration when starting out is your business name. You can trade under your own personal name, or you can use a non-personal name i.e. a business name.

   If you do decide to use a business name, your personal details must be disclosed to your clients and suppliers, so that they know with who they're doing business. The information you need to disclose is:

- your full name; and
- an address at which your business can be contacted and have any legal documents formally served.

What's more, this information has to be:

- displayed in a prominent position in all business premises to which your clients and suppliers have access; and
- included legibly on all your business documents, including:
  — letters
  — orders for goods or services;
  — invoices and receipts; and
  — demands for payment.

Also, it has to be displayed prominently on your website[9] and provided immediately in writing to any client or supplier who requests it.

   Unlike companies, you don't need to satisfy a registrar that your name isn't already being used. However, you still might run into legal issues if you're not careful. In particular, you need to bear in mind the old common law of 'passing

---

[9] The Electronic Commerce (EC Directive) Regulations 2002 (SI 2002/2013) reg.6.

off'. This is where you can be sued for having a name that is identical (or similar) to that of an existing business, such that it could cause confusion in the market place.

Key features

If you become a sole trader you won't have a legal existence separate to that of your business. Let's take a quick refresher on the concept of separate legal existence (otherwise called "separate legal personality"). Every person has what's termed 'natural legal personality'. Your legal personality is what makes you a valid person in the eyes of the law. It's the thing that lets you own property, enter into contracts, sue people, and so on.

4–34

In 1897 it was established, in the famous case of *Salomon v Salomon & Co Ltd*, that companies (as opposed to sole traders) have their own, separate, legal personality.[10] The judge in that case, Lord Macnaghten, formulated the classic definition:

"The company is at law a different person altogether from the *subscribers to the memorandum*; and, though it may be that after incorporation the business is precisely the same as before, and the *same persons are managers* and the same hands receive the profits, the company is not in law the agent of the shareholders or a trustee for them. Nor are the subscribers as members liable, in any shape or form, except to the extent and in the manner provided by the Act." [Emphasis added.]

What does this all mean? A company's owners (its shareholders) are regarded as being separate from their company. In other words, a company is just like a newly born child; it is its own person. Consequently, if something goes wrong with a company then its shareholders (generally, but not always) will have no personal liability for any of the consequences (like legal actions, financial losses etc.).

Let's go back to you as a brand new sole trader. Sole traders are not companies. They (you) are normal human beings with natural legal personality. Another way of looking at it is that you and your business are actually one and the same person. In consequence, as a sole trader you're personally liable for all your business obligations (contracts etc.) and all your debts. You need to pay your debts out of your own pocket, with no cap or limit on what you potentially might have to shell out. This is called unlimited liability, and it can sometimes force sole traders into personal bankruptcy.

Let's look at some other key benefits of sole traders.

1. Generally, only a small amount of capital is required to start-up (usually provided by you).
2. Your wage bill is low because there are few (or no) employees.
3. Your business is easy to control, because you've hands-on control and can make decisions quickly, without having to consult anyone else.
4. The ease of decision making makes it a nimble vehicle, quick to respond to business opportunities and market changes.
5. No public filing of accounts is required, so you can keep all your key financial information private from your competitors.

[10] *Salomon v Salomon & Co Ltd* [1896] UKHL 1.

There are some disadvantages.

1. You've no one to share the responsibility of running your business—you're on your own.
2. You can end up working long hours, and also you might find it difficult to take time off.
3. Growth potential is limited by the amount of capital available. As—by definition—there aren't any shares that can be offered to potential investors, any growth has to be funded by a bank or family loan (the former which, almost certainly, you would need to guarantee personally) or from your own private funds.
4. Unlimited liability means you technically can be forced to sell your personal assets to cover your debts.

Compliance

4-35 There aren't any special rules for ongoing compliance, bar a requirement to prepare a set of annual accounts for HMRC and to pay whatever personal tax you owe. As regards the Law Society, you need to hold a full practising certificate, have personal indemnity insurance and must pay into the master policy. You also need to fulfil the various regulatory roles required by the Law Society (which we look at in Ch.1 (Becoming a lawyer)) and deal with all ongoing continuing professional development (CPD) requirements yourself.

Tax

4-36 As a sole trader you pay personal income tax on the net profit from your self-employed income. This is what's known as Schedule D tax. You must fill in a self-assessment tax return each year, detailing all your income (fees, commission and bank interest) and expenses. You also need to register as self-employed with HMRC as soon as you start to trade. If you don't do this within the first three full months of becoming self-employed, you face a penalty of £100.

The current rates of personal income tax are set out in Ch.18 (How to understand financial services). If you've (or expect to have) a turnover exceeding £83,000 per year, you also need to apply for a VAT number, and then charge VAT to your clients, complete VAT returns and send VAT payments to HMRC. You also can voluntarily register for VAT. This has the merit of enabling you to reclaim all the VAT you pay out (input tax) against the VAT you charge your clients (output tax). Some business commentators argue that being VAT registered can help to make you look more professional in the eyes of your clients (the assumption being that you're doing really well and must be effective).

Finally, as a sole trader you've to make National Insurance contributions if you make a profit of £6,205 or more a year.

Other

For certain types of work a sole trader might need a licence from a local authority. Restaurants and taxi drivers, for example, need to have a local authority licence. In addition, your qualifications and business premises may be inspected to ensure you comply with certain regulations.

4–37

Advantages and disadvantages

Advantages

- No regulatory hurdles for start-up.
- Small amount of capital is required at inception.
- Low wage bills.
- Nimble response to opportunities and market changes.
- Limited on-going regulation.
- Privacy of financial information.
- You're your "own boss" and can work flexibly.

4–38

Disadvantages

- Day to day management rests on one set of shoulders.
- Long working hours.
- Need to deal with Law Society regulation by yourself.
- Need to arrange CPD training by yourself.
- Personal liability for business obligations and debts.
- Lack the power and spend of established big players.
- Challenging to grow due to difficulty in leveraging investment.

4–39

Partnerships

The basics

This business vehicle has been around a long time. In fact, the UK has regulated partnerships since 1890 (via the Partnership Act of that year). Even today, in 2016, it's still a popular structure for a lot of law firms. The essence of a partnership is that a firm's partners (its owners) share with each other the profits (and losses) of the business, in which they've all invested. Partnerships often are chosen for tax reasons, because the vehicle does not incur any tax on its profits before they're distributed to its partners (i.e. there is no equivalent of corporation tax). Overall, a partnership is a relatively simple way for you, along with one or more others, to own and run a business together.

4–40

Business planning

The advice is the same as per sole traders (see above).

4–41

Formation

4-42   If you want to set up a partnership, there is no formal process of incorporation to follow and also no form filling to be done. Quite simply, you become a partner of a partnership when you, together with one or more people, come together and start to trade with a view to making a profit (we'll look at this in a little more detail shortly). You still need to know exactly when you start trading, however, because HMRC will need this information.

When does a partnership exist?

4-43   The essential elements of a legal partnership are that it must:

- have more than one person;
- carry on a business; and
- have a profit motive.

In other words, you can't have a partnership all by yourself (although nowadays, conversely, there is no upper limit to the number of partners that you can have). You also have to be working towards making a profit. A charity can't be a partnership.

There's no requirement to have a formal partnership agreement. However, unless an agreement is in place, it makes working out when exactly your partnership comes into existence rather difficult and, generally speaking, not having one is considered to be undesirable. Ultimately, whether there is a partnership is established by reference to the legal test set down in s.2 of the Partnership Act 1890.

1. An interest (either joint or common) in property does not create a partnership (so, owning a flat with your partner, husband or wife) does not create a partnership).
2. Sharing gross returns doesn't create a partnership (you need to have made a profit).
3. Sharing of net profits is evidence of partnership (subject to some exceptions).

Or, if you share your net profit with one or other people, this is evidence of the existence of a partnership.

Before you start

4-44   If you're thinking of going into business with someone, then you need to think things over carefully. You won't be a sole trader making all your own decisions and controlling your own destiny. As we saw in 4-13, a rogue partner can bring down a global business. It pays dividends to research your proposed business partner(s). For example, you might instruct a search via Experian or Equifax, to see if they've good credit. It's also worth a general internet search, as this can throw up a wealth of information. If your proposed partner also is (or has been) a company director, search Companies House and download their latest company accounts. How well are they doing in their other ventures? Ask around also; it's amazing what your friends and colleagues might know. In other words, go into any partnership with your eyes (and ears) open.

Business name

You need to choose a sensible name for your partnership, and the general advice is the same as for sole traders. There is no central register of partnership names and no requirement to register your name. However, it's still a good idea to check the internet, domain name registries, phone books, trade journals and the trademarks registry to see if any other business is already using your proposed name.

4–45

While company names can be checked at Companies House with ease, it's much more difficult to check on partnerships, so the sorts of searches suggested are essential. If your preferred name appears to be available, you should lodge details with a solicitor to establish the date from which you commenced using it, in case this is challenged at a later date. Your trading name can be a combination of your partners' surnames, or you can use a non-personal name (i.e. a business name). Once again, if you do decide to use a business name, you and your partners' personal details nonetheless must be disclosed to your clients and suppliers (in the same way as per sole traders). This rule also applies if your firm's name includes your surname and your partners' surnames, but also with other words (for example, 'Sim and Todd Legal Services').

In the interests of practicality, however, the requirement does not apply if your firm has more than 20 partners, subject to:

- a list of the names of your partners being maintained at your principal place of business;
- none of your partners' names appearing in documents (except in the text or as signatories);
- all your documents state clearly your principal business address (and that the list of your partners' names can be inspected there); and
- the list being available for inspection during office hours.

If your firm uses a business name (i.e. it does not trade under the names of the partners), it must also conform to Pt 41 of the Companies Act 2006. This says that you can't use a business name if:

- its use would be a criminal offence;
- it includes words and abbreviations that denote a particular type of business, if the business is not in fact of that type—this include things like "limited", "public limited company" and so on (clearly your firm cannot be a limited company or a Plc);
- it suggests a connection with the Scottish or UK Governments;
- it suggests a connection with a local authority or a specified public authority;

- it includes a sensitive word or expression (without the approval of the Secretary of State).[11]

Finally, the common law rule of passing off applies to partnership names, in exactly the same way as for sole traders.

Key features

4–46   To an extent, a partnership is recognised as being independent. Unlike you as a sole trader, it has what is termed "quasi" separate personality. As such, your firm can:

- enter into contracts;
- sue or be sued;
- be declared bankrupt;
- own property in its own name.

Unlike a company's shareholders, you and your fellow partners are still liable for all the debts of your partnership, jointly and severally. This means that if one partner can't contribute to expunging your firm's debts, you and your other partners must bear his or her share. Once again, your liability is unlimited.

Let's look at some of the other key features of partnerships.

- Your business is easy to start—you simply commence trading.
- Your partners bring a variety of skills and ideas to the table.
- Decision making can be easier, with more people to work to solve problems.
- You share responsibilities and duties, so the burden does not rest on just your shoulders.
- With a division of labour, your working hours should be less (and holidays easier to arrange).
- Pooled resources give you a marketing clout that rivals established big players.
- Growth potential is better because equity (in the form of a partnership share) can be offered to potential investors.
- Law Society regulatory matters are dealt with by a bigger team.
- There is no need to deal with CPD training by yourself.
- No public filing of accounts is required, so you can keep all your key financial information private from your competitors.

In other words, partnerships retain a lot of what is good about being a sole trader, but also deal with some of the negatives that come with that vehicle. There are some other disadvantages.

- Unlimited liability means you technically can be forced to sell your personal assets to cover the partnership's debts.

---

[11] See ss.54 and 1194 of the Companies Act 2006.

- There is greater scope for management disputes to arise, among partners, which clearly can lead to problems.
- Growth options are not as flexible as with limited companies.
- There is no continuity of existence; your partnership actually dissolves if one partner dies, resigns or becomes bankrupt (unless you've a partnership agreement in place that specifically exempts you from this rule).

Partnership agreement

Before starting up, it's clearly advisable that you and your new business partners should sign a comprehensive partnership agreement. A typical agreement contains the following:

4–47

1. names of all your partners;
2. commencement date;
3. duration of the partnership;
4. business to be carried out (exactly what your firm will do);
5. firm name (and importantly who owns that name);
6. initial investments (how much each partner will invest);
7. division of profits and losses (what proportion of the profits each partner will receive, and the proportion of the losses each partner will bear); and
8. provisions regarding the winding up of the business.

As regards point seven, the normal starting point is that all profits and losses are divided equally. However, that might not be fair, if some partners contribute more capital than others. Any inequity can be dealt with easily. One option is to have different grades of partner (equity and non-equity/salaried), with only your equity partners sharing the net profit.

As regards point eight, the usual options are: assets are converted to cash and divided among the partners (in proportion); one partner purchases the others' shares at value; or the assets are not sold, but simply divided among the partners.

Your partnership agreement is also a useful way of dealing with what can be major disagreements, namely how new partners are assumed and how existing partners might be removed (e.g. if they under perform, or are guilty of some misdemeanour). In addition, it also sets out what should happen if one of your partners simply wishes to leave, and move on to pastures new. In this scenario, a well-drafted agreement might contain a so-called restrictive covenant clause. This has the effect of preventing your departing partner from participating in a similar business, within a certain geographical proximity and for a particular period. You've got to tread with care, however, because although these clauses are enforceable, if the terms are too onerous they can be struck down as anti-competitive.

Compliance

As per sole traders, there are no special rules for ongoing compliance, bar the requirement to prepare annual accounts for HMRC and to pay whatever personal tax you owe (but see further, below). As regards the Law Society, you and your

4–48

partners need to hold full practising certificates, there needs to be personal indemnity insurance in place and your firm needs to pay into the master policy. Once again, you all need to fulfil certain regulatory roles and deal with your ongoing CPD requirements.

Tax

4–49   As a partner of a partnership you pay personal income tax on your share of the partnership's net profit (your so-called drawings). In other words, you're treated as if you're self-employed, and so you pay Schedule D tax.

You must fill in a self-assessment tax return each year, detailing your income (which in this case is your share of the net profit) and any expenses that are incurred in running the business. You still need to register as self-employed with HMRC as soon as you start to trade, and the same penalty rule applies as for sole traders.

In addition to paying your own personal tax, you need to register your partnership with HMRC and submit a partnership tax return. This is the case even though your firm (unlike limited companies) doesn't actually pay any 'partnership tax'. In fact, it's really a way for HMRC to understand who the partners of your firm are, what your firm earns and what each partner draws from the business. In turn, it knows what to anticipate in your fellow partners' personal income tax returns. You need to appoint a nominated partner whose job it is to manage your firm's relationship with HMRC. That partner also must send HMRC your partnership return.

If your firm has (or expects to have) a turnover exceeding £83,000 per year, you also need to apply for a VAT number, and then charge VAT to your clients, complete VAT returns and send VAT payments to HMRC. As per sole traders, you also can voluntarily register for VAT. Remember, this has the merit of enabling you to reclaim all the VAT you pay out (input tax) against the VAT you charge your clients (output tax), and it can help make you look more professional in the eyes of your clients.

The same rules that apply to sole traders as regards NICs (both Classes 2 and 4) apply equally to all the partners of your firm. The same rates and thresholds apply also.

Other

4–50   The need to be aware of the requirement for local authority licences applies to partnerships as much as it does to sole traders.

Summary advantages and disadvantages

Advantages

4–51   •   No regulatory hurdles for start-up.
        •   Still able to be nimble in response to opportunities and market changes (but perhaps depending on size).
        •   Multiple partners bring greater skills and knowledge base.

- Shared responsibilities and duties.
- Decision making can be easier.
- Growth potential is better, making it easier to expand.
- More economic strength.
- Division of labour can mean shorter hours.
- Little ongoing regulation apart from annual tax returns.
- Easier to deal with Law Society and CPD requirements.
- Privacy from competitors as accounts are not published on public registers.

Disadvantages

- Greater amount of capital is required to start-up (when compared to sole   **4–52**
  traders).
- Disagreements among partners can lead to problems.
- Unlimited personal liability for business obligations and debts.
- Still not as flexible as limited companies in terms of growth options.
- No continuity of existence (unless provided for in partnership agreement).

Limited liability partnerships (LLPs)

The basics

Over time (and with some hard work), the number of partners in your firm will   **4–53**
increase. That indicates real growth. However, it also comes with associated risk;
can you trust each and every partner not to make a mistake that could cost you a
lot of money via joint and several liabilities? One solution is to set up an LLP, or
to convert your existing ordinary partnership to an LLP.

The LLP is a relatively new vehicle in the UK, first introduced in 2000 by the
Limited Liability Partnerships Act of that year. It's an entirely separate legal
entity. If you choose this vehicle, your firm can:

- enter into contracts;
- sue or be sued;
- be declared bankrupt; and
- own property in its own name.

However, unlike ordinary partnerships, this is no "halfway house"; LLPs have
full separate legal personality and you, as its owners, enjoy limited liability. This
limited liability protects you from losing your personal assets if your firm goes
under.

Business planning

The advice is the same as per sole traders (see above).   **4–54**

Formation

4–55 If you want to set up an LLP, there is a formal process of incorporation that you must follow (we'll look at this in a little more detail shortly). With this vehicle, things are a little more involved, however, compared with the sole trader and ordinary partnership vehicles.

Essential elements

4–56 Section 2(1)(a) of the Limited Liability Partnerships Act 2000 says an LLP must have "…two or more persons associated for carrying on lawful business with a view to profit".

In other words, you can't have an LLP by yourself (though there is no upper limit to the number of partners that you can have) and, once again, the requirement to have a profit motive would exclude a charity from using the vehicle. In addition, your LLP can't be set up and then just left dormant, as this would—by definition—be incompatible with the requirement to "carry on lawful business with a view to profit". This doesn't mean, however, that your LLP can't be dormant for a short while (e.g. due to the retirement of older partners and an influx of new partners).

Before you start

4–57 The same guidance applies, as for ordinary partnerships.

Business name

4–58 As always, you need to choose a good name, and the general advice is the same as for sole traders and ordinary partnerships. However, for LLPs there is also the central registry held at Companies House, and the requirement to register your name. Your LLP can't have a name to conflict with an existing entry on the register. Beyond that, you're largely free to choose as you please. However, the registrar will not register any name which is offensive or which would constitute a criminal offence.

Just as with partnerships, if your proposed name implies a connection with government or if it contains a so-called 'controlled word', it can only be registered with the approval of the Secretary of State. Controlled words are words that are deemed sensitive by the Secretary of State. The Secretary of State also can order your LLP to change its name within 12 months of registration, either if an objection is made by an existing LLP (or a company) or, if in his opinion, it's too similar to a name already on the index. That being said, the registrar is unlikely to take proactive steps unless some sort of objection is received. As always, it's open to any business to raise a 'passing off' action against your firm, if it feels that its rights are infringed.

Before filing in your application to start your LLP, it's vital to search the Companies House register of names. It's also a good idea to check the internet, domain name registries, phone books, trade journals and the trademarks registry to see if any other business is already using your proposed name.

Members

You must have at least two so-called 'designated members', at all times. They have extra responsibilities, including keeping the firm's accounts. You can have any number of ordinary members, however.

4–59

Forms

To get going, you need to fill in Form LL IN01. LL IN01 contains details about your members (i.e. your partners) and your firm's registered office. Under s.2 of the Limited Liability Partnerships Act 2000, a registration agent then submits all your incorporation documents to Companies House.

4–60

Companies House is the body responsible for: incorporation, re-registration, striking-off, and the registration of all documents required to be delivered under the Act. Registration is complete only when Companies House issues a Certificate of Incorporation. This is basically your LLP's birth certificate and bears the name of your firm, the date of incorporation and its registration number. Once your LLP is incorporated it's normal practice for your registration agent then to supply (in addition to the Certificate of Incorporation) a set of books including statutory and non-statutory registers, which are:

- Register of Members (not statutory).
- Register of Debenture Holders.
- Register of Charges Minute Book.

These registers are used to record information about the names and addresses of your members, and details of any and all capital contributions made.

Your statutory books must be kept up to date. Your company registration agent or an accountant, solicitor or professional advisor may take on this responsibility, on your behalf. Financial penalties can be imposed on you and your fellow partners for non-compliance. Keep in mind it's the members of an LLP who are penalised for non-compliance; you can't blame your accountant, solicitor or professional advisor.

The conversion of an ordinary partnership into an LLP is also a relatively easy process, with the assets owned by you and your partners simply being transferred to a new LLP, with you then becoming members of that firm.

Key features

LLPs enjoy all the general advantages of ordinary partnerships, so we won't list them again. The vehicle also addresses most of the downsides of operating either as a sole trader or an ordinary partnership. In particular, you and your fellow partners are not liable for the debts of your firm. In other words, you enjoy limited liability (to an agreed amount). The other key point is that because your LLP has full legal personality, it has what's termed 'perpetual succession'. In other words, it doesn't dissolve upon the death or bankruptcy of any partner.

4–61

Let's look at some of the other key features of LLPs.

1. Decision making can be easier, with more people to work to solve problems but also with the pressure of unlimited liability lifted from your shoulders.
2. Generally greater resources can give you even more marketing clout than ordinary partnerships and sole traders.
3. Growth potential is arguably better than for ordinary partnerships (due to limited liability and perpetual succession).

There are some other disadvantages.

1. Your business is a little more complicated to start—you've to go through a registration process with Companies House.
2. There is still scope for management disputes to arise, among partners, which clearly can lead to problems.
3. Growth options are arguably still not as flexible as with limited companies.
4. Public filing of accounts is required, so you unfortunately cannot keep your key financial information private from your competitors.

LLP agreement

4–62 Before starting, it's again clearly advisable that you and your new business partners sign a comprehensive partnership agreement. A typical LLP agreement sets out the powers of the LLP and also all the rules regulating its members' actions.

Your agreement (which incidentally isn't mandatory) should contain:

1. the name of your LLP (and who owns that name);
2. the names of all your partners (members);
3. the minimum and maximum number of members;
4. duties of members;
5. the address of your registered office;
6. the business activities of your LLP;
7. a procedure for appointing new members;
8. a procedure to remove problem members;
9. a procedure to deal with partners who die (including returning their capital);
10. the initial investments (how much each partner will invest);
11. the distribution of profit;
12. the contributions to the debts of the LLP on winding up;
13. a date for commencement of the agreement;
14. restrictions on members regarding competition and confidentiality;
15. provisions about insurance and pensions;
16. a procedure for issuing notices to members;
17. procedures at meetings; and
18. detail of partners' voting rights.

As regards profits and losses, the usual starting point is equal sharing. However, once again, any imbalance can be dealt with by having equity and non-equity/ salaried partners, with only your equity partners sharing the net profit (and contributing to any losses on winding up). Again, your agreement is the best way to deal with: the assumption of new partners; determining how existing partners might be removed; and the distribution of assets (and division of any losses) upon winding up. In addition, it can set out what happens if one of your partners simply wishes to leave (including a well-drafted restrictive covenant clause, which we discussed earlier).

If you don't have a partnership agreement, the Limited Liability Partnerships Act 2000 acts in a similar way to the Partnership Act 1890 (for ordinary partnerships) and various default provisions apply, which may not be suitable to your firm.

Compliance

As per sole traders and ordinary partnerships, you're required to prepare annual accounts for HMRC and to pay whatever personal tax you owe (see further below). **4–63**

As regards the Law Society, you and your partners again need to hold full practising certificates, there needs to be personal indemnity insurance in place, and your firm needs to pay into the master policy. And you all need to fulfil certain regulatory roles and deal with your ongoing CPD requirements.

Compliance for an LLP, however, is a little more involved. Every year, your firm must prepare and submit to Companies House a summary of its current members (together with a filing fee). Your first confirmation statement normally will be due on the anniversary of your firm's incorporation. Companies House does send a reminder, which contains information taken from the public record.

Tax

An LLP is transparent for tax purposes and no corporation tax is payable. **4–64**

As a partner of an LLP, you pay personal income tax on your share of the partnership's net profit (your drawings). In other words, you're treated like partners of ordinary partnerships and you pay Schedule D tax. Once again, you've to fill in a self-assessment tax return each year, detailing your income (your share of the net profit) and the expenses that are incurred in running the business. You still need to register as self-employed with HMRC as soon as you start to trade, as the same penalty rule applies. The current rates of personal income tax are set out in Ch.18.

In addition to paying your own personal tax, your firm needs to submit a tax return. This is the case even though your firm (unlike limited companies) doesn't actually pay any 'LLP tax'. You also have an obligation to publish your accounts via Companies House. However, if your LLP is small, it can file abbreviated accounts (which don't contain a full balance sheet and profit and loss account). The same rules about VAT apply, as they do to ordinary partnerships. Finally, the same rules that apply to sole traders and ordinary partners as regards NICs apply equally to all the partners of your LLP. The same rates and thresholds apply also.

Other

4–65   The need to be aware of the requirement for local authority licences applies to your LLP as much as it does to sole traders and ordinary partnerships.

Advantages and disadvantages

Advantages

4–66
- Full separate legal personality (with limited liability for members).
- Perpetual succession.
- Decision making can be easier, with more people to work to solve problems but also with the pressure of unlimited liability lifted from your shoulders.
- Multiple partners bring greater skills and knowledge base.
- Growth potential is better (arguably) than ordinary partnerships.
- More economic strength (arguably) than ordinary partnerships.

Disadvantages

4–67
- Formal process of incorporation.
- Greater ongoing compliance (with Annual Return).
- Greater amount of capital is required to start up (when compared to ordinary partnerships).
- Still scope for management disputes to arise.
- Still not as flexible as limited companies in terms of growth options.
- No privacy of key financial information from your competitors.

Limited companies

The basics

4–68   The final vehicle we're going to look at is the limited company. At the start of 2013, there were 1.4 million limited companies in the UK, with about 56% employing staff. This means that there are around 600,000 'one-man-band' limited companies in the UK.[12] It's worth noting that a proportion of these 600,000 companies may be in a dormant state (i.e. not actively trading). Limited companies are regulated under the Companies Act 2006. A limited company is also an entirely separate legal entity. If you choose this vehicle, your company can:

- enter into contracts;
- sue or be sued;
- be declared bankrupt;
- own property in its own name.

---

[12] Figure comes from evidence lead before the House of Lords: "Select Committee on Personal Service Companies Oral and Written Evidence" *https://www.parliament.uk/documents/lords-committees/Personal-Service-Companies/personalservicecompaniesevvolume.pdf* (at p. 170) (30 December 2013) [Accessed 17 April 2019].

With full separate legal personality again comes limited liability for you and your fellow owners (shareholders), this time capped at the amount unpaid on your shares.

Business planning

The advice is the same as per all the other vehicles we've looked at (see above). **4–69**

Formation

Before you start

The same considerations apply. If you're going to go into business with someone **4–70** then you need to think carefully. It pays dividends (literally, in the case of a company) to do research on your proposed new business partners. We gave you some suggestions as to how you might do this in the section on ordinary partnerships.

Promoters

To set up your limited company you need a promoter. This is the person who **4–71** carries out all the preliminary activities. There is no legal definition, but there is common law guidance. A promoter is:

> "...One who undertakes to form a company with reference to a given project and get it going, and who undertakes the necessary steps to accomplish that purpose".[13]

Promoters owe fiduciary duties (good faith duties) to your new company and any profit they make (or interest they might have in a transaction e.g. commission deals) must be disclosed.[14]

Pre-incorporation contracts

What happens if your promoter tries to enter into contracts before your company **4–72** is fully incorporated? They might, for example, want to make sure certain practical and logistical matters are bottomed out, so that your company can "hit the ground running". For example, they might try and conclude a lease, enter a utilities agreement, and so on. If your company isn't incorporated, however, it has no capacity to contract. In this scenario, your promoter is personally liable on the contract.[15] What's the work-around?

There are three solutions. Your promoter can:

1.   prepare a draft contract for your company to enter into, after incorporation;

---

[13] *Twycross v Grant* (1877) 2 C.P.D. 469.
[14] *Gluckstein v Barnes* [1900] A.C. 240.
[15] Companies Act 2006 s.51.

2.   enter into a binding contract and then change ('novate') that contract, after incorporation, with the consent of the third party, such that a new contract (on the same terms) is entered into between that third party and your company; or

3.   enter into a binding contract and then transfer only the benefit to the company, in exchange for the company's agreement to indemnify the promoter in respect of his or her liability to the third party.

Registration

4–73   What is the process by which your company becomes incorporated? First, your promoter has to submit several documents to Companies House.

1.   Memorandum of Association.
2.   Articles of Association.
3.   A statement of compliance with formalities.
4.   The registrar's fee.

The Memorandum of Association is simply a document (in prescribed form) that states that those who subscribe it seek to form a company. It has to include five things:

1.   your company's name;
2.   your registered address (to determine domicile);
3.   your business objects;
4.   whether your company is private limited or a Plc; and
5.   details of its share capital.

The Articles of Association, quite simply, is your company's constitution, and regulates its day-to-day operations. If you don't submit articles, Companies House will give you model articles (which may—or may not—be suitable for your company).[16] The registrar must be satisfied that your company has complied with all the provisions of the Companies Act 2006. The objects clause must demonstrate that your company is being formed for a lawful purpose. If not, your registration may be refused.[17] Upon registration, a Certificate of Incorporation is issued and—at that point—those who signed the Memorandum are members of a "…body corporate…capable of exercising all the functions of the incorporated company".[18] Your Certificate of Incorporation is conclusive evidence of compliance with the Companies Act 2006 during the incorporation process.[19]

Business name

4–74   The same general advice (provided elsewhere in this chapter) applies equally to companies. There is—largely—freedom of choice, but you can't have the same

[16] The Companies (Model Articles) Regulations 2008 (SI 2008/3229) Schs 1 to 3.
[17] *Attorney General v Lindi St Clair (Personal Services) Ltd* (1981) 2 Co Law Rev 69.
[18] Companies Act 2006 s.16.
[19] Companies Act 2006 s.15(4).

name as an existing registered company. Some names are barred by the Companies Act 2006, and the Secretary of State has the right to demand that you change your company's name if it is misleading, too similar, is offensive or amounts to a criminal offence. You're not allowed to choose a name that suggests a connection with government and (as with LLPs) certain names require the permission of the Secretary of State. Finally, the rules of "passing off" apply to companies.

Members

Your new company needs at least one member (i.e. one shareholder) and at least one director (an individual) to run it. Directors must be aged 16 years or over, but there is no upper age limit. Neither undischarged bankrupts nor disqualified persons can act as a director. It's normal practice to have a director's service agreement (a contract) between your company and each person who serves as a director. **4–75**

Forms

To set up your limited company, you need to fill in Form IN01. IN01 contains, among many other things (over 18 pages): **4–76**

- your proposed company name (including a declaration on sensitive words);
- the location of your registered office;
- a choice of three options for your articles (model, model with amendments, bespoke);
- details of your proposed officers (including directors);
- a statement of capital;
- the initial shareholdings;
- a statement of compliance.

Registration is complete only when Companies House issues a Certificate of Incorporation (bearing its name, date of incorporation and registration number).

Key features

Limited companies arguably enjoy all the tactical and human resource benefits of LLPs. As you know, they also have separate legal personality and you and your fellow shareholders enjoy limited liability (to the extent of the amount unpaid on your shares). **4–77**

Let's look at some of the other key features of limited companies.

1. Your company has perpetual succession.
2. Your business is a little more complicated to start—you've to go through a registration process with Companies House.
3. Decision making can be easier, with more people to work to solve problems but also with the pressure of unlimited liability lifted from your shoulders.

4.   Generally greater resources can give you even more marketing clout than ordinary partnerships and sole traders.
5.   Growth potential is arguably the best of all vehicles, with investors able to take shares (while not taking on any operational responsibilities as a director).

There are some other disadvantages.

1.   There is still scope for management disputes to arise, which can lead to problems (especially if the directors are not the same persons as the shareholders).
2.   There is more complicated ongoing compliance.
3.   Public filing of accounts is required, so you unfortunately can't keep your key financial information private from your competitors.

Compliance

4–78   As per sole traders, ordinary partnerships and LLPs, you're required to prepare your own annual accounts for HMRC and to pay whatever personal income tax you owe (see further below). As regards the Law Society, you and your partners —as directors—again need to hold full practising certificates, there needs to be personal indemnity insurance in place and your firm needs to pay into the master policy. And you all need to fulfil certain regulatory roles and deal with your ongoing CPD requirements.

Every year, your limited company must prepare and submit to Companies House a summary of its current members (together with a filing fee), called a confirmation statement. Your first statement normally will be due on the anniversary of incorporation. Companies House does send a reminder, which contains information taken from the public record.

Tax

4–79   Your company is taxed under a separate tax structure called corporation tax. In addition, all your shareholders are charged tax on dividends (the amounts paid to them from the company's net distributable profits). For this reason (the 'double charge' to tax), limited companies are not considered to be tax transparent. The current rate of corporation tax is set out in Ch.20 (How to understand financial statements).

As regards dividends, as of April 2018 a £2,000 tax-free dividend allowance was introduced. Dividends above this level are taxed at 7.5% (basic rate), 32.5% (higher rate) and 38.1% (additional rate). To declare your dividends, you have to fill in a self-assessment tax return each year.

Directors also are usually paid a salary. This is paid under the PAYE (Schedule E) scheme. Any such salary is liable for personal income tax (deducted at source). You also pay Class 1 NI (if you earn more than £155 per week) at a rate of 12%. The company also has to pay Employers' NI, at a rate of 13.8%. The same rules about VAT apply to limited companies. Lastly, your company's accounts must be filed at Companies House.

Other

The need to be aware of the requirement for local authority licences applies to   **4–80**
your company as much as it does to sole traders and ordinary partnerships.

Summary advantages and disadvantages

Advantages

- Full separate legal personality (with limited liability for members).   **4–81**
- Perpetual succession.
- Decision making can be easier, with more people to work to solve problems (but also with the pressure of unlimited liability lifted).
- Multiple members/directors bring greater skills and knowledge base.
- Growth potential is arguably the best of all the vehicles.

Disadvantages

- Formal process of incorporation.   **4–82**
- Greater ongoing compliance (with Annual Return).
- Greater amount of capital is required to start up (when compared to partnerships).
- Still scope for management disputes to arise.
- You can't keep your key financial information private from your competitors.

CHAPTER 5

Law firms and clients

INTRODUCTION

It's Thursday. You're in a meeting with a new client. Before you start discussing   **5–1**
what they need, your partner asks why the client chose your firm. The client says,
"A friend told me that your firm always stands up for people and doesn't back
down. You're like a dog with a bone—and I need a Rottweiler." Your partner
says, "You've come to the right place."
   You think, "Am I a Rottweiler now?!"

Most firms have a reputation. Schillings is known for defending celebrities   **5–2**
and others from libel and slander. Brabners are known for working with sports
people and sports organisations. Clients help firms gain a reputation. But they are
not the only source of reputation. Along with a reputation for working in certain
areas of law for clients, most firms have a reputation based on its staff, a
reputation for "how they carry out that work".

When Iain started his traineeship, he was told that his firm, a national firm,
wanted to recruit people who could show they were sociable, as well as
knowledgeable about their area of law. The firm wanted lawyers who could talk
to clients, not lawyers who'd have their nose in a book. The firm had a reputation
at that time not just for corporate law, but also for lawyers who were informal and
approachable.

You see a firm's personality when you start working and you deal with the
same firms, again and again. You might hear colleagues refer to one firm as
pedantic and unhelpful. Another may be referred to as only interested in fees.
Others are praised for working hard for their clients, and always pushing for a
better deal. Your firm's reputation is more than just pure technical knowledge. It's
everything about it. What does it do? How do its lawyers and staff act? What do
other people say about it?

Even appearances matter—law firms, like people, are judged on appearances.
If your shirt sticks out of your trousers, if your tights have a ladder, if your hair is
a mess, if you swear in a boardroom, all of these things change how clients view
you: "if they can't dress themselves how can I trust them with my business?" It's
the same for law firms. If your reception is filled with last year's magazines, if
your letters are sent on crumpled paper and if your website is still on Geocities,
clients might look down upon it: "if they can't send me a letter without spilling
tea on it, how do I know their advice is correct?" Knowledge, personality and
appearance matter for a firm and, as a trainee, they matter to you. Remember, you

don't start with a reputation. You rely on your firm's reputation while you build your own. That's why you need to know what it is, and how you can use it to benefit your career.

Outcomes

5–3   When we talk about a firm's knowledge, personality and appearance we're starting to talk about marketing and branding. Marketing is not just about adverts and signs. Marketing helps a business identify what clients want. This chapter introduces marketing by examining two techniques.

The first is called segmentation. This is a technique to identify what clients want by splitting large groups into smaller groups, based on shared characteristics. For example, if you work for a criminal law practice you might split clients into those who need legal aid and those who don't. You would then treat each group differently as you know you need to undertake extra work to comply with legal aid rules, for those clients who need legal aid.

The second technique is called the marketing mix. This is a technique used to identify what you can offer these smaller groups, once you know what they want. For example, if you know some of your clients need legal aid then, instead of explaining what it is each time, you might produce a leaflet explaining how legal aid works, which you can hand to new clients.

Most people think branding involves a logo. However, it's more than a logo. It's what your client thinks when he or she hears or sees your firm's name. These thoughts might be factual (for example, you have an office in Portsmouth with a blue sign above the door) and emotional (your firm's a Rottweiler). Your firm's name exists physically; people can see it. Your brand, however, exists in someone's mind. Thinking about branding, helps you to understand what other people are thinking.

This chapter will help you understand marketing and branding and, in doing so, it will help you understand how your clients think.

WHAT IS MARKETING?

5–4   At university you're judged on your knowledge of the law. It's an intellectual exercise, not an emotional one. No university awards first class degrees because they found your dissertation 'flirty' or your exam answer 'optimistic'. You're judged on your intellectual capability, reasoning and rigour. You're judged on your workings, not your conclusion: how you reach your answer is more important to academics than the answer itself.

Clients are different. They rarely need the curtain pulled back to see behind the scenes. They want answers, not footnotes. This creates a dilemma. If clients aren't interested in the detail of what a firm does, how does it build a reputation in any area of law? How did Schillings become known for its media law work? How did Brabners become renowned for sports law? This is a difficult question to answer. To help understand how reputations are created and developed, we must take a step back. We must ask a more basic question—what do law firms sell? If we say Schillings is excellent at media law, what does that mean?

What do firms sell?

Law firms are not shops. When lawyers open an office they don't sell eggs,   **5–5**
clothes or frying pans. We didn't sell anything physical at all, nothing that a client
could pick up and touch. Instead we sell something unique, namely the
information in our head, and our skill at turning that information into advice
clients can follow.

Compare lawyers with a shop. If you go into Tesco, you don't buy the store
manager's knowledge of stacking shelves or the checkout assistant's expertise in
packing bags. You're paying for a tin of beans, a box of cereal or a bottle of coke.
You're not buying something unique. These are ordinary items that you can touch
and feel. You can buy them in Asda, Waitrose or a corner shop. You're paying for
a product, not a service.

What's the difference between a product and a service?

In simple terms, a product is an object you can touch and hold, like a car, oven,   **5–6**
jacket or toaster. It's something you can see, feel, try, taste or otherwise use. It's
physical. A service, on the other hand, is an action that you undertake for
someone, like a haircut, car repair or medical diagnosis. Unlike a product, a
service doesn't physically exist. You can't pick up a haircut—it's an action that
you experience, and it's this experience that clients judge. And it's how a client
feels that's critical to how a firm manages its reputation.

How does a firm manage its reputation?

Just like you, your firm's reputation is based on its appearance and personality.   **5–7**
You might think it strange to think of a firm as having a personality, but think
about other businesses that you know. Apple is cool, Gucci is stylish, Ryanair is
cheap; each of these businesses has a personality. Law firms are no different and
they're judged on exactly the same criteria.

When clients walk into your office they don't appear by magic. The sign
above your door influences a new client; as does the look and feel of your
reception, how the receptionist treats them and what they think about the
boardroom they've been brought into. Before you open your mouth your client
will have started to form a view (rightly or wrongly) about your firm. Even a
client who phones you for the first time will have read an advert, or at least
checked out your firm's website. That client already has formed a view, just as
they would if they were walking along a high street before popping into an Apple
store or browsing the web and clicking on *https://www.apple.com*.

The best law firms—like the best businesses—know that everything it does or
says can influence how a client feels. When we say that Schillings has a
reputation defending reputations, what we're actually saying is that Schilling's
appearance and personality helps clients think that it has a reputation for
defending reputations. Just like wearing a wig and a gown makes someone
believe you are a lawyer or carrying a stethoscope makes someone believe you
are a doctor, law firm 'wear' a reputation. The trick is to understand what aspects
of its appearance or personality (a firm's marketing) influence how a client feels.

Introducing segmentation

Finding out how clients feel is difficult. Your firm must identify its current and prospective clients. If it doesn't know who its clients are, it can hardly make assumptions about how they feel. Identifying clients is difficult too. Your firm may have hundreds of clients. It's impractical to ask all of them how they're feeling. They would probably think it strange that they were being asked. Instead, your firm has to follow the adage that "you can't be all things to all people", and let that be its guide, because most businesses don't try and sell everything to everyone. Gucci sells clothes and accessories to people who want luxury items. Ryanair sells flights to people who want the lowest price. Even Amazon, which arguably does try to sell everything, doesn't sell to *everyone*. It only sells to people who can access the internet (though admittedly, this is a very large group).

All businesses divide their customers into smaller groups to help sell products and services. This is known as *segmentation*. Take Sainsbury's, for example. It doesn't just sell one type of tinned tomatoes. It has two. It has Sainsbury's own label, for customers who are willing to pay more for better ingredients. It has Sainsbury's Basics, for customers who want tomatoes at the lowest price. Sainsbury's has identified two groups of customers and has provided two different tins to help them. Imagine if Sainsbury's hadn't done this. If you want good tomatoes and Sainsbury's only offered Sainsbury's Basics, you would shop elsewhere. Equally, if you want the cheapest price but Sainsbury's only stocked Sainsbury's Basics you would also shop elsewhere. Sainsbury's would lose customers by only offering one tin. Separating its customers into two groups helps Sainsbury's sell to all of them.

In the same way, law firms need to segment clients into smaller groups to work out who their clients are likely to be and what they should offer them. We can see this in action when a firm opens a new office.

Segmentation

5–8   Imagine you're opening a new law firm. Where do you start? Theoretically you can act for anyone in the world, but you know you're never going to act for six billion people. Instead you need to narrow it down to something more manageable. Segmentation can help.

Step 1: As an English lawyer, you probably don't want an office in Alaska, Johannesburg or Beijing. You want clients based in England and Wales.

Step 2: Even in England, there are around 55 million people. You need to narrow your choices down and ask yourself what clients you want in England. Do you want to help people in a particular area? Do you want to help people who have a particular problem?

Step 3: If you decide to help people who have been accused of a crime, your choice narrows again. You've divided your clients into two groups: people accused of crimes in England, and everyone else in the world. You can forget about everyone else (they won't visit your office) and just concentrate on those who might be accused of a crime.

Step 4: You now have a manageable group of potential clients. When you ask yourself where you should open your office, you can further segment your clients by considering where potential clients would want your office to be. You can assume it's likely they'll want to visit an office that's close to a magistrates court, a crown court or the high court.

Step 5: Choose your office. You can choose from a small number of places that would be perfect for you to find clients.

Location

In the last chapter, William Slaughter could have opened his office anywhere in England. He could have acted for farmers in Shropshire or merchants in Hull. Instead, he decided to act for businesses in London. That meant he needed an office in the City,. This was Slaughter & May's first step in segmenting their potential clients. From being able to act for everyone in England, they were separating clients into people who lived in London (with access to their office) and those who lived elsewhere. Geography was helping dictate who they would act for.

5–9

We see the same thing today. While transport links and communication have made it easier to deal with people across the country, location still matters. Think of the firms you might join: a high street firm in Hull is not going to sell a house in Salisbury; a national firm in London is not going to deal with a breach of the peace on the Isle of Wight. Location matters, and a firm's choice tells you many things about it.

Type of work

Clients also choose a firm because they believe that firm can help. A law firm won't last long if it doesn't know the answers to the questions clients ask. If you're a criminal lawyer, you're unlikely to know corporate finance law. If you're a banking specialist, you're unlikely to know anything about custody hearings. This means that you want clients who need help in the areas you know. You segment potential clients into those you can help and those you can't. For example, in 2000, Clifford Chance moved to Canary Wharf because: "A number of our major clients are located at Canary Wharf, and more are likely to follow".[1]

5–10

Other factors

The location of your office and the work carried out are not the only factors that influenced law firms. You can split clients by any criteria you wish. Other examples are: nationality; age; sex; and lifestyle choices. For example, if you're a morning person then you may want a gym that opens early. If you like a lie-in, then you want one that opens late. Or you do what Pure Gym does and open 24 hours a day, so that both of you're happy. Your choice of how to separate clients is up to you, and the benefits of doing so are clear.

5–11

---

[1] The Law Society Gazette, Clifford Chance to quit City for Docklands, 7 July 2000, access from *https://www.lawgazette.co.uk/news/clifford-chance-to-quit-city-for-docklands/30007.article* [Accessed 23 November 2018].

Benefits

5–12   As we saw in Ch.2 (Clients), there are many different types of client. You can act for individuals. You can act for companies. You can act for local authorities.

Looking back, can you see that this chapter actually was an exercise in segmentation? What we did was to describe a number of smaller groups and the things we assumed they would want from their lawyer.

For clients, segmentation means that they get a lawyer who understands what they want and need, without them having to explain everything. If you're looking for a divorce you want to speak to a lawyer who understands family law. If you're looking to move house you want a lawyer who knows the area you're moving to. Segmentation helps clients pick the right firm.

THE MARKETING MIX

What is the marketing mix?

5–13   If you walk down a high street, every shop is different. HMV is piled high with DVDs and CDs. The Apple store is bright and clean, and filled with iPhones and iPads. Poundland contains a bit of everything. They all look different, but they're all based on similar ideas. They're the result of decisions made about: product, price, place and promotion.

Product

5–14   Every store has to decide what to stock. What should it sell? Is it phones, music or £1 bottles of Fairy washing up liquid?

Price

5–15   Every store has to decide how much it will charge. Is it £1 for everything or different prices for different products?

Place

5–16   Every store has to decide where it will be located. Should it be based on the high street, at a retail park, in a city or in small town?

Promotion

5–17   How does it tell customers what it sells? Does it need a logo? Does it need advertising? If so, what should it say or show?

5–18   These four categories (product, price, place and promotion) are known as "the four P's" and, when they're combined, form the ingredients of a marketing mix. The marketing mix is the combined effect on a customer of all the decisions a business makes about product, price, place and promotion. Let's look at an example of this in action by examining one of the world's largest companies, Apple.

How does the marketing mix work?

Steve Jobs, Steve Wozniak and Ronald Wayne founded Apple on 1 April 1976, to develop and sell personal computers. It's now one of the largest companies in the world and everyone knows its products: the iPod, iPhone, iPad, iMac and iWatch.   **5–19**

Over a million people visit an Apple store every day. It holds the credit card details of more than half a billion people, which is more than any other company. It brings in more money than Hewlett-Packard, Google, Intel and Cisco combined. It has twice the cash of the US. It managed to achieve all that by starting from nothing; just three men in a garage who followed three goals.

- It would understand its customers. It would know you as well as you know yourself.
- It would keep things simple. It would get rid of junk so that everything it did was needed.
- It wouldn't listen to the phrase "never judge a book by its cover". It would *always* judge a book by its cover. If something looks good, people think it is good.

It still follows these three rules today.

Product

Unlike other tech companies, Apple only sells a limited number of products. Compare that with Sony, which produces and sells a Sony version of almost all forms of electronic equipment, from bedside clocks to televisions, car radios, games consoles, cameras and Blu-ray players. Apple has fulfilled its second goal not just by producing products that are easy to use, but also only producing a small range. Its products are simple to use. They don't even come with instructions—Apple believes that its products should be that easy to use.   **5–20**

Price

Apple is an expensive product. It charges among the highest prices for a mobile phone or tablet. In return, it promises simplicity and quality. Its high price is one way to reinforce that quality: "my iPad must be better than an Android tablet—look at how much more expensive it is."   **5–21**

Place

Apple shops are simple, clean, and modern and designed to look better than any other shop on the high street. The stores are located on the most expensive streets: New Street (Birmingham) and Covent Garden (London). This reaffirms the idea that Apple products are better than those of competitors. Even staff are trained to   **5–22** live Apple's philosophy. If you want to become an Apple Genius you have to follow a book that tells you how to look, what to say (it warns you to avoid big words) and—even—how to stand. The Apple Genius employee guide tells staff that 'touching' and 'moving in closer' indicates acceptance and should be used to help clinch a sale.

Promotion

5–23   Apple spends millions of pounds creating classic ads to let you know what they sell and what makes them different. An advert like their classic advert featuring white headphones and black dancing silhouettes was used to sell iPods. It told you everything you needed to know about the iPod. It was music in your hand. (And it had white headphones—a then radical shift from traditional black). And it promotes itself based on the three values Apple set itself in 1979. It's simple, it looks good, and it gives customers what they want—all of their music in a small white box.

When taken together, the four ingredients of product, price, promotion and place all tell the same story. If you buy an Apple product you may pay a lot for it but you'll receive a phone, tablet or watch that is better, more stylish and easier to use than any other.

How does this use of marketing mix compare for a law firm?

5–24   Let's look again at Clifford Chance. We can see that choice of location is just one element of Clifford Chance's decision to open in Canary Wharf. Other factors that might have been relevant include:

Price

5–25   An office in the City is more expensive than one located in Canary Wharf. By choosing an office in a cheaper location, Clifford Chance could reduce its cost and increase its profits. We see similar moves with city firms opening regional offices. When Allen & Overy opened an office in Belfast it said: "We have to meet that challenge and proactively offer increased efficiencies and alternative resourcing to our clients."[2]

Promotion

5–26   With an office in Canary Wharf, Clifford Chance would have a presence in an area of the city that other rivals couldn't match. When a client in another office needs a lawyer, which name will they first think of? And will the fact that the office is on their doorstop influence their view of who they will use? To take an extreme travel example, Andrew can confirm that when asking national firms to bid to advise on listing on the AIM stock market, firms with offices in Scotland (where Andrew lives) had an advantage over firms that did not.

---

[2] Margaret Canning, *"Global legal firm Allen & Overy outsources to Belfast "*, *Belfast Telegraph*, *https://www.belfasttelegraph.co.uk/business/news/global-legal-firm-allen-and-overy-outsources-to-belfast-28586292.html* [Accessed 25 November 2018].

What is the most important factor about the marketing mix?

If companies' products define them, they must back up their claims. If Apple said   5–27
an iPod could hold your entire music library, when it could only store one album,
it would need to change its claim.

Secondly, the price of a product must reflect the budget of a company's
intended customers. If the iPhone screen were made of cheap plastic and easily
scratched, and not toughened glass, Apple would find it hard to justify sky-high
prices. Instead it launches the iPhone XR, as a more affordable iPhone with a
lower quality specification.

Finally, a company's marketing mix includes product packaging, public
relations and branding, as well as the sponsorship of well-respected people who
attest to the product's claims and benefits. Though this can go wrong, as Apple
found out when it gave away a free U2 album and tens of thousands complained
about receiving an album they didn't want on their iPhone. In short, the
marketing mix must be consistent. This is where law firms struggle. They don't
sell a product; they sell a service (their knowledge, personality and experience).

LAW FIRMS AND THE MARKETING MIX

You may have spotted that the four P's start with 'product', and you might ask   5–28
how this applies to law firms, which sell services. A product is something you can
touch and feel, sell and buy. A law firm doesn't sell products. We don't make
anything. We don't work in factories. We don't produce anything that clients
might pick up and touch. Law is a service and services are intangible. As we've
seen, services are more about how a client feels than what they can see. A GP
doesn't produce pills, they provide reassurance and advice. A travel agent doesn't
make two weeks in Magaluf, they provide advice on when to go and where to
stay. A service happens in the 'here and now'. It can't be repeated and it can't be
replicated.

Further, a service depends entirely on the person providing it. If we asked you
for advice, what you say and how you say it will be completely different from
any other person we ask. If law is not a product, then how do we apply the four
P's? A service is judged by three other factors: physical evidence, process and
people. The four P's become seven, when dealing with services. It is the seven P's
that define what law firms can offer to clients.

What are the seven P's?

A product is simple. You can pick it up and you can touch it. A service is more   5–29
complicated. We need to look at more than just product, price, place and
promotion, when we consider a service. We also need to examine how the service
is performed (the process), we need to check if it's intangible or whether it leaves
a physical trace (the physical evidence). Let's examine your new firm again, and
reflect on the seven P's. How does the marketing mix help you?

Product

5–30   You are not making a product. You are offering a service. We can't look at a box, or tin or plastic cover to judge this service. We need to look at the physical evidence, process and people involved.

Physical evidence

5–31   The second P is physical evidence. Just like a snail, services leave a trace behind them. As lawyers, you speak to clients to give them advice. You meet them in boardrooms. You call them on the phone. But that's not all that you do. You also produce letters, emails, contracts, advice notes, text messages and hand written notes. All of these extra documents are the physical evidence that a service has been performed and they can be just as important as the service itself.

Let's imagine you meet a client for the first time. You're charming and smart, and within 10 minutes you work out what they need. The next day you write a letter to them confirming what you said. This time, your letter is long, dull and filled with obscure legal jargon. It even has a passage in Latin. Now, instead of being charming and smart, the client has no idea what they've been sent or what it might mean. You are no longer the right lawyer for them.

Today, with the increased use of email to provide advice it's even more important that your writing is easy to read. You're judged more and more on how you write. Equally, as well as getting the content right, the physical evidence you leave behind should look good. Remember Apple? Appearances do matter. Even simple things like the font in your letters say a lot about your firm.

•   Is Times New Roman too boring?
•   Is Comic Sans too childish?
•   Is Arial Black too aggressive?

Everything your client sees and hears from your firm should be brilliant. Everything your client should see or touch should reinforce the reasons they have chosen you.

Process

5–32   As a lawyer you follow set processes. Sometimes these are formal. Your firm may have case management software that breaks down a transaction step by step, or it may follow checklists. Even if your firm doesn't, you'll soon find that you tend to do the same thing each time you deal with a similar transaction. If you're buying a house, for example, you'll ask the seller for titles, you'll prepare contract, have follow up questions on the title, prepare a report for your client, prepare for exchange, before dealing with cash and keys. It's the same process from A to B, each time.

Much of this process is hidden from a client's view. Your client won't see you pick up a title, read it, make notes on it, and report back on what it says. The decisions a firm makes about how it approaches these types of process can affect clients. A good example of how processes can affect a customer's view of a business is telephone banking. If you want to pay a bill from your account, banks have decided that—rather than phoning a branch direct—you need to phone a helpline. Banks also have decided that a real person doesn't need to deal with your request, and you can do it automatically via the helpline. On the one hand, banks argue that they have streamlined a process. On the other hand, how does that process make you feel? Do you like not having to queue? Or, do you hate having to constantly read out your account details to a computer?

Think about law firms. How do they deal with calls? Traditionally, if you called a law firm you either would speak to a receptionist or a secretary, before they put you through to a lawyer. Today, many firms list their lawyer's direct dial number on their websites. You can phone them directly. Law firms assume that clients value being able to speak to lawyers, as easily and quickly as possible.

Allen & Overy used process as part of its promotion strategy. When it set up the Belfast office, it was set up in part to cover high volume, routine work. It promoted that idea in the press. As a firm it was saying that its move and the processes behind that move would save clients' money. For cost conscious clients, that's a great message to hear.

Place

This is your firm's 'shop', the place you and your customers meet. For most of us this will be an office. Your office is your firm's chance to impress your clients. We've looked at location, already, but your office is more than just a location. It's also where you meet your clients, and they form a view of your firm based on what they see.

5–33

CMS Cameron McKenna Nabarro Olswang (CMS), opened a new office in London at Cannon Place in 2015. It is located above a tube station. It's surrounded by other global companies. It is one of the most impressive offices in London. As a client, if you walk into the reception area you might think: "this firm must be the best, to afford an office like this."

CMS had looked at location. Many of their clients are large corporates, so they need this office in London. They're in the City, where most of the biggest businesses are, so this office is the right one for them.

However, what if you're accused of a crime? Would you be impressed with this office or would you be too intimidated to go in? Or, if you were a small business that worries about costs, would you use a firm with an office like this? Decisions go back to what your clients want. The choice made should reflect the assumptions firms have made about their clients. We can see this clearly on the high street. Here you'll find that lawyers have offices on the busiest shopping streets. On the high street, law firms tend to be part of the community and so they want to be somewhere that you can pop into easily when you go into town. Many also have estate agents, so they'll have their property boards out so that people can see the homes (a product) for sale.

However, 'place' isn't just about offices. It's wherever you meet clients and 'place' also covers a firm's virtual reception. Your website and social media can all be used to 'host' your online office.

Promotion

5–34   Promotion covers everything you might say or do to raise awareness of who you are and what you do. This includes sponsorship (like Taylor Wessing sponsoring the internationally renowned Photographic Portrait prize), advertising in newspapers, PR and writing for the press, appearing on TV, winning awards, or attending events and meeting clients for coffee. It even covers adverts on the side of a double decker bus, like an advert CMS used in London to promote itself and the charity it supported.

Price

5–35   We're not going to say a lot about price at this stage as we cover that in Ch.10 (How to set fees). What we'll say is that one of the main debates about pricing for law firms is between charging a fixed price and hourly rates. Some clients hate hourly rates because they don't know what they'll end up having to pay. On the other hand, some clients hate fixed fees because the work may change, the fee may no longer apply, and the fee needs to be renegotiated to cover what the firm actually did.

        If you're listening to your clients—and you are because of segmentation— most of them will tell you they want a fixed fee. If you're creating a law firm, what kind of price should you offer? Ultimately it comes back to your client. Some clients are happy to pay more; some only want to pay the cheapest price. People don't change just because they're 'shopping' in a law firm, and not for tomatoes in Tesco.

People

5–36   For law firms this is the biggest factor. We've said a law firm is nothing without its clients. It's also nothing without people. If a client walks into a boardroom and there is no one to speak to them, nothing else matters. An office cannot provide advice. A letter doesn't write itself. Law firms need people. They need you. We'll look at what you can do in the next chapter.

Marketing mix summary

5–37   There are no right or wrong answers when considering the marketing mix. Each ingredient must be considered in light of the assumptions you've made about your clients. Equally, no one ingredient can influence a client, on its own. You may be the greatest lawyer in the world but if your website is on Myspace, no one will phone you. All of the ingredients of the marketing mix need to work together. Imagine a firm with an advert in the Northumberland News saying it's your local firm, but which only has an office in Abu Dhabi. That wouldn't make sense. It's the combination of all the factors—its brand—that make a firm's reputation, and yours.

Your firm's reputation

You've seen how segmentation works and how different firms have approached the marketing mix—now try two exercises. First, pick a law firm (your own or another) and try and carry out your own segmentation of its clients. Once you've thought of who they're and what they may want, imagine you're opening a new law firm. What would you offer those clients? Would you have an office? If so, where would it be? What kind of work would you cover? How would you deal with your clients? Would you have a secretary? Direct dial numbers? Would you make every lawyer be on Twitter? What kind of advertising would you have, if any?

5–38

Once you've thought of a few examples and you have an image of this new firm in your mind, carry out a second exercise and compare those with the real firm you've picked. Does your new firm match your firm? We bet it doesn't.

What you'll find is that most firms don't currently offer what their clients want. Firms with offices on the high street are finding their clients shop in huge supermarkets, on the edge of town. The high streets are dying and passing trade is falling away. Large corporates have expensive offices but clients want to pay lower fees, because of the recession. You'll find numerous examples where expectation and reality doesn't match and that's because most firms need time and money to change.

Segmentation and marketing mix is fine in theory, but in practice it can be a long, hard process to change around a firm to match what clients want. Halliwells opened an expensive office in Manchester. It wanted to emphasise it was a major corporate firm. Unfortunately, it paid a rent it couldn't afford and, as it was tied into the lease, it couldn't change. Its options were limited. It wanted to be a corporate firm, but when the corporate work dried up because of the 2008 recession, it was fatally exposed.

Let's look at Schillings. At the start of this chapter we said that it has a reputation for media law, built over a long period. We can see how they did this and how they maintain that reputation, by analysing the seven P's.

Place

They opened an office in London, not Manchester, Birmingham or Newcastle. They wanted to be near not just their clients—rich and/or famous people—but also near the Royal Courts of Justice in order to act quickly if litigation was required.

5–39

Promotion

Schillings rarely talks to the press. By not promoting itself, Schillings highlights its discretion and confidentiality. These are attributes its clients value.

5–40

People

Keith Schilling was one of the two founders. He was considered to be among the best litigation lawyers in London. The firm didn't start with a blank canvas. It

5–41

started with his names and reputation. Most firms start this way and most take the names of their founding partners. Examples include: (William) Slaughter & (William) May, (George) Allen & (Thomas) Overy and Keith (Schilling).

It's this final 'P' that becomes the most important element of how firms gain (and maintain) a reputation. As we said, you don't start with a reputation. You rely on your firm's reputation while you build your own. But this transfer is not just in one direction. Your firm needs your reputation, just as much as you need its reputation.

In the next chapter we look at the actions you can take as a trainee (or lawyer) to help your firm and your clients. As US author Maya Angelou said:

> "I've learned that people will forget what you said, people will forget what you did, but people will never forget how you made them feel."

SUMMARY

5–42   All law firms work with the same ingredients and largely follow the same recipe. A firm that deals in personal injury needs to know the same laws as any other, and the same processes for dealing with clients' injuries. Despite these similarities, firms nonetheless appear vastly different. At one end of the scale you have global firms like Clifford Chance and CMS. On the other, you have your local high street firm that deals with clients as and when they come through the door.

Knowing how those firms differ is an essential part of commercial awareness, as it shows how the legal market has developed based on how law firms react to clients (segmentation) and how it will develop to respond to client demands (marketing mix). Knowing segmentation and marketing mix is a critical element of the first definition of commercial awareness, namely knowing the legal market.

CHAPTER 6

Clients and you

INTRODUCTION

It's Friday. It's the end of your first week and you need to find the senior partner   **6–1**
to sign a letter that has to be sent today. It's only 2 p.m. but, when you speak to
their PA, they say, "The senior partner is on a course... a golf course that is.
They'll be back on Monday. You should know that the senior partner always plays
golf on a Friday afternoon with clients." And you think: "What a joke! Playing
golf while I'm stuck here doing their work... that can't be right. They're not even
working—are they?!?"

One misconception that students and new lawyers have about their career is   **6–2**
that partners must have the best legal knowledge. Many do. But many don't.
They have other skills that help bring in clients. They know how to sell
themselves and their firms as without clients law firms have no business. That's
why winning clients is one of the most important things a partner does. You can't
impress anyone with your legal knowledge unless a client walks through your
door and instructs you. If you're serious about your career, the ability to attract
clients to you and your firm is essential. It's a skill that has become more vital as
the legal market becomes more competitive. Clients have more choice, law firms
are more aggressive about approaching potential clients, and you can't expect to
become a partner unless you know how to bring in clients too.

In this chapter we examine a number of ways that you can build your
reputation to help you win business. We outline the traditional skills required to
network (and this doesn't involve learning to play golf, a largely outdated
stereotype), and to 'wine and dine' contacts over lunch, dinner or, most
commonly, for a quick catch up in a coffee shop. We cover the power of PR and
the traditional media and we examine social media and how it has created a
platform for lawyers to instantly connect to other people.

Outcomes

This chapter should be read alongside Ch.5 (Clients and law firms). As you build   **6–3**
a reputation, you're also representing your firm. If your firm is a traditional law
firm that still sends letters instead of emails, it's harder for you to gain a
reputation as being the cutting edge of social media. Equally, if you write an
article for the *Daily Star* when you act for FTSE 100 companies that are more
likely to read the *Financial Times*, your firm might not be happy. You need to
align your work with your firm's reputation.

In this chapter, we examine the steps you can take to create and build a reputation. We don't intend that you do all of the actions we suggest. Some people are great at networking; some hate it (even when they know what to do). Instead, they might love writing articles. This chapter is about opening the possibilities that you have so you can select the best way for you (and your firm) to build your (and its) reputation.

YOUR REPUTATION

Day one

6–4 On day one your reputation won't extend further than your desk. Colleagues may have an idea of what you are like from your CV and from your interview, but it's up to you to show them what you can do.

Back in 2000, Andrew was a trainee for McGrigor Donald (which merged with Pinsent Masons). He started in its corporate department. It was a fantastic experience. The first thing he was asked to do was to buy a football club. His first task was to research the current shareholders, for his head of department. He thought he'd done a good job and that was confirmed when one of the other partners showed Andrew an email the partner had been sent to all the other partners in the department. The head of department had written: "Use Andrew Todd. He's really good". The next day another partner asked Andrew if he could help with a share purchase agreement to buy a chain of shops, He said that even though Andrew was "just in the door" he could have a stab at drafting it. Andrew spent a week on that document, labouring day and night. It was going to be the best share purchase agreement the world had ever seen. It would be so good that not only would the partner email the rest of the team he'd be high fiving strangers on the bus.

Andrew was so proud when he handed it over. However, the partner took one look at it before giving it back, saying, "You know it's the seller and not the purchaser we act for? You'll need to change everything." How quickly reputations can change.

Changing reputation—you

6–5 At university you're judged on your knowledge of the law. You write essays and answer exam questions that test your ability to understand and interpret the law. It's an intellectual exercise, not an emotional one. And you are being judged on your reasons, not your conclusion. Clients are different: they want results, not reasons.

Think of a meal. Does a chef show you how he cooks your steak and chips? No. You judge them on what you eat. Just as they don't show you how the ingredients are transformed into a meal, so you're not expected to show every case, statute and textbook. A family that buys a house want to know when they will get the keys. A man accused of a crime wants to know if he's going to jail. A banker wants to know if the money she lends to a small business will be paid back. They don't want standard conditions, court procedure, or the finer details of the Companies Act. Clients don't want to see inside your kitchen—they just want to be fed.

Before they even meet you, your client has started to form a view (rightly or wrongly) about you and your firm. As we've said before, even a client who phones you for the first time has likely read an advert or checked out your firm's website. Before a word is spoken, your client has formed a view. Perhaps the biggest influence on them is that you're a lawyer: lawyers are trusted; lawyers are honest; lawyers keep secrets and put their clients' interests ahead of their own, because they follow professional standards.

All of these things—your professional reputation and the reputation of your firm—can be enhanced by your reputation. Once a client speaks to you, they're no longer judging you on how they expect a lawyer to behave, or what an advert about your firm may have led them to expect. They're judging you on your actions, words, advice and personality. It is up to you to protect and build your reputation, because it's the one thing you carry throughout your entire career.

Changing reputation—your career

There are different stages to building your reputation. As a trainee, your reputation is more about your technical knowledge and the people you work with. As a newly qualified lawyer, however, you should start to look at extending a reputation outside the firm to existing contacts and clients. As you become more senior, you're expected to build a reputation among your local community or the business markets you work in. Think of your reputation like throwing a stone into a pond. At first the ripples are gradual and small but as time passes they extend further and wider until they stretch from bank to bank. A small stone can create a big splash if you build your reputation through networking, PR, promotion and social media.

6–6

NETWORKING—NEW CONTACTS

Andrew once acted for the chief executive of a large property company. He was three years qualified and was buying a large office block. The transaction was a nightmare. Andrew would speak to the chief executive every hour, for days on end. He thought he was building a good relationship with him. However, when the deal was done, and Andrew phoned him and asked if he would like to meet for a coffee, the chief executive said: "No why would I want to do that? You're just a lawyer."

6–7

Rejection is brutal. It doesn't matter if you're sixteen and asking someone to the school prom, or twenty-six and asking a contact for a meeting. It's difficult not to take it personally. Yet, as trainees and new lawyers, you're often asked to go to business events and, afterwards, asked if you're going to meet anyone that you met there. It can be intimidating. If you go to a drinks reception or a local networking group, it can seem that everyone is much older than you and that they all know each other already. It's easy to hide and to only speak to people you know (usually some colleagues who have come with you). It's also easy to latch onto the first person who gives you the time of day and never let him/her out of your sight. We've all been there.

That's the thing. We've all been there because most people feel exactly the same way as you. When you go to an event most people don't know each other. They're in the same position as you. If they're talking to someone, it's usually a colleague from their office. They would welcome someone else to speak to—they've already covered all the office gossip. Just approach them. However, saying that is a lot easier than doing it. That's why we've set out some tips on how you can make 'networking' easier.

What is networking?

6–8   We don't like the term 'networking'. It suggests something formal and fixed, like telecom masts and underground cables. We prefer to think of it as something softer. Networking is simply meeting people, having a conversation and, if appropriate, keeping in touch afterwards. When people say they can't network, they're saying they can't talk. Of course, that is silly; we can all talk!

Meeting people takes many forms. It can be a cup of coffee, a drink after work, a round of golf, a formal lunch with a local chamber of commerce; even a lavish awards ceremony with everyone in black tie. However, at its heart, it's any place or time that you have a conversation with someone else. It can be on the street, coming back from Starbucks. Or, as Andrew once found, it can be naked in the shared shower of a local gym. If you meet someone you know or want to know, it's networking, no matter where it is.

Benefits of meeting people

6–9   Law firms need clients. We can't repeat this enough. Clients want lawyers who know them and can help them. This means lawyers who have the personality to relate to (and understand) clients. Meeting people is your chance to practice those skills with lots of different people, with lots of different personalities. You won't connect with everyone, no more than you are friends with everyone in your university class or law firm. However, the more you do it the easier it becomes as you share knowledge, identify opportunities, build connections and grow your confidence and reputation.

Share knowledge

6–10   Meeting new people is great for sharing ideas and knowledge. Ask questions of the people you meet. They'll be delighted to talk about themselves and their businesses. What are they currently working on? What are the current challenges? What are their recent successes? People like talking about themselves so, if you ask the right questions, you find out lots of information about them and you might see things from their perspective.

Let's assume you work for a high street firm. You go to a local business chambers lunch. If you talk to business owners you can find out which of them are busy, what they do, whether they have any problems they need help with, and whether your firm might be able to support them.

Andrew is approached regularly by law firms looking to work for a public limited company (plc). The meetings that go well are the firms that show a genuine interest in learning more about the company and who can then say: "if you're doing X have you thought about Y?"

Opportunities

It's natural that meeting people eventually will result in opportunities. The thing you won't know is when or how they'll materialise. It's rare that someone will say "I need a lawyer" or will look to instruct you straight away but, if you spot an opportunity, that's the time to say, "would you like to meet to discuss this?" or to make a mental note to follow up with them afterwards.

6–11

Connections

There is a lot of truth in the saying "if you scratch my back, I'll scratch yours". As a lawyer you meet lots of people with lots of different skills and knowledge. If someone you meet has a problem that you think one of your contacts can help resolve, suggest putting them in touch. If you do someone a favour generally, they feel obliged to return it in the future; when they meet someone, who may need a lawyer, it will be you they recommend.

6–12

Increased confidence

Meeting people, and pushing yourself to talk to them, helps increase your confidence. This is important, because your firm depends on you to make connections. The sooner you learn, the easier it will be to use these skills (especially as you become more senior).

6–13

Raising your profile

Being visible and getting noticed is a by-product of meeting people. By attending business and social events, people begin to recognise you. This can help you to build your reputation as a knowledgeable, reliable and supportive person by offering useful information or tips to people who need it. You're also more likely to get more clients, as you'll be the one that pops into their head when they are looking for help.

6–14

General tips to meet the right people

Select the right events

You don't need to be out every night meeting people. But, if you do need to 'wine and dine' then make sure you pick the right events for you, whether this is a cup of coffee or hosting a table at an event.

6–15

Attend events with a clear goal. That may be to find an opportunity to win some business, it may be to publicise you or your firm, or it may be to gather information from attendees. It's important that you know why you're going to an event. If you don't know, why go? Networking isn't compulsory. You have many other things you could do. So, our best advice, is to be specific when you want to meet people. Go to events that are likely to have the people you want to meet already attending. For example, if you work in corporate insolvency you may want to join the R3 group. This is a networking group dedicated to people who work in insolvency, such as administrators, accountants, bankers and lawyers. Alternatively, if you work in commercial property, you may want to attend the Investment Property Forum, because many of the big players in that industry attend their events. Going to random events is not smart. You might as well walk into any pub or restaurant and hope for the best. You want to go to events that you know will help you and make the best use of your time.

How do you know which events to go to? A good place to start with identifying the right events is to ask your supervisor or partner (since they might be going, too). Once you have identified an event you should prepare for it, just like you would any client meeting.

General preparation

6–16   The first thing to think about is whether you should discuss 'the law'. We say no—at least, not unless you're asked. Conversations are more effective if you look to build a relationship with the people you meet. A casual drink at an evening reception is not the place to discuss the top trends in international arbitration or changes to employment tribunal fees. Mechanics wouldn't talk to you about carburettors (at least we hope not). Lawyers don't need to talk about statutes and case law. Remember, potential clients (for that is what the people you meet are) are rarely interested in the nuts and bolts of what you do.

Instead, look to build a relationship by using small talk and asking general questions about them. Show that you're interested in their work. Remember that you're building a professional relationship, and not looking for a friend or partner. Some business relationships may evolve into that, but this is not speed dating for business people. In other words, approach it like you would any business task.

Make a list

6–17   Before you go to an event, try and find out if there is a list of guests (albeit data protection laws limit this now). Check the list and try to identify the people you might want to speak to. These could be people whom you already know, and who would expect you to introduce yourself. They may be clients of the firm who would expect you (as the firm's representative) to say "hello". It may be people who you don't know but would like to know. If you act for a lot of small businesses, then you may wish to speak to the directors of other businesses. If you deal with employment matters, you may want to speak to people in HR. In other words, be sensible. When compiling your initial list, try not to underestimate anyone's potential to be a knowledgeable resource. Don't be discouraged if you have only a few people on your list at first; each contact will direct you to more people and your numbers will soon multiply.

Conversation topics

You should always attend every event fully prepared, so that you don't waste anyone's time by asking him/her to explain basic details you could learn easily on your own. You wouldn't approach a doctor and ask them what they do, would you? You might ask instead if they specialise in a particular type of medicine or whether they are a GP, surgeon or anaesthesiologist. This doesn't mean you need to stalk people over the internet. You don't want to casually mention that you liked their photos of their holiday in Magaluf in July 2016. A simple Google search, or a search of LinkedIn, is enough to get started. And it's not too forward to check—when Andrew meets law firms looking to work with him, he always checks to see if they have read his LinkedIn profile so that he knows how diligent they are with their research. It's also worth checking with colleagues if they know anyone on your list. The chances are that some of the people who plan to be there will have been at events before, and your senior colleagues will know them.

6–18

Before going to any event, we would check news and sport. But only do this if you're comfortable talking about a particular subject. You don't need to know the latest scores from Match of the Day in order to have a conversation. Sometimes just saying, "I don't know much about football" (or indeed any other sport or topic) is a good way to change the subject to something that you're comfortable with. Most people are polite and will help change the subject.

At the start

You may want to start by talking to people whom you're comfortable with, such as colleagues or contacts that you already know. This is fine. Everyone needs to warm up and relax. However, don't stick with the same people all night. No one will take offence if you say, "it's been nice to talk to you; it's time to start mingling again". People expect everyone to move on and speak to others.

6–19

Introduce yourself

When you meet someone new, introduce yourself by making eye contact, smiling, stating your first and last name, and giving a firm but brief handshake. Listen for the other person's name (believe us, it's easy to miss this when you're nervous). Try and use it two times while you're speaking. This helps you to remember it. If you're not sure of their name, it's better to ask them to repeat it than to use it wrongly. No one minds repeating his or her name. In fact, they probably want you to repeat your name too as they won't have remembered it either.

6–20

Listen first

Let the other person speak, especially if you have approached them. No one wants to be approached by someone who only talks about him or herself. Ask

6–21

questions, listen carefully to the answers, and ask more intelligent questions about what you have just been told. Even if you're just asking about the weather it's flattering to be asked a question that seeks an opinion. Flatter the people you meet. Of course, there does come a point when too many questions will make you less a flatterer and more the Spanish Inquisition. Let the conversation develop naturally, and if it comes to an end then finish it politely and move on.

Follow up

6–22 The end of the event is not the end. It's the start. You should have met a number of people. You should have learnt something about them or their business. If you think it's appropriate you can drop them an email or give them a call after the event with anything that you think they may find helpful. If they've mentioned they've a problem with their landlord, you might have a useful note that they can read that explains the legal issues. If they mentioned that they're having problems with their tax return, you might recommend an accountant. If there is nothing immediate and the contact is someone you just want to keep in touch with, just look for other events that they may attend and make a note of some of the things they said so that next time you can show you remember them. The worst thing you can do is to do nothing. If you're doing nothing, then someone else (another firm) is contacting them instead.

Have realistic expectations

6–23 It's unlikely that someone will instruct you or your firm the first time they meet you. Relationships take time to build. It may be the third, fifth or even tenth time you meet someone before they think of something you can do to help. It may be never. However, the more people you meet and the more you show an interest in them, the more chance you give yourself to turn contacts into clients.

Be yourself

6–24 There's no ideal personality for networking. Being gregarious may get you noticed but equally it will drive many people away, those who might prefer a quiet conversation. Some people want to talk to someone witty; some might want a serious conversation; others may look for thoughtfulness. That's why it's easier to be yourself and not think that you need to be a particular type of personality. You find people who will want to talk to you because of who you naturally are and not who you pretend to be.

NETWORKING—EXISTING CLIENTS

6–25 The same tips apply for existing clients. The advantage of dealing with existing clients is that a lot of the hard work is already done. Your partner and colleagues should know a lot more about them and be able to recommend how to deal with them. For example, some clients hate black tie events, so don't invite them to a formal dinner. Others like an early morning coffee, before being caught by meetings and emails. Many public sector contacts, meanwhile, will have strict guidelines based on the Bribery Act 2010 about what they can accept as hospitality. They may need to pay, also, which may make them think twice about accepting your invitation for lunch at the Fat Duck.

As a trainee and new lawyer, the best way to meet existing clients is to piggyback a senior lawyer as they meet their contacts. You can learn from them how they network, and you can build your confidence knowing they're right beside you.

PR—ADVERTISING AND PROMOTION

Advertising is an effective way of telling people about your firm. We include it within this chapter, because if you're involved in advertising then you need to know that there are SRA outcomes that you must follow. These are:

- adverts must be accurate, not misleading and not likely to diminish public trust; and
- you must not make unsolicited approaches to members of the public.

6–26

PR—MEDIA, UPDATES AND WEBSITES

A good way to keep in touch with clients and contacts is to send them updates on the law that affect them. You can do this by writing articles for your website, a legal update or by writing for the local, national or business press. Identify where you want to be published. If it's your website, then you have full control over what you say and how you say it. If it's a third party website or the local, national or business press then you normally prepare a pitch before writing a full article. The pitch will be a short summary of your idea and why it's relevant to readers. For example, if you were writing an article for *Personnel Today*, a specialist employment magazine read by HR professionals, you would need to explain why your idea would interest an HR manager. It would not be enough to say that, for example, pensions law would be changing as a result of auto-enrolment, you would need to explain that auto-enrolment affects all businesses and that HR managers need to ensure their systems are updated to cover all their employees.

If you're targeting local or national press, you have to show why your idea is topical. The press is interested in current news, so your ideas need to reflect the latest developments. If, for example, the Supreme Court issued an important judgment, you would need to contact a paper the same day with your idea so that it can appear in the next day's edition. And remember that other people are doing the same thing—so if you're not first, you might get ignored in favour of the fifteen other firms that contact the press first.

Finally, if you're ambitious, you may want to write an academic textbook about a particular area of law. This is a serious statement that you're an expert in that area. It's a major undertaking, though, and maybe not one for your traineeship given the amount of work involved. You may want to wait until you have gained more practical experience as a lawyer.

6–27

PR—SPEAKING

6–28   Many people don't like public speaking but it's an effective way of gaining a reputation. If you stand up and speak then people assume you must be confident and that you know what you're talking about. They look up to you and, if they're interested in the topic, may seek you out for your opinion. There are a number of ways to find speaking opportunities. One is to organise your own seminar and invite clients and contacts to it. This could be on a hot topic, or a subject that you think they would benefit from hearing about. For example, every year the UK Budget and the Finance Act affects most businesses and people. You might want to organise a seminar that tells people—such as small business owners or companies in a particular sector—what the main changes are and how it affects them.

Alternatively, you might want to showcase your reputation for an area of law by taking part in seminars to the legal profession. Companies like Central Law Training or the events team at the Law Society are always looking for ideas for events. While you may not be talking directly to potential clients, speaking at such events is a powerful way to win over potential clients when you mention it to them. If you're teaching fellow lawyers about an area of law, then you must be a leading expert in that area.

The important thing is that you know what your audience comprises. Your talk about the UK Budget will be completely different if given to business owners than it would be if given to fellow lawyers. You can be more technical with lawyers. You need to limit yourself to potential impacts, when dealing with non-lawyers.

SOCIAL MEDIA

6–29   We love social media, but it's a difficult subject for many law firms given the risks that go with it. What if someone writes something objectionable? It's easy to do on a platform like Twitter; the 280 characters limit largely inhibits subtlety. Law is nuanced; Twitter is not.

Equally, Instagram allows you to publish photos instantly, but it's difficult to take a photo in a law firm. Confidentiality rules mean that you must be careful not to reveal any information which could be linked to a client. Even a computer screen in the background of your image could reveal information, were someone to zoom in. Think of the politicians caught out by long-range lenses, carrying papers into Downing Street. Facebook tends to be more personal. What you post is intended for friends and families, and the way you behave towards them is different to how you behave with a client.

Even LinkedIn, a platform for business contacts, can be misused, as the Charlotte Proudman incident demonstrated. Ms Proudman is a barrister and in September 2015 she received a message from a partner in a law firm praising her 'striking image'. She believed the message to be sexist and 'called the partner out' by publishing the message on Twitter. The national press picked up the ensuing debate about whether or not his behaviour was appropriate.

For those of you not into social media, we summarise the main platforms below (and give examples of how lawyers might use them).

Facebook

Facebook is the most popular social media service, with around 3/4 of people in the UK using it on a regular basis. Facebook is great for local firms that are looking to advertise and target local users. Check out the Facebook page of Stephens Scown, a firm based in Exeter, Truro and St Austell. Its Facebook page is an excellent showcase both of the firm's staff and the work the firm does. It's website is good too! In 2017 it was named as among the best in the world in the 21st Annual Webby Awards.

6–30

Larger firms also use Facebook for graduate recruitment. HR teams have a Facebook page to communicate with prospective traineeships. Check out the DWF Graduate Recruitment as an example of how a firm keeps graduates up to date with opportunities or Shoosmiths Live, a Q&A, streamed on Shoosmith's Facebook page. Shoosmith's Live is hosted by the firm's graduate recruitment manager Samantha Hope and guests.

We don't recommend that you use your personal Facebook page for business. Remember clients and contacts can 'Google' you too.

Twitter

If you use Twitter for business then you want to focus on showing authority in your area of expertise. Share links to information and give your own unique opinions too. The best lawyers on Twitter use it to comment on recent developments and provide commentary. While firms use Twitter to respond to client queries or to publicise legal news. CMS has different accounts to allow you to follow the latest news on employment or insolvency, for example. A good starting place to find accounts to follow can be found as *www.publiclawforevery-one.com* and the section on "Twitter & Blogs: A Guide For Law Students & Others". As with every other social network, the most important thing you can do is to be yourself. Think about posting opinions, news, and messages around your areas of interest. If you share information that is valuable to the people you want to talk to, they'll find you. It's also worth remembering that networking on Twitter is no different from meeting people face to face. Just as you wouldn't shout in someone's face at a drinks reception, so you shouldn't immediately tweet "FOLLOW ME, FOLLOW ME PLEAZ!". Just as you would if you meet someone in real life, you should find out what the person you want to talk to is interested in, be polite and then start a discussion with them. The only difference is that everybody can see your tweets. Quite often someone who is a follower of a 'friend's friend' will see your tweet and respond 'out of the blue.' Serendipity can lead to all kinds of unexpected opportunities.

6–31

LinkedIn

6–32   LinkedIn is different. It's designed specifically for professional networking (finding a job, connecting with potential business partners) rather than simply making friends or sharing photos, videos and music. To us, this makes it boring. What's the point of a social network that removes all the fun of being social? However, as young lawyers, LinkedIn does provide a useful way to keep in touch with contacts as they change jobs and roles. In your 20s your peers will change jobs frequently and it's easy to lose track of them. LinkedIn provides a good way to track changes as they're updated, and for you to get in touch and congratulate them (or offer support). It also provides a good way to contact recruitment agents, discreetly.

For general networking, Linkedin does have some value. Publishing articles and commentary to demonstrate knowledge and expertise is a traditional marketing tactic for law firms as we discuss above. Blogging has been effectively used by lawyers as a way of publishing their thoughts and insights without having to pitch to and/or pay third party publications for the privilege. LinkedIn takes pitch-free publishing a step further, with the distinct advantage of (i) automatically providing visibility to a user's connections and followers as new posts show up in their feeds; and (ii) giving people the ability to easily comment and interact with you. The important thing however is that whatever you publish is your comment. Even if it's just a 'this is interesting!' and a link to your firm's website. We've seen too many examples of lawyers on Linkedin posting the same comment as umpteen other lawyers at the same firm because, clearly someone in their marketing team has told them to do it. That's not showing who you are, unless who you are is a drone. You should be 'you' on social media.

The main thing to remember is that LinkedIn is one of the first places a business contact may look to find out more about you. Keep your profile up to date and make sure it has all the relevant information about you that you would want them to read.

YouTube (and other video sharing sites)

6–33   Firms have been slow to embrace video. The reasons are twofold. People are reluctant to appear on camera, and you need a certain level of skill to make good videos. However, with technology becoming cheaper and video editing simpler, it's a great time to experiment. Our only warning is that your video should look good—videos are visual, after all. Use proper lighting. Be engaging. Watch some 'how to' guides to 'vlogging' to pick up the basics. For examples of law firms using videos, check out Pinsent Masons' award winning HR Network TV, a news bulletin dedicated to employment law news.

These are all good examples of how firms use YouTube for their own purposes, but you should also be wary of appearing on it accidently. Building a reputation takes time, losing a reputation can take seconds. In 2013 a Clifford Chance trainee was filmed in Oxford, for a documentary video. He said, "I'm a City lad and I f******g love the ladness. I love the City." When he was asked what he meant by 'ladness' he said, "the ladness is just basically f******g people over for money." He was drunk and he wasn't at work. However, when Clifford Chance watched the video it released a statement:

> "The comments made are inappropriate and they're at odds with our principles and the professional standards we espouse as a firm. One of our trainee lawyers is the subject of our formal disciplinary procedures which may result in termination of the training contract with the firm."[1]

This trainee was probably playing up for the camera. However, when it comes to his leaving speech, do you think they'll mention his wonderful research skills, or his YouTube appearance?

This isn't just a problem for people caught talking about business. In 2015, US Law firm Goldberg Segalla sacked Clive O'Connell (a corporate partner in its London office) after he referred to Liverpool fans in a YouTube rant as, among other things, 'scum scouse idiots.'[2]

It didn't matter that he wasn't representing the firm, talking about clients, business or the law, when his comments were publicised.

It's not just firms that consider videos and not all YouTube videos lead to action. YouTubers are becoming lawyers too. And, as they graduate, as they get older, we've started to see stars of social media record their first steps into law. For a good example of how to use videos, check out future Magic Circle trainee, Eve Cornwell's videos on YouTube as she shares a day in the life on the Legal Practice Course at the University of Law or Angelica Olawepo's careers advice on her Angeliculture channel.

Blogs

Blogs allow you to discuss in detail particular aspects of law or practice. Given there is no restriction what (or how much) you can write your only challenge is to write engagingly so that people enjoy reading it. A regular blog can help build a readership that then will see you as an expert in your field. We refer you to David Allen Green's blog, "Jack of Kent" on Brexit and Brian Inksters' "Times Law Blawg" on the future legal tech. While for training contract advice we'd recommend Rosie Watterson's "Apply. Shine. Win."   6–34

Pinterest/Instagram/Snapchat (and other photo sharing sites)

A photo is worth a 1,000 words. The rise of Pinterest, Instagram and Snapchat evidence that we want to share photos of the things we like. While photo sharing sites may not be the first thing that pops into your head when you think of a law firm, they do allow firms to share photos of their people and offices to give you a glimpse of what it's like to work for them. Check out Urban Lawyers (which covers events for law students) and Tunde Okewale's musings on human rights.   6–35

[1] Jamie Hamilton, "Exclusive: Clifford Chance disciplines `f*ck people over' trainee", *http://www.rollonfriday.co.uk/TheNews/EuropeNews/tabid/58/Id/2909/fromTab/36/current Index/1/Default.aspx* [Accessed 17 May 2019].
[2] Andrew Harrison and John Hyde, "Should you be sacked for off-duty behaviour", *The Guardian*, *http://www.theguardian.com/commentisfree/2015/Nov/14/should-you-be-sacked-for-off-duty-behaviour-clive-o-connell-chelsea-scouse-scum* [Accessed 17 May 2019].

Even the Supreme Court has its own Instagram account. While Aberdein Considine, a Scottish law firm, uses Pinterest to sell homes.

SUMMARY

6–36   Business development and marketing skills set smart trainees and junior lawyers apart from your peers. Most lawyers will have the technical skills to do the same work as you – so, what sets you apart, is your ability to bring in, work with and understand clients.

PART 2

COMMERCIAL AWARENESS, KNOWLEDGE AND SKILLS

CHAPTER 7

How to write to emails, letters and reports

INTRODUCTION

Your partner asks you to write an email to a client. They ask you to show it to   **7–1**
them before you send it. After they review it, they return it, covered in changes.
They explain they've rewritten the letter in plain English: "Clients don't want
legal terms or long explanations", they say, "you need to keep things simple, so
they understand what they need to do. Remember, you are not writing an essay."

Words matter. As a lawyer, you should know this more than most. Not only do   **7–2**
words have a dictionary meaning, they may also have a meaning derived from
statute, case law, or both. Your choice of words in some way defines you, because
the majority of your work as a lawyer is spent writing emails, letters, contracts,
reports and other documents. Yet, it's the one skill that's not taught in all
universities.

This is an important point. Most universities judge you on what you write, not
how you write it. You need to show the depth of your research and the strength of
your arguments. Most clients are different. Every time you write to a client you
(clearly) know what you're talking about, but does your client? Have they spent
years at university? Do they know which laws apply to them? Or, do you need to
explain even the basic concepts? Even if your client is a lawyer, they'll still
appreciate a simple explanation more than one filled with big words, long
sentences and 'legalese'.

As an experiment, we asked the in-house team of a large public limited
company for examples of poor communication from their external lawyers. We
asked them for a Scottish litigation matter so that you don't have any existing
knowledge of the law discussed. This is the email they sent us—which they'd
received from a law firm:

> "Hi, just to update you: the defender's agent advised the Court that the defender's
> position is that the Answers to the Counterclaim do not present a substantive
> defence to the counterclaim. The defender is maintaining his criticisms of our
> principal claim and indeed the answers to the counterclaim, all as outlined in the
> defender's Note of Basis of Preliminary Plea and Supplementary Note of Basis of
> Preliminary Plea already forwarded to you."

They'd instructed a firm in Scotland to recover money. The particular lawyer who
received this missive was based in Leeds. He is an English lawyer and—
frankly—had no idea what it meant. Do you? What are "answers to the

counterclaim"? Why don't they amount to a "susbstantive defence to the counterclaim"? What is the 'counterclaim'?

Do you think that this firm would be instructed again, given that no one knew what it had done? Now think about your communication. Remember, you will write to people who don't have the same knowledge of law as you. Are you explaining things simply or clearly? Or are you sending them emails, letters or reports like this where you assume the person reading it will know the same things as you?

This is why we cover off some basic tips to help you improve your writing. This is not intended to be a comprehensive guide to construction and grammar. We assume you know the basics. Instead, we examine the main techniques used to make your writing easier to read, more direct and, most importantly, accessible to the greatest number of people. If you follow these steps you should never have a client phone you and complain: "I read your letter, now can you tell me what it means?"

Outcomes

7–3   By the end of this chapter you'll know four tips to improve your writing, including structuring your writing to make it easier for clients to understand what you're trying to say to them.

READABLE WRITING

7–4   *The Blah Story* by Nigel Tomm is a 23-volume novel. It's notable for having the longest sentence (and the longest word) in the English language, some 2,087,214 letters long. Here's an extract:

> "Blah intimidated, they blah to blah blah, where blah and blah passed a blah blah. Blah little blah that blah blah one blah surprised to blah what blah their blah were blah...[and on for over one million more words]".

All in all, it has almost 12 million words, 70 million characters and 18 thousand pages. It was never a bestseller. However, for everyone who thinks *The Blah Story* is one of the worst books ever written, someone else praises its attempt to challenge our perceptions of literature, by making the reader fill in the blanks, or the 'blahs'. One person's great work of art is another person's kindling, because writing is subjective. Everyone has different styles and different tastes. Some only read 19th century French literature, others only read Batman.

That's why this chapter isn't going to teach you about good (or bad) writing. Instead, what we'll do is share four techniques to make your writing more readable. Readable is different from 'good'. Regardless of what you think about the literary qualities of *50 Shades of Grey*, or the latest Jack Reacher, you can't deny that they're easy to read, and readable writing is the reason why millions buy them, while *The Blah Book* is only printed to order.

Why learn readable writing? What has readable writing got to do with being a lawyer? The answer is simple. 90% of your life as a lawyer is spent writing on a computer. You meet clients, you make calls, you go to court and you speak to colleagues, but the emails, letters and reports you write *are* your job. If you want to be good at your job you need to be able to write in a manner that the majority of your clients understand. Your hard work is meaningless if no one reads it. Or, worse still, it's read but without any understanding i.e. it's regarded as 'legal mumbo jumbo' or just 'blah blah blah'.

Take this extract from a client bulletin issued by a Magic Circle firm. The bulletin sets out to explain the difference between two common legal concepts, 'reasonable endeavours' and 'best endeavours'. This is the first sentence:

> "Some important distinctions arise throughout the delineation of these two terms, yet equally, courts have often been reluctant to affix unqualified criterion, rendering some such distinctions imprecise."[1]

We challenge anyone to understand this sentence without a clear head and a strong cup of coffee. Yet, this is a bulletin sent to clients, published on its website and—supposedly—meant to be helpful. It might be good legal writing and it might well be precise, but it sure isn't readable.

The following four tips will help make your writing more readable and easier for clients to understand.

TIP ONE: WRITE SHORTER SENTENCES

This is perhaps the greatest opening sentence of all time. It's by Charles Dickens and it comes from *A Tale of Two Cities*:

> "It was the best of times, it was the worst of times, it was the age of wisdom, it was the age of foolishness, it was the epoch of belief, it was the epoch of incredulity, it was the season of Light, it was the season of Darkness, it was the spring of hope, it was the winter of despair, we had everything before us, we had nothing before us, we were all going direct to Heaven, we were all going direct the other way—in short, the period was so far like the present period, that some of its noisiest authorities insisted on its being received, for good or for evil, in the superlative degree of comparison only."[2]

That's pretty good, isn't it? There's only one problem. It does go on a bit. It's over one hundred words long. We were bored by line three. We know it's considered a classic, but couldn't it just be a little shorter? How about: "Good times, bad times, just like today!" We're not saying that this is better than Dickens, but it does have a certain energy and directness that Dickens lacks. Arguably it's more readable, also, because you get the point without having to think about it as much. Some of the nuance and elegance is lost, but subtlety is what great literature is all about.

You, on the other hand, are writing to a client. You're not writing great literature. You don't need complex allegories, symbolism or a thesaurus (and your work should definitely be non-fiction). Instead, you need your work to be

---

[1] We don't wish to name the firm involved as we don't want to pick out this firm unfairly. There are many similar examples of technical language used in client bulletins and this was chosen purely as an example of a wider problem.
[2] Charles Dickens, *A Tale of Two Cities*, (Penguin Classics, 2003).

readable so that your clients understand you. The first lesson is a simple one. Short sentences are more readable than long sentences. How do you know if a sentence is too long? The trick is not to write with your hands. Instead, write with your ears. The simplest test of good writing is to read it out loud. If you're sitting in an office, perhaps do this under your breath so as not to disturb your secretary. You don't want to give her a fright when you start reciting:

> "It was the best of times, it was the worst of times, it was the age of wisdom, it was the age of foolishness, it was the epoch of belief, it was the epoch of incredulity, it was the season of Light, it was the season of Darkness, it was the spring of hope—[*BIG INHALE*]."

If you read what you write then you know immediately if any sentence is too long, because you'll run out of puff. How do you make your sentences shorter? The easiest way to write shorter sentence is take out all the "ands" and replace them with full stops. You'll make your work easier to say out loud, and to read.

TIP TWO: USE SHORT WORDS

7–6   This leads to our second tip. Use one short word instead of three longer words. You might think you sound smart when you use big words. That's drummed into you since childhood. The more words you know the smarter you must be. However, according to a study published in Applied Cognitive Psychology, the answer is an emphatic 'no'. Ironically, the title of the study was *Consequences of Erudite Vernacular Utilised Irrespective of Necessity: Problems with Using Long Words Needlessly*[3].

To be smart, you must stop *trying* to sound smart. Use short sentences and use small words like these:

Long	Short
At that point in time	Then
By means of	By
By reason of	Because of
By virtue of	By/under
For the purpose of	To
For the reason that	Because
From the point of view of	From/for
In accordance with	By/under
In as much as	Since
In connection with	With/about/concerning
In favour of	For
In order to	To

---

[3] Daniel M. Oppenheimer, *Consequences of Erudite Vernacular Utilized Irrespective of Necessity: Problems with Using Long Words Needlessly*, Daniel M. Oppenheimer, Applied Cognitive Psychology, Appl. Cognit. Psychol. 20: 139–156 [2006]

Long	Short
In relation to	About/concerning
In terms of	In
In the event that	If
In the nature of	Like
On the basis that	By/from
Prior to	Before
Subsequent to	After
With a view to	To
With reference to	About/concerning
With regard to	About/concerning
With respect to	On/about

For more examples read any article or book that discusses plain English. We also recommend the *Guardian* and the *Financial Times* style guides. These set out how these publications use language.

TIP THREE: GET TO THE POINT

Lawyers are bad at answering questions. It's not how we think. We prefer to set out arguments, a logical progression of thought and, finally, reach a conclusion. That's great for an essay, but awful in real life. Clients don't want to wade through your thought processes to get to the answer. They're shouting, 'get to the point!' If you're 'guilty', you don't want 10 pages telling you what happened. If your contract is unenforceable, you don't want 20 pages debating it. This doesn't mean you can't include some detail. Just be smarter about telling people what they want to know, first, and then tell them what they need to know (if they wish to read more).   7–7

Take Oscar Pistorius, the Paralympian athlete. He was accused of murdering his girlfriend. As you probably know, he was found guilty of culpable homicide. If you remember the trial, this decision took two days to reach. The judge set out the evidence before reaching a decision. But, if you face life imprisonment, would you want to wait two whole days before being told what will happen? Instead of taking two days to read out the decision, the judge could say, "I have found you guilty of culpable homicide and here's the reasons why."

Journalists, on the other hand, don't think like lawyers. They think in the opposite way, and give their readers all the information they need first. A process we can all follow by learning a technique known as the 'inverted pyramid'.

What is the inverted pyramid?

The inverted pyramid (also known as 'front-loading') is a style of writing where you include the most important details in the first paragraph. This is particularly important for web writing, where readers have short attention spans and more   7–8

125

often just scan articles. Pick any website, particularly news sites like the *Guardian*, *TMZ* and *Daily Mail Online*. Read the headline and first paragraph of any story. Then ask yourself if you know everything you need to know about the story? We bet the answer is 'yes'. The inverted pyramid has its roots in traditional media, dating back to the time of the telegraph and the early days of the newswire. One historian cites the reporting of the death of Abraham Lincoln in 1865 as one of the first examples of the inverted pyramid. *Associated Press* sent the following telegraph to all newspapers: "The President was shot in a theatre tonight and perhaps mortally wounded."

Contrast this with the *Daily Mail Online* story about the rapper, Kanye West:

> "Kim for First Lady? Kanye West announces he's running for president in 2020 during epic MTV VMAs acceptance speech (but admitted he smoked a joint before going on stage)".

We've given you examples of two stories. They're completely different, but each tells you everything you need to know in just its first line. Abraham Lincoln was shot and mortally wounded in a theatre. Kanye may run for president (but he might have been high).

Let's pick another article. This story, about Ukraine, comes from *BBC News*. The headline: "Russia sends 'aid mission' to Ukraine".

The first paragraph:

> "Around 300 lorries of humanitarian aid have left the Moscow area bound for eastern Ukraine, Russia has said."

The first paragraph gives us more information. 300 lorries of aid had left Moscow, bound for Eastern Ukraine. Then come some critical words: "Russia has said". This is a story about Russia telling the world it's sending aid to Ukraine.

The second paragraph:

> "Russian media said the cargo, including hundreds of tonnes of grain, baby food, power generators and medicine, will go to the civilians trapped by fighting in the area held by pro-Russia rebels."

The second paragraph expands on the first. We now know that it's the Russian media that has made the claim that the cargo is aid for Eastern Ukraine. We know more detail about the aid; it's hundreds of tonnes of grain, baby food and generators. It also fills in detail about who is receiving the aid: civilians trapped in areas held by pro-Russia forces.

As you can see, each paragraph adds more detail. It expands on the snappy headline. It doesn't build to a conclusion like a legal essay or a judicial decision. Ask yourself, what do your clients read? Do they read websites, newspapers, magazines and books? Or, do they read case reports from the Supreme Court and legal textbooks by academics? Then reflect on whether you should write like a Supreme Court judge, or like a journalist writing an article.

What's the benefit of the inverted pyramid?

The main benefit is that the readers of a paper can glean the gist of an article by reading only the first paragraph. This helps them to decide whether they want to read further. If they stop reading, they still have the key details of the article. From a writer's perspective, this style lets you engage your audience quickly and also to maintain their attention. In this age of short attention spans, readers are impatient, you need to get to your point quickly because clients expect information up front.

7–9

How do I write using the inverted pyramid?

This is easy to aspire to, but hard to achieve. If it were easy, we'd all do it naturally. Before starting any writing ask yourself who your reader will be. Is it a single person or a group of people? What do they want to know? Do you have something to tell them? Do you need information from them? Whatever it is that you need them to know, make sure you get that message out in the first paragraph. Use as many of the five 'w's' as you can (who, what, where, when, why), and also one 'h' (how). By addressing these points, you probably have summarised the article as a whole, in a few sentences. If not, go back and rewrite your introduction so that it does.

7–10

When writing to a client, start with the most important information first. Then go on to include more detail, until you finish with the least important information. In other words, get to the point.

EXAMPLES OF READABLE LEGAL WRITING

Shorter sentences and smaller words

This is an extract from an article on tax rules for limited liability partnerships (LLPs). Here's the second paragraph:

7–11

> "This [consultation] focused on two perceived misuses of the existing partnership tax regime: first, removing the presumption of self-employment for those LLP members who are 'salaried members' in order to tackle the disguising of employment through LLPs; and secondly, counteracting the tax-motivated allocation of business profits or losses in mixed membership partnerships (typically a mixture of individuals and corporates)".

Let's apply our first two tips to this passage. Shorter sentences and smaller words would give us this:

> "The Government's consultation did two things. It removed a presumption that some LLP members were self-employed. It revised rules for allocating business profits or losses in mixed membership partnerships".

The longest sentence is 13 words, the shortest is five words long. It's not interesting, but this isn't about being interesting. Rather, it's about readability. We could go further:

> "OMG! OMG! OMG! You won't believe what the taxman's done to LLPs—he's ripped up the rulebook. You need to watch out. Don't tell him you're self-employed when we all know you're fibbing. Don't fiddle with your profits—you'll only get caught. He's on the war path."

Clients expect you to keep things professional, so perhaps this isn't the style you should use. However, it does demonstrate that it's possible to make even the driest subjects into something that can be read by anyone.

Get to the point

7–12   Let's look again at the Magic Circle firm's article. You need to explain to a client the difference between 'reasonable endeavours' and 'best endeavours'. This is a fairly common question, when looking at a contract. This is how Andrew described it (in a contract with a landowner). He said:

> "I recommend we (*who*) use 'reasonable endeavours' (*what*) to get planning permission for X houses by January 2019 (*when*). This is because (*why*):
> 'Reasonable endeavours' is the weakest of the weak. All we need to do is to show we've done something—anything—to get planning. Doesn't need to be much, it just needs to be relevant.
> 'Best endeavours' is homemade hooch. Avoid. You'll go blind. It says we'll do everything we can just short of bankrupting ourselves to get planning."

As you can see, the second and third paragraphs expand on the first. There is no need to explain what 'reasonable endeavours' and 'best endeavours' are before you recommend one. The client may accept your recommendation without reading further. If they want to know more, they can read on.

WHY YOU SHOULD USE READABLE WRITING

7–13   It is just bad business to write badly. It's in everyone's interests that you communicate clearly so that your clients know what you're doing and what they need to do. If you don't, misunderstandings may occur, your client then is disappointed and you may lose business (or, worse, receive a complaint).

You can even test this scientifically. Readability tests assess the reading age someone needs to be to understand your writing, on a first reading. You can find free tests online. Just search for 'readability tests'. They work in a similar fashion, by counting the variables that have the biggest impact on readers: sentence length, number of syllables per words, and the number of passive sentences. Each formula works things out in a slightly different way, but most allow you to copy and paste a bit of text. A typical magazine has a reading age of 10 (or secondary school), a typical legal bulletin has a reading age of 24 (or post-graduate study). If you want your writing to be universal, then you want to be nearer to 10 than 24.

SUMMARY

Good writing is a joy, but we know it's a challenge. Five years of university is   **7–14** poor preparation for clear, direct writing. At university you're asked to write to a word count, and this can encourage padding. If you have 900 words written down, but a word count of 1000, you won't leave in all the 'ands', you may even add a few more. These are habits that you need to break. You're not writing for an academic, you're writing for a business woman who only reads the news on her iPad, a young father who left school at 16, a pensioner with poor eyesight—everyone, in fact.

That's why we encourage you to apply our four tips to your emails and letters. Try writing an opening sentence that tells your client everything he or she needs to know. Check those words and phrases that can be shortened. Your clients will thank you because they will understand what you are trying to tell them and they will know what they need to do next.

CHAPTER 8

How to meet clients

INTRODUCTION

You're meeting an existing client. They haven't told you why they want to meet. **8–1**
You think it may be to discuss funding options to expand their business. On the other hand, you've read that they have had problems with staff. They may want to meet to discuss an employment issue. You won't know until you speak with them. You think: "Wouldn't it be easier if everything was dealt with by email? Then I would have time to prepare an answer, rather than having to meet them and think of an answer on the spot? What if they ask me something I don't know?"

Words matter—not just when you write them down, but also when you say **8–2**
them out loud.

If you say the wrong thing, you can start wars. If you say the right thing you can make someone fall in love with you, and, while we don't expect you to start wars or seduce people in the office, your words have a powerful effect. Just think about the fuss over the legal advice for the Iraq War or the legal effect of the Brexit backstop. Lawyers' words matter. Clients make life-changing decisions based on what you tell them. They'll change their plea and go to jail, they'll divorce partners, they'll cut family members out of wills, they'll sue for millions or make radical changes to their business based on what you say. That's why before you say anything: (i) you should know what you should say to your clients (and others) and (ii) you should consider carefully how you should say it.

Outcome

Speaking to clients involves a range of knowledge and soft skills. What follows is **8–3**
a mixture of theory, business advice and practical exercises, all of which are focused on helping you to develop an understanding of what you need to do to become better at speaking to clients, and managing and leading meetings. We look at the practical steps you should take before arranging meetings. We then look at how you should start meetings; how to listen and ask sensible questions; how to end meetings effectively, and how to take the right actions afterwards.

STARTING OUT

8–4   How do you start speaking to clients? It's easy. Just open your mouth and talk. However, you're a professional, you have a reputation and you don't want to open your mouth and say anything. You want to provide clear and clever advice. But, how do you do that? Where do you start?

What is a client?

8–5   In this chapter we talk about speaking to (and meeting) 'clients'. However, our advice applies generally, for example to agents, intermediaries or other solicitors. We refer to clients only for simplicity's sake.

What is a meeting?

8–6   When we say 'meeting', what comes to mind? You may think of two or more people sitting at a boardroom table. However many meetings take place by telephone, conference call, video call, Skype or Facetime. Quite simply, how we meet has changed. Equally, when you think about meetings, you might be of the view that they must always take hours. You might think that meetings inevitably are long and complicated, with an agenda to follow and rituals to observe about who can speak and when. Yet, this too has changed. Most modern meetings are informal and happen rather quickly. People don't want to sit or speak for hours. They've got other things to do and places to be. When we refer to meetings, we're referring to anything from a 30 second call to just one person, to all day meetings with 20 or more people in a boardroom.

Whatever type of meeting you have, you should prepare in the same way. You can make just as good or as bad an impression in 30 seconds as you can in a day. If you phone someone and get his or her name wrong, ask a stupid question or give them wrong information, you damage your reputation just as much as if you turn up at court without your papers.

How do you prepare for meetings?

8–7   You need to prepare. You need to know what you want to say before you walk into a boardroom, pick up a phone or connect to a video call. You should know why you're speaking to a particular client or contact, what you hope to achieve, what they want to achieve and how you wish to present yourself. There are some simple, practical steps you can take so that you don't make basic mistakes. For example, go to the right place at the right time; make sure you phone the right number; speak to the right person, and so on. These steps (and many others) are set out in the following table, and should be your starting point for all meetings.

Practical steps checklist

Confirm people	This may seem obvious, especially if you're only speaking to (or meeting) one person. However, as your meetings grow larger it's easy to miss people out. If you do, they may feel miffed and might become difficult, even if they agree with you.	8–8
Confirm time	For formal meetings and calls, confirm a date and time. Send a meeting appointment if you can, so that they can be added to diaries.	
Confirm location	Confirm the location (whether physical, online or on the phone). Some law firms have more than one office in the same city so it's worth double-checking where you'll be.	
Confirm meeting arrangements	If appropriate, provide map directions to your attendees, or instructions as to how to join your conference (or video) call. If you're driving, make sure you know when you need to leave to get to your meeting early. Most sat navs let you look up traffic problems and congestion, prior to starting your journey. If you don't have a sat nav then check Google maps for traffic information. If you don't know about parking arrangements, check to see where the nearest car park will be.	
Prepare	Regardless of where your meeting is, review your notes, file and any legal aspects that might be relevant (we'll look at this in more detail, a little later).	
Research	Do some basic research on the people you're going to meet, especially if this is a first appointment. Try and know the basics about everyone who's going to be there. There are loads of resources to trawl, including Google, Twitter, Facebook and LinkedIn. Ask your colleagues, if you're meeting an existing client. We know one property lawyer who invited a blind man to view a property. If only he had asked a colleague, he would have avoided an awkward faux pas.	
Get ready	Pack everything you need to take with you well before you leave, to ensure you don't forget anything. Do this the night before if you've got a morning meeting, or first thing in the morning if it's an afternoon meeting.	
Last minute check	Scan the news before you leave, to see if there's anything happening that might relate to your client's business/industry. If there is, then you'll come across as sharp and savvy.	
Be a good host	On the day itself, if you're meeting in your office, make available some refreshments e.g. tea, coffee, water and biscuits.	
Don't be late	Most importantly, start on time. Clients can be late—you can't.	

This checklist may seem overkill if you're just phoning a client. Do you need to confirm when you're going to speak and how you'll do it? We argue 'yes'. A former colleague started all his calls with, "are you free to speak?" and, while most times the client could speak straight away, the question would often be followed by, "when would be a good time to call you?".

Equally, if you're making a call, you may only intend to ask your client one question. However, your client doesn't know that. He or she might take the opportunity to ask you about other matters. Having your client's file available (whether a paper copy or on screen), means you have the answers to hand.

Using our checklist (even for the simplest of calls) will help you develop good habits when meetings become longer, more complicated and involve more people.

What should you think about before a meeting?

8–9   Along with these practical steps, you should think about what you want to get out of the meeting, what your clients want to achieve, and how you intend to carry yourself.

What's your purpose for speaking to the client?

8–10   Be clear in your mind why you're speaking to your client. If something ancillary comes out of it, that's fantastic, but have a clear objective. If you're meeting a client for the first time, your main objective may be to get information from them. If you're phoning them to discuss a particular issue with a case, your objective may be to get instructions. More likely, your conversation will have multiple objectives (for example, to progress a particular legal issue and also to develop your relationship with them). Consider how you might further all objectives in the one meeting. One common way commercial lawyers build relationships is to hold important meetings at the client's office. By meeting the client at their office, they are not just providing advice they are also reducing the time the client needs to be away from their business, and they're getting a chance to learn more about that business while they are there.

What's in it for them?

8–11   We examine some possible benefits you can offer clients later, but for the moment just keep this in mind. Every client (existing or prospective) has an agenda. Spend as much time thinking about what your client will say, as you do in thinking about what you'll say. Consider the different ways your client might react to the information you're going to give them. Try and consider the business and/or personal pressures the client might be under.

How are you going to help them? You might be looking for instructions, but they may want reassurance that they've done the right thing in even raising a claim. They're often less interested in what you plan to do than in how confident you're about their prospects. A meeting that consists of, "well, we could do this, or we could do that or we could do this other thing, what do you think?" won't reassure a client as much as, "you have two options. I will discuss both, but I think the second will raise the stakes and make them more likely to agree with us".

How are you going to present yourself?

This links you back to your reputation (see Ch.6 (Clients and you)). How do you want a client to see you? Will you be happy and chatty, or serious and to the point? What is your personality and will it suit the meeting? A discussion about adoption is likely to require sympathy and empathy. A call to ask for money laundering information may require humour to point out the absurdity of asking a client who's been with the firm for 30 years to confirm his or her identity.[1] Equally, it's easy to be a nodding dog and agree with everything a client tells you, but are you prepared to act as devil's advocate and challenge their views? Are you willing to question assumptions? This can be the hardest part of taking meetings as a new lawyer.

    Remember, you have a duty to offer independent advice and to act in your client's best interests. This sometimes means giving them bad news or disagreeing with what they tell you. This can difficult, at first, especially when you're trying to tell someone who may be older than you that they're wrong. In these cases, a good way to approach this is to phrase your response in hypothetical language: "have you considered what will happen if that is not the case?" and, "let's assume for the sake of argument that you can't do that, we would then need to consider . . ." etc. Thinking not only about what you'll say but how you might say it, will make your meetings more effective.

8–12

WHY YOU SHOULD MEET CLIENTS

As a new lawyer, you might wonder why you need to meet clients at all. It can seem a distraction from getting on with the important contracts, cases and paperwork that "must go out this afternoon". This thought is short-sighted. No one gets promoted because they can draft a contract without spelling mistakes. People get promoted because of their reputation, and that comes from what your clients say about you after meeting you and speaking to you.

8–13

Your benefits

You should see the benefits of meetings as:

8–14

Enhanced confidence

Often new lawyers feel anxious. However, by regularly leading client meetings, you'll overcome (or at least control) your nerves.

8–15

---

[1] Not that the money laundering regulations are absurd—but you'll find that some clients find them to be when asked for ID.

Develop your leadership and team working

8–16   When you take a client meeting, you are acting as a leader. You're leading a meeting by keeping to an agenda; shaping the meeting's structure and outcomes; asking questions; and bringing it to a conclusion. By taking meetings, you build up your leadership skills.

   Meetings also encourage teamwork. If you're working with a colleague (for example, a year one trainee) you're actually building and managing a small team in your meeting. After your meeting, you might have that trainee do some work. You may ask a typist to prepare an email, report or letter etc. In other words, you'll be delegating, which is a key management skill.

Networking

8–17   Every client meeting is a window to a potentially influential person. It's your chance to shine. You never know where your career might lead you. You're not just gaining exposure to your own network, you're also building connections with your network's network. If your client knows a third party who has a need that matches what you can offer, assuming you've made a good impression then you may get an introduction.

Enhances your reputation

8–18   If you can upsell (and cross-sell) (see paras 8–22 and 8–23) you'll create a good impression in the eyes of your partner. You'll be seen as someone who can leverage increased business from existing clients and generate business from new clients.

Meet targets

8–19   This is a related point. If you upsell, you generate more business for yourself and so you can more easily meet your billing targets. As a young lawyer, this is a serious measurement of your performance.

Firm benefits

8–20   There are also business benefits for your firm:

Information sharing

8–21   This is a key advantage. It can be as simple as your client sharing updates about their business financials, new deals they're involved with, new start-up projects, and so on. With this information you can better judge if your clients are going to be good prospects. Your firm might be able to get involved with their new projects. You might also get an early warning of any problems they're facing which might impact on them paying any outstanding fees (which, in turn, helps inform a decision whether to take on new work). They might inadvertently leak information about your competitors; you might get nuggets about the services they offer, their charge out rates, their relationship with clients and so on. If a client recently has used another firm, it's also your chance to ask them why they did not come to you.

Upselling

Upselling is where you identify additional needs that your client might have and then you provide a service that fulfils them. For example, your client might ask you to draft a lease for a new rental property. What else might you ask them? What other services could you sell? He or she might need you to review the planning history of the property or check the property tax position. If you convince them that they need to cover these areas too, your £5,000 fee might just have doubled. But you can't really unlock that potential by email; you have to meet them to discuss what they need.

8–22

Cross-selling

Cross-selling is where you identify a client's additional needs and then you bring in someone else from another team within your firm to provide the service. You even, at a push, bring in an acquaintance from another firm altogether (for example, for specialist tax advice). It's basically upselling, but done horizontally as opposed to vertically. In other words, you don't get the extra business yourself but your firm still benefits. Many firms will recognise this cross selling

8–23

Let's assume that your client wants to lease a new property. However, you know that she wants the property in order to set up a new business. You persuade her that it would be safer for her to set up a new company to operate the business and take the lease. You can bring in a corporate colleague to help set up the company.

Downsides

Not every meeting leads to work and nor is every meeting productive. Even, if the meeting is about a current transaction, they can be time consuming. Some clients like to talk, and if you phone them to ask a simple question you can still be on the phone 30 minutes later. Andrew had one client who would take 45 minutes per phone call no matter the subject. If you're working on a fixed fee basis, you can appreciate how meetings like that eat into your time (and profit).

8–24

STEP ONE: PREPARE AN AGENDA

You know the benefits. You've reviewed the checklist and you know what you want to say, how you want to say it and how a client might react. Let's consider in more detail the practical steps you can take to make your meetings more effective. A good first step is to prepare an agenda. An agenda is important because it lets you and everyone you share it with, know what to expect in the meeting.

8–25

In particular, an agenda:

- provides a focus for your meeting;
- can be used as a checklist to ensure that all required points are covered;
- lets clients know what's going to be discussed, giving them the opportunity to come prepared and better informed; and
- gives you the opportunity to impose controls (especially relating to time, if you have other commitments that you can't change).

What should an agenda contain?

8–26   Here are our eight top tips:

- Send an email confirming your meeting, its goal (or goals) and all the administrative details (when, where etc.).
- Ask those invited to accept or decline the meeting. You can use free online applications, like Doodle, to help.
- Consider the agenda items you want to include.
- Ask everyone who's coming to contact you (say no later than two days before) with any agenda items they want to add.
- Once all agenda requests have been submitted to you, summarise them in a table format with suitable headings:
  a.   agenda item;
  b.   presenter (who'll lead the discussion on the point); and
  c.   time allocated.
- Ensure each agenda item relates to the goals of your meeting. If an inappropriate request is made, suggest that this be discussed at another meeting.
- Be realistic. Don't cram too much into a one-hour meeting. When people (especially colleagues) accept a meeting, generally they expect to be finished on schedule. It's better to under-play the time available, leaving a small amount of time (say 10 minutes) to spare.
- Send your agenda to all participants the day before, with a reminder of the goals (also location, time and duration). At this point, check with the presenters (if there are any) that they're happy with the order in which they'll be speaking, and the amount of time they have been allocated.

Do you always need an agenda?

8–27   Yes. While you may not need to follow all eight steps to prepare for a simple meeting, it's still worth working through them, each time. You may not prepare a full agenda but you may want to write a couple of notes on your note pad as a reminder of what you'll say, what you need to cover and who you need to speak to. You can then refer to the note, to make sure that you get everything you need.

Working with colleagues

8–28   Don't forget to send your agenda to any colleagues if they're going to join your meeting. This is important because, not only will they want to know what you're going to talk about, it also helps:

- establish clear roles for each person—this avoids duplication and also the embarrassment of both of you talking over each other on the same points;
- identify someone to observe and take notes—this may be you in your first meetings as a trainee, and, if so, use this opportunity to observe how others act in meetings;
- consider whether the mix of your team members will provide a suitable range of knowledge and skills; and
- consider if everyone needs to be there—a common mistake is to invite everyone to a meeting when some people may only be needed for part. This is particularly important when you meet a client for the first time. You may think they will need to speak to a team of people but the client may be overwhelmed if they find themselves facing a 'mob' of lawyers.

STEP TWO: STARTING MEETINGS

You've arranged a meeting and you've thought about what you want to say (and how you plan to say it). You've drafted an agenda and circulated it. You've turned up on time ready and raring to go.   **8–29**

The next issue is how best to start. Take it as read that you need to smile and shake your client's hand. What we're getting at is what you should do once your client is ready to talk. Basically, your client wants to know two things. Firstly, why am I here? Secondly, why should I care?

Meeting steps

To help you answer these questions, there are four steps you can take. You should: **8–30**

- inform;
- excite;
- empower, and
- involve.

Inform

This is where you let your client know the purpose of the meeting and the expected outcomes. An agenda helps. You can run through it and ask your client to confirm they're happy with it. If you don't have an agenda, you might say: "the purpose of this meeting is . . . when we're finished, we'll have achieved…".   **8–31**

Excite

You may have your client in the room, more in body rather than in soul. How do you excite them? You make statements that answer the question, "what's in it for me/why should I care?" Compare these two openings. Which does the better job of 'exciting'?   **8–32**

Example 1:

> "Good morning, it's a pleasure to meet you. Let me start by reviewing why we're here. The purpose of this meeting is to sort out a draft will and power of attorney. I suppose you have to do these things, don't you?"

Example 2:

> "Good morning, it's nice to meet you. Let me start by reviewing why we're here. The purpose of this meeting is to sort out your new will and power of attorney. By the end of the meeting we'll have all the information we need to prepare the documents which will help protect you and your family."

The second is by far the better statement. It does a neater job of describing various benefits to your client. Notice another thing: excite statements tend to contain a greater number of the words 'you' or 'your'. They serve to tie a client into a meeting; they get the client excited about being there. In other words, the key to getting your clients excited about participating in a meeting is to explain clearly what's in it for them.

Empower

8–33 You describe to your client the role he or she will play during the meeting. The goal is to ensure that your client (or potential client) is clear on the power that they have. You see, when people feel empowered, they tend to be much less hesitant about participating and are much more willing to open up and be collaborative.

Often, a single empowering statement is sufficient. Other times you might find that multiple statements are needed to empower a client who is used to being told what to do (especially if it's a corporate client).

Examples:

> "Just stop me if you want me to go over anything, or explain anything."

> "You have a choice between court and arbitration. As I explained, a court could be costly but it will provide a definitive answer. Arbitration is cheaper but there's no guarantee it will work. Which option do you prefer?"

Involve

8–34 Get your client involved immediately using 'engagement questions' to ensure they are involved in the meeting. There are a few different ways you can do this.

- Key topics approach: you think about the purpose of your meeting and build a list of key topics with your client. You might say, "if we're going to be successful today, what do we need to cover? Let's make a list first so we have a checklist of what we'll need to cover today."

- Personal outcomes approach: you visualise how a successful meeting would go. You might say, "given your objectives, what are the outcomes you personally would like to see come out of today's meeting?"
- One-minute check approach: this works well if you meet a client regularly. You could say, "it's been several days since we were all together. Let's start with each person giving a quick update from the last time we met." While another option might be, "we were last together on 1 December. Since then, there probably have been some significant events that have occurred. Can you update me?"

STEP THREE: LISTEN AND ASK QUESTIONS

Once you've started a meeting you should be using your listening and questioning skills to help you get the information you want.

8–35

Listening skills

The following exercise—for which you'll need a friend to volunteer to help you—demonstrates just how critical it is to listen.

8–36

Get your friend to go away and prepare a short, three-minute talk. He or she will speak to you about something that has interested them recently (be it an experience, their last holiday etc.). While they speak, every time something interesting arises (that makes you want to ask a question or makes you tempted to react in some way), raise your hand for five seconds and then put it back down. Do this throughout the entire conversation. You're not allowed to interact with your friend. You can't ask questions, nor can you affirm your understanding. You must remain totally silent. As well as raising your hand, try deliberately to lose focus. You can do this by staring out the window, or by becoming transfixed with a detail on their jacket. The aim is to create a distraction to your listening.

Once the three minutes are up, ask your friend how they felt talking to you. What emotions were evoked? You can expect answers to include statements like, "I didn't feel listened too", "I didn't understand why you were putting you hand up", or "you distracted me." Try repeating this exercise with different people. You'll come to appreciate why active listening is important.

Questioning skills

This next exercise demonstrates why good, open questions are essential if you're going to elicit information. In fact, developing a list of possible questions is something you can (and should) do as part of your pre-meeting preparation.

8–37

Firstly, think of a famous person (but clearly don't tell your friends who it is). Start a timer. Each of your friends then asks closed questions, in turn (for example, "are you a man?" or "are you an actor?"). Their aim is to work out who you are. Gradually, they'll narrow the possibilities and eventually arrive at the correct answer. This illustrates a point: closed questions get you nowhere (fast) if you want to gain information.

The second part of the exercise is to put your friends into pairs. Each of you then has 60 seconds (in your pairs) to take turns in asking open questions of each other. The aim is to find out five things about the other person, in the time available. Make sure you write them down.

What you'll tend to find with these short exercises is that if you ask open questions you get lots of information, in a short period of time, compared to the amount of time it takes to find out just one piece of information using closed questions.

What are close-ended questions?

8–38   Close-ended questions are those that can be answered by a simple 'yes' or 'no'. "Did you get here by car?" "Would you like a cup of tea?" These can be answered with a yes or no. If your client arrived by train and would prefer a coffee, your conversation will seem curt if they keep saying 'no'.

What are open questions?

8–39   Open-ended questions are those that require more thought, and certainly more than a simple one-word answer. "How did you get here today?" "What do you like to drink?" Your client can give you more information. "I got the train from Victoria as the roads were gridlocked" or "could I get a coffee, no milk or sugar?"

These are simple examples, but the distinction becomes important when you're trying to get information from a client. You want to start by asking open questions, such as "how can I help you today?" and "is there anything else I should know?", so that you can find out as much information as you can. You only ask closed questions if you want to confirm something specific. Here's an example:

"How can I help you today?"

"I've recently been made redundant by my employer and I don't understand why they've done this."

"Who is your employer?"(You are now asking for specific information.)

"Company X."

"And what do you think they've done wrong?"(Opening up the conversation again to try and understand how the client thinks.)

STEP FOUR: NON-VERBAL COMMUNICATION

8–40   This is an important aspect of your behaviour. We communicate non-verbally all the time. Non-verbal communication includes: eye contact, body language, facial expressions, mirroring, approach, face to face (proximity), senses and silence. Let's run through each of these.

Eye contact

It's really important for sincere communication that you give your client your complete attention. For this you need lots of appropriate eye contact. This shows respect and helps you connect to that person.

8–41

Body language/facial expressions

When we communicate with people, they derive information in the following proportions:

8–42

- 7%—words;
- 38%—vocal characteristics (tone, volume, inflection); and
- 55%—body language and facial expressions.

Does your face match your words? When you aren't speaking, what does your face say to those around you? You have to match your body language with your intent. Know that your client is always watching you, albeit he or she might be speaking.

Approach/proximity

Both are forms of communication. Clearly, you should approach everyone from the front and be aware of just how close you are when speaking, especially when someone is seated. Applying that to meetings, don't ambush your client and make sure that the meeting space is set up appropriately.

8–43

Senses

Again, just be aware that you can communicate with other senses: smell, sight and taste. What do you think we mean by smell and sight? Keep stocked up on soap and shampoo, and make sure you're well turned out. This might sound like something your mum would say but she says it because she's right—and it's just as true in the office.

8–44

Silence

Silence is unsettling. If you're trying to get information out of a client during a meeting this can be a useful way to do this. If you leave a silence, someone will feel an urge to fill it. However, it is best avoided in some circumstances as it can make people feel uncomfortable. It's also worth using sparingly otherwise people will just think you have nothing to say if you fall silent every five minutes.

8–45

STEP FIVE: ENDING MEETINGS

8–46   Earlier we said that an agenda is a really useful tool to help you to end your meetings on time. After all, you've got other things to deal with. Ending a meeting on time also educates your client that your time is valuable. How do you do it without appearing to be rude? When you feel that all the business aspects have been dealt with, consider these different approaches to end on a positive note:

Verbal cues:

- reassure your client they're on the right track;
- perhaps congratulate them on their decision;
- explain the next steps;
- mention each agenda item and review the decisions made, or actions required; or
- make a defined closing statement, like "I've got one final question before you leave …".

Give physical cues:

- close your file and move it off to the side;
- extend your hand for a handshake, giving a verbal cue (like "thank you for coming in today");
- change the subject to something generic, like the weather; or
- as a last resort, stand up and your client (should) follow your lead.

STEP SIX: AFTER THE MEETING

8–47   Arguably this is the most important step. If you don't do what you say you'll do, you undo all your good work. Imagine meeting a lawyer who is charming, smart and knows exactly what you need to do. Imagine that lawyer not doing anything for six months. What do you think of them now?

After the meeting may be the final step yet it's so often forgotten. It includes:

- dictating the minutes of your meeting (or write a file note);
- working out your next actions;
- working out any actions that your client needs to take;
- reviewing any deadlines;
- writing to your client, setting out the agreed next steps (with timelines);
- putting key dates in your diary (e.g. intimation dates etc.);
- allocating work across your team (if necessary); and
- arranging your next meeting.

Minutes/file note

You need to record the discussions that take place in every meeting, as well as all the decisions reached. It's important to detail, also, any disagreements (especially if you have recommended a course of action that your client has overruled). It's important to set down tasks that need to be actioned. This should include what the task is and can also include what the outcome of that task will be (e.g. a document, a report etc.). It's essential to record the name of the person who is assigned to a particular task. **8–48**

Delegation

Delegation is a managerial skill. We deal with it in depth in Ch.16 (How to delegate work). If you're going to delegate tasks that arise in the course of a client meeting, you need to think about your team member's suitability. Think about whether he or she has the knowledge, skill and experience to do what you're asking of them. If not, consider whether there is time to put in place appropriate training. If not, it ought instead to be completed by someone that already has experience. **8–49**

SUMMARY

Meeting clients and contacts and other solicitors is a vital part of being a lawyer. Every criminal case has at least two people: the crown and the accused. Every house sale has a seller and a buyer. Every sale contract, a seller and a buyer. And, for all of them, every lawyer has a client. You'll always need to speak to someone—and the more you prepare the more confident you'll be when you meet them. **8–50**

CHAPTER 9

How to negotiate

INTRODUCTION

You act for client in an employment dispute. You've raised a claim against their **9–1**
employer and immediately received good news. Their former employer is
prepared to settle and pay compensation. Their lawyer sends you a compromise
agreement, to confirm the terms and compensation. However, your partner takes
one look at it and shouts, "completely unacceptable!" They tells you to, "arrange
a meeting with their lawyer and negotiate better terms. Our client can do much
better than this." But how do you negotiate new terms?

Over the course of your career, you'll be asked to negotiate many agreements **9–2**
and documents. It might be a settlement offer; a contract; financial matters
following a divorce; a commercial deal; a personal injury claim; or a lease for a
new property. Whatever it is, you'll be asked by clients to negotiate on their
behalf.

In many ways a negotiation is just like any meeting: it could take place in the
formal setting of your boardroom, or it could be a 30 second telephone call. Just
like in the last chapter, while the format can change, the principles remain the
same. You'll either be trying to persuade someone to accept what you say, or
you'll be trying to reach an acceptable compromise.

In our scenario, let's say that your client has been offered £20,000 by way of
compensation, but has been asked to sign a restrictive covenant that will prevent
her working for a rival firm for five years. Your client is happy to accept £5,000
in compensation (as she has raised her claim as a point of principle) but wants to
start work after six months. You have parameters in which to negotiate and, while
you know where you want to end up, it's up to you how you get there. Do you
offer £5,000 straight away? Do you ask for more (say £10,000) and see how they
respond before moving to your actual position? Tactics matter and, depending on
what tactics you use, they could mean the difference between reaching
agreement, accepting less, or, ultimately everyone walking away. As a new
lawyer, negotiations can be daunting, but if you follow the principles set out in
this chapter you'll know how to prepare and how to handle yourself, so that you
can achieve the best results for your client.

Outcomes

This chapter looks at the theory and practice of negotiation. We explain what we **9–3**
mean by negotiation and we look at the tactics and skills required to negotiate
successfully.

NEGOTIATIONS BASICS

9–4   Those new to negotiation are often anxious about a lack of experience. If that's you, relax. In actual fact, everyone has some experience of negotiation:

- when you buying something from Gumtree ("I'll give you £90 instead of £100, and I can come round tonight and pick it up");
- when you haggle over a bill with friends ("I should pay less as I didn't have any cocktails");
- when you were young and wanted to stay out late ("If I can stay out until 11pm I promise to keep my mobile switched on at all times");
- when you're older and married, and still want to stay out late ("If I can stay out until 11pm I promise to keep my mobile switched on at all times"—this never changes);
- when on holiday, bartering in a street market; or
- negotiating your new mobile phone contract when you need to decide between different options.

In other words, the fact that you may never have led a formal negotiation is not something to worry about. You already know how to negotiate. You do it all the time. But what is negotiation?

What is negotiation?

9–5   Negotiation is what happens when people who disagree try and agree something together. If you prefer a formal definition then negotiation is the process by which you seek to achieve a mutually beneficial agreement on a matter (or a number of matters) with someone else (your opponent, if you will). This other person will have different needs and goals to you and negotiation is the process by which agreement is reached. Every negotiation is unique. Each differs in terms of its subject matter, the number of participants and your approach. One day it's Gumtree, the next it's a multi-party compromise agreement. Regardless, your approach is very similar.

Why negotiate?

9–6   Good negotiations contribute to your success in any business, not just the law. Firstly, they help to create enduring, mutually respectful relationships and, secondly, they enhance existing relationships. In other words, if you get your negotiation right, your opponent will be much more inclined to do business with you in the future. It's worth remembering that you are part of a relatively small legal profession, so if you're a nightmare to deal with or if you use underhand tactics, other lawyers will talk about you. You want to be someone who, when named, others lawyers say, "they're good to deal with" and not, "oh no, not them."

Where do you start?

In terms of procedure, negotiations are incredibly flexible. You're free to shape them in accordance with your needs and those of your opponents. You and the other parties may want a formal meeting, or you may just want a phone call. It's entirely up to you to agree. What you'll find is that formal meetings happen less and less. A lot of documents are negotiated by phone or email before any meetings take place. We've assumed in this section that you're preparing for a meeting, but the tips are just as relevant for email and phone calls. You may not go into as much detail, but the process is a good one to know. Better to know too much and to cut down what you need, than to know too little and miss something.

    In terms of representing clients, you need to be clear about your mandate to lead any negotiation and also about your opponent's authority. Do you have the power, either within your firm or from your client? Always be wary of negotiations involving companies and their agents. Your opponent needs to have express or implied authority from the company he or she claims to represent. In other words, do they have the power to broker a deal, or not?

9–7

What do you need to watch out for?

No negotiation can guarantee the good faith or trustworthiness of its participants, though you can reasonably expect every lawyer to act in good faith (if they're to meet professional standards). Some clients however may say 'black is white' and 'white is black' to get a deal done (and then completely ignore everything you've agreed). If you have clients like that, you need to make sure that you maintain your own standards by remaining objective. You'll have many clients, but you only have one reputation.

    An example of bad faith would be to use a negotiation as a stalling tactic, either to delay you or your client from moving forward with, for example, litigation. Usually this becomes apparent, as meetings will rehash the same issues again and again. If this happens, you either call the other side on it by asking, "do you actually want to do a deal?" or you revert to your Plan B and continue with your client's claim.

    Finally, you need to understand that some issues simply are unable to be negotiated. There is little chance of an agreement if, for example, you and your opponent are divided by diametrically opposed beliefs which leave no room for concessions. It's possible that from time to time your negotiations might just break down. The absence of a neutral third party as arbiter sometimes results in parties being unable to reach an agreement, because quite simply they might not be able to work co-operatively. What's more, that lack of an arbiter might actually encourage your opponent to be overly aggressive, in an attempt to take advantage of you.

9–8

SUCCESSFUL NEGOTIATION

It's fair to say that a successful negotiation is one that:

9–9

- generates the best possible deal in the circumstances;
- avoids litigation;
- achieves a workable, lasting agreement;
- establishes or maintains a client relationship; and
- maintains professional standards and ethics.

Interests v positions

9–10 A key point when working towards a successful outcome is to understand the difference between interests and positions.

Many commentators believe that negotiations stand a much greater chance of success when parties adopt an interests based approach. If you focus on mutual needs and interests, and use objective standards (as opposed to subjective standards), there is a greater chance of reaching an agreement that meets the needs of both you and your opponent. This is sometimes called a "win-win" approach.

What's the difference between interests and positions? Interests tend to be long-term. They relate to your overall situation, and might develop and change over time. Positions, by contrast, tend to be short-term and focused more specifically (indeed, narrowly) on a particular issue. Let's look at a simple example. A plumber is needed to do a job in a hotel. The plumber wants a minimum of £100 to put down his remote control on a wild and windy night; the hotel is willing to pay a maximum of £100. In this case the positions are the same and a deal can be struck. What if the hotel has a policy of paying only £80 in call out charges? If this negotiation were purely positional (specifically cash positions), there could be no agreement. The plumber would simply say no. However, the plumber has a wider interest, namely developing his business. If the hotel were to take the plumber's interests into account it could offer, for example, to put him on its approved suppliers list. This would cost the hotel nothing but might allow it to fulfil its interests too i.e. having its premises maintained in good order.

Let's look at our example. Your client is young and she has a long career ahead. She doesn't mind taking a short break, as long as she receives some compensation. Equally, she doesn't want her employment restricted for five years as that would affect her career prospects. Her long-term interest is to win her case, but not have it affect her career. A short-term position (to win £20,000 at all costs) will not help her achieve that. While she might get £20,000, she may live to regret it. However, were your client in her 60s and not bothered about another job, her interest would be to get as much money as possible to help her retirement. She would be willing to sign anything to get £20,000.

Understanding your client's interests helps you judge whether their stance is likely to be helpful. When advising them you can say, "I think this is a good offer because it will give you a good nest egg for retirement and you won't have to give up anything important in return" or "I think this is a bad offer because while it's a big amount now, think about what will happen in two or three years. You still won't be able to work in a similar job—and £20,000 doesn't stretch that far."

Ethics

9–11
We've touched on professional standards and ethics. Remember, as a solicitor you have ethical obligations that include, for example, an obligation not to mislead fellow solicitors. You must bear this in mind, if negotiating with another solicitor on behalf of a client.

Turning to corporate bodies, since the inception of the Companies Act 2006 s.172, directors must promote the interests of their companies in good faith. This includes having regard to:

- the likely consequences of any decision in the long term;
- the interests of the company's employees;
- the need to foster the company's business relationships with suppliers, customers and others;
- the impact of the company's operations on the community and the environment;
- the desirability of the company maintaining a reputation for high standards of business conduct; and
- the need to act fairly as between members of the company.

These arguably can be said to be a form of corporate 'ethics'. It may be that your firm is a limited company, in which case you're bound by the terms of s.172. Corporate clients, almost certainly, won't be impressed if you behave unethically acting on their behalf. We repeat again, clients may be unethical—but you can't be.

STYLE

9–12
You can be two main types of negotiator. The first is a co-operative (interest based) negotiator who:

- tends to be friendly;
- tries to avoid conflict; and
- makes concessions to reach an agreement.

Is this you?

The co–operative negotiator

9–13
This sort of negotiator always starts from the premise that negotiations need not be 'zero sum' (i.e. the gains of one party shouldn't be at the expense of the other party). Mutual interests are identified and objective standards are used. The goal is to reach an agreement acceptable to all participants.

You know that your client's employer doesn't want her to start working immediately for a competitor. You know that your client is happy to take a short break. When you propose a one-year break (and they propose three) you might ask questions about which competitors they don't want her to work for. From this, you can identify that they're only concerned about her working for their main rivals. Perhaps, then, your client might indicate that she has no intention of working for those firms and is happy to accept a longer restriction for those two, provided she can work for other firms after one year.

If you adopt this approach, it has the advantage of creating joint benefits. However, some disadvantages are: your concessions might not generate agreement; you might be vulnerable to exploitation and might not recognise it when it happens; your opponent may think you're not 'fighting their corner' and regard you as weak; or you might react emotionally to your opponent's competitiveness and 'lose face'. Allied to this is the concept of the principled negotiation. Those who favour principled bargaining believe that being positional can lead to situations where parties will be stubborn ('hard bargaining') or accept big, unilateral losses ('soft bargaining') in order to reach agreement. Principled bargaining attempts to reconcile the interests underlying the positions. This form of negotiation is increasingly popular. It could be called co-operative 'plus'.

The competitive negotiator

9–14   The second type of negotiator is the competitive negotiator. This type of negotiator:

- treats opponents as adversaries and they play to win;
- keeps the pressure on;
- can be perceived as quite threatening; and
- demands concessions yet makes no concessions.

Is this you?

If you adopt this approach, you try to maximise your advantage at the expense of your opponent. Mutual interests are eschewed, in favour of a positional stance. The advantage of this approach is that it minimises the risk of exploitation. The main disadvantage, however, is that increased tension (caused by brinkmanship) inhibits the mutual trust that is required to unlock joint gain. This tends to cause a breakdown of negotiations.

Let's go back to our example. Let's say you insist that your client wants £20,000 and a one-year restriction, or else you'll take her claim to the employment tribunal (which will be public and could be bad PR for her employer). Even if the employer responds with—say—£10,000 and a one-year restriction, you still push for more, and that's when they walk away.

A further disadvantage is that, over time, your reputation for being competitive precedes you and you tend to conclude fewer deals. Why? Past opponents are less inclined to do business, as they don't see any advantage in negotiating with you.

THE STEPS TO NEGOTIATION

A great negotiation involves lots of preparation and planning, both on your own and with your team. You need to marshal all your facts and arguments. During a negotiation you'll need to question your opponent, listen, think and even discuss various matters with your team (and client).

9–15

Step one: process v act

Firstly, you should treat negotiation as a process rather than an act. Processes can take place over a period of time, or last just a single session. They're inherently flexible. If you view negotiation as an act you'll tend to consider it a 'one off' and immediately be time-bound, putting yourself under pressure to conclude an agreement in one session. That, in turn, can encourage you to be positional. Positions, after all, can be accepted or rejected quite quickly. Interests, on the other hand, can take time to be fully articulated, explored and aligned.

9–16

Think about Prime Minister Theresa May's Brexit negotiation with the EU. This was not a one off process. She and her advisors met repeatedly with the EU's chief negotiator and with other European leaders in the run up to the final withdrawal agreement. They'd spent time speaking to every interested party to test what he would offer and what they would accept in return. The final meetings it took a single day to complete (with offers and counteroffers). Whether you think the outcome was successful is a matter for your own personal politics. However, in terms of process, Theresa May treated the negotiation as a process lasting months and not just a single meeting in November 2018. You can learn a similar lesson in even the simplest of negotiations.

Don't assume that one meeting will deal with all points that might need to be negotiated. You and your client (and the other party and their solicitor) may need to reflect on what was said and what was offered. You may want to change your position based on what you learn.

Step two: assessment

Your negotiation begins with a communication (either from you or your opponent) indicating a willingness to bargain. Since negotiation is a voluntary process, the first step has to be to assess whether your opponent is serious.

9–17

Factors that might help you make that assessment are:

- whether a negotiated solution is in their interests;
- their credibility (perhaps elicited from previous dealings);
- whether there's a disparity such that it would be impossible to negotiate equally; and
- whether that person has the authority to enter into negotiations and to conclude an agreement (especially if they're representing a company).

Step three: practical steps

Once you've green-lit a negotiation, you need to start preparing.

9–18

- Agree the purpose of your meeting. What are you intending to achieve? What is the scope of the negotiation? Is this a preliminary meeting, or is it being held with a view to concluding an agreement?
- Agree an agenda. This brings a structure to your negotiation. It also helps you exercise control. You don't want to be taken by surprise and forced into a bargaining situation where you feel you need more time or information.
- Agree a timetable. Remember, a negotiation is a process (not an act). What will the frequency of your negotiations be, and how long will they last?
- Work out who will be present at the sessions.
- Choose a venue (preferably a neutral location).

Getting the preparation right is not only good business practice, but also helps to reinforce your credibility (and thus contributes to establishing confidence and trust).

Step four: preparation

9–19   The next step is to plan your strategy. Thorough preparation is the key. In no particular order, you need to:

- marshal your arguments;
- find out as much as possible about your opponent (including any information about how they have conducted negotiations in the past);
- ensure that everyone in your team is on the same page (internal disagreements work against you by undermining your authority);
- work out what questions you might ask;
- anticipate the questions you'll be asked and work out how you'll handle difficult questions;
- decide how your negotiation will be handled—will it be just you talking, or will your colleagues contribute?;
- consider when and how you'll call a private team meeting (a 'time out') that will interrupt the negotiation (this might be appropriate if a new issue emerges);
- consider how best to play to your strengths and to exploit your opponent's weaknesses;
- remember that your opponent will have "monkeys on his or her back" i.e. the external pressures that are on a person to reach an agreement; and
- check if there are any critical dates you will need to know.

Step five: consider your BATNA

9–20   You need to give consideration to your best alternative to a negotiated agreement (your so-called 'BATNA'). BATNA is a benchmark that protects you from accepting terms that are too unfavorable, but also from rejecting terms that would be in your interest to accept.[1]

Quite simply:

---

[1] BATNA is a term coined by Roger Fisher and William Ury in their 1981 bestseller, *Getting to Yes: Negotiating Without Giving;* (London Random House Business, 1st edition, 2012).

- if a proposed agreement is better than your BATNA, you should accept it;
- if a proposed agreement is worse than your BATNA, you should continue your negotiations; and
- if you cannot improve the proposed agreement, you should consider withdrawing from negotiations and pursuing your BATNA.

Having a well worked out BATNA increases your negotiating power. If you know that you have a really strong, viable alternative, you don't need to concede as much and—in fact—can push your opponent harder. Why? You simply won't care to the same degree as you would if you didn't have that great alternative.

If your BATNA isn't strong, however (or if it's non-existent), your opponent will be able to make demands that you'll likely have to accept, because you don't have a better option. Let's assume your client is broke. She owes £5,000 on credit cards, £2,000 on her overdraft and is three months behind on her mortgage. This example also shows the importance of timescales and key dates. If your client has a mortgage to pay and no money to pay it, this limits your tactics.

The opposite is true, too. Your BATNA may make it easy to negotiate. Your client may be a millionaire. She's not suing for the money, but instead for principle's sake: employers should not get away with treating people unfairly. While not her first option, she might be happy to see the case go to a tribunal and have it heard in public, so that people can find out how her employer has acted. Her BATNA means that if she's offered an unattractive deal, she's able to reject it, even if it risks a breakdown of the process.

It's important to improve your BATNA wherever possible. If your BATNA is strong then it's worth revealing it to your opponent, early on in the negotiation. If it's weak, it's much better to keep it quiet. Always try and work out what your opponent's BATNA might be.

Step six: the negotiation

What follows are our top tips for the negotiation, itself.   **9–21**

- Agree the facts. This helps to foster a spirit of co-operation and also ensures that you're not working at cross-purposes.
- Agree common interests. The objective here is to make everyone feel that they're striving towards a common goal (that is, if you're being a co-operative negotiator).
- Question and listen. Negotiation requires great questioning and listening skills. Using them effectively helps you obtain extra information and also lets you assess how your opponent is approaching the negotiation. Listen for clues as to what your opponent's interests are, and to what they might be prepared to agree. Often, if you just listen, people give away more than they intend to.
- Before you amend your position on any point, consider why you're doing so. Try not to move unless you're sure there is a positive benefit.
- If you're negotiating several terms, think of them as a package, like 'juggling balls' in the air. There is a benefit in playing different terms off

155

against each other. However, if you let your opponent negotiate each term individually and sequentially, you can't revisit them later (without looking unprofessional).

- Summarise and recap regularly. This helps you to slow the pace down and take back control (which is useful if you need some breathing space and/or thinking time).
- Record your agreement. This seems obvious, but a note summarising the points that have been agreed is always worthwhile.
- After the event, analyse your negotiation. Think about what you thought would happen and what actually happened. Why did things perhaps turn out differently (whether or not in your favour) and how could you manage the process better the next time?

Step seven: the offer

9–22   This is the big one. At some point in your negotiation, someone is going to have to make an offer. The timing of that offer, and the question of which party should make it, is often determined by the overall dynamic of a particular situation. However, if you end up breaking the ice, always give your reasons first and then make your offer. If you do it the other way round it weakens your position, because it appears apologetic. It then seems to your opponent that you're justifying yourself (or making an excuse). In response to your offer, you should always be able to answer the question "why?", or "how did you arrive at that figure?" To be credible, it's best to be able to refer to objective criteria. For example, you could refer to similar products, previous agreements your firm (or your client) has entered into, current market practices and so on.

It's also worth considering making a hypothetical (rather than a real) offer. This means if you make a proposal you should be able to retract it, if it's rejected, without revealing your true position (or having to reveal you were bluffing). The following two examples demonstrate the difference.

Example one

9–23   You tell the employer's solicitor that your client is prepared to accept a two-year restriction and £10,000 compensation. You've told your opponent two things: the length of the restriction and the amount of compensation that your client is willing to accept. They could say, "we'll accept a two-year restriction but we can only offer £5,000." But when you say you'll accept £5,000 in return for a one-year restriction, they'll likely say, "you've already admitted that your client can accept two years, so we're only negotiating on price now."

Example two

9–24   You tell the employer's solicitor that *if* the employer were to offer a two-year restriction *and* £10,000, *then* your client would consider it. If they offer £5,000 and try to hold you to two years, this time you can ask for one-year. You can justify it because you've linked your position to a hypothetical offer, and you said only that your client would *consider* it, not accept it.

Finally…

Throughout your negotiation, remember to remain within the limits of your authority (or your client mandate). Ensure that there's constant communication with your client (if applicable). You must be certain that you've specific instructions as to whether to conclude a proposed agreement. At the end of the day, it may become necessary to end negotiations, having carefully examined your BATNA and concluded that this is the best course of action. **9–25**

TROUBLESHOOTING

There are some common issues that crop up in negotiations that are worth considering. These are teamwork and standard negotiating tactics. **9–26**

Teamwork

If you're working with others in a team, always resolve disputes well away from the negotiating table. You must avoid revealing any hint of disharmony to your opponent through body language. Brief your team to keep their poker faces on, at all times. **9–27**

This can also apply to your client. You don't want your client looking at you in surprise when you make your latest offer or, worse, saying something along the lines of, "I said I didn't want that much" or "why are you asking for that?" Make sure they know how you want them to react. An unpredictable client can work in your favour. Andrew had one meeting with a client who threatened to throw himself out of a top floor window unless the lawyers "got a bloody move on." What was turning into an all-day meeting was then wrapped up in 30 minutes. We don't recommend this as your standard tactic though.

Standard negotiating tactics

Your opponent may try to use a variety of tactics to obtain an advantage. These might include pressure tactics (attempting to force you to accept specific terms), intimidation (implicit or explicit), ambiguity about the scope of their mandate, and even unethical behaviour (e.g. misleading you), though they shouldn't, as this would be a breach of professional standards. Preparation is the key to responding effectively. Previous experience of your opponent can yield useful information. Good communication techniques and, specifically, strategies on how to communicate with difficult people can also be helpful. **9–28**

Ultimately, how to respond is a question of your personal judgment. What may be an appropriate response in one situation may, in contrast, be a bit heavy handed in other circumstances. Below we give you a range of common mistakes and problems, along with our suggested strategies/responses.

Tactic	Possible responses
"Take it or leave it"	• avoid and move on to another issue; • ask to justify the statement; • call their bluff.
Silence	• meet with silence; don't be intimidated; • ask a pre-planned question to fill the silence; • don't start talking to fill the silence (a natural tendency).
Be specific	• don't say "about X or Y" as it reveals latitude in what you might settle for.
Sun in your eyes	• move seat; • draw it to the attention of the other party; • don't be intimidated.
Travel plans	• think about keeping your return travel plans a secret as your opponent may "run the clock down" to put you under pressure to conclude.
Large demands	• ask to justify the demand; • counter with similar demand; • call their bluff.
Lack of authority	• question the extent of opponent's authority; • seek to reconvene.
Feigned surprise	• stick to your guns.
Anger/threats/personal attacks	• defuse the situation if you can; • don't be drawn in to a fight; • remain professional; • move debate on; • if necessary, end the session.

SUMMARY

9–29   Negotiation is a skill, and one that requires you to change your tactics and approach each time you do it. The more you practice, the better you'll get. By following the processes set out in this chapter, you'll develop into a good negotiator who can—more often than not—get the results your clients want.

CHAPTER 10

How to set fees

INTRODUCTION

A transaction ends. Your partner asks you to review the file and raise a fee. **10–1**
"Check what we've agreed with the client and let me know how it compares with
the work we've done. We don't want to lose money on this, so I may need to speak
to the client about an increase." When you check the file, despite weeks of work,
a large team, and three departments involved, you see the fee was fixed at
£20,000. You check the system and your time alone is £15,000. It looks like the
firm is going to lose a lot of money if your partner can't agree an increase...!

Every business must make money. If it doesn't, it'll soon be out of business. **10–2**
Law firms are no different. We have bills to pay every month. Rent for an office,
money for office supplies, wages to staff. All of this takes money, and most law
firms make money by charging clients a fee for carrying out legal work.

Charging fees was simple. Traditionally, you charged by time. A client would
be charged by how long it took you to carry out work for them. If it took ten
hours, and you charged £250 per hour, your fee would be £2,500. However, as the
economic landscape has evolved and as clients expect greater value and as
competitors have become—well—more competitive, the fees we charge have
changed.

Today, clients want more nuanced options. They want to know how much
they'll be charged in advance, so they can budget with greater certainty. In
response, firms offer fixed prices or other alternative fees. If they don't, clients
choose firms that do. Imagine you go to a restaurant and the waiter tells you that
they charge £5 per minute for every minute you eat. Would you eat there? Or
would you pop down to your local McDonald's where you know a Big Mac will
cost you £2.69 and you can sit as long as you like? The restaurant may have a
better reputation but at McDonald's you know what you will get and how much it
will cost you. We know which one we'd choose.

In this chapter, we examine the main ways you can fee clients and why clients
might choose one option over another.

Outcome

By the end of this chapter, you'll understand the difference between hourly rates, **10–3**
fixed fees and other alternative fee arrangements. We examine the link between
what you do and how much you fee, and we look at how the way you work
influences the final fee paid by clients.

PRICE AND COSTS

10–4   If you walk into your local Tesco, you know exactly how much everything costs. If you want a four pack of Granny Smith apples you pay £1.99. If you want a bag of satsumas, you pay £2.99. What's more, if you want to compare apples and oranges, the prices are on the shelf, in big letters, making it easy to judge.

Try walking into a law firm. Do you see any prices? Do you know how much it costs to speak to a lawyer? Let's go back to your first week as a trainee. This time imagine you're a client. You walk through the door, you sit in a boardroom and you meet a young lawyer. At the end of the meeting, you ask that lawyer perhaps the most important question you have: "how much will this cost me?"

As a lawyer, how do you answer? If your client has an employment claim, then tribunals can be complex. Depending on the evidence involved, the witnesses called, and the time required preparing, you could be talking 50 hours, or you could be talking 200 hours. That's before you know how the employer will respond. Will they be fast or slow? Will they keep to the main issues or will they try and introduce new ones? You want to give your client a rough estimate, but how can you when there are so many variables? And, all the time you're thinking "what is the right fee for this work?" your client is thinking "I only have £2,000—I wonder if that will be enough?"

What is a price?

10–5   Before we examine how you set a price, let's answer a simple question. What is a price? A price is the amount of money expected, required, or given in payment for something. In your case, your 'fee', your price, is the money you expect to be paid for providing legal advice.

How do we set a price?

10–6   This is where things become more complicated. Prices can be set in a number of ways. We'll look at three: cost, by competitor and value.

Pricing by cost

10–7   This is one of the simplest ways to price something. You set your price based on how much it costs. Tesco sells milk and let's say that every two litres costs 79p; this is the cost of a farmer milking cows, the cost of packaging and transport to a local store. Knowing that the milk costs 79p, Tesco set a price of 99p. The extra 20p is Tesco's profit.

It's the same with a television. If all the components of a television cost £700 and it costs £50 for fixed costs (like premises and staff) then John Lewis has to charge more than £750 to make a profit. In each case, shops look at how much it costs to sell something and then charges more, to make money.

You might think that it must cost more than 79p to produce two litres of milk? In fact, doesn't it cost more than 99p? There were news reports in 2016 suggesting that it costs more to make milk than the price paid by Tesco for it.[1] That's true, but the principle is the same. In this case, Tesco pay farmers 79p (Tesco's cost) so that they're not the ones losing money. Why might they do that, though?

Pricing by competitor

In the past Supermarkets have been involved in price wars. In 2016 Tesco was in the midst of one. Asda, Morrisons, Sainsbury's and others were charging 99p for milk. If Tesco charged more, its customers would switch to a rival. Tesco's prices were dictated by what its competitors were doing. In other words, it's not looking at cost any more. Instead, it's competing on the prices set by others. This is a dangerous path because you might not be able to sell at the same price as a competitor.   **10–8**

Let's assume you're a small newsagent, selling milk at £1.29. Tesco opens next door, selling milk at 99p. You know you need to drop your price, but how can you? Tesco can buy in bulk and pay less under economies of scale. You have to buy a single crate. You can't save money; it costs you £1.20 for each bottle of milk, and that's that. If you try and compete, you'll lose money. What can you do? Our third option, pricing by value, might save your business.

Pricing by value

Pricing by value means charging a price based on what your customer is willing to pay. If you have a newsagent, you may have customers who don't want to stand in line at a self-service check-out. Instead, they want someone who can help them shop and they're willing to pay more for that help. Pricing by value is much harder than pricing either by cost or competitor. Pricing by cost is the easiest. You sit down and work out how much something costs you to make or do, and then charge a higher figure. Pricing by competitor is easy too. How much do your competitors charge for the same thing? And you either charge the same or less. Pricing by value means you need to understand who your customers are, what they want, and what they're willing to pay. You might think that having someone help with a till is worth paying more but your customers might be willing to use a self-service till if you charge too much for this extra service.   **10–9**

How do law firms set prices?

Let's examine how law firms might use each of these options.   **10–10**

Law firms setting price by cost

Part of the reason for using hourly rates is that hourly rates are based on cost. A law firm should review its costs regularly. These include rent, bills and other costs and can be worked out for a week, month or year. Let's say for your firm the   **10–11**

---

[1] BBC News "Q&A, Milk prices row and how the system works" (11 August 2015), *BBC.co.uk*, *http://www.bbc.co.uk/news/business-18951422* [Accessed 7 April 2019].

figure is £250,000 annually. That means your firm needs to fee at least £250,000 before it makes any profit. (For larger firms, multiply these figures by 10 or even a hundred for the Magic Circle).

Let's assume that your firm consists solely of you and a partner. Each of you can work eight hours a day (you may work more, but most hourly rate calculations assume a normal working day). Excluding weekends and holidays, there are 253 working days (506 days if you include you and your partner). That means that you and your partner must fee £62 per hour. How do we know this?

£250,000 divided by 506 days divided by 8 hours in each day = £62 per hour

£62 per hour generates the £250,000 needed to pay all your costs. However, you want to make money, so you charge £70 per hour. This means that you make £283,360 per annum, creating a profit of £36,360.

£70 multiplied by 8 hours multiplied by 506 days = £283,360 per annum

This is a simple example. In real life, a client wouldn't expect to pay the same for a partner as for a trainee. A partner can charge more to reflect skill and experience. However, this example does illustrate the problems with hourly rates. These are:

Maximum profit

10–12   There are only 24 hours in a day. If you charge an hourly rate then the most you can ever charge is 24 times your hourly rate (assuming you're working all night and don't go home, have lunch, dinner or even a toilet break).

Limited time

10–13   To be realistic, you need to assume that you won't work on client matters every minute of the day. You might chat with colleagues, check the news, catch up on social media, and, more seriously, have admin to deal with.

You also can't charge clients for everything. You might start drafting a contract only to realise that you're using the wrong template. You might want to read a case in full, even though you know it, just to check you have it right. That's why most firms that use hourly rates also have another target such as utilisation. Your utilisation rate is the percentage of time each day that your firm reasonably assumes can be charged to clients. Your utilisation target might be 75%, with 25% of each day accepted to be time that you cannot charge to clients. In an eight-hour day, only six hours will be assumed to be chargeable.

Client time

10–14   Your firm assumes that not every client will pay for every hour you spend on their work. Some files may take longer than expected. If you expect a contract negotiation to take five hours and you tell the client in their engagement letter that you'll charge them five hours, they may not agree to pay for six hours. Why should they pay more if your estimate is wrong?

Utilisation includes an element of non-chargeable time. Firms also assume that not every hour of that chargeable time will lead to a payment. A client may refuse to pay, a client may become insolvent or a client may complain a fee is too high

162

and you agree to reduce it. The amount of money you receive will be less than what you charged. The percentage of money received to money charged is your *realisation* rate.

Going back to your average day (eight hours) you may lose almost half that to work that you can't charge for. In our example, our utilisation ratio of 75% means in an eight hour day we typically only spend six hours on potentially chargeable work. If we now assume that our realisation rate is also 75%—because we know from previous files that we tend to record more time against a file than we can charge to the client—then, of those six hours, we are only paid for four and half hours (75% of six hours).That's part of the reason why firms have looked at alternatives, such as billing by value. Firms want to make money and not be limited by the number of hours in the day that their lawyers can bill.

Billing by value

You don't expect to walk into your local Tesco, pick up your shopping, take it to the checkout and only then find out how much it costs. You want to know the prices up front. Clients are no different. They want to know how much it'll cost to hire you. You might say that your fee will be calculated by reference to hourly rates, inevitably the next question is still: "can't you tell me how much I will pay?"

10–15

Billing by value means setting a price that a client is willing to pay. For many clients, especially since the 2008 recession, that means a fixed price. In other words, you (and they) agree a price for your work before you start. Your fixed price might be based on cost. One way to fix a price is to work out how long it'll take you to do the work and then base your price on that. For example, if a client asks you to prepare a lease, you might assume (from your previous lease work), that it'll take you ten hours. You can then tell the client that it'll cost £2.000 (i.e. ten hours at £200 per hour). If you complete the work in nine hours, you make a £200 profit. If you take eleven hours, you make a £200 loss. The faster you complete the lease, the more profit you make. The longer it takes, the more you lose.

Your fixed fee doesn't need to be priced on cost. You could price it on the value the work has to your client. For example, if you're client is caught speeding and they face losing their driving licence, you might consider how much that licence is worth to them. If the client is a salesperson who has to drive every day to different offices, then she may well be willing to pay a premium, if you can help her retain her licence. Even if the actual work takes just five hours, you could charge £5,000, because you know how vital it is to them.

No win/no fee is partly based on this principle. If you don't get a result for your client then you haven't done anything valuable for them, so why should you be paid? If you're paid by cost, then you should be paid a fee for the work you've done.

Billing by competitor

It's easy to compare different types of milk. It's not so easy to compare law firms, because clients are not comparing 'like with like'. You're not the same lawyer as

10–16

the trainee in the firm down the road. Your partner is not the same as other partners. You both might charge £55 per hour, but are clients buying the same thing?

This is why you need to know who your competitors are and how clients choose between firms. Your knowledge of clients (see Ch.2 (Clients)) should help you to identify who your clients are, and what firms make up the competition. You can then identify the prices they charge. Do they offer a fixed fee of £199 for conveyancing? If so, it's going to be difficult for you to charge £200 per hour without good reason. You need to understand what your competitors' prices mean, also. It might be the £199 only applies to homes that are on the Land Registry and worth less than £200,000. You, on the other hand, might specialise in commercial leases, and so this fee doesn't apply to you. You're not comparing 'like with like'.

10–17   The Solicitors Regulatory Authority's Price Transparency Rules has, as a by-product of improving pricing for consumers, made it easier for firms to check other firm's prices. In December 2018, the SRA required law firms to publicise their prices for the following services:

- Residential conveyancing—freehold sales, freehold purchases, leasehold sales, leasehold purchases, mortgages and remortgages.
- Probate—uncontested cases where all assets are in the UK.
- Motoring offences—summary only offences.
- Employment tribunals—for claims of unfair or wrong dismissal or, acting for a business, defending claims for unfair or wrongful dismissal.
- Immigration—excluding applications for asylum.
- Business debt recovery for up to £100,000.
- Licensing applications for business premises—both new or varying existing licenses.

The rules require firms to publish price information in a prominent location on its website, and it must be easily accessible and easy for website visitors to find. Or, if a firm doesn't have a website, the information must be available on request in an easy to read format.

What price information should be included? Key information includes:

- Overall, there must be a clear guidance of what exactly is included in the displayed price.
- The firm must list the services, that are included in the price displayed along with a typical timescale and key stages.
- Services which are not included in the price which a consumer might reasonably expect to be included should be highlighted.
- The firm should confirm who will act for the client including details of their experience and qualifications.
- The price must state if it includes VAT.
- If a range of prices is published, then a basis for the charges must be set, and this should include all hourly rates or other factors which are considered in determining the final price.

PRICING OPTIONS

Setting a price requires information. If you're setting a price based on cost, then   **10–18**
you need to know the cost of what you're providing. If you're setting a price by
value, you need to know what your client's value and what they might pay for it.
And, if you set a price based on what your competitors charge, you need to know
what their prices are and what they offer for it.

Can you spot the problem? You need information to set a price, and a good
deal of that comes from third parties, clients and competitors. That's part of the
reason why charging by the hour has been popular. You work out your price (and
your potential profit) based on information that you control (as your firm should
know its own costs). However, basing a price just on costs isn't necessarily what
clients want. They may want a fixed fee. They may want you to offer a no win/no
fee arrangement, as they won't have any money to pay you unless they're
successful.

When you're asked to agree a fee, you have to decide what information you
have (on which to base your judgment) and what you can offer (relative to your
competitors). We can see this clearly, below, when we examine each of the
options. These are broken down into hourly rate, capped fees, blended rates, fixed
fees and success fees.

Hourly rate

What is it?

You charge clients by the amount of time that you work on their files.   **10–19**

Advantages

It's simple to implement and easy for clients to understand.

Disadvantages

It rewards inefficiency; the longer you spend the more you can charge. There is
no incentive to finish work quickly.

Capped rate

What is it?

This is a variation of the hourly rate. It caps the rate so that fees are not unlimited.   **10–20**
This cap could be daily, so that you can't charge more than eight hours in a single
day or no more than 20 hours in a week, no matter how long you actually work on
a file. To take it a step further, the cap might be a total figure that you can't charge
above. For example, you might agree an hourly rate of £150 per hour, with a total
cap of £20,000 to cover all work.

Advantages

Your clients can set limits so that they know what the highest likely cost will be.

Disadvantages

Your cap needs to be one that still lets your firm make a profit. If you agree a daily cap of two hours a day, but it regularly takes you four hours of work each day, you're giving a client two free hours (and you're not able to use that time to do work for another client who would pay).

Blended rate

What is it?

10–21 This is a variation of the hourly rate. Normally, every lawyer has a different rate. A trainee may be charged at £150 an hour, an assistant at £200, a senior associate at £250 and a partner at £300. A blended rate gives a client one rate for all fee earners (for example, everyone is charged out at £210 per hour). This means a client receives a discount if senior lawyers are involved, as they don't need to pay £300 for a partner. However, if junior lawyers do the bulk of the work, the firm clearly is paid more.

Advantages

The big advantage is simplicity; your client receives one rate for everyone.

Disadvantages

There is a conflict between the firm's interest in making sure junior lawyers are profitable and a client's desire to see senior lawyers working on their file (giving them a real term discount). It can be difficult to reconcile this conflict and not have the client say: "why didn't the partner do all the work as they knew what they were doing? I'm paying the same price for them, after all!"

Fixed fees

What is it?

10–22 This "does what it says on the tin", as the advert goes. You set a fixed price for all (or part) of your work. For example, if a client asks you to help them with an employment tribunal, you could offer to do it all for £9,000 regardless of how long it might take.

Advantages

Your client knows exactly what they must pay.

Disadvantages

Your client may not know what they're paying *for*. In your engagement terms you list all the assumptions that apply, in order that you might offer a fixed fee. For example, for an employment tribunal you assume that there will be less than three witnesses. If there turns out to be 300 witnesses, you need to change your fee because you're doing 100 times more work. Your client may not appreciate that because the underlying assumption has changed, their fee should change. They still believe they're paying £9,000. A fixed fee requires you to calculate exactly what you've got to do for a client. This may not be easy.

Fixed fees (weekly, monthly, annual)

What is it?

Most fixed fees are based on individual pieces of work, like a lease or a contract. However, a number of firms offer clients the option of paying a fixed fee to cover all of their legal work for a fixed length of time. For example, Tyco pays Eversheds Sutherland an annual fee to provide legal advice. Many employment firms offer a hotline service where HR managers pay an annual fee and then can phone as often as they need to, without incurring any additional fees. This is what Andrew uses for two subsidiaries who don't have a dedicated HR team. For a fixed cost all employment contracts and policies are kept up to date.   **10–23**

Advantages

Your client knows exactly what they're paying for and your firm knows it has a guaranteed fee for the year. It doesn't need to rely on winning each piece of work, individually.

Disadvantages

Your firm needs a lot—and we mean a lot—of information before it can set a fee. It needs to know exactly what legal advice a client might need during the period. This information might be based on historic legal costs, but it also needs to predict what might come up. It also needs to make a large number of assumptions. For example, an appeal to the Supreme Court action can torpedo any budget. As you can imagine, these assumptions create the same problems as for normal fixed fees, a client may not appreciate that assumptions sometimes have to change and then dispute changes to their fees.

Contingent fees—success fees

What is it?

A contingent fee is linked to the successful conclusion of a piece of work. If a client is suing for compensation, you might agree that you'll only fee their file if you're successful. On the flip side, there are also abort fees. These are fees that   **10–24** are agreed if your client is unsuccessful. For example, if your client doesn't succeed in buying a business, you might agree that you only get 20% of the fee you would have charged

Advantages

A lot of legal work is risky. There's no guarantee that a client will win a case, get their house, sell their business or complete a deal. This risk has to be at the front of your minds. Many clients won't have the money to pay for a court case, even if they have a good legal reason for raising it. That's why, for individuals, no win/no fee arrangements are attractive. They allow the client to take a risk.

For corporates, a success fee also is attractive. They see the lawyer sharing in their risk. If corporate clients only make money if their deals are a success, they won't like a law firm that renders fees regardless. It's much easier for you to ask the question: "can you pay this bill?" when your client is ecstatic that a deal has been done (especially if they're richer for having done it).

Disadvantages

This is the same as for fixed fees or hourly rates (depending which you're using). You need to make sure that any success fee is profitable and that an abort doesn't lose you too much. You need information about your client to know what success actually means to them. You don't want to be saying that your success fee kicks in as soon as an employment tribunal gives its decision, if your client believes success is only demonstrated once they know that the decision isn't going to be appealed.

DON'T FORGET ABOUT COSTS

10–25 Regardless of whether you're setting a price based on value or competitors, never forget that you need to recover the cost of your work. You can match a competitor's price, or you can charge a price your client is willing to pay. However, if that price does not exceed your costs, you lose money. This is why (regardless of the fee option) your firm needs you to record your time accurately (as we see in the next chapter). Your firm can use that information to work out if it's making money.

For example, you may have quoted a fixed fee of £500 to complete a small claim, but it ends up taking you £1000 of time to do it. Your firm needs to know this so that either it can increase its price the next time, or it can streamline its workflow to ensure that a similar job is completed within a £500 budget (for example, by having someone else do the work or by improving process or by using more IT).

DON'T FORGET ABOUT PROFESSIONAL STANDARDS AND CLIENT BUDGETS

Remember that you have a professional obligation under rule 8.7 of the SRA **10–26** Code of Conduct for Solicitors to provide clients in their engagement terms with the best possible information about you intend to charge (or how you calculate fees). You also have an obligation to tell them if any assumptions change and that you plan to propose a change in their fee. We recommend that you're always open with your clients about fees; don't put off having a discussion until the last minute. Your clients have budgets and definitely won't appreciate you changing a fee late in the day. They may not have the money to pay it or may need to obtain fresh board approval (if a corporate client). The sooner you discuss fees, the easier it is to agree changes. Andrew always tells firms that he understands that scopes can change but, because budgets are set early, he has no power to change a fee at the end of a transaction—only if it's brought to his attention during the transaction.

SUMMARY

Setting a price is hard. It requires information, informed guesses and an ability to **10–27** see the big picture. As a new lawyer, it's worth spending time examining the various options and how they might apply to your clients. You may be able to offer a different option that is more appropriate (and better for your firm) than just hourly rates. And, if so, you'll be able to offer clients more options and better value.

CHAPTER 11

How to record time

INTRODUCTION

Your partner has agreed a fixed fee of £1,500 (excluding VAT and costs) for a
small matter. Your hourly rate is £150 per hour. After one week, you've spent five
hours working on it. By the end of the second week, you've spent 10 hours, and,
by the time you've finished, you've spent 20 hours.

    When your partner asks how long you worked on it, you say '9 hours'—you
haven't recorded your time and you think that if you say it took you 20 hours,
your partner will think you're slow.

    Your partner is happy: "Excellent. The fee was spot on—if we get another, we
can charge the same amount and still make a profit". However, are they right,
considering you've spent twice as long on it as your partner thought?

11–1

    Setting fees requires information. If your firm uses hourly rates then, as
discussed in the last chapter, it has to set a rate that recovers its costs and
generates a profit. Equally, once a piece of work is complete, your firm will want
to charge for all the time that you and others have spent on it. If you don't record
your time accurately then your firm won't have the right information to work out
what to charge your client.

11–2

    Different firms have different ways to record time. Some depend on you
writing notes on files, some have electronic systems, others do it automatically by
monitoring how long it takes to write emails or letters. Regardless of how
sophisticated a system is used, the principle behind time recording remains the
same. How long does it take you to complete a particular piece of work? As the
saying goes, 'time is money' and, for most law firms, money is time.

Outcome

By the end of this chapter, you'll understand time recording, common
time-recording errors and the different processes of time recording.

11–3

TIME RECORDING BENEFITS

Time recording is the act of recording all of the time you spend on a client's file,
together with a short description of what you have done.

11–4

    Why do you need to record your time? There are a number of benefits:

Benefit One—Evidence

11–5 Recording your time provides financial information for you and your firm. If you time recording is linked to your hourly charge out rate. It helps you know at a glance what you are working on and how much it should be charged. This potential chargeable work is known as your 'work in progress' (your WIP). Most firms expect you to meet an annual WIP target. This might be anything between 1,200–2,000 hours annually. As reported on *www.rollonfriday.com*, Ashurst has an annual target of 1600 chargeable hours. Herbert Smith Freehills has a target of 1700 chargeable hours. Trowers and Hamlins has a target of 1,550 chargeable hours. If, during the year, you meet your targets you increase your chance of a pay rise, a bonus and promotion.

Accurate time recording also helps clients. Some lawyers send clients a breakdown of the time they've spent, so that the clients can see what they've done. This is useful if you spend more time than you expect; you might want to let a client know that he or she is getting a discount if you've agreed a fixed fee and your actual time is more than the price agreed. This can help with repeat clients who'll then be more willing to pay more next time, knowing how hard you worked. Some clients will ask for a breakdown of your time. Accurate time recording (with a good narrative) enables you to provide clients with detailed answers about fees.

Benefit Two—Reduces Complaints

11–6 Time recording shows the time you have incurred on a job, which, in turn, forms the basis of your fee note. Fees that can be linked to objective time recording are, by their nature, transparent. This helps reduce the number of potential client complaints and, if they do arise, it helps deal with them effectively.

Andrew was once challenged over a £20,000 fee based on hourly rates. The client argued that it was too much. Because he had recorded his time, Andrew was able to send them a note of the time including a narrative for every day within minutes of receiving the complaint. The client was able to see why the fee was justified and paid it.

Benefit Three—Accuracy

11–7 Time recording is the basis of your work in progress. WIP, however, is not cash. You can't spend WIP. It won't pay the rent. It's only potential profit. It doesn't become cash until you convert your WIP into a fee invoice that is—in turn—paid by your client.

An example might help demonstrate the difference between WIP, profit and cash. Let's assume you've worked ten hours. Your charge out rate is £200/hour. Based on the time you've spent, your WIP is £2,000. However, this isn't profit, because you haven't raised a fee invoice. You suggest to your partner that the file be charged at £3,000 to cover all the time you have spent on it. However, your partner knows your client won't pay more than £2,500, no matter how complicated the work might have been. Your potential profit is based on the £2,500 actually invoiced, rather than the WIP time you spent on it. Now, let's assume the client disagrees with the invoice and only pays £1,500. Your WIP is £3,000. Your potential profit of £500 was based on a £2,500 invoice. But you won't actually receive that profit—£500—as cash until your client pays the whole invoice. Instead, the client is only paying £1,500. And your profit on paper has turned into a loss when the invoice was paid. Good time recording always gives you an accurate WIP figure that allows you to start the process of working out how much of that WIP will be invoiced and, ultimately, how much of it will become cash.

Benefit Four—Increases profits

Accurate time recording increases your firm's profits. How? In a bid to secure work in a competitive market, fee earners sometimes underestimate their time when issuing an estimate or a quote. It's easy to understand why: you don't want your existing clients to leave you for another firm. You also want to be competitive in order to tempt new clients to come to you. **11–8**

However, it can be a trap and it can lead you into situations where you end up working extra hours you haven't quoted for, meaning you end up with a much smaller profit margin. By recording your time you can see exactly how long the same (or similar) work should take. If you know how long it will take, you can quote much more accurately. To put it another way, you cannot price for profit if you do not know how much the work is costing your firm to do. For example, you agree a price for £20,000. You record £18,000 in WIP. But one of your colleagues, who worked on the file, forgets to record some of their time. If they had, the WIP would have been £22,000.

By recording time accurately, you know the work should be charged next time at more than £22,000 to make a profit. Accurate time recording helps you make smarter decisions. Even picking up one extra 6-minute unit of time a day, over a year, will increases your profits.

Benefit Five—True cost of time

If all time is recorded, then you can calculate the true cost to your firm of any piece of work that you do. This is especially important when you're working for fixed fees. Your hourly cost rate includes a nominal allocation of rent, other fixed costs, heat/light and—of course—wages. If you render fees that don't make back the hourly cost rate, then your firm won't stay in business very long. **11–9**

Benefit Six—Trends and future planning

This continues benefit five. Good time recording helps to spot trends and highlight work that you should not be doing using fixed fees. Let's say, for example, that you price a particular service at £5,000. Your charge out rate is £100 per hour (to make it simple). Over a financial quarter your time recording routinely shows that you take 55 hours to complete that service. What does this trend tell you? It tells you that each time you take on this work you'll lose £500 for your firm. **11–10**

Benefit Seven—Performance

11–11   You can use time recording information to assess how long a fee earner takes to complete a piece of work. If necessary, your firm can help with further training to improve his/her performance.

Imagine we have two lawyers. Both do the same type of work. Iain always fees ten hours and Andrew always fees twenty hours. Your partner might want to speak to both to explore why there's such difference. Perhaps Iain doesn't record his time accurately and he should be recording twenty hours? Perhaps Andrew needs extra training to help him understand the contracts involved so that he can deal with them faster. Accurate time recording allows you and your firm to ask the right questions and then look for ways to improve.

UNDERSTANDING FEE RECOVERY

11–12   We talked in the last chapter about how a fee deals with two types of money. The first is to pay for your firm's costs (including you and your time). The second is your profit, everything you earn after your costs are paid.

Full cost recovery is where you recover the total cost of your services. That is to say the cost of your time (your salary etc.) and also your share of costs that are not directly related to delivering a service, but which are necessary to run your firm (office rent, heating, lighting etc.). The aim is to avoid running at a loss because the true cost of providing your service hasn't been met. This requires some mathematics. You need to work out what your hourly cost rate is and then make sure you render fees that at least cover these costs or, better still, exceed them. You only make a profit if your fees exceed costs.

What is Your Realisation Rate?

11–13   Your realisation (or recovery) rate is the percentage of your WIP that is invoiced to a client. This should be an easy calculation. If your WIP is £20k and you invoice £20k then your realisation rate is 100%. Over a year, you may have some files that will fee at more than 100%, you may have other which are written off. Provided your WIP is more than 100% then you will know that you have covered your costs and you will have generated a profit (assuming your hourly rate includes an element of profit).

The following tips will help ensure your WIP is invoiced and paid.

Interim fees

11–14   You don't need to wait until the end of your work before issuing a fee. Many legal tasks last months, if not years, and clients may prefer you to issue smaller regular bills than to receive one large bill at the end.

Interim fees:

- boost cash flow (so you can pay office rent, staff salaries and other bills);

- reduce the risk of your clients trying to negotiate you down (or even refusing to pay) a single, large fee at the end of a long transaction; and
- deal with real-world market volatility. If one of your clients runs into financial difficulties, then you'll struggle to get back anything like the amount you're owed. Instead, you may get nothing. Interim fees help avoid exposing you to clients with financial problems.

Shedding clients

This might sound a little counter-intuitive but it can be effective. Often the time spent in arguing over fees is just not worth the aggravation. You can spend a lot of time and money to recover only a little bit more than you spend.   **11–15**

The idea behind shedding is to identify and remove the worst performing 1% to 5% of your clients every year. In year one this makes little difference but over a five-year period you'll dramatically change your client base. What you're looking at is how much money they bring in to your firm and how long they take to pay their fees (indeed if they pay at all). This only works if you have good quality new clients coming in. This is why keeping in touch with potential clients is important, even when you're busy.

Fee promptly

You should always raise your fee notes promptly after a transaction concludes. Bear in mind the 'gratitude curve'. This assumes that a client's willingness to pay fees diminishes as time passes, no matter how happy they are with the quality of your service at the time. Andrew is occasionally asked to pay a fee for matters which finished more than 12 months before. Usually, the firm apologises for forgetting to raise it sooner. But, while the fee may be reasonable, and the work should be paid for, it can present Andrew with problems if budgets have closed and need to be re-opened. A fee that would have been paid without thought 12 months ago now becomes a problematic fee just because of the firm's delay.   **11–16**

Elasticity

If you increase your prices by 10%, what percentage of your clients do you think will leave? The answer for most firms is almost none. Generally, the demand for professional services is inelastic for two reasons. Firstly, clients want to deal with you because they trust you and it takes time to build that trust. Secondly, even with a 5% to 10% increase, the size of your fee is often just not enough for them to worry about. Just bear in mind that there is a "glass ceiling" above which the client drop-off rate increases dramatically. The point, here, is that by increasing your fees a little, your good payers will—to an extent—help to cancel out those who either don't pay or who want to negotiate.   **11–17**

Staff training

Your firm should have procedures in place to recover fees. Make sure you know what those are and, if not, ask for training.   **11–18**

175

How to recover costs

11–19   It's not just time that needs to be recorded. Your fee should also record all your costs, including bulk photocopying, scanning, IT systems and transactional costs such as court fees, search fees or other costs.

In a 2012 article for *LegalTechnology.com*, Stewart Hadley noted that in 2002, 97% of firms billed clients for photocopying and almost all of those bills were paid.[1] By 2012, only 87% of firms were billing for photocopying. Today, scanning is common (and there are associated costs e.g. cloud data storage). Lots of documents are also printed to a network printer. However, only 51% of law firms recover printing and only 36% recover scanning.

Your fee needs to include all costs. Otherwise you are losing money by paying for things that you could charge to your client. In order to recover these costs you need to record them accurately. Modern systems will let you capture this. Some firms will record client matter numbers when printing or photocopying. Others will only let you incur costs if a matter number is provided. Either way, your firm wants all costs to be paid by clients so that it doesn't have to pay for them itself.

When considering how to recover costs you may want to consider how many sheets of printing are being charged to "firm expenses" rather than to your clients? Are you even tracking your printing? Are you charging for scans (to take account of server space)? What about data rooms? With on-line data sites becoming more prevalent, are you charging for the server costs or IT support the same as Dropbox or Google Drive would charge for using large amounts of server space? Are you capturing other "hard costs" such as taxis and couriers? Which teams are systematically charging costs such as travel or printing and which are not? Which of your team has the highest write-off percentages?

Remember: you can't manage what you don't measure.

Financial leakage

11–20   Not recouping otherwise recoverable legal fees and client costs is called 'financial leakage'. At one end of the spectrum it can be down to you as a fee earner not taking care in assigning a correct matter number when recording time. At the other end, it can be indicative of a general resistance to recovery. You should now appreciate that if a recoverable fee or a recoverable cost isn't clawed back then it's lost profit.

COMMON TIME RECORDING ERRORS

11–21   Common time recording errors include:

---

[1] See: *http://www.legaltechnology.com/latest-news/the-changing-face/* (17 October 2012) [Accessed 3 January 2019].

Failing to record time

Some lawyers don't time record at all. They claim that they don't have the time to   **11–22**
do it, they're too busy. For all the reasons given in this chapter, you should
understand why you must record your time.

Failing to provide a narrative

Some lawyers don't provide a narrative, or only record a partial narrative. As we   **11–23**
discussed above, it's important, to make sure you write down what you do for
your clients. It provides you with the information to confirm fees when
challenged.

A warning—make sure what you write is appropriate. You shouldn't write
anything in a fee narrative that you wouldn't write in an email. Clients can—and
will—read the narratives to see what they're paying for. One trainee we know,
after a week of photocopying evidence for an important case, wrote as their
narrative for the day, "eight hours of ****." The client read it, demanded both an
apology and discount, and got both.

Human error

The best example of human error is using the wrong matter number. To get all the   **11–24**
data you need to correctly set fixed fees (or to adjust your hourly billing rates),
you need to allocate your time (and all client disbursements) against the correct
matter number. It's just a case of taking care.

Not recording chargeable time

This is where lawyers try and reduce their time in order to appear efficient by   **11–25**
allocating otherwise chargeable time inappropriately to, for example, admin. This
happens if bonuses are based on hitting targets such as 85% realisation across all
files. If recording time accurately means missing targets, because your extra time
is routinely written off when invoiced, then some will omit any time which could
reduce their realisation rate.

Delaying recording time

Sometime lawyers wait several days to record their time. Everyone's busy, but   **11–26**
you need to record either as you go or at the end of your working day. If you wait
too long you will not remember how long everything took you.

Forgotten time

This flows from the previous point. If you don't record your time regularly, you   **11–27**
may forget not only how much you did but also what you did entirely, and not
record time against a file. You might then under-record.

TIME RECORDING PROCESSES

11–28   There are many ways you can time record. They all have different pros and cons. Whatever you choose it should be applied and used consistently.

Back of a napkin

11–29   We're only half joking when we suggest this. It may be basic but at least it's better than not recording your time at all.

Paper

11–30   With this method you keep a template at your side, filling it out as you move from one project to the next.

Pros

The only plus, in this day and age, is that you can use paper recording when your IT goes down. At the end of a day, if you've shut your PC down and a client calls, you can also make a quick paper entry, to save time logging back on.

Cons

There are several: lawyers often forget to fill out paper timesheets, or they try and play catch-up at the end of a day. If you don't use this method in real-time it becomes difficult to use accurately, with each passing hour.

It's also hard to track time on paper accurately if you're jumping around from file to file. Paper timesheets also can only account for so many matters. There will be days (we hope) when you'll deal with more projects than you can physically fit on a sheet, leaving you using multiple sheets (one of which, according to sod's law, ends up being lost). Finally, this information is limited unless entered into software that can run reports.

Microsoft Excel spreadsheets

11–31   With this method you use a software spreadsheet.

Pros

Using spreadsheets overcomes most of the drawbacks of paper entries. In addition, you easily can run reports with Excel spreadsheets. As they're digital files, they can be backed up and archived more effectively than your paper timesheets. Excel is universal and your learning curve, if you haven't used it, will be small.

Cons

There are a few drawbacks with Excel. If you use it, you'll be entering lots of data into spreadsheets every week, eating up a few hours of your time. If you need more sophisticated add-ons, you'll spend a significant number of hours customising your templates.

Software/apps

This is where you do your time recording on your PC, tablet or smartphone using a software package or online, cloud-based app.

11–32

Pros

Using software and apps overcomes most of the drawbacks of using paper time recording sheets. It retains the benefits of Excel based time recording, but also deals with the downsides associated with spreadsheets. Some firms have increased their profits after incorporating software time recording into their workflow. Why? They start to pick-up time that wasn't tracked before. Software lets you keep track of multiple client matters at once, making it easier to switch between them without losing time. Packages also make generating detailed reports easier. Lastly, since data is tracked in real-time, you can record at the click of a button or tap of a finger. No more daily or weekly data entry.

Cons

The first drawback is cost. Packages with multi-user licences are expensive. Cloud based packages (or computer based packages with cloud back-up) should keep your data secure in the event of IT failure, but you may still need to keep a hard copy.

   Some software that monitors your computer cannot distinguish between work and personal use. If you check BBC News every couple of hours, when you get a report at the end of the month, you may find you spent more time on BBC News than any other client. Equally, if you open a file in MS Word and switch to work in MS Outlook, because you haven't closed MS Word the software can struggle to identify what you are doing and record you still working on MS Word even though you've switched to another matter. As software becomes more sophisticated, we expect these problems will be addressed.

IMPROVING TIME RECORDING

Culture

Your firm's culture plays a part. Your firm needs to encourage a culture of time recording. Often lawyers will say that time recording is tedious; your firm needs to ensure that its system is easy to use and your firm or team needs to encourage you to use it.

11–33

Incentives

11–34   Incentives work; some firms reward those who time-record on a daily basis (e.g. a monthly prize). We're not a fan of this approach. Time recording should be a requirement of all lawyers, you wouldn't expect a bonus for turning up to the office on time, so you shouldn't expect one for recording your time. Instead, a number of firms set-up their system to stop time sheets being submitted until all hours are accounted for. In extreme cases, they even stop fee earners from saving to electronic files. Sometimes, a stick helps more than a carrot.

Quick improvements

11–35   Quick improvements with time recording are easy. It could be as simple as setting yourself the following goals:

- record one extra unit of time per day (that otherwise would be allocated to client admin or firm admin);
- time record at the end of each day; and
- provide a better narrative.

Commit to introducing one of them each week. After three months, print off your reports and look to see just how much you have improved. You'll be surprised the difference that small changes make.

SUMMARY

11–36   Becoming good at time recording requires training and a consistent approach. It's about forming good habits. If you record time after each piece of work, it becomes a natural part of your work. And you'll see the benefit when you fee clients as you will set fees which are clear and accurate.

CHAPTER 12

How to manage your time

INTRODUCTION

You're working on five client matters today, another dozen need looked at this   **12–1**
week, there are ten unanswered emails in your inbox and your calendar reminds
you that you have a half-day holiday tomorrow (to take your parents out to
lunch). You're working flat out yet your partner keeps giving you more work. The
senior associate wants you to join a three-hour conference call tomorrow
afternoon and the admin assistants are refusing to draft simple letters because
they're preparing a data room. You don't think you have a choice: you'll have to
tell your parents that lunch is postponed and you'll need to cancel your time off.

Your contract may say that you work Monday to Friday from 9am to 5pm.   **12–2**
But, more often than not, you'll work later or on weekends. It's simply a fact of
life that if you act for clients then you don't work regular hours. On the high
street, a client can phone at 4:55pm with an urgent question and you need to deal
with it. In legal aid firms, your clients are not just accused of crimes during
working hours. In corporate firms, your clients may not even be on the same time
zone, as you deal with people across the world. Your 'home time' could be your
American client's breakfast call. While, as you gain responsibility, you'll find that
bringing work home on a Saturday or Sunday helps you feel like you have a head
start on the week.

This doesn't mean that you've signed up to be a lawyer 24/7. You just need to
understand that other people and events dictate what you do. It's why it's
important that you plan your time effectively. You don't want to spend every
waking hour at work.

Outcomes

By the end of this chapter, you'll know what time management is and how you   **12–3**
can take practical steps to work more efficiently. We set out the key steps required
to identify the reasons why you might not be using your time effectively. We then
suggest ways in which you can tackle these issues.

WHAT IS TIME MANAGEMENT?

12–4   Have do some people seem to have the time to do everything that they need to do? Are you one of the many who feels that you're rushing around, always struggling to meet deadlines? Ever wondered why that might be? The reason, simply, is that people who appear to be in control are good at using time effectively. For them (and you), time management means that the right amount of time is allocated to the right activity, at the right point.

EFFECTIVE TIME MANAGEMENT

12–5   The key to using your time effectively is to understand the difference between tasks that are *urgent* and those that are *important*.

Urgent or important?

12–6   An urgent task is one that can be classed as requiring immediate attention. However, whether you actually give it that immediate attention may (or may not) matter. An important task is one that always matters. Not doing it will have big consequences for you and/or your firm. Let's look at some examples:

Answering the phone—urgent or important?

12–7   If you don't answer your phone the caller may ring off. You won't know why they called. It might be a new client. Or it might be your mum just wanting to check if you'll be home at the weekend. Answering your phone is urgent, because it requires your immediate attention, but it is not yet important because ignoring the phone may have no consequences. The caller may ring back, they may leave a message, they may text you.

Going to the dentist—urgent or important?

12–8   If you don't go to your dentist you might suffer dental problems. On that basis, going to the dentist is not urgent. You don't need to immediately go the dentist to avoid dental problems, you should just aim to go regularly. It is important, but, unless your teeth start falling out, it's not urgent.

Checking social media—urgent or important?

12–9   Do you check social media at the start of each day? Do you check it regularly during the day? Perhaps checking social media is neither urgent nor important? Understanding the distinction between tasks that are urgent and important is the key to prioritising your time and managing your workload. That, in turn, comes down to:

- using time management tools, like a priority matrix (if you don't know what that is, then we look at this next);

- a good time management attitude; and
- controlling your environment.

We'll examine each of these in the next section.

MASTER TIME MANAGEMENT

Step one—use time management tools—a priority matrix

A priority matrix is an easy to use, intuitive grid that lets you organise your tasks   **12–10**
into four categories:

- do first;
- do next;
- do later;
- don't do.

It has scales for 'urgency' and 'importance'. At a glance, you can see which tasks are both important and urgent, and those that are neither important nor urgent. An example of the form is included in Appendix 2.

You can use a matrix for your daily tasks and—zooming out—for weekly (and even monthly) tasks. Its application is limitless and it only takes a couple of seconds to draw a grid on a piece of paper, and then update it as necessary. Or, if you don't have time to be so structured, just ask yourself: "Is this urgent or important? And is it more urgent or important than the other work I have to do?". You will soon start to rank the work you need to do first.

We issue one health warning: 'urgency' and 'importance' are not set in stone. Remember the example we gave you about answering the phone? Things can gradually—or suddenly—change from being urgent to important. A client phoning once might be urgent. The same client phoning you three times in 10 minutes is probably both urgent and important.

Step two—develop a good time management attitude

The next aspect of effective time management is to develop the right attitude.   **12–11**
Let's examine three different factors:

Schedule work for when you are strongest

Are you a morning person or a night person? You will have a time of day during   **12–12**
when you tend to work best. Andrew prefers drafting long documents first thing in the morning before starting any other work so as not to get distracted. Iain prefers working in the evening once all the smaller tasks have been completed. Whatever you are, make sure you schedule your most difficult tasks for that time.

Avoid multi-tasking

12–13   Generally, people are not good at multi-tasking, because it causes you to split your attention between two or three things, to the detriment of each individual task. From a time management point of view, it's better to finish one job before moving onto another. You can only do one thing at a time. When you're doing something, don't worry about anything else. You can't answer two phones at once. You can't draft two documents at the same time. Do one thing. Finish it. Move onto the next.

Keep everything in perspective

12–14   You need to keep a sense of perspective. If you try to accomplish too many tasks at once, you can feel overwhelmed. That's why you should always try and do one thing at a time. Your brain may try and tell you to do more, but you've only got two hands, one keyboard and one phone.

Keep in mind that the sun won't fall out of the sky if you fail to complete that last task of the day, or if you hold it over until the following morning, especially if it's part of a well thought out prioritisation strategy. Getting an early night, so that you're fit for work the next day, can be a better option than meeting a self-imposed deadline.

Avoid dithering

12–15   Do you find yourself doing anything other than a task you know you need to do? Is it a case of, "I'll do it tomorrow, there's still plenty of time"?

If you use a priority matrix, it's reasonable to plan certain tasks to be completed at a later time. You've made a decision that they're neither sufficiently urgent nor important. This isn't dithering; this is planning (to help get more important tasks completed first). However, if a job is considered to be both urgent and important, and you keep putting it off, then you're dithering. Why might this be? We'll tell you after a short coffee break. We might even walk our dogs for half an hour. Hang on, now we're dithering...

The classic reasons are:

- a task seems unpleasant;
- you might not know where to start;
- you're a perfectionist. People who tend towards perfectionism often feel they just don't have enough time to complete a task perfectly and, if they can't do it perfectly, they prefer to put it off until such time as they can.

There are some practical tips, to help you prioritise:

12–16   *Start with the hardest task*—do a task you don't want to do first and then reward yourself with something you do want to do.

12–17   *Consider timing*—if you're a morning person, cover off your tough tasks in the morning, when you're fresh. If you're an evening person, do it last, so that you know it's done before you go home.

Write it down—it's much harder to ignore a task once you have written it on a 'to-do' list (especially if it's a list of things to do that day). Andrew keeps a list on a spreadsheet on Microsoft Excel, split into different categories. He prints out one copy which he keeps in his day book and writes on it as new tasks come up. He then then updates the spreadsheet monthly so that he knows from month to month what tasks have been completed and which still require attention. And, the act of ticking an item on the list, or deleting it from a spreadsheet, is a satisfying way to show yourself that a task is done. 12–18

Involve others—do unpleasant jobs with colleagues. People tend to complete jobs when working together, to avoid letting colleagues down. 12–19

Question yourself—Ask yourself: "will things get better if I put this job off?" The answer 99% of the time will be a resounding 'no'. This is a good way of persuading yourself to do small (but unpleasant) jobs, like corporate admin and approvals, ordering searches or filling in forms. 12–20

Reward yourself—think about how good it'll feel when you've completed a job; the simple joy of ticking it off your 'to-do' list; and that feeling of job satisfaction. The key is to focus on the end goal, not on the task needed to accomplish it. 12–21

Break it down—carve up large tasks into smaller bite-sized chunks. This makes even the most complex tasks seem more manageable. 12–22

The two-minute test—if you have natural down time during the day (for example, between meetings) then make a list of the small jobs that will take you less than two minutes and complete them when you have a spare moment. 12–23

Reverse psychology—think about the pain of not doing something. Just as people are motivated by reward, they can be motivated by a fear of loss. 12–24

Step 3—Controlling your environment

The third aspect of effective time management is to learn how to control your environment, so as to minimise distractions. 12–25

Phone

If you're busy, turn your phone off or switch it to silent. You should use voicemail (with a message you update each morning) and set aside a time in the day to return your missed calls. 12–26

When you're on the phone, always be polite but avoid excessive small talk, to keep calls as short as possible. This can be tricky, some clients love to talk, but, remember, you're their lawyer, not their friend.

If you have a mobile handset or mobile phone, try taking your calls standing up. People who stand when on the phone tend to keep their conversations shorter.

Email

This is a difficult one. All your instincts tell you it's wrong, but try only checking your emails a couple of times a day. Close email when it's not being used, because new messages flashing up are a real distraction. Alternatively, switch off notifications so that you only see new emails when you check them. 12–27

Everyone tends to check emails constantly. If checking-in a few times a day is just too much for you, you can set up preferences to filter your mail. You should delete your spam and any irrelevant emails immediately (including general emails that don't actually relate to you). If appropriate, forward emails to colleagues who can provide a better response. Once you open up a message, we suggest that you handle it once: read, respond, file. In other words, deal with it. Don't have your inbox cluttered with 'read' messages. Finally, be wary of emails marked 'urgent' or 'high priority'. They may be important to the person who sent it, but that doesn't necessarily mean that they are to you. Some people mark all their emails urgent, even when they're not. Don't be afraid of making so-called urgent emails less of a priority than they might first appear.

Tidy your desk

12–28   Keep your desk tidy. Clutter is a distraction and, actually, is quite depressing. Allied to that, the act of tidying your desk improves your sense of motivation. You'll find it easier to stay on top of your work. This could be one of your two-minute procrastination busters?

Mail

12–29   Aim to handle each letter just the once. It's the same process as email: read, process and reply (or action).
    We suggest that you keep three piles: keep, give away and throw away.

- Keep—when you need something for your paper file (if you are using one, or scan into an electronic file), or you need to act on it.
- Give away—when it's work that can and/or should be delegated.
- Throw away—when the mail has no value to you or anyone else, bin it.

Meetings

12–30   You should only attend meetings that are relevant to you. If you get an invite, ask yourself, "is this necessary?" and "what is it for?". If you need to be part of it (as trainees or new lawyers you may not have a choice), arrive on time. You should know the purpose of each meeting you go to, by getting an agenda in advance. We suggest that you always use a timed agenda (especially for longer meetings, or where the chairperson is less effective). Don't be afraid to leave early, if your meeting is only partially of relevance. We know though this can be difficult when you're the most junior person at the table. As you gain experience, however, you can speak up and say if you don't have anything else to add. And, if you're planning to do this, let everyone know before the meeting too, so it doesn't come as a surprise.

Other

12–31   Try and:

- turn off instant messaging applications;
- close documents when you have finished (and file them away);
- close webpages after you have finished with them;
- log-out of social media at work and ensure personal phones are not nearby your workspace to prevent distractions.

SUMMARY

Managing your time is more than just scheduling your day and setting out a list of tasks. It's about changing your priorities as emails arrive, colleagues ask for help and the phone rings. Controlling your environment helps ensure that you have won't have needless distractions, so you can concentrate on your work. Mastering time management will help you work faster and smarter (and get home earlier). **12–32**

CHAPTER 13

How to delegate work

INTRODUCTION

You are fast and efficient. Most days, you go home at a regular time. It almost feels like you have work under control when your partner tells you that a colleague is leaving, and it will be six months before they're replaced. Your partner wants you to take responsibility for your colleague's files. You have no idea how you'll find the time to deal with them. You're already working at capacity. What do you do?

13–1

If you're good at your job, your colleagues and clients will want more from you. It's flattering, but it can make you overloaded with work. In turn, this can make you feel pressured and stressed. When you're overwhelmed, you end up not being able to do everything that everyone wants, this may leave you feeling that you're letting people down. To avoid this, you need to learn to delegate.

13–2

Delegation is the process of transferring a task from you to someone else. Normally, delegation is vertical (manager to subordinate, such as partner to assistant), however it can be horizontal (peer to peer, such as assistant to assistant). It's important that you understand that when you delegate any work, you remain accountable and responsible for it. If you ask a trainee to complete a contract, it's up to you to make sure they do it right.

Delegation is an important skill for all lawyers, because it's with delegation you can—almost—be in two places at once.

Outcome

In this chapter we examine 12 tips for effective delegation so that both you, and the person you ask, gain from it.

13–3

DELEGATION SKILLS

How to delegate

If you work on your own, there's a limit to what you can do, however hard you work. We know that two hands are better than one, and four hands are better than two, but how often do we put that into practice by asking other people to help us? Not delegating is a particular problem for lawyers, because we tend to work on

13–4

'our files' for 'our clients'. We tend to avoid delegating because we feel the need to deal with our files and clients *ourselves*.

There are times when you can't do everything. You need to delegate because you're running out of time or because it's cheaper or faster for someone else to do the work. There may only be 24 hours in the day, but that's 48 hours for two people and 72 hours for three people. You can't make more time, but you can do more in the time you have, if you delegate.

12 delegation tips

13–5   There are 12 'golden rules' for effective delegation:

One—delegation benefits you and your colleagues

13–6   Delegation is a two-way street. It's meant to benefit you and your colleagues. You need to consider what you want to delegate, and why. Are you delegating to get rid of work you loathe, or are you trying to help a junior colleague develop? If you're delegating to avoid something you don't like or don't understand, then you shouldn't be delegating it to someone else. Andrew is company secretary for a group of companies. His background is in conveyancing, not corporate law. However, until he understands how to complete all Companies House filings, he doesn't delegate this work to his trainee, even though it's not complex or difficult. Until he understands what to do, he doesn't believe he should be telling anyone else to do it for him.

Two—use a delegation matrix

13–7   If you want to be structured in how you delegate work you can use a delegation matrix. A delegation matrix is a tool which can help you decide what to delegate. You'll see a simple one in the appendix. A basic delegation matrix has four quadrants and two scales. They're easy to use. You place the work you're thinking of delegating into the appropriate quadrant. You can even take it further by adding numeric scales (1-10) and placing work tasks even more precisely within the quadrants. Ultimately, however, the point is that—at a glance—you can see the work you need to keep doing, and the work you definitely can/want to delegate first.

We suspect that most people won't need a matrix. You will know yourself whether you are delegating something you shouldn't. You'll probably feel guilty when asking for help.

Three—is the work suitable to delegate?

13–8   Make sure that any work you intend to delegate is suitable to be delegated. There are certain things only you should do. For example, if you've prepared for a five-day hearing, you know all the evidence inside out, you don't delegate it the day before to a trainee who's never seen a court room.

Four—be clear about what you are delegating

Be clear about what you're asking someone else to do. Poor delegation is to say: "I want you take this file and finish it off", without saying what needs done. Good delegation is to say: "I want you to take this file for the lease of a shop and finish it by completing the SDLT return. You'll find the information you need to complete the form in this document. Can you prepare everything in draft then show it to me. Once I've checked it, we'll then arrange for payment. I'll then explain what you need to do to arrange payment".

13–9

Five—select the right person

Select who should take on a task, but make sure you can answer the question: "what are they going to get out of it?" If the work you delegate is obviously a task that will help a colleague to develop, they are more likely to want to help.

13–10

Six—select a person with the ability to undertake the work

Make sure you consider your colleague's ability and training needs. Can they complete the task you want them to do? If they don't know that VAT stands for Value Added Tax then they'll struggle when you ask them to examine the correct status of an exempt supply.

13–11

Seven—explain what you need that person to do

Explain clearly the reason for the work you're asking your colleague to do. Explain why it's being delegated and how it fits into the wider legal project. No one wants to work in the dark or be told "just do it because I told you to do it." Also, they may have better ideas about how to do it and letting them know the context might lead to a different way of acting. For example, when asking his trainee to send a due diligence questionnaire to different managers, Andrew asked her to split the list into separate documents. He explained that he wanted to show which questions were relevant for each department without overloading them with the rest of the questionnaire. His trainee suggested using Microsoft Excel instead with a pivot table to categorise questions. Instead of spending half a day creating separate documents, the task was completed within an hour.

13–12

Eight—set an overall outcome

You need to be clear, also, about expected outcomes. Explain how you plan to measure progress. Sometimes it's good to ask your colleague to recap in his or her own words, so you're clear that there hasn't been any misunderstanding. This is particularly important with timescales. You don't want any misunderstandings. If you need to prepare a claim by the end of the week then you don't want to find that your colleague thought you wanted the claim prepared by the end of the month.

13–13

Nine—Provide the right resources

13–14 Discuss the resources that your colleague thinks will be required (whether they relate to location, time, equipment, materials and money etc) and make sure they are in place. There's no point asking a trainee to help set up an electronic data room which will store a large amount of data if your firm doesn't have one or doesn't have a subscription for a service like Dropbox.

Ten—set realistic timescales

13–15 Agree a deadline. Make sure you include a means to monitor and measure progress. And make the deadline realistic. You are only setting someone up to fail if you ask them set up a data room by 9am the next day when they have 200 folders of documents to scan in first… and only one scanner.

Eleven—inform relevant people

13–16 Update anyone else (for example, your client, other staff/teams etc.) so that they also know that you're delegating work. This helps to avoid situations where colleagues also might want to delegate work, leading to someone becoming overworked.

Twelve—provide feedback

13–17 Let people know how they're doing and that they're achieving the goals that you've set. This feedback will ensure that next time you delegate the same or similar work to then, it will be easier and faster as you both know what is required to be done.

Levels of delegation

13–18 There are different levels of freedom that you can confer on a colleague. The more experienced and reliable your assistant is, clearly the more you can safely delegate. It's good to explore with your colleague the level of authority they actually feel comfortable being given. Some people are confident, others less so. Since you're retaining accountability for work, it's your responsibility to delegate at an appropriate level. But why guess? Involve your colleague in establishing their comfort zone.

The following statements help to illustrate the different levels of delegation. These are simplified for clarity. These also are not exhaustive. There are shades of grey. As you read through the list, you'll see each statement offers your colleague more freedom. Level one is the lowest level of delegation, level 10 is the highest level:

- Level 1. "Do exactly what I say." This is an instruction, with no freedom for someone to think or act themselves.

- Level 2. "Look into this and tell me the situation. I'll decide." This is asking for investigation and analysis, but no recommendation. You will assess the options and make the decision.
- Level 3. "Look into this and tell me the situation. We'll decide together." This is subtly different to number two, with the decision being a shared process (which can be helpful when you're trying to develop people).
- Level 4. "Tell me the situation and what help you need from me in assessing and dealing with it. Then we'll decide." This opens the possibility of greater freedom for analysis and decision-making.
- Level 5. "Give me your analysis of the situation (reasons and options) and a recommendation. I'll let you know whether you can go ahead." This seeks analysis and recommendation, but you will check the reasoning and make the final decision.
- Level 6. "Decide, but wait for my go-ahead." The other person is trusted enough to assess the situation and make a decision in principle. However, you prefer to keep control of timing ("wait for my go-ahead"). This level of delegation can be rather frustrating for people, if used too often. The reason for controlling the timing needs to be explained. If someone has a good idea then they usually want to act on it straight away. It can be frustrating to be held back.
- Level 7. "Decide and go ahead unless I say not to." Now, the less senior person is starting to control the action. This subtle increase in responsibility will save you the time of making a decision. The default is positive, rather than negative.
- Level 8. "Decide and let me know what you did (and what happened)." This, as with each notch up the scale, saves even more time. This level of delegation also enables a degree of follow-up by you as to the effectiveness of execution of the delegated responsibility.
- Level 9. "Decide and act. You don't need to check back with me." This is the greatest freedom that can be given, while you retain overall responsibility. A high level of confidence, clearly, is necessary.
- Level 10. "Decide where action needs to be taken and manage the situation. It's your responsibility now." This is generally not used without a formal change of the other person's job role. This basically amounts to assigning part of your job. You'd use this highest level of delegation when, for example, you're developing your successor.

HOW TO GIVE FEEDBACK

An essential element of delegating work is to give feedback to people after **13–19** they've worked for you. If you don't give feedback how will they know if they've done a good job—or if they need to improve? It's always a pleasure to do this when the going is good and targets are being met.

However, when someone hasn't done what you want, if they are underperforming, the process needs to be handled with care. That's why you should always give *constructive* feedback and avoid *praise and criticism*.

What is constructive feedback?

13–20   Constructive feedback is objective. It's based on information and observations.

What is praise and criticism?

13–21   Praise and criticism is your own personal judgment about someone else's performance. The information is general and vague, based on your opinions or feelings. The process is subjective and may even be coloured by your own personal prejudices. This method should be avoided.

How do you give constructive feedback?

13–22   The following tips will help you give constructive feedback.

- Be direct. Whether good or bad, feedback should be given in a straightforward manner.
- Avoid mixed messages. These are sometimes called 'yes, but' statements. For example, "Iain, you've worked hard on this, but…." What then follows usually is negative, and yet is the intended point of the message. The word 'but,' along with its distant relatives 'however' and 'although,' create contradictions. In essence, you're telling your colleagues, "don't believe a thing I said before."
- In positive feedback situations, certainly you can (and should) express appreciation. Appreciation alone is merely praise and should be tied to constructive feedback.
- With negative feedback, you should try and convey concern. An empathetic tone communicates a sense of caring. Ultimately, the purpose of negative feedback is to create an awareness that then will lead to improvements in your colleague's performance.
- Give all your feedback in person, not by email. The nature of constructive feedback is that it's given verbally and informally.
- Your feedback should be given as close as possible to when performance occurs so that events are fresh in everyone's minds. Delays lessen the value of any feedback.
- Try and give your colleagues constructive feedback regularly. Even a simple "You did that well – the report was very concise with everything the client need to read in the first paragraph" helps reinforce good habits.

WHAT STOPS YOU DELEGATING?

13–23   There are some factors that might discourage you from delegating.

- A feeling that you can do the job better yourself. This is almost certainly true. After all, you shouldn't be delegating work that you can't already do yourself. And, you are probably more experienced than the person you are delegating to. You should be faster. The question to ask yourself, however, is: "should I be doing this work myself or is it better for me (and the firm) to delegate it to someone else?". In 2017, Andrew recruited a trainee. For six months he delegated work to her and would spend longer giving her instructions and reviewing her work than it would have taken carrying out the work himself. However, once she knew what to do, he only needed to spend a small amount of time checking her work was okay. The relatively small time spent on training has meant that he is able to delegate work that he would previously have had to done himself and saved himself hours each week.

- A fear of failure. It can be hard to delegate when you're not 100% sure of what you're doing yourself. You don't want someone to know that you might have doubts in your ability. This fear is natural. We all feel like we don't know what we're doing.
- Envy of your talented assistant, whose ability shines through. The solution is to let that talented assistant do the work. The truth is they'll make you look like a leader who can use the talents of his or her staff effectively.
- You don't want to give up something you actually enjoy. There are aspects of every job that are more enjoyable than others. The question here is the same as above, should you be doing it?
- A fear of losing control. Don't fall into the trap of becoming a micromanager, with all of its downsides. By all means, establish check-in points so you can monitor progress. However, don't over-monitor your colleagues or you'll end up causing frustration.

Overcoming these obstacles is critical. If you can't delegate work effectively, your partner might criticise your inability to use your colleagues efficiently. That, in turn, can exclude you from further opportunities. On the other hand, if you do delegate effectively, partners and senior colleagues will note your ability to get the best out of the team. You'll be earmarked as a leader, deserving of higher levels of responsibility.

SUMMARY

If you delegate, you can increase the amount of work that you can deliver and decrease the amount of time you need to do it. And if you can reduce time, you may also reduce costs and increase your firm's profits. That's why you should choose the right tasks to delegate, identify the right people to delegate to, and delegate in the right way by following the 12 tips. If you do, you'll achieve more than working on your own. **13–24**

CHAPTER 14

How to manage teams and projects

INTRODUCTION

You've had your first review. Your partner is impressed that you've decided to focus on time management and delegation as "those are really important skills to develop as a new lawyer—but I think you can do more. I want you to set yourself the goal of becoming a legal project manager. I want you to start thinking about not just how you can work smarter and faster but also how the whole team can work smarter and faster."

14–1

Usain Bolt was the fastest man in the world at 100 metres and 200 metres but, when he ran in a relay, it didn't matter how fast he ran, he didn't win a gold medal unless everyone in his team ran fast too. A relay team is only as fast as its slowest member.

14–2

The same is true for law firms. You might be in full control of your time, working efficiently and smartly, but, if you delegate work to a trainee and they take 40 hours on a 30 minute task, then you've lost all the time that you thought you'd saved—and even worse, they charge your file for all of those hours and your £1,000 file suddenly has 40 hours of time recorded on it

As a new lawyer, you're more likely to work on your own files or as a team member for others. As you become more senior, you'll take on more responsibility and you'll delegate more work to others. Ultimately, you'll have your own clients and those clients may have lots of different legal needs. A small business may need advice to take out a loan, buy a property, licence a product and sue a supplier. It doesn't necessarily expect you to deal with all of this work, but if you're their lawyer, it'll expect you to lead and manage a team who will. That means, as you gain responsibility you also need to spend more time managing others than doing the work yourself.

Equally, as you become more senior, your work will become more complex. Even a single instruction, such as raising an employment claim against an employer, might involve a number of people, from paralegals to trainees and assistants, all of whom need to be managed and led. That's why, as time management and delegation have grown in importance for individual lawyers, project management has also grown in importance so that lawyers can manage everything that a project will need, including scoping it correctly, allocating the right people to it, picking the right fee for it, and completing the work efficiently and smartly.

In this chapter we'll examine what it takes to become a legal project manager. This may sound complicated but, at its heart, a legal project manager is simply someone who thinks about the firm and their team first rather than themselves—and uses all the resources of your team or firm to provide the most efficient service for a client.

Outcome

14-3 In this chapter we're going to examine how you can manage legal work (projects), whether a whole file or part of it, so that you're in full control of it. This is partly about time management, both for yourself and others, but also about managing people, managing budgets and managing clients (and their expectations). It's starting to pull together all the skills and knowledge you've covered so far.

WHAT IS A PROJECT?

14-4 This is a sensible first question. Projects are unique, with specific objectives and are usually never repeated in the same way. For this reason, you're as much a project manager as anyone else. How so? Every client matter has its own unique factors, whether it's a capital market fundraising, a major trial or a simple executory. What's more, because of these unique factors, it's unlikely that any transaction you're involved with will be repeated in exactly the same way.

Think of two semi-detached houses side by side on the same street. They're both for sale and you act for both sellers. While the process will be the same: you'll negotiate a contract, discuss title and prepare for completion, the day to day details will change. One purchaser may accept a contract with minimal changes. The other may argue over every clause. One purchaser may be happy with the title, the other wants you to confirm various easements within it don't apply to them. One file takes 10 hours. The other 30 hours. Both transactions are the same, but they're not repeated in exactly the same way. Every file could be a project.

WHAT IS PROJECT MANAGEMENT?

14-5 Traditionally, lawyers would think about themselves first. Not in a selfish way, don't get us wrong, rather they would think that because a client had asked them for help, then they should be the one to provide that help. If you go to see your GP you wouldn't expect her to call in the practice nurse or, worse, the receptionist, to speak to you. You would expect to just deal with the GP. It's the same attitude for lawyers. A client asks you for help then it's you they want, not the rest of the firm.

Modern lawyers realise that clients are not asking specifically for you and, when a client asks for help, you might not be the best person to deal with all or parts of your response. When a client asks for help, the whole firm can help, not just you. Project management is about changing your thinking from thinking about yourself first, to thinking about the firm first.

What skills and knowledge does a legal project manager need?

Project management is about all the skills and knowledge you and your firm need to move a specific task, event or duty toward completion. In the above example, the aim of your 'project' is to sell a home. If your client was raising an employment tribunal then the aim of your project will be to reach a settlement or favourable decision from a tribunal. Your aim should match what your client is trying to achieve. Chapter 15 (How to set goals) will help you here.

14–6

Legal project managers also need to master a mix of hard skills and soft skills. The hard skills include the use of tools and techniques such as the use of Gantt charts (we'll look at this at the end of the chapter), resource allocation and risk management (which we look at Ch.16 How to manage risks).

Soft skills include managing teams, negotiating with clients and external parties, and juggling multiple projects (time and personal management). We have already looked at these in the preceding chapters.

The overriding aim of acquiring and using these skills is to help you:

- achieve the desired aim (sell the house, reach a settlement etc); and
- be efficient and use the best value resources.

Or, that is to say, your matters (your projects) should be delivered on time, on budget (if you've quoted for the work) and in a way that always meets (or exceeds) your clients' needs.

Because, in the end, you never want to give a client the impression that his or her matter has been completed successfully only because you worked a huge amount of overtime and, in so doing, became so stressed that you drank 12 cups of coffee a day and forgot to feed your cat. Instead, if you look at client matters from a project management perspective, it doesn't mean that you'll never experience problems. However, it'll help you manage and control any unforeseen eventualities—it's the difference between planning and managing, on the one hand, and fire-fighting and reacting, on the other.

HOW DO YOU PLAN AND MANAGE A LEGAL PROJECT?

Overview

Every project has a lifecycle, certain steps that recur in every project. There are striking similarities between generic project lifecycles and legal transactional lifecycles. A typical cycle might follow this path:

14–7

Step one: management (conceptual)

There has to be a management decision to appoint you as the fee earner to lead on a file (i.e. your appointment as a legal project manager). This could be as simple as your partner passing you a file and telling you that it's yours. Or, it could be as complex as being appointed as an 'official' legal project manager for a large deal involving many different teams and offices.

14–8

Step two: scoping and setting goals

14–9   The work that's required by your client has to be scoped and appropriate engagement terms agreed. This scoping exercise should be as thorough as you need it to be for the project you're dealing with, so that you can identify the outcome your client wants. Are they looking to buy a house? Sell a company? Sue their employer? Go to tribunal or reach a negotiated settlement? The scope provides the final aim of your project.

It'll be possible to have different aims. You don't need to just have one. Your client may want you to go to an employment tribunal and, if so, to win. But they may also accept that if compensation was offered, they would want you to negotiate the right to work for a competitor company.

Step three: basic planning

14–10   Once you know your destination, you need to work out how you'll get there. You need to do some basic planning. At this stage you would break up large projects into manageable chunks (this involves you applying your goal-setting knowledge) and start to set key diary dates. If you know you need to sell a home on the 1 March then you know you'll need to:

- Step 1—Initial instructions from client (start)
  To begin the conveyancing process of buying a house you need to receive your initial instructions. You will ask the client to complete initial paperwork and provide you with a form of identity. You will need to diarise time to meet the client, to prepare the initial paperwork and to ask for and receive their identity information.
- Step 2—Receive draft contract
  The draft contract will be completed by the seller's solicitors. You will need to receive it, or chase to receive it, so that you have enough time to review it, take instructions and revise it.
- Step 3—Searches and investigation of title
  You will carry out searches and you will review the title. If you have any queries about the property or paperwork you will contact the seller's solicitor and the solicitor may need to refer to the seller. This process can be quite lengthy depending on a number of enquiries you need to raise. You will need to diarise time to begin this process in enough time to receive and order the searches, to review the title and to give you time to deal with any unexpected issues. This is not something you want to do the day before you exchange contracts.
- Step 4—Report
  Once you have received replies to all enquiries and the results of the searches, a report can then be created on the property and sent to the client along with their mortgage offer. The financial side of the transaction will be set out by you, providing the client with a completion statement highlighting the total amount due from them. This should be sent in enough time for the client to ensure all funds are in place before completion. Again,

you don't want to tell the client the day before completion that they need pay many thousands of pounds they may not have expected.

- Step 5—Signing

    When the paperwork is agreed, you can arrange for the client to sign and a completion date is agreed.

- Step 6—Exchange of contracts

    The transaction and completion date become legally binding on the exchange of contracts. A deposit will be sent to the seller's solicitor and a request for the client's mortgage advance will be paid from their lender. At this stage you will be diarising the dates required for money to be in your account so that it can be paid to the seller on time for completion to take place.

- Step 7—Conveyancing process for buying a house (finish)

    Completion happens, keys are handed over, the client moves in and the purchase price is transferred to the seller's solicitor. You need to make sure that all steps take place and that everyone knows what to do and where to go e.g. remember to tell the client which estate agent holds the keys!

Step four: review resources

This is where you start thinking about the firm. You need to assess whether you **14–11** have the people, resources and IT systems for the job in hand. This could include things like access to online resources (for example, Westlaw). If your firm doesn't have the necessary subscriptions to let you research the latest position on a highly specific point, good project management would suggest that either these be put in place or you withdraw (rather than carry on and risk an SRA complaint, or worse). In our conveyancing example above, one of the resources you might review is whether you are the best person to deal with all of the seven steps. A conveyancing transaction may have a fixed fee. If you have a paralegal who could undertake some of the steps then you could reduce your cost and make the transaction more profitable.

Step five: detailed planning

This is where you consult all relevant people and develop a full understanding of **14–12** your client's requirements. For example, at this stage, this may just involve the client, and you could have a lengthy, detailed client meeting. However, you could also consult with your partner and start to build your project team (for example, pulling in a paralegal to order and review the searches as you already have many other tasks to do the week that will be required).

Step six: execution

You then undertake the client's work, keeping him or her fully informed and **14–13** updated.

Step seven: review

14–14   You need to constantly review your work so that you avoid 'scope creep'. This is where clients ask for more work beyond the scope that you originally agreed. If you're a good project manager, you will recognise and identify scope creep when it arises, so that you can deal with it and your work becomes more profitable. For example, you might start with a simple conveyancing but, it turns out the title contains a number of easements that need to be removed. You may need to raise this additional work with your client and agree a new fee as your original fee had assumed the title would be straightforward.

Step eight: evaluation

14–15   Projects, ultimately, are meant to bring about a good outcome for your clients (and your firm). The benefits of the work you've just completed need to be measured. You also need to evaluate the benefits you've derived against the investment of your time and your firm's resources. This could be as simple as sitting down with your partner, after your fee invoice has been sent out, and assessing how profitable the project has been.

We'll look at each of the stages in more detail.

THE LEGAL PROJECT LIFE CYCLE

Step one: management (conceptual)

14–16   Files that need a project manager typically fall into two types: one, volume work, and two, complex work.

Volume work files are files that are similar and recur frequently. For example, a personal injury firm may receive a lot of claims for slips and trips. A conveyancing firm in Birmingham may receive a lot of instructions to sell flats, a rural firm will mainly deal with houses. A high street firm may receive a lot of instructions for simple wills from husband and wife leaving everything to their spouse. The work required by these files may not be complex but, in their sheer volume, they may require someone to project manage them to make sure they're all completed on time and on budget.

The second example of work, complex work, requires a project manager to help ensure it's dealt with in the best way possible for the client and your firm. A surgeon wouldn't start an operation without knowing what they'll do and what people they'll need with them at the operating table. You shouldn't start any complex legal work without knowing what you'll do and who you'll need before you start. By planning what you'll do in advance you can plan what to do so that, just like a surgeon, you can act without making any unnecessary mistakes.

The first step in project management is to identify the need for a project manager. This may be something that you suggest, or it may come from your partner. And, while it could be formal, it could equally just be a thought in your head that you need to approach a new piece of work with your project manager hat on. And you may find that you approach all new work like that. Either way, you've identified a need to use your project management skills, so what next?

Steps two and three: scoping and planning

Scoping and planning both cover a similar thought—do you know what you'll do for your client before you start working for them? This is a thought you should cover in your engagement terms but, as project manager, it's one that you should examine further. An engagement letter may tell your client *what* you'll do, but it doesn't tend to tell them in detail *how* you'll do it. A client is not interested in whether you're using a template for your contract or drafting it from start. Nor is a client interested in knowing which particular trainee or assistant may help you in the background. However, a project manager will care how the work is done and will plan for it.

    Let's examine a house sale to show the difference between what you might write in an engagement letter and what you'll cover in your planning. In your engagement letter you may explain to the client that you'll "negotiate and conclude a contract on their behalf." However, your plan may show: "a trainee will draft a contract offer in the firm's style. You'll review it before it is sent to the seller's solicitor. You'll review any changes required by the seller. You'll conclude the contract." You're describing what you'll do and how you'll do it.

    At this stage you may also start working out how long the work will take and how much you can charge for it. For example, your plan might say: "a trainee will draft a contract in the firm's style (two hours at £100 per hour). You'll review it before it is sent to the seller's solicitor (one hour at £150 per hour). You'll review any changes required by the seller (two to four hours at £150 per hour). You'll exchange the contract (30 minutes at £150 per hour)." Your plan is telling you that if you follow this plan then it'll take a trainee two hours of time and £200 and it'll take you up to six and half hours of time at £825 to draft and conclude a contract. This doesn't include the time it'll take to review titles or complete the sale. And you know your fee is £500. What do you do?

Step four: review resources

Your next step is to consider if you have the resources to carry out your plan. In practice, this would form part of your planning as you would be thinking of resources at the same time as you scope and plan the work. You wouldn't think of using a trainee if you didn't have one—though you might as Andrew did, before starting an IPO listing, hire one to help out. When you review resources, you're testing your plan and considering alternatives. In the example of our house sale your initial plan shows that you'll make a loss on the sale. You'll spend more time on the sale than you'll recover in a fee. You need to reduce the time you'll charge to the file.

    If this is volume work, you might think it would be good to spend time creating a template contract and to use document automation software to help tailor clauses quickly. While the time spent creating the template may take a long time, let's say 40 hours of time, it'll save almost two hours in every transaction

14–17

14–18

because the contract can be produced in five minutes rather than two hours. You're saving almost two hours for every file after that initial work.

Alternatively, you might consider whether you should negotiate the contract. Your trainee is smart, they know what to do and although they're not as fast as you, you think they would still only take five hours at most to complete the negotiation. Your cost of negotiating the contract is £500 at most, instead of £600. You've saved £100.

Step five: detailed planning

14–19 This is where you start to finalise your plan and go into detail into exactly what you'll do. You may start to speak to your partner to check that you can use the trainee to help you. You'll speak to the client to explain that you're using a new template, which will help speed up the sale, and you're getting their feedback.

Your partner may tell you that the trainee will be on holiday when you need them. The client may want you to handle all of their work and they don't want anyone else dealing with it. If so, you'll need to change your plans again.

Step six: execution

14–20 You and your team do the work. Though that doesn't mean blindly following your plan, as you'll need to review it.

Step seven: review

14–21 Things change. Your client may give you new instructions. The other lawyers may raise points you've not considered in your plan. Even the simplest house sale can turn into the most complex property deal when you find out the title is missing access easements, the extension has no planning permission and the seller wants to implement a tax saving scheme to help reduce its tax liability.

When you review your plan that means going back to step two and thinking through again what you need to do, who needs to do it, what resources you have for it and who do you need to speak to in order to agree it. This review also includes effective supervision. Are your team performing as expected? If not, do you need to speak to them or, ultimately, change them to make sure you get the result you need?

When Andrew was working on the regeneration of former council housing, an unexpected issue with procurement meant the entire project had to be rethought. He had to change his project plan to include procurement specialists in his team, while the project team had to revise deadlines, inform third parties involved and review the budget to make sure the project was still profitable.

This review is a vital step, if you need to take a different course you need to tell your client, just as a pilot would tell you if your flight changed direction. You're the pilot, the client is your passenger and you need to let them know what's happening—especially if you need to change your fee later.

If your fee exceeds the fee agreed with your client, your clients will not consider your work to be a success (even if you've delivered on time). That's why you need to manage your budget. Here are four tips that will help you avoid increased cost.

- Review your budget regularly—checking your work in progress prevents budgets getting too far out of hand. How much time has your team incurred? Does that figure change your view as to how much time you need to complete your project? And are they recording all of their time?
- Review your team—just as a budget needs to be revisited to keep it on track, you need to do the same for your team, since the people working on your project clearly add to its cost. Do you need an extra trainee or newly qualified support? Do you still need a specialist to attend every meeting, or has their role ended? The former will add to your budget; the latter will help you bring your legal project home under budget.
- Keep your team updated—we recommend sharing your budget with your team so that they can manage their time and see how it links to the overall project. It will then be clear, along with their scope, what they're intended to do as they might think that they're providing a full due diligence review when the budget makes clear you only want them to carry out a headline review.
- Manage your scope of work carefully—scope creep is perhaps the number one cause of project overruns. Unplanned work means hours are racked up, and your budget goes out the window. Some clients will always try and push their luck and ask for more work. In the face of client pressure, you need to be firm, and make sure that you agree any changes and any fee increases for any work that isn't covered by the initial scope. These new instructions (signed off by the client) give you a new budget to work to.

Step eight: evaluation

Once complete you want to review what you've done to see if there's anything you can repeat for similar transactions (or avoid). This is particularly important for volume work as five minutes saved in one file could be hours and days saved across all files if repeated. A proper evaluation will take place as soon as possible after the work has completed and will ask: "what worked well?", "where could we improve?" and "what lessons, documents or process can be shared or replicated?"   **14–22**

CHOOSING A TEAM

We've looked at the steps you should take as a project manager. In a law firm, one of the most important steps is choosing your team. People are the most important element of legal work and having the right people is the most important part of your project. However, building a team for the first time might seem rather daunting.   **14–23**

What is a team?

14–24 Your team is a group of people organised to work together to accomplish a set of objectives that you otherwise can't achieve alone. Even in small firms, you can't function without your secretary. In this example, your team is just you and your secretary. It's also important to realise that you can have different teams for different client projects; your teams won't be the same each time. But how do you select your team?

Choosing a team

14–25 There are thought to be three attributes required in order to be a great team member:

- business or commercial skills (professional orientation);
- time and cost awareness (goal orientation); and
- the ability to work with different types of people (team orientation).

Dr Meredith Belbin is a pioneer of 'team-role' research. In 1993, he published his theory that a good team player is someone who has the ability to co-operate and interrelate with others in a particular way.[1] He suggested that there are four principles that can help you design and build a good team.

- A balanced team—There has to be a good balance in the team roles you designate, and their corresponding functional duties/responsibilities. In a legal project this means making sure that you the right mix of experience and skills. When buying another housebuilder, Andrew selected a team that would be able to provide property, corporate, employment and IP advice. He knew that while property might be the most time consuming task—as more than a dozen sites would be reviewed—the corporate team was the most important as the purchase required stock market investment, which would be critical to raising funds. When selecting the team, he knew he would need an experienced corporate partner but that the property work would be carried out by assistants. He was selecting a team to reflect the responsibilities required.
- A strong team—Your team members need to be able to adjust to relative strengths within the team, both in expertise and also in the ability to engage in specific team roles. You want your team to be flexible to reflect how projects can change.
- A team that can work together— You need to understand that personal qualities fit some team roles while limiting the chance of success in others. Andrew works with a board of directors that believes in plain English and meetings that get straight to the point. Before introducing any partner to them, Andrew checks to make sure they know how to speak simply and directly. If not, Andrew knows that it doesn't matter what they say, they

---

[1] R. M. Belbin, *Team Roles at Work* (2nd Edn, Abingdon, Oxon.; New York: Routledge, 2010).

won't be heard. Selecting a team that has the personal qualities to succeed with a client is just as important as selecting a team with the legal experience to succeed.

- A team with the right skills—Your team can only use its resources to the best advantage when it has the right breadth and range of team roles. In other words, you need to plan to ensure that your team is properly equipped from a human resources perspective. This is similar to points 2 and 3. Make sure you have the right people doing the right things at the right time.

Another common question is whether people in teams all need to get along. Do your team members need to be Facebook friends? Do they need to go to the pub on a Friday and then play golf at the weekends? Do they need to 'like' each other? Surprisingly, the answer appears to be 'no'[2]. Instead, the best teams work together by sharing a common goal. That's why it's so important that you share that purpose with your team and keep them updated throughout the project.

We'll examine goal setting in the next chapter.

SUMMARY

Project management is a process, a way of thinking, to help you think about how you deliver legal services using all of your firm's people and resources. You may ask if project management is just a way of making legal services cheaper so that firms may make more money. That is true, if your sole goal is to reduce costs then project management will help you identify where savings can be made. However, as a solicitor your ultimate aim is provide effective legal advice following professional standards. That doesn't always mean providing a service at the lowest cost. Instead, we want you to also think about using project management to provide a better service to clients.

14–26

BACKGROUND INFORMATION: INTRODUCTION TO GANTT CHARTS

Project management is a way of thinking but it also has its own tools that can help you organise your thoughts. This section is for those looking for advanced skills and knowledge. The first tool, and one that many project managers use is a Gantt chart. This is a form of advanced diary management. Gantt charts are incredibly useful in showing planned, essential activities (i.e. your project's various tasks and events) as against a timeline.

14–27

There are many free templates available online, in Excel format, and we have also included an example of one in Appendix 4. If you haven't seen a Gantt chart before then take a minute to review it.

---

[2] See Chs 3, 4, 6 and 8 in J. Katzenbach, The *Wisdom of Teams: Creating the High-Performance Organization* (Boston, Massachusetts: Harvard Business School Press, 1993).

Format

14–28   The format of Gantt charts is pretty much standardised, regardless of the template you use. Usually on the left of the chart (the vertical) is a list of all the actions that are needed in order to complete your legal project. Along the top (the horizontal) is a time line. Each activity (or event) is represented on the chart by a bar. The position and length of the bar reflects the start date, the duration and the end date of each activity. Taken together, this graphical interface allows you to see at a glance:

- what all your various activities involve;
- when each needs to begin (and end);
- how long each is scheduled to last;
- if any activities actually overlap with others (and if so, by how much);
- the start and end date of your entire legal project.

Your Gantt chart will show you what has to be done (your activities) and when (your schedule). Nowadays, since they usually come in Excel format, Gantt charts can be created and then updated easily.

Project plan

14–29   How do you go about even starting to make a Gantt chart for a legal project? It's simple.

   The first thing you need to do (before you even open your Gantt chart file) is to complete a detailed project plan. Your project plan simply is your list of the all the tasks that you think will need to be performed, and in which order they need to be completed. For example, let's say you're moving into a new office. You can't start re-designing your office space before your lease has even been signed. In this example, your project plan would be: sign lease, re-design office space, move equipment in, and so on.

   The next point to keep in mind is that your project plan should have a start date that matches the starting point of your first task (e.g. signing your lease—seems sensible) and an end date that corresponds to the completion of your last task (e.g. moving into your new office).

   One trick when creating your project plan is to use what is called a work breakdown structure. This is a simple technique for splitting big tasks into smaller sub-tasks, and creating a task hierarchy (i.e. an order of what is most important, second most important, third, fourth, and so on). Good Gantt chart apps generally will let you reflect your project hierarchy in the task list, on the left hand side.

Data entry

14–30   Once your project plan is complete, you simply enter all the data from the plan into your Gantt app. A sensible method for inputting the data would be:

- Set your start date and end date. The default scheduling method usually is forwards from your project start date. In this mode your tasks are scheduled to start as soon as possible, which means that your whole legal project will finish at the earliest possible date.
- Define your project calendar. This is where you specify the number of working days in the week (and the number of working hours in each day) that you'll work on your legal project.
- Enter all your tasks (and their durations).
- Set up a resources list and then assign resources to tasks. Although you can often define your resources as and when you need them, it's usually much quicker to start by setting up a global list from which you can then select your resources.
- Create links to specify any dependencies between project tasks (i.e. task three might depend on task two being completed and—in turn—task one might depend on task two being completed).
- Set constraints on your tasks, as necessary (and we'll look at these in more detail just shortly).
- Make any final tweaks and adjustments to your legal project plan.

Your app will then automatically create a graphical Gantt chart for you.

Timings

Any change that you make to the timing of a task will affect all the tasks that are dependent on it. If a task runs ahead of schedule, your Gantt application will automatically recalculate the dates of the other tasks that are dependent on it, in order to take advantage of the time gained. Conversely, if a task is delayed, all the tasks that depend on it will automatically be pushed back, which may or may not—depending how well you pad your timelines—affect the end date of your legal project. **14–31**

As you go along, you can easily add or remove tasks, adjust the duration of tasks (i.e. the length of the bars), link tasks (for example to make one task follow immediately after another) and add constraints (for example, to specify that a task must end "no later" than a given date).

Constraints

By default, your tasks usually will be linked from 'finish to start'. This means that the first task you select (the so-called "predecessor task') must end before the next task you select (the so-called 'successor task') can start, and so on. This typically will be shown on your Gantt chart by lines with little arrowheads, joining each task to its successor. The arrowhead simply indicates the direction of the link (predecessor to successor). **14–32**

Constraints are handy. They define the degree of flexibility available to your Gantt app when scheduling (or rescheduling) tasks, by imposing restrictions on start dates and end dates. Two 'constraints' are so flexible that they're generally not regarded as constraints at all.

- As soon as possible (ASAP)
    a. This is generally the default when you schedule a project from its start date, as is normally the case. To make life simple (and we like simple), try to keep this default whenever possible, as it gives your software the most flexibility.
    b. If you apply this 'constraint' to an unlinked task, that task will be scheduled to start at the project start date. If you apply it to a linked task, however, it'll start as soon as its predecessor task is finished.
- As late as possible (ALAP)
    a. Generally, this is the default when you schedule your project back to front (i.e. from its end date).
    b. If you apply this to an unlinked task, that task will be scheduled so that its end date coincides with the end date of your overall project. If you apply it to a linked task, however, it'll be scheduled to end when the successor task needs to start.
    c. On the whole, try to avoid this option. It doesn't give you any extra slack time to deal with problems that might arise. And problems often do, in the most unexpected ways.

There are other, more sophisticated constraints that you can use within your Gantt app. When you're just starting out and getting comfy with Gantt charts, however, it's best to keep their use to a minimum.

- Start no earlier than
    — A task (whether linked or not) can't start before a date you specify. However, your Gantt app has the flexibility to start it later.
- Start no later than
    — A task (whether linked or not) can't start later than a date you specify. However, your app has the flexibility to start it earlier.
- Finish no earlier than
    — A task (whether linked or not) can't end before a given date. However, your app has the flexibility to end it later.
- Finish no later than
    — A task (whether linked or not) can't end later than a given date. However, your app has the flexibility to end it earlier.
- Must start on
    — This rigid constraint means that a task (whether linked or not) must start on a specific date. Even if its immediately preceding task is completed earlier, your app will not bring forward the task to take advantage of the time gained.
- Must finish on
    — This is another rigid constraint. A task (whether linked or not) must end on a specific date. As above, even if its immediately preceding task is completed earlier, your app will not bring forward the task to take advantage of the time gained.

If you do decide to apply any constraints to your tasks, it's a good idea to add a brief comment to your Excel to explain why. If a constraint causes scheduling conflicts later on, as your legal project evolves, you'll be able to refer to your notes to decide whether to: keep a constraint in place, change it to a different constraint, or remove it completely.

CHAPTER 15

How to set goals

INTRODUCTION

You start a large transaction. Your client wants you to complete it by the end of   **15–1**
the year. Your partner asks you to prepare a project plan and timetable setting out
what you and the rest of the team will need to do. How do you turn this aspiration
to complete this year into practical steps that you, your partner and your team
can understand? You need to set some goals.

Everyone needs goals. Imagine setting off on a journey across an ocean, but   **15–2**
without a set destination in mind. You might have a sense of the general direction
you want to go but, if you have no specific destination, how will you know when
you reach the end? As the late baseball legend, Yogi Berra, once said: "If you
don't know where you're going, you might end up someplace else".

Not having goals, whether at work or at home, is just like embarking on this
imaginary journey, with no destination in mind and no compass to guide you. If
you like, you can simulate it by trying to drive across London without GPS. How
far did you get? How long did it take? And, after the umpteenth roundabout, did
you find yourself back exactly where you started? If you know where you're
trying to get to then you go plan how you will get there.

That's why goal setting is an important skill for lawyers managing projects.
Your goal might be a general one: to sell a home; win a case; or obtain funding
for a client. But goal setting is about splitting that general goal into smaller
specific steps you can take. If you need to obtain funding for a client then you
might need to agree a facility letter with a bank's solicitor; you may need to agree
supporting documents such as company minutes confirming the funding, if your
client is a company. Knowing your goal, you can work out how you will achieve
it. Perhaps you will take the lead on the facility letter while you ask your trainee
to pull together minutes. The facility letter is a complicated document and
requires a senior lawyer with experience to review and negotiate it. The minutes
are standard documents that a junior lawyer can prepare. Goal setting helps you
plan your 'project'.

Equally, just as a flight to Australia might involve a stop in Hong Kong, so
your goals might also have interim steps. If you're preparing a facility letter, then
you may need to provide some due diligence documents as part of the funding
requirements. This might be a valuation or some other documents. An interim
goal for you will be to obtain that valuation from your client so that you can
provide it when required to draw down funds. Clever goal setting helps you see
not just the ultimate destination but also the steps that will help you get there.

213

Outcomes

15–3   By the end of this chapter you'll understand how setting goals can help your career. You'll know how to set appropriate goals and how to avoid unrealistic ones.

WHAT IS GOAL SETTING?

15–4   Let's start by examining goal setting in general, so that you understand the principles that apply and the benefits they bring.

Why do we set goals?

15–5   There are five key reasons for setting goals:

Reason one—goals are motivational

15–6   Let's return to sailing on the ocean. Visualise yourself on your boat, in the middle of that ocean. Do you have a clear idea about the purpose of your trip, your direction or where you're going? Without any additional information, we'd expect the answer to be 'no'.

Imagine that someone asks you to sail to Canada, within 90 days, to deliver a ship filled with Union Jack flags. What's the difference? You have a clear sense of purpose (to deliver the flags within 90 days) and a clear direction (to sail to Canada). This is more likely to encourage action. You now know what you need to do and when you need to do it. In other words, well-stated goals provide a sense of meaning, purpose and direction; they motivate you.

Let's think how this translates to your firm. You have been asked by your partner to sell a small company with a turnover of £10m. The sale must take place by the end of the year—31 December. This gives you a purpose. However, it's not yet a fully developed goal, because goals also need to set clear expectations.

Reason two—goals should have clear expectations

15–7   If you set a goal of selling the company by 31 December, this is rather vague. You need to be more specific. Exactly how will you sell the company? You might decide that you need to agree a share purchase agreement, you need to provide the purchaser with information about the company so it can complete its due diligence review and you need help from other departments to deal with employment, tax and IP issues. Your developed goal might be to speak to the other departments by the end of the week; to provide the purchaser with due diligence information by 1 December and to sell the company by negotiating a share purchase agreement by 31 December 2018. You not only have a purpose, you know what steps you need to take to realise it.

Reason three—goals drive performance

When your goals are clear and measurable, they invigorate you. You're able to check if you're meeting your goals. In our example, in one month's time you can look back and check. Do you have a team? Do you have the due diligence information? Or, are you falling behind?

15–8

Reason four—goals enable teams to work towards a common purpose

Your goals are not just for you. If you share your goals with your team (even if it's just you and a trainee), they'll better understand what you're trying to achieve and why. This reduces the likelihood of team members being pulled in different directions, working on irrelevant activities, or getting into disputes. Sharing goals is vital when managing a team. If your goal is to open the data room on 1 December then you need to tell your employment colleagues that they need to have all employment contracts scanned and uploaded by 1 December too.

15–9

Reason five—goals support a firm's culture

Lastly, and this applies more for your personal performance than a project, it's not just you who sets goals. Your firm (via partners and senior lawyers) sets firm wide goals, normally as part of the appraisal process. These goals can help you. For example, if teamwork is particularly important to your firm, then firmwide goals that are designed encourage this can support you as your entire project as your colleagues should already be thinking collegially. Alternatively, you should try and avoid goals that contradict any firmwide goals. You'll be less likely to have support if your goal is to "get documents out today, regardless of what state they are in, so as to show the client we can move fast" when you have goals that require a thorough review of drafts by supervising partners or more senior colleagues.

15–10

Goals to avoid

Are there goals you should avoid? Yes. Everyone wants to make a meaningful contribution. If your goals either are not essential to your strategy (or your firm's strategy), a project or a piece of work, don't set them. Nothing is more frustrating than working on something that lacks purpose. Let's look at common mistakes in goal setting.

15–11

Setting unrealistic goals

Make sure that your goals are realistic, and that you actually can achieve each goal in the time frame you've set. For example, a realistic personal goal might be to lose one stone in a month. It would be unrealistic to try to lose that weight in two weeks. Equally, setting yourself a goal to finish all your work before you go home is likely never going to be achieved; you'll have too many interruptions. Instead, finishing all essential work is a better, more realistic goal.

15–12

Underestimating completion time

15–13   How often has a task taken longer than you thought? Probably more times than you can count. If you don't estimate completion times accurately, it can be discouraging when things take longer than you expect. This can sometimes cause you to give up. Always build in time for unexpected delays. You'll feel less pressure and you're more likely to achieve your goals by your target date. Plan a few hours each week for the unexpected. If you think the data room will take 10 hours of your time to complete, plan to have it done in five days, not two. That gives you two hours each day, with extra time to deal with calls, emails, interruptions and urgent tasks that you hadn't anticipated. You might not know what the additional time will be spent on, but you know something is likely to arise. The important thing is that you build in a sensible buffer for the unexpected client call or partner request that must be dealt with urgently that day.

Not appreciating failure

15–14   No matter how hard you work, you'll fail to achieve some goals. We've all been there. However, failures ultimately shape your character more than anything else. They teach you lessons, if you're minded to learn from them. In other words, don't be upset if you fail to achieve a goal. Instead, take note of where you went wrong and then use that insight to reach your goal next time.

Perhaps the data room was ready on 1 December but you still hadn't received employment contract for the company's staff. You have asked for this information but you haven't pushed for it. In fact, you've not asked for it again in the previous week. In future you will know that you may need to remind clients if information is missing.

Not reviewing progress

15–15   It takes time to accomplish any goal and, sometimes, you might feel that you haven't made progress. That's why it's important to take stock on a regular basis. You need to set staging posts and make a point of celebrating your successes. That's why having interim goals helps. Celebrate the fact the data room was provided on time. You may not have sold the company yet, but you've taken a major step on the way to achieving that. Regular reviews also help you to analyse what you need to do to keep moving forward. Goals are never set in stone, so don't be afraid to amend them if required.

Setting "negative" goals

15–16   How you think about your goals influences how you feel about them. For instance, have you ever set yourself the goal of losing weight? This sort of goal actually has a negative connotation; it's focused on what you don't want (i.e. your weight). A positive way to reframe this goal would be to say that you want to 'get healthy'. That way your weight-loss becomes part of a more positive goal.

Negative goals are emotionally unattractive, which makes it harder for you to focus on them. Reframe all your negative goals so that they're positive. Don't make your goal, for example, to produce a first draft share purchase agreement without any mistakes. Instead, set goals that help you become faster and more efficient. Draft a share purchase agreement that includes the main terms. Focus on the general requirement, not on getting every word correct.

Setting too many goals

You've got a fixed amount of time and energy. If you try to focus on too many goals at once, you won't be able to give each individual one the attention it deserves and – indeed – requires. Instead, use a 'quality, not quantity' rule when goal setting. Work out the relative importance of everything that you want to accomplish.

15–17

HOW DO YOU CHOOSE THE RIGHT GOALS?

When it comes to appraisals and setting goals, it pays to be S.M.A.R.T. A SMART goal is S-pecific, M-easurable, A-ttainable, R-ealistic and T-imely.

15–18

Specific

You have a greater chance of accomplishing a specific goal than a general goal. To set a specific goal you need to answer the six 'W' questions.

15–19

- 'Who' needs to be involved, to help you achieve your goal?
- 'What' do you want to accomplish?
- 'Where' are you going to carry out all the required actions?
- 'When' will you achieve your goal by (time-frame)?
- 'Which' requirements do you have to succeed (plus constraints)?
- 'Why' do you want to accomplish the goal (benefits)?

Example

An example of a general goal would be to 'record time'. However, a more specific goal would be to record time at the end of each working day.

Measurable

As you know, you need to measure your progress towards the attainment of every goal you set. When you measure your progress you tend more to stay on track and achieve your target dates. In turn, you experience a sense of achievement that motivates you to keep going to reach your ultimate goal. Ever heard of the self-fulfilling prophecy? If your goal is measurable, it answers the "how" questions.

15–20

- 'How' much?
- 'How' many?
- 'How' will I know it has been achieved?

Attainable

15–21   You can attain almost any goal you set for yourself. You're the only one, however, who can decide just how high your targets will be. The sky's not the limit; you are. Interestingly, an ambitious goal often is easier to attain than an unambitious one. Why? A lower goal exerts only a low motivational force. Some of your biggest accomplishments, in retrospect, may seem easy, but that's precisely because they motivated you in some way. As you become more successful, goals that previously had seemed out of reach suddenly become attainable, when viewed with fresh eyes, not because they have become diluted in some way, but because you have developed to match them.

That being said, however, the concept of attainability is exactly the principle we looked at, earlier, whereby you should not set yourself unrealistic goals. One way to work out if your goals are realistic is to reflect on whether you've accomplished anything similar in the past.

Relevant

15–22   Your goals should be relevant both to you and your firm. A relevant goal is one in respect of which you can answer in the affirmative, the following questions:

- Is your goal worthwhile?
- Are you the best person to be trying to achieve the goal?
- Is the timing right?
- Does your goal align with your own needs and those of your firm?

Time

15–23   Your goals need a timeframe. Without it, you have no sense of urgency. For example, if you want your trainee to help produce the corporate documents required for the sale then you won't want them appearing on your desk at 5pm on 31 December. You need time to check and review them. You might set a goal of receiving the documents on 15 December so that you don't have to spend time on them in the days between Christmas and New Year.

SMART goal setting exercise

15–24   It's time to do a bit more work. It's a simple enough exercise, and it won't take you too long. You can use the grids provided in Pt 1 of the Appendix to help you.
Here's how you do it:

- choose a current piece of work (conveyance/estate/criminal work/trust etc.);
- undertake a SMART analysis and create some key goals;
- answer the 'what' questions;
- answer the 'how' questions;
- assess:
  — attainability;

—   relevance; and
—   time-frames;

• using SMART analysis, identify any obstacles that might impede your progress;
• develop a simple action plan to achieve your goals; and
• identify the people who you can turn to for advice and support.

SUMMARY

We started this chapter by saying that you need goals. We concluded by saying that you need SMART goals. Now, when setting off on your journey across the legal ocean with your clients you'll have a set destination, a specific route to follow—and, to misquote Yogi Berra: "you'll end up *exactly* where you want to be."   **15–25**

CHAPTER 16

How to manage risks

INTRODUCTION

You've missed your alarm and slept in. You tumble out of bed and rush to the shower. You don't check the temperature of the water before you jump in. You might not realise it, but you've just taken a risk.

    You know that you'll struggle to make it through rush hour traffic in time for your 9.30am team meeting, so you text your colleague (all the while doing 45mph in a 30mph zone); more risk.

    You get to the office. It's 9.15am—you've made it. However, you've been lucky. You could have had an accident. You could have been caught by the police and charged with speeding or using a phone while driving. You swear you won't ever do any of these things again. You should know better. You're a lawyer. However, even as you promise you're going to change, you know this will happen again. Doesn't everyone check their phone or breach the speed limit now and again?

16–1

    This chapter is about managing risks. Already, from this simple scenario, you can see that your personal life is full of risk. Some are inherent (the risk of scalding as you jump in the shower), others are man-made (deliberately driving over the speed limit). However, risk doesn't stop when you enter the office. It affects your professional life in a number of ways. You're exposed to the risks that flow from dealing with new clients and new retainers (money laundering). While going back to our scenario, your personal actions can expose you to ethical risk (a driving conviction could be a matter for the SRA).

16–2

    In all cases, risks can be identified, assessed and reduced. This becomes more important as you rise through the ranks. As a trainee (or new lawyer), you're supervised. As you gain experience, you become the supervisor. Ultimately, you could manage your own teams, departments or the entire firm. You need to understand the risks that you and your team face, so that you can plan ahead. Imagine, for a second, you're the partner of the lawyer in our scenario. Imagine they hasn't come to work that morning and let's say that lawyer had been due to attend court. What do you do? Do you have a plan in place when someone is absent? Risk management is all about assessing what might happen, so that you can plan ahead.

Outcomes

In this chapter we examine what we mean by 'risk'. We review different ways to identify risks and manage them appropriately. We then look at a number of management theories, illustrated by examples of common legal risks.

16–3

UNDERSTANDING RISK

16–4   Let's start with some theory.

What is risk?

16–5   Risk is the possibility that something (normally bad or unpleasant) will occur. If you advise a client to sue a competitor, there's a risk they might lose. If you walk across a road there's a risk you might be hit by a car. Risks are all around us; you can't avoid them. Instead, what matters is that you understand how to identify risks, how to measure them (the likelihood that a particular risk will materialise), how to estimate their impact on you (and your clients), and how to develop appropriate responses. For example, if there's a risk your client may lose then you may want to tell them up front that court actions aren't always successful, so they don't blame you if it doesn't go their way. Risks can be managed.

What is risk management?

16–6   Risk management is defined as "[t]he identification, analysis, assessment, control and avoidance, minimisation or elimination of unacceptable risks."[1] Note that this definition refers to *unacceptable* risks. There are, by definition, acceptable risks. You take acceptable risks every day. Every time you write an email to a client giving them advice, you're taking a risk. However, you tend not to think about it in that context, because it's just part of your job.

    Sometimes you might draft an email, aware that the advice within is going to have a big impact on your client. You swither about pressing "send", and so you seek a second opinion from a colleague. In other words, an everyday acceptable risk has become unacceptable. But, by speaking to others and getting that second opinion, you've managed the risk. You can go ahead and send it.

    You could avoid all risk by not doing anything and never leaving your house. If you don't send any emails, then you'll never give any wrong advice. However, if you adopted that approach to every risk, you won't be a lawyer for very long. Clients want your advice. If you don't send an email or speak to a client, you'll end up doing nothing. Risk management is all about understanding how to identify risks and how to deal with them.

Effective management

16–7   Let's consider some theory again. Effective risk management involves "…risk assumption, risk avoidance, risk retention, risk transfer, or any other strategy (or combination of strategies) in proper management of future events."[2] We look at risk assumption, avoidance, retention and transfer later on. However, these all pre-suppose that you have some sort of strategy. The International Organisation

---

[1] Definition from *Businessdictionary.com*, *http://www.businessdictionary.com/definition/risk-management.html* [Accessed 19 January 2019].
[2] Definition from *Businessdictionary.com*, *http://www.businessdictionary.com/definition/risk-management.html* [Accessed 19 January 2019].

for Standardisation (ISO) has identified 12 principles that underpin every good risk management strategy.[3] We think nine are worth you considering:

Principle one—create value

The value principle says that the resources you invest in dealing with a risk ought to be less than the consequences that would flow from inaction. In other words, the gain for dealing with a risk should exceed the pain of a risk happening. A famous example is the RMS Titanic. When the Titanic was built, her designers decided that to save deck space they would forego lifeboats for all the passengers. Since the ship had a double hull, the White Star Line proclaimed her 'unsinkable'. In this case, the consequences outweighed the cost of installing lifeboats. With the benefit of 20/20 hindsight, a different decision would have been taken.

    This is an important principle to consider when managing a project. If you need to draft a board minute, then there is a risk that it could be drafted incorrectly. You might want a partner to draft the minute so that there are no mistakes. However, a partner will charge £750 per hour and, if you get the minute wrong, the only downside is the embarrassment of asking your client to sign it again. You might decide that asking a trainee at £150 per hour to draft the minute is acceptable even though there is a greater risk that the minute could be wrong.

16–8

Principle two—organisational ethos

The ethos principle says that your strategy needs to be part of your firm's culture. Since your partners are the biggest influencers of a firm's culture, by definition the strategy must be implemented at the top and then cascaded down. That's hard, because if you think about it, most firms are pyramid shaped, with a few partners at the top and more and more (increasingly junior) solicitors beneath them. The minority has to influence the vast majority.

    A famous example is the 1987 sinking of the Herald of Free Enterprise in Zeebrugge . Sir Barry Sheen, who conducted the subsequent public enquiry, concluded that the company had a 'disease of sloppiness'. Indeed, a request to put an indicator on the ship's bridge that would have shown the position of its bow doors had been rejected by management on the basis that it would be wasteful to spend money on equipment that effectively would show that employees had failed to do their job properly.

    We touched on this in Ch.14 (How to manage teams and projects). If you're managing a team, you need your team members to follow you. If you ask construction to review building contracts at least 48 hours before your meeting with a client, but your firm has a culture of working at the last minute, then you're not going to receive their report until the client is walking into your reception.

16–9

---

[3] ISO 31000:2009, *Risk management–Principles and guidelines.* Available at: *http://www.iso.org/iso/home/standards/iso31000.htm* [Accessed: 19 January 2019].

Principle three—integrated to decision making

16–10   Your firm's culture can influence staff. For example, if there is enormous pressure of time (for instance, due to high billing targets), staff might tend not to assess risks as rigorously and diligently as otherwise they might. External factors can have the same effect. Financial downturns are the classic example, where staff becomes fixated on billing to the exclusion of all else.

A risk assessment strategy should be integrated into your firm's internal processes, so that assessments are—in effect—compelled. For example, to combat the risk of taking on an unacceptable new client, you might use an anti-money laundering system that won't let you record time against a client matter unless and until "red flags" are lifted by a central registrar. These only would be lifted upon verifying that all AML checks had, in fact, been completed.

Principle four—uncertainty and assumptions

16–11   You need to be clear about the assumptions (if any) that you apply to your risk assessments. Are there any factors that you consider might make your assessments inherently uncertain? Alternatively, are you satisfied that your assessments are reasonably robust and accurate? For example, if you're planning a civil court action on behalf of your client, you may assume the other party will want to move quickly to reach a decision. Instead, your assumption was wrong, they use every tactic to delay and run up costs. You realise you should have considered they may have used this tactic to try and persuade your client to settle for less.

Principle five—systematic and structured

16–12   This is intuitive. Your risk assessment system needs to be structured in such a way that anyone in your team can use it with ease. In addition, a structured system helps to ensure that the results it generates are (as far as possible) standardised, regardless of who is using it. We'll look at an exercise in how to do this in para.16-31.

Principle six—best available information

16–13   You need the best information to make any risk assessment you undertake as accurate as it can be. Turning to anti-money laundering, there is a sound rationale to "know your client". If you know a client's personal and business circumstances, the work that he or she is asking you to undertake can be assessed. If you don't know them, or don't carry out a proper assessment, then you increase the risk something will go wrong.

It is worth saying that you can have too much information. Andrew worked with a US bank. Before it would discharge a mortgage, it wanted to know the source of funds for paying the mortgage. Most banks accept funds that are sent by law firms as they know the law firm has carried our anti-money laundering checks. This bank wouldn't accept this. Instead it wanted a full review of all funds, including asking if anyone involved was related to a US Supreme Court judge as part of it's check on political connections. Unless it received a written confirmation that no one was related to Ruth Bader Ginsburg, it wouldn't discharge the mortgage! The best available information requires a balance.

Principle seven—customised

This is another intuitive point. Whatever system you choose must be able to be customised to suit the particular circumstances of your assessments. The US bank's question might be appropriate in the United States but it wasn't appropriate for discharging mortgages in the UK.

16–14

Principle eight—responsive to change

This says that your system must be able to move with the times. For example, the risk a particular client poses (or that a transaction poses) can evolve over time. Something that starts innocuously can change, so as to give you cause for concern. Your system needs to be able to detect emerging risks. Good communication is vital here as you may not realise that risks have changed. Your construction colleagues may have found penalty clauses in every building contract that trigger substantial payments if work is not completed on time. You know from speaking to your client that they have had some delays. You need to speak to your colleagues regularly, so you can pick up risks as you get more information.

16–15

Principle nine—reassess risks

It's not just your system that changes, the world (and the legal market) is ever changing. So, too, are the range and nature of possible risks. For example, the risks of hacking (with its implications for client confidentiality and data loss) are rising. Five years ago, a company may not consider its customer database to be a big risk. Today, with a new focus on protecting people's data, your client may see your database as its biggest risk and it wants you, as it's lawyer, to help them manage it by putting in place the right legal protections. Just look at the example of Mossack Fonseca and the leak of the 'Panama Papers'. Over 11 million documents were hacked from the firm revealing financial secrets of more than 200,000 offshore companies (and some of the famous names reputedly behind them).

16–16

HOW DO YOU IDENTIFY RISKS?

Step 1: select type of risk

Let's consider how risks can be identified. Risks are potential events that, if they happen, will cause you, your team or your firm problems. Hindsight is useless. Instead, you're trying to look into the future. There are two types of risk identification that can help you: source analysis and problem analysis.

16–17

Source analysis

16–18   With source analysis, you're looking at a bigger picture. You're looking at potential sources of risk, whether internal or external. An internal source of risk could be your employees, or even your clients. An external source might be the economy. With source analysis you're not identifying specific risks or specific problems. Instead, you're identifying the root of potential problems. As such, it's quite general.

Problem analysis

16–19   With problem analysis, you're taking out your microscope and examining particular problems that might arise. Again, these can be internal or external. However, they'll be much more specific than the broader brush of source analysis. Examples include a breach of confidentiality or an infraction of the AML regulations.

Outcome

16–20   Once the sources of risks are identified, the events that any particular source might trigger can be investigated. Similarly, once specific problems are highlighted, the events that can lead to a particular problem can be examined.

Step 2: identify outcome required

16–21   Once you've chosen your general approach (whether source or problem analysis) you need to select a more specific formula to home in on—and identify—risks. The formula you choose largely depends on your firm's culture and prevailing standards identified by the SRA, Legal Ombudsman and others. Let's look at some, before you do an exercise.

Objectives-based risk identification

16–22   This is where any events that endanger achieving your objectives are classed as risks. For example, your firm might have an objective of improving its fee income. Any event that might impede that (whether partially or completely, internally or externally) would be classed as a risk. An example might be clients not paying their fees; clearly that's going to reduce any fee income.

Scenario-based risk identification

16–23   In scenario analysis, different scenarios are envisioned. These are your alternative ways of achieving your objectives. Any event that triggers an alternative to your desired scenarios is classed as a risk.

Taxonomy-based risk identification

Taxonomy-based risk identification is a breakdown of possible risk sources (a form of detailed source analysis). It's based on knowledge of best practices within an industry or profession. Using that knowledge, a questionnaire is compiled, and then your answers to those questions help you detect and uncover risks. **16–24**

Common-risk checking

Some industries (for instance, chemical engineering) have lists with known risks already available (developed in the light of experience). Each risk in the list can be checked for whether it might apply to a particular situation. **16–25**

According to Marsh, a professional indemnity insurer, some of the leading causes of claims include: **16–26**

1. communication failures;
2. failing to examine and/or report on documents;
3. delayed or missed time limits;
4. errors and/or omissions in drafting;
5. errors in law or incorrect advice;
6. fraud; and
7. a failure to generally identify risk for clients.

While other commonly reported issues include: reading confidential documents (or having conversations) in public places; using portable devices in such a way other can see your data and losing documents.

Risk charting

This combines the above approaches and displays risks graphically on a risk matrix. It's a hybrid of risk identification and risk assessment. We look at a risk matrix in just a short while. **16–27**

Risk identification exercise

What we want you to do is a simple exercise. This is about getting comfortable with the ISO principles and, secondly, having a go at some basic risk identification. **16–28**

When you're completing the exercise, reflect on the degree of risk management that you think might be commensurate with the risks that you identify. In other words, at one end of the spectrum will you use a sledgehammer to crack a nut, or (at the other) will you readily accept risks (even if they're identified by a rigorous process)?

Reflect, also, on your own appetite towards risk and give yourself a risk-score, out of 10 (with one meaning you're extremely risk averse and—at the opposite end—10 meaning that you're extremely relaxed about risk).

The "4 Cs" task

16–29   The task is called '4 C's'. You're going to do it in the context of planning a short trip away. Most people can relate to planning a trip. It's easy to do.

1.   Identify everything that you might want to pack for a two-mile walk in the country, on a warm day. Write your list on a post-it note.
2.   Then consider:
    a.   Costs—what will it cost you to take each item? Write this down on a separate post-it note.
    b.   Consequences—what might the consequence be to you of not taking each item? Again, jot this down on a post-it.
    c.   Context—keep in mind the context of the exercise (in this case a two-mile walk in the country). This is important; risk identification depends heavily on context. Relating that back to your work, a small rural firm might identify something as a risk that a large city firm might not.
    d.   Choice—make your final choice as to what you will pack, based on an informed balance of cost versus consequences. Create a final, edited list on a post-it.

After you've completed the exercise, repeat it by changing the parameters (you could make it a 10-mile hike or a week-long trip to the mountains, in winter). What you find is that your lists get longer as you prepare for more and more eventualities.

One fascinating aspect relates to your personal risk-score. In a recent continuing professional development (CPD) training session, a group of five solicitors undertook this exercise. Each participant reflected on his/her appetite for risk and selected a personal risk-score. On the day, each of the cohort gave themselves either a 'five' or 'six'. Yet, in the plenary, it transpired that each had made quite different choices about what he/she would pack. This illustrates how difficult it is to calibrate risk assessments.

Step 3: assess risks

16–30   Once you've identified risks (such as those above) you then need to assess them as to the potential severity of their impact (generally negative, such as damage or loss) and also the probability of them occurring. If you take the example of an AML risk assessment, risk assessment is what you do once you've ingathered all the relevant information from your client, on a customer due diligence questionnaire. You're analysing that information and making an assessment of risk.

The potential severity of impact of any risk either can be easy to measure (for instance, the value of your firm's building if it's destroyed by fire) or it can be impossible to know, especially in cases where there is a low probability of occurrence (after all, if something has never happened, it's difficult to judge what its effect might be were it to arise in the future).There can be a real difficulty in determining occurrence, because statistical information is often not available for past incidents. After all, why would a business publicise things that have gone wrong? Best-educated opinions likely will be your primary sources of information. When trying to assess risk, a useful tool is the 'risk magnitude' formula. This gives you a magnitude score for each risk that you identify. You work it out by multiplying the rate (probability) of occurrence of an event, by its impact.

Probability is assessed on a scale from one to five, where one represents a low probability of the risk actually occurring, while five represents a high probability. Impact, likewise, is assessed on a scale of one to five, where one and five represent the minimum and maximum possible impact. Once you've got a whole raft of risk magnitude scores, you can plot them on a chart called a composite risk index.

As we've mentioned, impact can be impossible to predict if the rate of occurrence historically has been low. Probability, also, can be difficult to estimate, since historic data often is not readily available.

Keep in mind that your magnitude scores can change. For example, you might change a score because of the way a retainer evolves, or because of changes in the external business environment. This is why it's necessary to periodically re-assess your risk assessments and then either intensify or relax your mitigation measures, as necessary. In August 2018, you might have viewed a no-deal Brexit as a high impact but low probability event. One that you didn't need to cover in your contracts. However, by November, you might be saying to your client that the contract should have an option to pull out if the client wasn't happy in March 2019. And you now have changed it again when Brexit has been delayed further.

Risk assessment exercise

It's time for you to complete a second exercise. This time, you're going to assess **16–31** impact and probability for a range of scenarios. You're going to plot them on the blank composite risk index (below). The exercise is designed to make you aware about the breadth of different risks that can arise and also to get you to start to assess risks. Try the exercise twice. First time assume you are a partner in a high street firm. Second time assume you are a partner in a global firm. Consider how your assessment varies.

1.   A major client joins a rival firm.
2.   An associate is headhunted.
3.   There is a fire in the office, causing it to burn to the ground.
4.   A client file turns up on the train and the press find out.
5.   An inspection reveals a £100,000 client account shortfall.
6.   You're sued for £1 million due to a missed deadline in your litigation department.
7.   Your server malfunctions and goes offline for two days.
8.   A client defaults on a substantial fee owed to your firm.
9.   Your trainee is arrested for drink driving.
10. A partner has posted offensive material on social media.

Step 4: deal with risks

Risk management options

16–32 Once you identify risks and you understand how to assess them (using magnitude scores) the next thing you need to do is to work out how to manage the risks you identify and—then—whether you apply these management measures immediately, or above some sort of threshold.

Risk management measures are usually based on one or more of the following options:

- avoidance (withdraw from or don't become involved);
- reduction (mitigate);
- sharing (transfer); and
- retention (accept).

The ideal use of any of these strategies might not be possible. Some of them may involve trade-offs that simply are unacceptable to you or your firm. Let's look at each in turn.

Avoidance

16–33 This involves not performing an activity that could carry risk. An example would be not buying a property so as not to take on any legal liability that might come with it. Another example would be not to fly, in order not to take the risk that your plane might crash.

Avoidance can seem the answer to all risks, but avoiding risks also means losing out on the potential gains that accepting (or retaining) risks may yield. To re-iterate an earlier point, it is not possible to avoid all business risks unless you're going to shut up shop. That's why we say that the optimum use of each strategy might not be possible. The following two example puts this into context.

- A study by the Virginia Tech Transportation Institute (VTTI) reported that a driver's risk of collision is three times greater if they text. A risk avoidance strategy would stop you driving. Risk reduction, however, means you'd still drive but would, instead, simply not text.[4]
- According to the Centre for Disease Control, falling out of bed accounts for 1.8 million accident and emergency visits in the USA, each year. A risk avoidance strategy would stop you sleeping in your bed and, instead, have you sleep on your floor. Risk avoidance can go too far.

Now think about winning work. Some of the biggest companies in the world are technology companies—Apple, Facebook, Alphabet (the parent company of Google). Wouldn't you want one of them as your client? Think of all the legal work they require. Yet, if you want to win new tech companies you are presented

---

[4] "New VTTI study results continue to highlight the dangers of distracted driving" (29 May 2013) Available at: *http://www.vtti.vt.edu/featured/?p=193* [Accessed 21 January 2019].

with a risk. 90% of all tech start-ups fail.[5] A risk avoidance strategy would tell you to not act for any start-ups given the risk that they might fail and they might not be able to pay you. Yet, you would also be giving up the chance for others to get in at the start and forge relationships with potentially global companies.

Reduction

Risk reduction involves accepting a risk, but then reducing either the severity and/or likelihood of loss. For example, sprinkler systems are designed to put out a fire, reducing the risk of total loss. The risk hasn't gone away but it has been managed.   **16–34**

That could involve only accepting a small number of clients in the tech start up business so as to reduce the risk of a single failure affecting the firm. Or, it could be only providing a certain amount of legal work before the client would need to pay all their bills to date so that the firm only carries a small risk.

Outsourcing is another example of risk reduction, particularly, if the outsourcer can demonstrate a higher capability at managing or reducing risks. For example, a business might outsource its customer service delivery to another company. This way, it can concentrate on its core activities without having to worry about managing a call centre team. Many law firms use outsources for administration, payroll, document management/mail room, facilities/office services, IT project management, legal research, networks and security, training, and word processing.

Sharing

The term 'risk transfer' is often used in place of risk sharing, in the mistaken belief that you can transfer a risk to a third party through insurance or outsourcing. In practice, if an insurance company or a contractor becomes bankrupt, the original risk may revert to you.   **16–35**

Retention

Retention is where you accept the loss caused by a risk crystallising. This is a viable strategy for small risks, where the cost of insuring against them would be greater than the total losses that would be incurred were they to arise. It also covers risks so large that they just can't be insured against, such as war. Insurance companies won't cover you for losses incurred during a war. These have to be retained by you. Any risks that are not avoided or transferred are—by default—retained, albeit they might be controlled (i.e. risk reduction measures are put in place).   **16–36**

[5] Neil Patel, "90% Of Startups Fail: Here's What You Need To Know About The 10%", Forbes, *Forbes.com*, *https://www.forbes.com/sites/neilpatel/2015/01/16/90-of-startups-will-fail-heres-what-you-need-to-know-about-the-10/#b6decef66792* [Accessed 21 January 2019].

CREATE A RISK MANAGEMENT PLAN

16–37   When reviewing risks, you may want to create a risk management plan for your team or firm. A risk management plan involves selecting appropriate measures to contain the risks that you identify. It needs to be approved by the appropriate level of firm management (following on from our point about ethos, earlier). For instance, a plan to deal with the risk of money laundering needs to have all of your firm's partners backing it. However, a plan that addresses the risks that might flow from a firm's marketing might only require the approval of the marketing partner.

A good plan should contain a schedule for implementation, and it should also identify the staff responsible for any actions that are required. When Andrew worked on his company's IPO, one of the tasks required was the creation of a risk register (another way to describe a risk management plan), which was published in its admission document. This is an example of how one risk—land may decrease in value—was described:

> "There is an inherent risk that the value of land owned by the Group may decline after purchase and this would have an impact on the value of the Group's current land bank which could materially and adversely affect the Group's business, financial condition and results of operation. The valuation of property is provided by independent surveyors. Factors such as changes in regulatory requirements and applicable laws (including in relation to building and environmental regulations, taxation and planning), political conditions, the condition of financial markets, the financial condition of customers, potentially adverse tax consequences, and interest and inflation rate fluctuations all mean that valuations are subject to uncertainty. Moreover, all valuations are made on the basis of assumptions which may prove inaccurate and there is no assurance that the valuations of land will reflect actual sale prices of either the land itself or any developments built thereon.
>
> To mitigate these risks, the Group utilises its in-house legal team and in-house land and planning team. Both teams are positioned to consider potential future changes when purchasing land."[6]

In short, in order to reduce the risk of land decreasing in value, it uses independent external valuers to check priced are realistic and it uses its in-house land and legal teams to check contracts are flexible to cover any potential changes.

SUMMARY

16–38   We take risks every day. When you walk across the road you take a risk. When you give advice to clients you take a risk. When you stand on one leg on a chair, while trying to reach a file at the top of the cabinet, you take a risk. Managing risks allows you to take risks, in greater safety. It helps you prepare for what might happen so that you have a back-up plan for the unexpected. The more senior you become the more you need to plan ahead. This means thinking about

---

[6] Springfield Properties plc, Admission Document, p.34 available from *https://www.springfield.co.uk/assets/0001/8651/Springfield_Properties_Admission_Document.pdf* [Assessed 21 January 2019]

not just the good things you'd like to happen but also the possibility that something bad or unpleasant will happen.

The key thing is that good risk management helps you manage risks and prevent (or at least reduce) undesirable outcomes. It helps you change something that you otherwise might avoid into something you can manage and control. In short, it can change a risk to be avoided into an opportunity to pursue.

CHAPTER 17

How to design legal services

INTRODUCTION

17–1 *For three months you've worked on a large transaction. It's turned out to be more complicated than expected. You have a pile of paperwork that's threatening to break your desk. You've juggled numerous contracts and you've endured countless meetings. You're proud of how you've dealt with everything and your partner has congratulated you on a job well done. You've used your commercial awareness skills to keep costs under control and you've hit your fee targets.*

Then, unexpectedly, your client complains to your partner. The client says that nothing is happening; they don't understand why they should pay a large fee when you haven't done anything for them.

Before responding, your partner asks you to set out step by step what you have done. Something has gone wrong, but what?

17–2 Before we talk about legal design and how it can help you improve the way you work, let's start with an analogy. Think about a magician pulling a rabbit from a hat. You've seen this trick, haven't you? A magician reaches into a hat and pulls out a rabbit. Were you impressed when you saw it? Or has the trick become so clichéd that it barely registers? You know exactly what's going to happen. It's like hearing the punchline of a joke you've heard a million times. There's no longer either a sense of surprise or a sense of wonder. While it may take the poor magician two months to train his rabbit to stay still and not jump out of the hat (and another two months to practise pulling it out of the hat without revealing the secret compartment inside) you simply shrug your shoulders and demand something more impressive: *"Make the Tower of London disappear! Pull an elephant out of the hat!"*

Repetition perhaps has rendered the extraordinary mundane. However, that's not the only reason for your lack of interest. Without knowing the effort required to perform the trick, you—the audience—are unable to appreciate the skill required to control the rabbit and make it appear flawlessly. Is it any wonder that magicians swap rabbits for inanimate objects that don't need trained or fed such as flowers or flags, and pull these out instead?

There is a similar dilemma with legal services. Clients don't recognise the hard work involved in the work that you do. They turn around at the end of a transaction and shrug their shoulders. They don't understand why they're paying for hundreds of hours of work when all they saw were a few emails. Yet from your perspective, however, you remember the late nights and weekends working on their files. You know you could have charged more for the many, many hours that you devoted. The conflict between the work actually undertaken and the service your client perceives he/she has received can be avoided if you can start to understand exactly what a client sees, hears and feels when you advise them. By understanding what they see, you can improve the way you work.

Outcomes

17–3   We conclude this section of the book by examining a way of thinking that can help you understand the difference between what you do and what a client experiences. If you understand this difference, you can make meaningful changes to the way you work.

THE CLIENT EXPERIENCE

17–4   Clients don't sit beside you when you work. They don't listen to your phone calls. They won't read most of the emails that you send, and they may not even read the contracts and papers you write. Instead, they judge you on the conversations you have with them and the documents that they choose to read. Depending on the particular task, this may only be a small fraction of the work you *actually* do for them.

It may take you half a day to prepare questions to interview a witness, a full day to speak to them and, finally, another full day to ensure that you have all the relevant information you need. If you multiply this by fifteen witnesses, you've spent more than a month on just this one task. Yet, your client knows little about it.

When you tell your client that you spoke to fifteen people, they probably imagine that took you only a day. Perhaps they think you phoned them, one after another, and it only took a couple of hours. No wonder they complain if they don't hear from you for a month. You might well be busy working for them, but they don't know that unless (and until) you tell them. If you're vigilant and highlight what you're doing, from first instruction to the moment they pay their final bill, a client always feels more in control. They won't complain about your work or your bill, and they are far more likely to use you again (and indeed to recommend you).

You should place yourself in your clients' shoes and identify what works, what doesn't and what needs to change. By doing so, you can provide your clients with the best service.

How do you put yourself in your clients' shoes? How do you identify when it's appropriate to advise them of any changes? We believe that you do this by preparing a 'roadmap' of the work you intend to do. You identify the steps that you propose to take and decide which of these will be visible to your client. Much like a magician, you work out what is going to happen backstage—behind the red curtain—and what is going to be visible onstage. We'll review two examples to show how you can achieve this.

Background information

The idea of separating work into backstage and onstage actions was conceived some 30 years ago by Lynn Shostack, in an article published in *The Harvard Business Review*.[1] She put forward the idea of a 'blueprint'; a document that sets out in visual form how a customer (client) and service provider (law firm) interact. Broadly, a blueprint helps you identify what clients experience when they instruct you.

17–5

- Start onstage by identifying all the events the client experiences e.g. when they receive documents from you, when they give you instructions, the documents they see etc.
- Move backstage by identifying what you need to do to ensure these onstage events occur. For example, if a document is produced, how is it produced? Is the person who sends it out the same person who drafted it? Is your library involved in the research? Are precedents used or is the document drafted from scratch?

FIRST EXAMPLE: USING A LEGAL DESIGN BLUEPRINT TO IMPROVE A MAGIC TRICK

Step one: identify what the client will see, hear or experience

Let's return to our example of the magician pulling a rabbit from a hat. How might we visualise this? We can sketch out the steps required to perform the trick. We've included an example of this in Appendix 3.

17–6

- As you can see, steps one to five represent the onstage action (what the audience sees).
- Backstage, you can see the steps required to perform the trick in public (whether it's finding a venue, buying supplies, training your rabbit or practicing the trick).

Sketching out the actions isn't the end of the process, however. Once you know what your client sees, you can work out how to improve the experience for them.

---

[1] G. L. Shostack, "Designing services that deliver", Harvard Business Review, January 1984, No.62. Available at: *https://hbr.org/1984/01/designing-services-that-deliver* [Accessed 10 January 2019].

Step two: identify how you can improve what they see, hear or experience

Fail points

17–7   After identifying what occurs onstage and backstage, you can isolate the fail points. These are the parts of the process where events might go awry. If you can predict what the fail points are, you can build in preventive measures to prevent service failings later.

Timing

17–8   The process can be given approximate timings. Improvements can then focus on those parts of the process that might reduce the time required to complete a transaction. For example, if you have an audience that is impressed regardless of what comes out of your hat, you could decide that the time spent training your rabbit is unnecessary when you could use a plastic flower instead. Alternatively, you might seek to innovate and restore the wonder of the trick by replacing your rabbit with something more implausible, so that audiences once again gasp: "how did they do that?!"

Visible innovation

17–9   By identifying what your client sees (and the work required to achieve it) you can consider improvements to those parts of the process that are of the greatest visual value to your client. For example, buying better carrots to feed your rabbit won't improve how your audience perceives the trick. It's the focus on your client as the reason for innovation that gives blueprinting its greatest value.

SECOND EXAMPLE: USING LEGAL DESIGN BLUEPRINTS TO IMPROVE LEGAL CONTRACTS

Step one: identify what the client will see, hear or experience

17–10   Let's examine part of a typical transaction e.g. negotiating and concluding a simple contract. How can you visualise this as a blueprint again? Remember, you sketch out the steps required.

- Once again, steps one to five represent the onstage action (what your client actually sees).
- Backstage, you see the internal actions required to conclude the contract.

Step two: innovation and legal services

17–11   If you review the blueprint, you can identify the fail points, timings and visible innovations that can provide tangible benefits to your client.

Fail points

You can appreciate, in steps one to five, that your client might only see a small   **17–12**
number of documents during the transaction (perhaps a first draft, a summary of
any changes and then a final draft). In order to improve your client's experience,
many partners insist that they review your documents before you send them out.
In particular, when you're a trainee, senior lawyers will check your work.
Equally, larger firms are adopting quality assurance programmes to ensure that
documents are reviewed to reduce the chance of mistakes creeping in. For
example, spelling a client's name incorrectly is one of the most basic (but also
most noticeable) errors that you can make. Another is to send an email to the
wrong person. Autocomplete makes it very easy to pick up the wrong email
address. To fix this, one firm we know has updated its Outlook programme to
always ask "Are you sending this to the right person?" before it will let you send
an email. This simple question ensures lawyers always think about their emails
before they hit "send".

Timing

Your client might be under pressure of time to complete a contract swiftly. It's   **17–13**
important that you're able to support them. By examining how long it takes to
produce a draft, you can start to see that there are things you could introduce to
produce a first draft faster. For example, you might set up a template for future
adaptation (to save drafting from scratch). You might use document automation to
populate multiple documents with the same information. Alternatively, you might
work with your IT team to create an AI program to deal with contracts
automatically, so that they are created by the client answering a few questions.

Visible innovation

Let's stay on the example of using a template. If you don't tell your client that   **17–14**
you have created templates, he/she won't ever know the time saving mechanism
you have introduced for their benefit. You might say to them at your first
meeting, "we can deal with this quickly because we have templates that can
easily be tailored for you. This will save you money."

It's important to mention that service blueprinting doesn't advocate pulling
back the curtain *completely* to reveal everything that you do backstage. Clients
won't thank you for showing them every due diligence bundle and every internal
email.

Service blueprints highlight those parts of a transaction that could be
mentioned onstage, so that your client is fully aware of the work involved (and
what their fees are paying for). If you don't tell them about the complex titles
before producing a report on them, and if you don't share the nightmare due
diligence bundles you have received, your client's perception of your service is
then biased. You can understand why he or she might say, "all I got was an
email". Conflict, then, becomes inevitable. By placing yourself in your clients'
shoes, you can consider how much of the curtain you want to draw back so that
your service (and value) can be recognised.

LEGAL DESIGN BENEFITS

17–15   A blueprint identifies the work you do that your clients actually experience. It helps you highlight the actions that matter to them. By identifying what actions are taken "onstage" and what are not, you can appreciate the importance of communicating to your clients exactly what is required of you to perform the services that they're paying for. And, if you consider transactions from your clients' perspective, you realise that what they *see* of a transaction is entirely down to what you choose to reveal.

SUMMARY

17–16   The art of the magician is the art of visual manipulation. In card tricks, a magician diverts your attention so that cards can be palmed, decks stacked and coins dropped. For the magician, each pass of the hand, flick of a wrist and tap of a wand is choreographed so as to provide the maximum value to an audience.

Remember, you are a lawyer working for clients as part of a business. When designing legal services, if you want to maximise the value of your services, the secret lies in what to reveal. When you start working as a lawyer, you may not be able to sketch out a transaction fully; you may not have sufficient technical and practical knowledge. As you gain experience, you'll be able to identify when you should be onstage and when you should pull back the curtain to reveal what happens backstage. No matter what level you're at, you should always consider your client's point of view.

PART 3

FINANCE

CHAPTER 18

How to understand financial services

INTRODUCTION

You are three-years qualified. You've paid off your student debts and you've **18–1**
started to think about buying a flat, starting a pension and perhaps saving some
money each month. But where do you start? Should you speak to a financial
advisor?

Financial advice can appear complicated. It's filled with jargon and acronyms. **18–2**
Should you take out an ISA? Should your mortgage be capped, fixed or tracked?
It can be difficult to know where to start and you may feel that you need to speak
to an expert. The only problem is that many clients think that *you* are that expert
when they seek financial advice. That's why we started this chapter with an
example of how you approach your own financial decisions. You need to be
confident in your own ability to understand finances before you can speak
confidently to clients.

And clients will ask for your advice. If clients buy a house they may ask you
for advice about taking out a mortgage; when they invest money in a trust they
may assume that you'll tell them if it's a good idea; when corporate clients take
out a loan from a bank they'll expect you to understand what they're doing and
that you'll keep them right. That's why you need to know how money works. You
should understand the basics behind giving financial advice, as well as some of
the main products such as shares, pensions, loans and insurance. We'll cover
everything you need to know in this chapter and the way that we'll do that is by
looking at how finance affects you.

Outcomes

To help you understand finance, we've addressed this chapter to you first. If you **18–3**
don't understand how your own finances work then you'll struggle to translate
that to clients. Everything we talk about in this chapter, though, applies equally to
clients. We start by examining the concepts behind financial advice. These
concepts are simple and, once you know them, you'll be able to understand how
one financial product differs from another. We'll examine the main financial
products used by individuals and companies and the differences between them.
We'll examine how governments help protect financial decisions—and how you
can protect them through using insurance. We finish by looking at how these
products are then bought and sold in the 'financial markets'.

THE BASICS OF FINANCE

The money in your pocket

18–4   All financial decisions can be viewed in two ways. Either you're moving money from the present into the future, or you're moving money from the future into the present. In short, finance is about time travel. You don't create money from thin air, you move it through time to when you need it.

Imagine you have £100 in your pocket. What can you buy with it? Perhaps you can buy a new coat, or an expensive meal? In fact, you can buy anything up to the value of £100. Could you buy a MacBook Air (£1,000)? No. Could you buy a Fiat 500 (£10,000)? No. Could you buy a flat (£100,000)? No. You have only £100, and once you've spent it, it's gone.

Let's imagine that you've started work and you earn a salary of £24,000 a year. Let's forget about taxes and assume that every month you receive £2,000. Each month, you have £2,000 in your pocket. Could you buy that MacBook Air? Yes, it's only £1,000 and you have enough cash in your pocket to pay for it. Could you buy the Fiat 500? No. It's £10,000, which is still £8,000 more than you have. However, you know that in five months you'll have £10,000 (five months' salary of £2,000 a month). If you could only send that money back from the future, you'd be able to buy that car today.

It's the same for the flat. In four years and two months you'll have £100,000 (50 × £2,000). If you want to buy it today, again you need to send that money back from the future. Either that, or you have to wait for 50 months.

That's why financial products can be viewed as time machines. They move money from one point in time to another point in time. This can moving savings from the future to you today to spend. Or it could be about moving money today into the future so you can spend it later. Think about a pension. You might be earning £2,000 a month today but, when you retire, you'll be earning nothing. Future You would love to have £2,000 a month to spend after they retire. So, Present You invests in a pension to help Future You when you retire.

You're a time traveller again. Moving money from one point in time to another. Most investments work like this. When you invest money in a savings account, or a pension or just in a piggy bank, you are taking the money you have today and using it so that you will have it in the future. Loans work in the opposite direction. You move money from the future back to today. A bank may give you a mortgage to buy a house. It may pay you £240,000 because it assumes that you will earn at least £24,000 annually for the next twenty years. It then assumes that you will need £12,000 for other costs. You will have £12,000 to pay for the mortgage each year. It then lends you £240,000 over 20 years assuming that you will have money to pay it over that 20 years. Loans and investments are money time machines, and we look at how they work in the next section.

INVESTMENTS: INFLATION AND INTEREST RATES

You have £100 in your pocket and £2,000 in your bank account, from your first **18–5** salary. After paying your rent, buying food, going out for drinks and buying some new clothes you have £1,000 left. You decide to be sensible and keep it. You have a choice. You could stuff it under your mattress or you might invest it. But why would you invest it rather than keep it under your mattress?

Introducing inflation

Let's start with a simple analogy. Remember when you were a child? How much **18–6** did a bag of crisps or a Mars bar cost? Was it 50p? How much is it today? 75p? The price has increased. Imagine if you had £100 in your pocket, when the bag of crisps cost only 50p. You could have bought 200 bags. Today, because crisps are 75p you can only buy 150 bags. In the future, if prices keep increasing, your £100 will buy fewer and fewer bags. But why have prices increased? There are two main factors:

- costs increase; and
- demand increases.

Cost increase

Costs can increase for various reasons. The main ingredient of crisps is potato. If **18–7** the price of potatoes increases, then manufacturers (like Walkers) have to increase their prices in turn.

The same applies to: the cost of plastic to make the packets; the cost of the flavouring to make the crisps taste of salt and vinegar; the electricity to power the factory; taxes to pay the government; even Gary Lineker's salary to star in the latest advert. As any cost increases, the price of the end product may need to increase.

Demand increases

There are a finite number of potatoes in the world. In turn, there's a finite amount **18–8** of crisps. The scarcer something is, the more people are prepared to pay for it. So, as demand increases (or as the supply of goods decreases), the price increases.

Let's assume there are 10 people in your office who love crisps. Let's assume your local corner shop has 1,000 bags of crisps. If only 10 people want those 1,000 bags, the shop may need to drop its price. Fast forward a week and the crisps are half price; 500 people want the crisps. However, if it's just one bag of crisps (and 10 people want it) the shopkeeper can raise the price. These changes in supply and demand lead to price increases and decreases.

The housing market is a good example of supply and demand. The UK is an island. There is only a limited amount of land and a limited number of homes. House prices rise as the number of people looking for homes increase. House prices fall as the number of people looking for homes decrease.

What is inflation?

18–9   Inflation is simply the percentage increase in prices each year. It's measured monthly and it tracks price increases over a 12-month period. Inflation can be measured in a number of different ways. The most frequently quoted (and most significant) are the Consumer Prices Index (CPI) and the Retail Prices Index (RPI). Each looks at the prices of hundreds of items we commonly buy (including bread, cinema tickets, pints of beer and bags of crisps) and tracks how they've changed over time. The inflation rates are expressed as percentages. If CPI is 4%, this means that on average, the price of products and services bought is 4% higher than a year earlier. Or, in other words, you'd need to spend 4% more to buy the same things you bought 12 months ago.

Can prices go down?

18–10   Yes. This is known as deflation. If prices are not going up, then economists assume people are scared to buy things. This is bad for the economy. If people are not buying, then companies are not getting paid. In turn, companies may become insolvent and employees made redundant (with a rise in unemployment). Inflation is a sign of a healthy economy; deflation is the sign of a poor economy (though too much inflation can also be unhealthy).

Why is inflation important for investment?

18–11   If we didn't have inflation then you could stuff your money under your mattress, take it out in 40 years and buy exactly the same things you can buy, for the same price. However, inflation means prices increase. Your money, over time, becomes worth less, until it's worthless.

To avoid this scenario, you need to invest your money in a way that it increases in value by *more* than the inflationary rate. If, for example, inflation is 3% per year, you need your money to increase by at least 3% so that it retains its value. The more you can increase the value of your money, the better your investment.

The following example shows how this would look if you had £100 in your pocket and inflation is 3%:

Year	To keep up with inflation (3%) you'll need	If investment returns 2%	If investment returns 4%
One	£103	£102	£104
Two	£106	£104	£108
Three	£109	£106	£112
Five	£116	£110	£122
Ten	£138	£122	£148

After 10 years, to keep up with inflation your £100 needs to become £138. If your investment increased by 2% you end up losing £16 after 10 years. If it increased by 4% you gain £10.

Introducing interest rates

We've looked at inflation. We know that it can change the value of the pound in your pocket over time. However, what we need to know, is how do you 'beat' inflation? As we showed you above, you need to invest your money. The simplest way to invest is to invest it in a bank. A bank will pay interest and you want this interest rate to be greater than inflation.

18–12

How are interest rates set?

Every month the Bank of England sets a base rate. Banks and building societies use this base rate when calculating their interest rates. These rates are the rate of interest you get each year if you invest your money with them. So, if the interest rate were 3% (assuming inflation is also 3%), your money would be safe—it would neither increase nor decrease in value. If the interest rate were 4%, your money would increase in value. On the other hand, if the interest rate was 2% (with inflation at 3%) your money would decrease in value.

18–13

Interest rates are also used for loans, and we look at this in more detail later.

Why does the Bank of England set interest rates?

The Bank of England is the UK's central bank. A central bank is a public institution that manages the currency of a country (or group of countries) and controls the money supply (literally, the amount of money in circulation). The central bank of the EU is the European Central Bank. The Federal Reserve is the central bank of the US. One of a central bank's functions is to ensure that economies are stable. In the UK, one of the main ways the Bank of England tries to achieve this is to ensure that inflation doesn't increase by more than 2% each year.

18–14

The bank can control inflation by increasing or decreasing interest rates. When interest rates are low, people are less likely to save money because they can make more money spending it or saving it elsewhere. When rates are high, people are more likely to save as they know the bank will give them a good return. This is a constant balancing act as the more people spend, the more inflation is likely to rise—the central bank has increased demand. The less people spend and the more they save, the more likely it is that inflation will fall—the central bank has decreased demand.

This balance between interest rates and inflation is one that is debated each month by the Bank of England's monetary policy committee, leading to an announcement about the interest rates.

INTRODUCING INVESTMENTS

18–15   Assuming you or your client want to save their money, and move it from today to a future date, how do they go about doing this? You have a number of options. You could save it in a bank or building society; you could save it with the government; you could buy a bond; or you could invest it in shares, property or other assets.

INVESTMENTS: SAVE IT IN A BANK OR BUILDING SOCIETY

18–16   Think of a deposit as a safe that you put your money in, which you'll open in the future. When you open it, you want the money inside to be worth as much as when you put it in, and, hopefully, even more. However, because your money is in a safe, it's not doing anything. And, because it's not doing anything, it's harder for it to grow in value. Would someone pay you if you put your feet up all day? No. So, why should your money be any different? It's not doing anything in the safe. That's why we have different types of deposit, or different types of safe. These are current accounts and savings accounts.

Current accounts

18–17   This is the most common type of deposit. Most people have a current account. A current account is a deposit account designed for everyday transactions. You access it most days to pay in your salary, to set up direct debits for bills and, importantly, to take out cash from ATM machines. These accounts usually yield only a low rate of interest (if indeed any) on the money deposited (also known as your *capital*), because you can withdraw the money at any time. The money always has to be in your "safe", because you may need it at any time.

Saving accounts

18–18   If you want a higher interest rate, you need to let the bank use your money. A savings account is an account that is harder to access. You may not get a debit card and you may even need to give the bank notice before you can take your money out. 60 to 90 days' notice is normal. Since the bank doesn't need to give you your money instantly, it can take the money from your 'safe' and invest it itself. It then returns that money to you with a higher rate of interest as a 'thank you' for letting them use it. Notice accounts are also referred to as term deposit accounts.

INVESTMENTS: SAVE IT WITH THE GOVERNMENT

18–19   When you place your money in a 'safe' you want that safe to be secure. You don't want to give your money to someone who might run off with it, who won't return it to you, or won't invest it wisely. Banks and building societies are authorised by the Government to deal with money. You know they're safe because the Government stands behind them.[1] You may, however, wish to invest in the government directly, particularly after the banking crisis that started in 2008. You may believe that the Government represents the safest place to keep your money. The interest rates offered usually are lower than those of a bank of building society, but your money is more secure.

National Saving and Investment

The UK Government provides deposits through National Saving and Investment (NS & I), an executive agency of the Chancellor of the Exchequer. NS & I provides the following options: **18–20**

Current account

The NS & I Investment Account is an instant access account offering varying rates of interest, depending on how much money is invested. The product offers higher returns for larger investments, with a maximum investment of £1,000,000.   **18–21**

Saving account

The Direct Saver is a savings account which pays a variable rate of interest. The Direct Saver account pays interest gross. This is, in turn, taxable and must be declared to HMRC.   **18–22**

Pensions

Strictly speaking a pension is no different to any other investment. You're taking cash you have today and sending it to future you, to use when you retire. You could do the same thing by converting your cash into a deposit, you could buy shares or you could buy assets. So why have pensions at all? We didn't always have pensions. Either you worked until you died or your family would step in and care for you. The Government wouldn't help. In fact, it created laws to make begging a crime and forced the poor into workhouses. That changed at the turn of the 20th century.   **18–23**

In 1908, David Lloyd George, in a Liberal government led by Herbert Asquith, determined to take action to "lift the shadow of the workhouse from the homes of the poor".[2] He believed the best way of doing this was to guarantee an income to people who were too old to work. In 1908, he introduced the Old Age Pensions Act and created the pension, worth about £23 a week today. In the years since, to encourage people to take charge of their own pension arrangements, successive governments have created tax breaks and incentives to encourage companies to offer workplace pensions.

---

[1] Every UK regulated account usually gets £75,000 protection. If a bank fails, the Government will pay you back within seven days.
[2] Ben Johnson, Lloyd George, Historic UK, see *http://www.historic-uk.com/historyuk/ historyofbritain/lloyd-george* [Accessed 13 February 2019].

18–24   There are two types of pension. There is the state pension, which is provided by the UK Government and paid for through your National Insurance contributions (NICs). There are also private pensions, which are arranged by you or your employer. We'll look at private pensions later in the chapter.

State pension

18–25   The basic state pension is a regular payment from the government that you get when you reach the state pension age. The State Pension age is currently 65 for men. It's increasing for women from 60 to 65. From 2019, the state pension age will increase for both men and women to reach 66 by October 2020. The Government is planning further increases, which will raise the state pension age from 66 to 67 between 2026 and 2028. To get the pension you must have paid (or been credited with) National Insurance Contributions (NICs).

The most you can receive is £164.34 per week as at January 2019. The actual total is based on how much you have contributed through national insurance. The basic state pension increases every year by at least 2.5% or, if higher, the highest of:

- earnings—the average percentage growth in wages (in Great Britain); and
- prices—the percentage growth in prices in the UK as measured by the Consumer Price Index (CPI) (to beat inflation, as we discussed).

INVESTMENTS: BUY A BOND

18–26   Instead of investing your money in a steel safe by saving it, you may want to make your money work by lending it to someone else to use. In return you get an IOU. This IOU promises to return your money at a certain time, and it promises to pay you a set rate of interest each year. This type of arrangement is known as a bond. In some ways, it follows the same principle as a savings account. However, instead of a bank, you're letting someone else use your money, when you don't need it. The main differences are that instead of having to give notice to get your money back, you agree a date upfront for when it'll be returned. Secondly, you can sell the bond to other people as the IOU is valuable. How valuable depends on who has granted it.

If a government issues the bond, you know it's safe. If a bank issues a bond, it should be safe. If a company set up last week issues a bond, you may never see your money again. Would you accept an IOU from someone you didn't know? However, for a high rate of interest you might be willing to take that risk.

Bonds take a number of forms. The most common forms are:

Gilts

18–27   If the government issues a bond it's known as gilt-edged securities or 'gilts', because originally the security had a gilded (or gilt) edge. Gilts can be bought in two ways. Firstly, the Treasury issues gilts to raise money for the Government. Since 1993, this has been done by way of an auction, whereby potential investors bid for gilts. Secondly, gilts can be bought and sold on the London Stock Exchange. Investors simply instruct a broker to buy and sell at a particular price, and settlement happens the following day.

Corporate bonds

Also known as 'stocks', corporate bonds are fixed interest securities. They're similar to gilts, but issued by companies. As such, they're riskier than gilts and offer a higher interest rate, to attract buyers. Corporate bonds offered by blue chip company trading on the FTSE 100 should be safe and will offer a lower interest rate than a bond offered by a company formed last week.

18–28

Income Bonds offered by NS & I

Income Bonds, as their name suggests, provide a monthly income from the underlying capital. The minimum investment is £500 and the maximum is £1,000,000. The interest rate varies. Interest is paid monthly, without deduction of income tax, but is still taxable (and so must be declared to HMRC). Capital may be withdrawn without notice. Anyone over 16 can open an account and an investment can be made in trust for someone else.

18–29

Savings Certificates offered by NS & I

Savings Certificates either are fixed rate or index linked and provide a guaranteed return at the end of the term. They're issued for periods of three or five years. However, if they're cashed in before the end of the term, a penalty might be applied. The return is tax-free. There are no new Certificates currently on general sale, but existing Certificates can be renewed at maturity either for the same (or a different) term.

18–30

Children's Bonds offered by NS & I

These provide a tax-free return for children under 16 (even if the child becomes a taxpayer in the meantime). There is a guaranteed return for each period of five years, until a child reaches 21. The maximum investment is £3,000 per issue, per child (with a minimum investment of £25). Parents, legal guardians and grandparents can invest on behalf of a child. They can be cashed in early, with a penalty equivalent to 90 days' interest.

18–31

Premium Bonds offered by NS & I

Bonds can be bought in multiples of £100. They allow an investor to be entered into a draw, every month, to win up to £1,000,000. There are 1,500,000 prizes awarded every month, all of which are tax-free. Interest is not paid on these bonds, as such, and the initial investment can be withdrawn at any time. The maximum investment is currently £50,000.

18–32

INVESTMENTS: BUY SHARES

Ordinary shares

18–33   Companies, to raise money, issue ordinary shares. Shares carry with them ownership and a right to participate in any profits the company makes (usually by the company paying a dividend). Larger companies may choose to trade their shares on the stock market and become public companies. These companies are referred to as *quoted companies*, as opposed to companies that choose to trade their shares privately (*unquoted companies*). Unquoted shares cannot be bought and sold on the stock market, making them harder to sell (or less 'liquid') than quoted shares.

Larger firms with good track records often have little problem finding people to buy their shares. Companies like these are called "blue chip companies" and would include most of the large Plcs such as banks, industry leaders such as BT Plc, and major corporates such as Tesco Plc or Next Plc. Their shares are traded on the London Stock Exchange (we look at exchanges later in the chapter).

The London Stock Exchange is not the only place to buy and sell share. Shares can also be bought through the Alternative Investment Market (AIM). Companies on the AIM don't have to meet the same requirements as the London Stock Exchange. If London Stock Exchange is Ebay with strict rules about selling, then AIM is Gumtree, where anyone can post with fewer checks. Another advantage of AIM is that it costs less to use it. This means that smaller companies can raise money on AIM than the London Stock Exchange. Andrew is company secretary for an AIM listed plc. Although rules are less strict than the main market there are still many additional regulations that must be followed. If you have a client that is subject to London Stock Exchange rules then you should try and become familiar with the main rules so that your advice is tailored to cover the additional requirements that may apply. For example, depending on the transaction, your client may be bound by strict confidentiality rules and may expect their lawyers to use project names and information barriers to restrict access.

The performance of shares in the UK is measured using various indices like the FTSE 100. The FTSE 100 is an index of the leading 100 companies in the UK. As well as the FTSE 100, there is also the FTSE 250 and the FTSE all-share index. The FTSE 250 is an index of the 250 shares below the top 100 and the all-shares index is an index of the leading 850 companies in the UK.

Every country has its own indices for measuring the performance of its stock market. These include the NASDAQ and Dow Jones, in the USA, the Hang Seng in Hong Kong, the Nikkei in Japan, the DAX in Germany and the CAC in France.

There are two advantages to buying shares. Some shares are known for paying large dividends. Investors may choose these if they're looking to provide themselves with extra income. The second advantage of shares is the scope for the share to increase in value. As a company grows in reputation and stature, there should be an increase in the number of people wanting to buy shares, which then pushes up the market price. Another example of how demand can increase price.

As share prices change over time, based on the company's reputation and financial performance, most shares are considered to be a long-term investment.

Companies don't make money overnight. They grow gradually and it's rare for a company to suddenly make money. It takes time for sale and reputations to grow.

Preference shares

Other kinds of shares, such as preference shares, are appropriate for particular clients. Preference shares pay out a fixed rate of dividend, which is declared before any dividend to ordinary shareholders. There are several kinds of preference share. Some are cumulative, meaning that if a company doesn't have enough profit to pay a dividend in one year, it's rolled into the following year. Non-cumulative preference shares, however, often lose the dividend right altogether, if a company simply can't afford to pay. An investor must be wary about which kind of shares he or she is purchasing.   **18–34**

Ordinary shares offer potential for high growth and a big return, but you must always bear in mind that the opposite can be true. Dividends might not be paid for a long time and a company can fail completely. Individuals with limited capital (and those who can't afford to lose their initial investment) should not invest directly in the stock market. Preference shares are less of a gamble and the reward from them is usually less.

INVESTMENTS: BUY PROPERTY OR OTHER ASSETS

When you buy something (like a bag of crisps) you haven't lost your cash. You've just converted it to something else. You can convert it back, if someone will buy the bag of crisps from you. Instead of investing your cash by depositing it with a bank or building society, or buying a bond from the government, you could instead buy an asset in the hope that when you need cash in the future, you can sell the asset at a profit. Perhaps the most common asset is property. For example, you buy a house for £100,000 and, 10 years later when you want to move, you sell it for £150,000.   **18–35**

You can also invest in gold and other metals, oil and even in wine and whisky. The principle is the same; you're buying something in the hope that it'll be worth more when you sell it in the future.

Also, assets may give you an income. Think of a flat. If you buy a flat, you can rent it out to a tenant. You've not only gained an asset, which can increase in value, you've also gained a monthly rent. This type of asset is known as an income asset.

We look more closely at property when we discuss loans (and mortgages).

INVESTMENTS: INVEST IN A PRIVATE PENSION

There are two main types of private pension: defined benefit (also known as a final salary pension, for reasons which will become apparent) and defined contribution.   **18–36**

Defined benefit

18–37   A final salary pension is one that promises to pay out an income when you retire, based on how much you earn. For example, if you're paid £20,000 a year (as at your retirement date) your pension will pay £20,000 a year, until you die. This type of pension is the easiest to understand. Your employer automatically deducts part of your salary to pay your pension. When you retire, it then continues to pay you your final salary.

Defined contribution

18–38   Defined contribution schemes pay an accumulated sum when you retire, which you can use to secure a pension income (by buying a product called an annuity or by income drawdown). You can also take the lot as a lump sum, but may face a hefty tax bill. Your employer can arrange either type of pension (a workplace pension) or you can make arrangements directly with a provider. Your pension provider invests the money you put in. The value of your pension pot can go up or down, depending on how these investments perform.

Private pension—how much will you receive?

18–39   A final salary pension is easy to work out. When you retire, you're paid your final salary.[3] A defined contribution scheme is harder to work out. It's an investment, like any other, and what you get depends on how much you've paid in, how well your investments have performed, and how you choose to be paid. You can choose to be paid regular sums, a lump sum or even smaller sums. You usually get 25% of your pension pot tax-free.

Private pension—when can you receive payments?

18–40   The state pension starts when you're 63 or 65, depending if you're male or female. A private pension is not linked to the state pension age. Instead, you get paid based on your scheme's rules. This may allow you to be paid earlier (though rarely less than 55) or it may be linked to other conditions.

Private pension—what happens if my employer no longer exists when I need my pension?

18–41   Although your employer might run your pension scheme, your funds don't form any part of your employer's finances. Instead, funds are managed by a pension trust or pension provider, on behalf of the company.

---

[3] This is not strictly your final salary as shown on your last payslip. If it were, an unscrupulous employer could reduce your final wages. Instead, it's calculated using an average so that you receive a fair figure for your final salary.

Why would you use a pension instead of another investment?

A pension is a tax efficient way to invest for your retirement. A pension lets you take up to 25% of your investments out tax-free. This is a big saving, compared to direct investments.

18–42

We've looked at investments and what happens when you want to send money into the future. We turn to what happens when you want future you to send money back to you.

INTRODUCING LOANS

A loan is the opposite of an investment. Instead of sending your money from the present to the future, you're sending money from the future back to the present. Think about your student loans. These are based on the idea that once you graduate you will earn a salary that'll help you pay them off. Future Employed You is sending money back to Student You.

18–43

Loans take many different forms. In this section we look at two of the most common loans: personal loans and mortgages.

LOANS—PERSONAL LOANS

A personal loan from a bank, building society, company or individual usually consists of four things:

18–44

1.	the amount loaned (let's say £1,000);
2.	the interest rates (let's say it's 10%);
3.	when it needs to be repaid (let's say in 10 months' time); and
4.	how it is to be repaid (monthly at £110 per month).

A lender needs certain pieces of information. They may want to know Future You will have at least £110 per month, to pay off the loan. They may want evidence that you have a job, that your salary will cover the repayments and that you don't already have any other debts. Using this information, a lender can build up a picture of what future you will be like and—on that basis—they can decide to lend.

A personal loan is a risk for any lender. It's giving you money now, on the understanding that future you will pay it back. However, Future You could take ill, lose your job, you might stop paying or you could die. There are all sorts of things that could stop a lender from getting repaid. That's why personal loans tend to be for smaller amounts (perhaps £1,000 to £10,000) and the interest rates are higher.

If you need more money (for example to buy a house) you would apply for a mortgage. This is a form of personal loan. It has the same four elements (set out above). The main difference is that your bank will ask for a security over your property. If you can't pay back your loan, it can use that security to sell your property and recoup its money that way.

LOANS—MORTGAGE

18–45   For most of us, mortgages are necessary if you want to buy your own home. Homes are expensive, the average price in the UK is more than £200,000, and it would take years, if not decades, to save enough money to even buy a one bedroom flat. Without mortgages, we would not be able to afford to buy a home.

How do you arrange a mortgage?

18–46   A mortgage is just a type of loan. As with a personal loan, the lender (a bank or building society) will want to know that you can pay it back. They'll consider your borrowing capability and examine income, liabilities, employment and whether you have any money to pay a deposit or part of the price already. They also consider how much the home is worth as, ultimately, they could sell it to recoup their loan.

Traditionally, when working out how much you can pay, lenders applied income multiples when deciding how much to lend. This is a simple calculation. The lender asks how much you earn and then multiplies it by a set figure to let you know how much you can borrow. Before 2008, this could be as much as five times your salary, for one person applying for a mortgage; while, in the case of joint incomes, a lender might take the higher salary and apply the appropriate multiple and then add the lower salary. When lenders calculate income, they're looking at guaranteed income, such as your basic annual salary, while excluding things like bonuses, which could be discretionary. Proof of income is necessary; pay slips are usually required for at least three months. If you're self-employed (which you may be if a partner in a law firm), your accounts for the previous three years will be needed. As well as your income, the lender may also want to know how much you owe. The lender may ask for details of any credit cards, hire purchase agreements or overdrafts.

Your credit score is also relevant. In extreme cases a low credit score might prevent a mortgage lender even considering lending to you. Alternatively, a low score might mean that a lender applies a lower multiple.

However, these rules have changed and many lenders only use income multiples as an indicator now to show the maximum they'll lend. This is in light of new rules for mortgage lending that came into force as a result of the Mortgage Market Review, a comprehensive review following the property crash in 2008 which introduced new rules for mortgage lending on 26 April 2014. These rules impose an obligation on a lender to also conduct an 'affordability test' for every mortgage application.

Affordability assessment

18–47   A lender must verify your income and demonstrate that a mortgage is affordable. It does this by checking your income (such as your salary), your costs (such as credit cards), personal loans, hire purchase, but also other costs such as basic household expenditure (food, utilities, insurance, clothes and household goods). The lender is checking whether, after you spend your salary each month, you have enough money left to pay your mortgage.

Interest rate stress test

Along with checking your income and costs, the lender must also take into account the impact on mortgage payments of future interest rate increases (over a minimum of the following five years). You might be able to afford a mortgage today, but could you afford it if interest rates increase and your monthly payments increase? This test is to check that the mortgage remains affordable. **18–48**

How much will the lender lend?

While the maximum a lender will lend may still be linked to a multiple of your salary, there's also another important check that the lender will carry out. It wants to know that the property is worth more than what they're lending you to pay for it. This test is known as the loan to value (LTV) and is simple to calculate. A surveyor will value the property (let's say they value it £200,000) and the lender will compare that with the amount you have asked as a loan to give a percentage value. If you ask for £150,000 then the LTV would be 75%. If you ask for £100,000 the LTV would be 50%. Lenders always specify an upper LTV limit for each of their products, and its rare now for any lender to lend any more than 95%. This doesn't mean that they'll always lend this amount. That depends on a borrower's credit score, income and outgoings. **18–49**

The lower the LTV the more likely it is that you will receive a lower interest rate. LTV shows the lenders risk if property prices fell. If a lender has an LTV of 95% then if prices fell by more than 5% it wouldn't be able to recover all of its loan by selling the property. However, if a lender has a LTV of 50% then the price would need to fall by 50%, which is unlikely, before it was at risk of not being able to recover all of its loan by selling the property.

Repayment options

Various kinds of mortgages are available: **18–50**

Capital and interest repayment

A sum of money is borrowed for a fixed period. Let's say £200,000 again and you agree to pay it back over 25 years. Monthly repayments are scheduled to pay back the £200,000 plus interest. By the end of 25 years, if payments have been kept up to date, the mortgage is paid back in full. **18–51**

Interest only mortgage

With this kind of mortgage, the loan capital is not paid back until the end of a fixed period. If you borrow £200,000 then you would only pay the interest, and, at the end of 25 years, you would still need to pay £200,000 back. This means you need to take out some other form of investment to cover this final payment. An interest only mortgage is risky. You're assuming that you will be able to **18–52** invest money to pay the capital at the end of the term. If you don't have the money to pay the capital, the lender could sell the property and you could be left with nothing.

Flexible mortgage

18–53 This is a hybrid of the two kinds described above. Repayments can be larger than first contracted, so that a mortgage can be repaid more quickly. It may be possible to have "holidays" during which no repayments are made, and the term extended so that final repayment is deferred.

Interest rate options

18–54 The type of interest rate selected at the outset of a mortgage has a large effect on the subsequent repayments. The choice depends on your risk profile and whether you need certainty about how much the repayments will be, over the term of the loan. The most common are:

Tracker: As the interest rate of the Bank of England changes, so the interest rate of the loan changes (over the term). Trackers are available for different terms (most commonly two or five years). You can get term trackers (for the life of the loan). The rates for trackers tend to be lower than fixed rate deals. The danger is that interest rates rise quickly and that monthly repayments increase substantially.

Fixed rate: The rate of interest is fixed for a set period of time (typically one to five years). For that period, the borrower pays the same amount each month, regardless of what happens to the Bank of England rates. For some, this helps with budgeting. Once the fixed rate period is over, the rate reverts to the lender's variable rate. It's common for an agreement to stipulate that the borrower is tied into the variable rate for a fixed period too.

A potential problem is that interest rates might fall and the borrower is stuck paying much higher rates of interest.

Discount: Trackers aren't the only variable mortgage. Discount mortgages are linked to the lender's standard variable rate (SVR). The SVR can change even if there is no change in the Bank of England base rate. Discount mortgages are available over different terms (usually one to five years).

Offset: This is a more complicated mortgage. It links the borrower's savings to the mortgage debt. Interest on savings is offset against the loan, so the borrower pays less interest on the debt. There is the flexibility of keeping monthly payments constant (even when savings are rising) with the consequence that the mortgage is paid off more quickly and a substantial amount of interest saved.

In addition to the potential interest saving, there is also a tax benefit. Ordinarily, income tax is paid on interest earned on savings. With an offset mortgage, you don't earn interest so there is no income tax to pay. An offset can be particularly attractive for people in the higher or top rate tax brackets. The disadvantage with offset mortgages is that the rates tend to be higher.

CORPORATE FINANCE

So far we've just looked at individuals. We've asked how you can manage your money and, indirectly, demonstrated how you can help clients in similar situations. However, many of your clients will be companies, partnerships, public bodies and other corporate entities. We need to consider how those entities can raise money. **18–55**

Corporate investment

The principles are the same as per individuals. Just like an individual, a company needs to beat inflation by choosing the best investment options. This means it might also look at depositing cash in current and saving accounts. The options are, in general, no different to an individual (though some specific options may not be open to it, like premium bonds). **18–56**

Corporate loans

Most corporate bodies are financed by their owners or by loans from banks (or other institutions). **18–57**

Financed by owners

When a company is formed it issues shares. Every subscriber owns a share of the business. If a company issues 100 shares, equally, to two subscribers, each is a 50% owner. As a company grows, however, it may need cash. To leverage new investment, it might ask its original owners to purchase more shares, via a rights issue. A rights issue gives a company's owners the right to buy new shares, to the extent of their existing holding (to keep the relative percentages the same). **18–58**

For example, if our company wants to issue 1,000 shares, it must offer 500 shares to each of its two original owners. This maintains the balance; they each would have 550 shares (500 + original 50) of 1,100 shares (1,000 + original 100). If they decline to buy the new shares these can then be sold to others.

In practice, the Companies Acts 2006 gives directors the right to impose rules on how shares are allotted, so our simple scenario might end up being more complicated. For example, The Rangers Football Club Limited, has a prohibition on issuing new shares to anyone other than existing shareholders—even if they decline—without prior approval.

Can you see a potential problem with rights issues? There's no guarantee a company's owners will have the cash to increase their investment. Equally, they may not want new people owning shares. Imagine you're a shareholder in your family business; every share is owned by a family member. Even if you're penniless, do you really want to invite non-family members to effectively co-own your family business?

Further, if you're asked to invest, you may need to buy a certain percentage of shares to ensure that you have a say in what the company does. If you own the

259

company, then presumably you'll want to be able to decide what it does. That means you may need to own at least 25% of the shares (to have any real influence).

Financed by lenders

18–59 The alternative is that a company seeks a loan from a bank or third party (such as a private equity house). Once again, these can include loans for property, or loans direct to the company. As for individuals, a bank or other lender will attach conditions and almost certainly seek securities, for protection. This might be in the form of a personal guarantee from a director, a security over heritable property, a floating charge over moveable property and/or insurance.

INVESTMENT RISK

18–60 Some people are more adventurous in their investing, and other people prefer a more cautious approach. There's no right or wrong way—just the way that's right for you or your client. This balance between risk and reward is managed by investing across a range of investments and across a range of assets within those investments to build up a portfolio that will strike the right balance between risk and return to help you achieve your financial goals. Just as you wouldn't put all eggs in one basket, so you shouldn't put all your nest eggs into one investment.

For example, if you want to save money for your retirement you might invest in a pension which is low risk as it's backed by the UK Government. However, as it's low reward, you may also invest in some shares in new or risky companies which are higher risk but promise high rewards if the companies are successful. Finding the right balance is an essential part of your own personal investment and the advice you may give a client.

TAX

18–61 Two things are certain in life: death and taxes. While we can help little about the former, there are many highly paid accountants who will try and help you with the latter. Just ask singer Gary Barlow, comedian Jimmy Carr or Google. People and companies will try and do everything they can to reduce the tax they pay through lawful means (tax planning or tax avoidance) or unlawful means (tax evasion). As a lawyer, you'll find you'll be asked to advise clients who'll be following (or even want you to suggest) ways to help them reduce their tax. It should go without saying that you should never be involved in tax evasion, however, you may be asked to advise on tax planning. This could involve suggesting ways to invest money in a trust, to setting up companies or following certain courses of action which attract lower taxes than others. It's important that you know your way round the various taxes that can apply to you and your clients. This section will examine the main taxes and what they do.

A full discussion of tax is beyond the scope of this book and we always recommend that you either read the most recent textbook that you can or, better yet, read the law and guidance set out on the HMRC (for England & Wales) and Revenue Scotland (for LBTT and income tax in Scotland) websites before you advise anyone on tax. Tax laws and guidance change frequently, and you should make sure you're always up to date. As Gary Barlow, Jimmy Carr and Google have found, the taxman may come back for more money (or worse) if he doesn't think he's been paid correctly.

Direct tax

Direct taxes are directly paid to the government by the taxpayer. It's a tax applied on individuals and organisations directly by the government. The most common direct taxes are:

18–62

Income tax

As an individual, you're responsible for paying taxes on any income that you earn in each tax year (from 6 April to the 5 April the following year). Income includes not just your salary and is calculated based on:

18–63

- how much of your taxable income is above their personal allowance (the amount you can earn as income before you're taxed); and
- how much of your taxable income falls within each tax band above your personal allowance.

The personal allowances and tax bands for 2018–2019 are:

	2018/19
Personal allowance	£0 – £11,850
Basic rate band	£11,851 – £46,350
Higher rate	£46,351 – £150,000
Additional rate	Over £150,000

The personal allowance and rates bands are the same across the UK. The rates paid, however, are set independently by the UK Government for England, Wales and Northern Ireland and the Scottish Government for Scotland.

In Scotland, the Scottish Rate of Income Tax (SRIT) is set at 10% for all bands. The Scottish Government can then vary the UK rate. Any change affects all bands equally, so a 10% rise in basic rate from the UK rate would also need a 10% rise in higher rate and 10% rise in additional rate. As you'll see from the table below, a 10% rise means Scottish tax payers pay the same as the rest of the UK. This is the rate for 2018/19.

UK rate for England, Wales and Northern Ireland	Income band	UK rate paid in Scotland	Scottish rate	Total rate for Scottish taxpayers
Basic rate 20%	£11,001–£43,000	10%	10%	20%
Higher rate 40%	£43,001–£150,000	30%	10%	40%
Additional rate 45%	Over £150,000	35%	10%	45%

However, if the SRIT was set at 9%, the income tax rates for Scottish taxpayers would be:

- basic rate—19%;
- higher rate—39%; and
- additional rate—44%.

Corporation tax

18–64   Corporation tax is like an income tax for companies. The UK Government taxes companies on the money they make, and this is calculated based on their worldwide profits (for UK companies) or for their trading profits in the UK (for non-UK companies). In simple terms, Google and Starbucks seem to pay little tax because they argue they only make a small profit in the UK and, instead, their profits are generated in other countries, such as Ireland.

The main rate of corporation tax is currently 19%. It will fall to 18% for the year beginning 1 April 2020.

National Insurance

18–65   NICs are payable by employees at rates of 12% on weekly income between £162 and £892 and 2% on income above this limit. Employers also pay NICs on employees' earnings above £155 per week (at 13.8%). This includes benefits in kind. Your NICs help pay for your state pensions as discussed above.

Capital gains tax (CGT)

18–66   A capital gains tax (CGT) is a type of tax on capital gains incurred by individuals and companies. Capital gains are the profits that you make when you sell a capital asset for a price that is higher than the purchase price. For example, if you buy a flat as an investment for £100,000 and you sell it for £200,000 you have made a profit of £100,000. That profit would be subject to CGT.

CGT is charged at two rates. Those who pay basic rate income tax pay CGT at *18%*, but higher rate taxpayers are charged CGT at *28%*. Lower rates (and reliefs) are available to support entrepreneurial and business activity.

The annual exempt amount (currently £10,900) and the exemption for your main home (which is why we used the example of a second home above), ensures that most people don't, in fact, pay CGT.

Stamp taxes

Stamp taxes apply to transfers of property. There are four types: **18–67**

Stamp duty: this applies to shares and securities sold using a stock transfer form. It is charged at 0.5%.

Stamp Duty Reserve Tax (SDRT):   this applies to shares and securities sold electronically. It is charged at 0.5%.

Stamp Duty Land Tax (SDLT):   this is a tax on property sold or leased in England and Wales.

Land and Buildings Transaction Tax (LBTT):   this is a tax on property sold or leased in Scotland. While the rules are similar to SDLT in England and Wales, and may lead you to think they're connected, there are enough differences that you should not rely on any SDLT guidance when reviewing LBTT.

Other business taxes

There are local property taxes that are paid on non-residential properties. These   **18–68** are called Business Rates or Non-domestic Rates. These are set by the UK Government for England and Wales and the Scottish Government for Scotland. The rates are collected by local authorities, to pay for local services. The rate depends on the value of the property that is used for business purposes.

Indirect taxes

Someone other than the Government collects indirect taxes before it's passed on   **18–69** to the Government. The main indirect tax is VAT and we'll examine how it's collected below.

What is VAT?

Value Added Tax (VAT) applies in all countries in the EU. VAT is added to most   **18–70** goods or services sold by businesses as a 20% charge (subject to certain exception) on the price of goods or services sold by them.

How does VAT work?

18–71   VAT is collected on behalf of HMRC by companies. A company pays VAT to HMRC by calculating the amount of VAT charged to customers (its output VAT) minus any VAT it has paid on its own purchases (its input VAT). Every quarter, a company will pay HMRC the difference between its input VAT minus its output VAT. If it has paid more in input VAT on its own purchases than it received from selling goods or services to customers from output VAT, it can ask HMRC to reimburse it.

Does VAT apply to all goods and services?

18–72   Certain goods and services are exempt from VAT (i.e. there is no VAT on the supply, but also no refund of VAT incurred on the costs of supply), while others are charged at a reduced rate (5%). Uniquely, the UK also has a broad range of zero-rated supplies, including books, newspapers, magazines and children's clothes, which means VAT on the supply is 0%, but input tax may be reclaimed.

How does VAT affect businesses?

18–73   As a general rule it should not affect any business that sells goods or services. It can recover any VAT incurred in making these supplies. VAT only becomes an issue if it sells goods or services which are exempt as it can't then recover any VAT it was charged to make those goods or services.

WHO PROTECTS THE FINANCIAL SYSTEM?

Governments and regulators

18–74   If you carry £100 in your pocket, you always know where it is. You can keep it safe. However, as soon as you give that £100 to someone else, it might not be quite so secure. If you give it to the Government, there's nothing to stop it investing in an MP's duck house. If you give it to a bank, it could be spent on a chief executive's scallop kitchen. If you give it to a company, it might become part of the chairman's bonus. The next thing you know, the government changes, the banks collapse or the company is liquidated. Your money is gone. To build confidence in the financial system, the Government has created laws and appointed regulators to ensure the system works correctly. The most important regulators are the Financial Conduct Authority (FCA) and the Prudential Regulation Authority (PRA), discussed below.

Legal system

18–75   The UK is regarded as having a stable legal system in which rights are enforced, debts settled and contracts honoured. That makes the UK a good place to do business. Increasingly (particularly in relation to financial matters) there is a push for greater standardisation of law across various countries. This means that some principles (such anti-money laundering—as we saw in Ch.6 (how to open files) will be the same regardless of the country you're in. However, even with harmonisation there are some countries which are more stable, more reliable, and better to do business in than others.

Regulators

If you have laws and rules you need the means to enforce them. This means you need an effective court system and government bodies and independent regulators who will ensure any laws and rules are enforced.   **18–76**

The Financial Services Act 2012 came into force on 1 April 2013. The Act created a new regulatory system which:

- gave the Bank of England (through a new Financial Policy Committee) responsibility for oversight of the UK financial system as a whole—it has powers to monitor and respond to risks;
- set up a new regulator of safety and soundness in the financial services sector, the Prudential Regulation Authority (PRA), working under the Bank of England, to supervise all firms that manage significant risks as part of their business—banks and other deposit takers, insurance companies, and large investment banks; and
- established a new business regulator for financial services, the Financial Conduct Authority (FCA), that protects consumers and supervises all firms to ensure that business across financial services and markets is conducted fairly.

Together these regulators 'police' the financial markets.

Insurance

Every investment is a risk. Share prices may go down as well as up. If you buy a home, it could burn down before you pay off the mortgage that helped you buy it. Running a business also involves risk. Whether it's the risk of fire, the risk of damage to goods or the risk of natural disasters, all these incidents may have a financial impact on your business.   **18–77**

If you want to reduce the risk of your home or office burning down, you could install smoke alarms and sprinkler systems to reduce the damage caused by fire. However, you may also want to protect yourself against the financial impact of a fire—e.g. the cost of repairing or rebuilding. Most financial risks can be protected by insurance. Insurance is the transfer of risk from themselves and on to someone else. You cannot avoid all risks but you can protect yourself against them by transferring those risks to someone else. This transfer of risk is the principle behind insurance.

How does insurance work?

An insurer is someone who agrees to take on risks on behalf of a company or individual, in exchange for a fee. It does this by providing the business or   **18–78** individual concerned with an insurance contract, sometimes called a "policy". This policy covers a person or business for many of the costs they have to meet as a result of a risk occurring, and provides the policyholder with some security should the worst happen.

How is the insurer paid?

18–79   The insurer is paid an insurance premium. This is the sum of money paid by you in return for the insurer giving you a policy. The sum depends on how much the policy will pay out and how likely the insurer will need to pay out. The greater the likelihood of a pay out the more the premium will be.

Think about car insurance. It will replace your car if it's stolen. If you have a second hand Mini worth £1,000 then the cost of replacing it is small. If you have a Porsche worth £100,000 then the cost of replacing it is high. Because the Porsche is faster and more desirable, it's more likely to be stolen. So that increases the premium too. It's a riskier car to own. Every time you take out insurance the insurer calculates the risk of paying out. That's why it asks hundreds of questions when you apply. It's trying to work out how risky the policy is based on statistics.

Who are the main insurers?

18–80   There are three main types.

- Insurance companies—mostly owned by shareholders, but policyholders own 'mutual' insurance companies. In other words, when you take out a policy you're also becoming an owner in the business itself. 'Specialists' offer one type of business, (e.g. life insurance), while 'composites' offer a range of insurance products.
- Lloyd's of London—not an insurer itself, but an organisation providing a building (the Lloyd's building in London) and facilities for its underwriting members to do business.
- Reinsurers—for large risks, insurers may insure some of it, then seek cover for the remainder—called reinsurance—from other insurers.

What are the main types of personal insurance?

18–81   Insurance can cover anything. John Schnatter, founder of the pizza chain, Papa John's Pizza, has insured his hands for $15 million,[4] Sebastian Michaelis, a tea blender for Tetley, has insured his taste buds for £1 million,[5] while supermodel

---

[4] A. Victor, "Papa John's pizza founder has his hands insured for $15 MILLION . . . putting him in the same league as Heidi Klum's legs and Madonna's breasts' (8 July 2015), *Dailymail.co.uk*, *http://www.dailymail.co.uk/femail/food/article-3153322/Founder-Papa-John-s-pizza-hands-insured-staggering-10-MILLION.html* [Accessed 19 January 2019].

[5] L. Hyslop, "Tetley insures tea blender's taste buds for £1m' (26 November 2016), Telegraph.co.uk, *http://www.telegraph.co.uk/foodanddrink/foodanddrinknews/11252789/Tetley-insures-tea-blenders-tastebuds-for-1m.html* [Accessed 19 January 2019].

Heidi Klum has insured her legs for £1.2 million.[6] However, these are extremes. The most common types of insurance are:

Life insurance: Life insurance pays out if you die (or, for some policies, if you also suffer a terminal illness). This ensures that you can help partners or relatives if you were to die unexpectedly. For example, if you own a home with a partner, you may take out a life insurance policy so that you know that they'll have money to pay the mortgage if you die. The two basic types of life insurance are *traditional whole life* and *term life*. Simply explained, whole life is a policy you pay on until you die and term life is a policy for a set amount of time. Life insurance will increase in price as you get older or if you suffer from any illnesses or disabilities which could reduce your life expectancy.

Health insurance: Health insurance will pay to cover any medical treatments you require.

Home insurance/contents insurance/car insurance: These all cover things that you own: your house; your furniture, television, jewellery, laptops, bikes etc.; and your car.

Travel insurance: This will pay for health cover, cancellations and theft while you're abroad.

What are the main types of business insurance?

A business can insure against the decisions it makes, the products it produces, the advice it gives and the possibility that an employee or other person could sue them.   **18–82**

Key person insurance: Many businesses rely on one or more people to be successful. For many years former Apple chief executive Steve Jobs was the face of the company. He was seen as instrumental in creating the iPhone and iPad. When he died, Apple were seen to have lost a vital part of their success. Without Steve Jobs' vision, Apple's shares fell by 5%.[7] The company lost billions. To protect against this risk, many businesses will take out key person insurance to cover them against losing key people. In a small business, this is usually the owner, the founders or perhaps a key employee or two. These are the people who are crucial to a business—the ones whose absence would sink the company.

Directors' and officers' liability insurance: Directors' and officers' liability insurance—also known as D & O insurance—covers the cost of compensation claims made against a business's directors and key managers (officers) for alleged wrongful acts. Wrongful acts include: breach of trust; breach of duty;

[6] L. Milligan, "Heidi's Legs" (20 September 2011), *Vogue.co.uk, http://www.vogue.co.uk/news/2011/09/20/heidi-klum—legs-insured-not-worth-the-same-amount* [Accessed 19 January 2019].
[7] J. Kollewe, "Apple stock price falls on news of Steve Jobs's death" (6 October 2011), *TheGuardian.com, http://www.theguardian.com/technology/2011/oct/06/apple-stock-steve-jobs* [Accessed 19 January 2019].

neglect; error; misleading statements; and wrongful trading. If directors did not have insurance they might refuse to act as directors. The insurance helps protect them against the risk that someone may accuse them of a wrongful act by covering their legal costs to defend any claim and by paying for compensation if any claim is successful.

Employers liability: Employers' liability insurance covers the cost of compensating employees who are injured at or become ill through work.

Public liability: Public liability insurance covers the cost of claims made by members of the public for incidents that occur in connection with your business activities. Public liability insurance covers the cost of compensation for: personal injuries; loss of or damage to property; and death.

Product liability: Product liability insurance covers the cost of compensating anyone who is injured by a faulty product that your business designs, manufactures or supplies.

Professional indemnity: Professional indemnity insurance covers the cost of compensating clients for loss or damage resulting from negligent services or advice provided by a business or an individual.

How do you know insurance companies will pay out?

18–83   Insurance companies make money in two ways. Firstly, they pool all of the premiums paid by everyone taking out insurance policies. For example, if you take out travel insurance for £40 to go travelling this summer, the insurance company will add that £40 to everyone else who has also taken out travel insurance from them. If 100,000 people take out travel insurance, then the insurance company has £4 million. However, not everyone will make a claim under that policy. The insurance company is calculating that if 100,000 take out travel insurance for £4 million, only a few will actually raise a claim—and those few will be paid less than £4 million. The difference between the insurance premiums collected and the policies paid out is how the insurer makes money.

The second way the insurer makes money is by using the money it's collected to invest. As you know from earlier in the chapter, if you don't invest your money it'll start to lose value because of interest rates. Insurance companies will use part of the money it collects and it'll invest it to make more. This return is known as 'the float'.

Provided the insurer has calculated its risk correctly, it should always have more money than it pays out, as the pool (the total of money collected) should be greater than the potential claims (the total of money paid out), and the float (investment return) should ensure that the pool doesn't lose value over time.

THE FINANCIAL MARKETS

Before we end this chapter its worth spending some time reviewing how financial markets work. How do banks, building societies, pension or insurance companies make money? They don't just keep your money safe, they use that money to make more money on 'the market'. **18–84**

What is the market?

In general, the market refers to the financial markets. A cattle market sells cattle and livestock. A farmer's market sells meat and vegetables from local farmers. The market refers to a market that buys and sells financial products. The main markets are: **18–85**

The capital and money markets

This is where people buy and sell investments such as shares and bonds. The capital market deals with long term investments, including shares. The money markets deal with short term investments, typically bonds which have less than 12 months before they're paid back. If you've ever bought shares in a company you've participated in the capital and money markets. **18–86**

The foreign exchange market

This is where people buy and sell currency such as the dollar and the euro. When you change money before going on holiday you're participating in a money market, albeit on a much smaller scale. If you're travelling to Paris, you offer to buy euros at the rate of, for example, 75p for every euro. When you return, you offer to sell the euro back to the travel agent for £1. You're buying and selling currency—and, depending on the price, you can make a profit or a loss when the price changes. If, when you return, the travel agent will accept £1.10 then you will have made 10%. If, and more likely for a travel agent, they only offer to buy it back at 90p, you've lost an additional 10p. The secret of the money market is to buy currency that will increase in value so you can then sell it for a profit. **18–87**

The debt capital market

This is where people buy and sell debt. If a company owes money, then this debt can be sold by the person who is owed it. **18–88**

The commodities market

This is where people buy and sell assets, mainly raw material such as steel, minerals, gold and oil, and agricultural products such as a wheat, coffee and sugar. **18–89**

How do the markets work?

18–90   The markets operate through exchanges. Exchanges were originally physical places where buyers and sellers could meet to trade. The London Stock Exchange was founded in 1801 at Paternoster Square close to Saint Paul's Cathedral in London. Today there are more than a hundred exchanges throughout the world including the New York Stock Exchange and the NASDAQ stock exchange (both based in America, and the two largest exchanges in the world).

    Exchanges are more than physical locations. They set the rules that govern trading including centralising all information about trades so that no one receives information before anyone else. That way, everyone has the same opportunity to buy and sell on the exchange. Think of it like eBay. If you ask a question on eBay any answer will be published on eBay for all to read. An exchange ensures everyone can see all information at the same time.

How do you buy and sell on an exchange?

18–91   As part of controlling information, an exchange centralises the communication of bid and offer prices so that everyone can see who is selling and what they're selling. You can then respond by buying at one of the prices quoted or by replying with a different quote. Depending on the exchange, you can respond by voice, hand signal, a discreet electronic message, or computer-generated electronic commands. When a buyer and seller reach agreement, the price is then communicated throughout the market. The result is a level playing field that allows anyone to buy as low or sell as high as anyone else, as long as the trader follows exchange rules.

Do you need to be in the exchange to take part in trades?

18–92   No. Electronic trading has meant that many traditional trading floors are closing, and all communication takes place electronically. The London Stock Exchange is completely electronic.

What is "the City"?

18–93   The City refers to the City of London, an area of London which is also known as 'The Square Mile' because it is 1.12 square miles in area. The City of London is the traditional home to the UK's trading and financial services industries, including the London Stock Exchange. When people refer to 'the City' they're using it as shorthand to refer to the UK's main financial services industry.

What does "how will the City/the market react" mean?

18–94   Every day market traders try to interpret news and events to work out how to make money. When commentators refer to the reaction of the City or the market, they're principally looking at whether people are buying or selling. If more people buy, prices tend to increase, and this shows confidence. If more people sell, then this shows less confidence as people try and recover their money. A good example was when the then Chancellor, George Osborne, announced a 'sugar tax' as part of his budget statement in April 2016, the markets instantly reacted by selling shares in soft drink manufacturers such as AG Barr, the makers of Irn-Bru. Commentators would say the market reacted badly, because it started to sell as many shares as it could in companies affected by the sugar tax.

How does the market link to you and your clients?

Every time you or your clients invest money with a bank, building society, pension or insurance company, you give money for that bank, building society, pension or insurance company to invest in the market. In this way, the money in your pocket is directly linked to how the market performs. If the market does well, and you have invested in it, then you will do well too. If the market turns, as we saw in 2008 with the financial crash, then you will lose money too.   **18–95**

SUMMARY

Time travel is not real. However, financial advice is perhaps the closest you get to it, because you're trying to move money from the present to the future, and from a possible future to the present.   **18–96**

We cannot predict the future, so we need to protect our money. The government can do this by putting in place laws to protect individuals and companies. It can appoint regulators to oversee these laws, and it can enforce them so that no one ignores them. However, even with all these protections, you can still do more by, for example, taking out insurance. Together, you can move money to when it's needed and protect you and your clients from the financial impact of any wrong decisions. And, when you move money, you're giving it to companies either directly or indirectly to invest in the financial markets.

CHAPTER 19

How to read financial accounts

INTRODUCTION

You've been promoted to a senior associate and you're on track to become a   **19–1**
partner. You know that becoming a partner will make you financially responsible
for the firm so you want to know more about the firm's finances before you put
yourself forward. As your firm is a limited liability partnership (LLP) it has to
publish its account annually. You download last year's accounts from Companies
House. It contains a profit and loss statement, balance sheet and cash flow
statements, filled with numbers. Where do you start your review?

Every number tells a story. If you have £100 in your pocket today and £5 in   **19–2**
your pocket tomorrow, then you may ask what happened to £95? Did you spend
it? Did you lose it? Did someone steal it from you? Whatever happened, those
two numbers are the start of a series of questions that eventually tell you a story
about what happened to the £95.

In this chapter we look at how you turn numbers into information. This
requires you to understand the following points.

- Accounts have a set format. We look at two formats in this chapter (*profit and loss* and *balance sheet*) and one other format in the next chapter (*cash flow*). Between them, they tell you the main things you need to know.
- Accounts are based on certain *assumption*s. You need to know the assumptions before you examine the numbers.
- You need to know how to ask the right questions. These can take the form of calculations (also known as *ratios*). We examine how you use ratios later in this chapter.

You may ask why people keep accounts. There are four good reasons. The first
three are regulatory. You have to do it because others demand it. They are:

1. The SRA Accounts Rules 2018 compel you to keep accounts for your firm.
2. HMRC needs to see a partnership tax return each year (albeit your firm doesn't pay "partnership tax").
3. Companies House requires accounts to be lodged (if your firm is a limited company or an LLP).

The fourth reason is equally as important.

4.   Your accounting documents are an early warning system. Good quality accounts tell a story and they'll help you predict the future. They'll tell you if your firm is making money, they'll warn you if you're losing money. They can even point out where you can improve your business. You just need to know how to translate the numbers into the information you need.

We can't deny that understanding financial accounts will involve a calculator and some work on your part. Once cracked, you'll be able to run your firm confident in the knowledge that you know exactly what it's doing and whether or not it's making money

OUTCOME

19–3   In this chapter we'll review the basic assumptions that apply to accounting, we'll introduce you to profit and loss and balance sheets, and we'll look at how you can use ratios to ask questions of financial information. Accounting is a complex subject. For ease, and to help introduce the concepts used, we've taken a broad view on how the various accounts work to help show concepts in action. Just like law, there is a lot of detail in accounts once you start to dig into them more closely. This chapter and the next is intended to help you start that process.

ASSUMPTIONS

19–4   Imagine a house. What do you see? Does it have four walls and windows? Does it have a roof and a front door? Now imagine your parents' home. Do you see the same house? What about the Queen's home, Buckingham Palace, and the White House? Further afield, what about an Eskimo's igloo? Whilst these are completely different, they are all recognisably 'homes'.

Accounting is no different. Accounts may change, they may look different but, because they're based on common standards and assumptions, they're all recognisably the same. That's why, before we start looking at any numbers, we should start by looking at the assumptions that apply to accounts. These provide the conceptual framework of accounting. Just as you would expect a house to have a doorway, so you expect accounts to show certain things too. There are a number of assumptions. If followed, all accounts, no matter who prepares them, will be recognisably the same. The main assumptions are:

True and fair

19–5   'True and fair' is not defined in statute, but accountants take it to mean that your financial statements should be drafted in accordance both with Generally Accepted Accounting Principles (GAAP) and their professional judgment. They are a common set of accounting principles, standards and procedures that companies use to compile their financial statements. This means that accounts should be the same around the world provided they all follow GAAP. (Note that some companies elect to use IFRS (International Financial Reporting Standards), which serve much the same purpose.)

Materiality

How accurate do your firm's financial statements need to be before they give a 'true and fair' view? The materiality principle states that an accounting standard can be ignored if the impact of doing so has such a small impact on the financial statements that a reader of the financial statements would not be misled. A rough rule of thumb is that an amount less than 5% of the result before tax is considered unlikely to impact on an account's reliability.

19–6

Consistency

Your accounts should be consistent both internally and also with your accounts from previous years. You should only change an accounting principle or method if the new version in some way improves your reported financial results.

19–7

Prudence

Profits should not be recognised until your firm is confident that they will arise; losses, on the other hand, should be accounted for as soon as anticipated.

19–8

Matching

Your income and expenditure should be matched to the period to which they both relate.

19–9

Going concern

Your accounts should be drawn up on the basis that your firm will be trading for the foreseeable future.

19–10

KNOW THE TERMINOLOGY

Just as you have technical language that describes what you do, so accountants have certain phrases which they use to describe what they do. These include:

19–11

Fixed and current assets

A *fixed asset* is something acquired by your firm for long term use (generally considered to be more than 12 months from date of the accounts), with a view to earning profits. It includes things like computers, printers and furniture. In short, you are buying fixed assets to use, not to sell.

19–12

Your *current assets* are the opposite. They are items you plan to use or convert into cash in the short term (i.e within 12 months). Current assets include cash in your bank accounts and any fee (i.e. debts) that your clients owe your firm also are treated as current assets.

Fixed and current assets can also be divided further. They can be divided into *tangible* or *intangible* assets. Tangible assets are obvious; you can touch them. Intangibles are items you can't touch, and include things like your firm's intellectual property.

Liabilities

19–13   Liabilities are sums of money that your firm owes to others; they either are short-term (current) liabilities or long-term (non-current) liabilities. They include *accruals*. Accruals are liabilities that exist, but for which no invoice has been receive. For example, you use electricity in the final month of a trading period, but don't receive your bill till the following month. The amount used but not billed is classed as an accrual. It is a liability that you expect to pay, even though you don't have official confirmation of it yet.

Many clients will treat court actions as accruals. They know they might have to pay compensation or a disputed debt if they lose a court action, but until they lose that action, no compensation or debt is due. The client may have an accrual in its accounts to show the potential liability.

Values

19–14   The values of your firm's assets and liabilities are obtained from its records. The basis on which your assets are valued is usually 'at cost' (i.e. the amount your firm paid for them), with depreciation ("wear and tear") over their estimated useful life factored in. For example, you might 100 computers at £50,000. However, as you use them, they lose value. You would value these at cost (£50,000) less a depreciation of £200 per year per computer. After 12 months, your computers are worth £30,000 (£50,000 minus £20,000 in depreciation).

What is capital?

19–15   Your firm's capital is the residual claim on the business by its partners. When solicitors start a firm, the capital they introduce is the total value that they've committed to the business. For example, if you start a firm with ten partners and each invests £100,000 then the total capital will be £1m and each partner's capital will be £100,000.

It's important that any contribution is quantified in monetary terms, to establish his or her true capital input. If a partner removes an asset for private use (e.g. a computer), or withdraws cash, then their capital is reduced by the relevant amount.

As you firm makes a net profit, this has the effect of increasing your firm's overall capital, while a loss will reduce that capital.

Double-entry bookkeeping

You don't need to worry too much about this. However, this is the system that **19–16** underpins the creation of your final set of profit and loss accounts. Basically, an account is created for each item (or group of items) of assets, liabilities, capital, income and expenditure that you have. Each account records changes (whether an increase or decrease) in the monetary value of each item concerned. An increase in one account will be matched with a decrease in another, hence the name 'double entry' book keeping.

Trial balance

A trial balance allows you to check the accuracy of your individual accounting **19–17** records. Once a month each account is balanced-off—checked against each other to make sure they are accurate—and then the full trial balance is created. It's a summary of all of your balances.

PROFIT AND LOSS ACCOUNT

Your firm needs to have access to its most recent set of annual accounts, **19–18** comprising a:

1.   profit and loss account (P & L account); and
2.   balance sheet.

Your P & L account tells you whether your firm is profitable. It's a summary of income and expenditure, over a financial period (usually a year). Income is accounted for only if earned (irrespective of whether it has been received) and so is expenditure. In other words, if you render an invoice and it's not been paid, you still need to add it to your income for the period.

This is an important distinction and can be summed up as *profit doesn't equal cash*. Cash flow (which we examine in the next chapter) is the lifeblood of any business. A business can survive for a period of time without profit but it can't survive without cash. Like it or not, cash is how a business keeps afloat. If you don't have enough cash on hand, you can't pay your suppliers, your employees, or the bank. Without cash, you'll go out of business.

Profits are different. You may have acted for lots of clients and have a heap of invoices to show for it, but you can't spend those invoices. Paying staff and suppliers requires cash. Those invoices are profit, but they're not cash.

Figure 1 will give you an example of a P & L account for a fictional law firm Sim & Todd.

	2017 £		2018 £		2019 £	
Income						
Fees Rendered	1,500,000		1,350,000		1,250,000	
Commission	125,000		95,000		68,000	
Bank Interest	8,125		7,225		6,950	
Add: Increase in WIP	100,000					
Less: Decrease in WIP			-20,000		40,000	
		1,733,125		**1,432,225**		**1,364,950**
Less: Expenses						
Wages and salaries	725,000		805,000		875,000	
Office rent and rates	66,000		78,000		78,000	
Heating and lighting	35,250		38,925		41,135	
Telephone	9,995		11,995		12,495	
Post and stationery	20,475		18,775		16,985	
Insurance	5,205		8,875		11,750	
Professional subscriptions	3,750		4,425		4,995	
Travelling expenses	11,200		15,475		19,960	
Bank charges	22,195		24,295		25,295	
Motor car running costs	22,450		25,650		28,230	
Bad debts w/o	35,000		48,000		56,000	
Equipment repairs	1,500		1,750		1,680	
General expenses	4,800		3,760		5,245	
Depreciation charges:						
Motor car	2,500		1,875		1,406	
PCs	2,000		1,500			
Less: Sundry Expenses						
Loss on sale of PCs					2,500	
	967,320	-967,320	1,088,300	-1,088,300	1,180,676	-1,180,676
		765,805		**343,925**		**184,274**

Figure 1: Sim & Todd LLP—Summary Profit and Loss Accounts for the Periods from 2017 to 2019

Geography

You're probably wondering what all the numbers mean. Along the top (the horizontal, or left to right) you have a time line. Our time line runs from 2017 until 2019. This is a technique used by lots of accountants to let readers see patterns really easily. You can spot incoming going down, or expenses going up, easily, if the numbers are side by side.

    On the left hand side (the vertical, up and down) you have a:

- list of all your income (your money coming in);
- list of all your expenses (your money going out); and
- total (income minus all expenses).

Your income figure includes everything you've earned, including fees, commission and bank interest. It also includes any increase or decrease in work in progress (and we look at that a little later).

    The expenses column lists all your outgoings, like wages, heating and lighting, telephone and postage etc. It also includes an allowance for bad debts, depreciation and any gain or loss on the disposal of an asset (keep reading to find out what we mean by this).

ACCOUNTING ADJUSTMENTS

So far it's been just a case of simple arithmetic i.e. deducting the sub-total of your expenses from the sub-total of your income. However, you can't leave it there. There are five accounting adjustments you need to be aware of:

1. depreciation;
2. the disposal of assets (leading to a gain or loss being incurred);
3. bad debts;
4. accrued and pre-paid expenses; and
5. work in progress.

Depreciation

Depreciation is the measure of the wearing out, consumption or other loss of value of your fixed assets, whether arising from their use, the passing of time or good old obsolescence. It's worked out using either the straight line or reducing balance method.

19–19

19–20

19–21

Straight-line method

Formula:

19–22

> Original cost of asset—[residual value/useful life]

Worked example

19–23 A car costs £12,000 and has an estimated residual value of £2,000. Its useful life is four years. The workings are:

> (£12,000 – £2,000) ÷ 4 = £2,500

The annual depreciation charge (from years one to four), therefore, is £2,500.

Reducing balance method

19–24 The more commonly used method is called "reducing balance". This assumes that the cost of owning an asset is actually loaded towards the earlier years of its life. This leads to a higher depreciation charge in the early years, with a lower charge in the later years. The formula is:

> Carrying value of asset × percentage (%) charge

Worked example

19–25 A car costs £10,000 and the firm decides it should be written down at 25% per year (using reducing balance):

> Year 1 £10,000 × 25% = £2,500
> Year 2 £7,500 × 25% = £1,875
> Year 3 £5,625 × 25% = £1,406
> Year 4 £4,219 × 25% = £1,055

See Figure 2.

Income	2017 £	2017 £	2018 £	2018 £	2019 £	2019 £
Fees Rendered	1,500,000		1,350,000		1,250,000	
Commission	125,000		95,000		68,000	
Bank Interest	8,125		7,225		6,950	
Add: Increase in WIP	100,000					
Less: Decrease in WIP			-20,000		40,000	
		1,733,125		1,432,225		1,364,950
Less: Expenses						
Wages and salaries	725,000		805,000		875,000	
Office rent and rates	66,000		78,000		78,000	
Heating and lighting	35,250		38,925		41,135	
Telephone	9,995		11,995		12,495	
Post and stationery	20,475		18,775		16,985	
Insurance	5,205		8,875		11,750	
Professional subscriptions	3,750		4,425		4,995	
Travelling expenses	11,200		15,475		19,960	
Bank charges	22,195		24,295		25,295	
Motor car running costs	22,450		25,650		28,230	
Bad debts w/o	35,000		48,000		56,000	
Equipment repairs	1,500		1,750		1,680	
General expenses	4,800		3,760		5,245	
Depreciation charges:						
Motor car	2,500		1,875		1,406	
PCs	2,000		1,500			
	967,320	-967,320	1,088,300	-1,088,300	1,180,676	-1,180,676
Less: Sundry Expenses						
Loss on sale of PCs					2,500	
		765,805		343,925		184,274

Figure 2: Sim & Todd LLP—Summary Profit and Loss Accounts for the Periods from 2017 to 2019

Disposal

19–26 When one of your firm's assets is sold, the accuracy of its depreciation charge can be assessed. If the charge that has been applied over the years matches the disposal proceeds, no further action is required. However, if the two figures don't match then some further work needs to be done. Either you've not depreciated the asset enough, or you've claimed back too much. The formula is:

> A gain on disposal is shown as income in the P & L
>
> A loss on disposal is shown as an expense in the P & L

Worked example

19–27 Four computers cost £8,000. They are sold at the end of year three for £5,000. Accumulated depreciation is £3,500. The workings can be shown as follows:

> Total proceeds = £5,000 + £3,500 = £8,500
>
> Cost = £8,000
>
> Gain = £500
>
> This is shown as *income* in the P & L account

Let's say your computers sold at the end of year three made £2,000, but the accumulated depreciation is still £3,500. The workings are now as follows:

> Total proceeds = £2,000 + £3,500 = £5,500
>
> Cost = £8,000
>
> Loss = £2,500
>
> This is shown as an *expense* in the P & L account

Factoring in disposals, the P & L account now looks as in Figure 3

Bad debts

19–28 This one's easy. If it becomes apparent that one of your clients simply isn't going to pay his or her invoice(s) and all reasonable steps have been taken to recover the outstanding amounts, the fee can be written off as a bad debt and then charged as an expense to your P & L account. The P & L account shows it as in Figure 4.

	2017		2018		2019	
Income	£	£	£	£	£	£
Fees Rendered		1,500,000		1,350,000		1,250,000
Commission		125,000		95,000		68,000
Bank Interest		8,125		7,225		6,950
Add: Increase in WIP		100,000				40,000
Less: Decrease in WIP				-20,000		
		1,733,125		**1,432,225**		**1,364,950**
Less: Expenses						
Wages and salaries	725,000		805,000		875,000	
Office rent and rates	66,000		78,000		78,000	
Heating and lighting	35,250		38,925		41,135	
Telephone	9,995		11,995		12,495	
Post and stationery	20,475		18,775		16,985	
Insurance	5,205		8,875		11,750	
Professional subscriptions	3,750		4,425		4,995	
Travelling expenses	11,200		15,475		19,960	
Bank charges	22,195		24,295		25,295	
Motor car running costs	22,450		25,650		28,230	
Bad debts w/o	35,000		48,000		56,000	
Equipment repairs	1,500		1,750		1,680	
General expenses	4,800		3,760		5,245	
Depreciation charges:						
Motor car	2,500		1,875		1,406	
PCs	2,000		1,500			
Less: Sundry Expenses						
Loss on sale of PCs					2,500	
	967,320	-967,320	1,088,300	-1,088,300	1,180,676	-1,180,676
		765,805		**343,925**		**184,274**

Figure 3: Sim & Todd LLP—Summary Profit and Loss Accounts for the Periods from 2017 to 2019

283

Income	2017 £	2018 £	2019 £
Fees Rendered	1,500,000	1,350,000	1,250,000
Commission	125,000	95,000	68,000
Bank Interest	8,125	7,225	6,950
Add: Increase in WIP	100,000		40,000
Less: Decrease in WIP		-20,000	
	1,733,125	**1,432,225**	**1,364,950**
Less: Expenses			
Wages and salaries	725,000	805,000	875,000
Office rent and rates	66,000	78,000	78,000
Heating and lighting	35,250	38,925	41,135
Telephone	9,995	11,995	12,495
Post and stationery	20,475	18,775	16,985
Insurance	5,205	8,875	11,750
Professional subscriptions	3,750	4,425	4,995
Travelling expenses	11,200	15,475	19,960
Bank charges	22,195	24,295	25,295
Motor car running costs	22,450	25,650	28,230
Bad debts w/o	35,000	48,000	56,000
Equipment repairs	1,500	1,750	1,680
General expenses	4,800	3,760	5,245
Depreciation charges:			
Motor car	2,500	1,875	1,406
PCs	2,000	1,500	
Less: Sundry Expenses			
Loss on sale of PCs			2,500
	967,320	1,088,300	1,180,676
	-967,320	-1,088,300	-1,180,676
	765,805	**343,925**	**184,274**

Figure 4: Sim & Todd LLP—Summary Profit and Loss Accounts for the Periods from 2017 to 2019

284

Pre-paid expenses

Clearly some expenses are going to be pre-paid. For example, it may be that your rent is paid quarterly, in advance. Let's say your rent for the period from 6 April to 5 May is paid in the March, then that payment shouldn't be included in your P & L account to 6 April. **19–29**

Even though the money is paid in March, it relates to the *following* tax year and—to apply the principle of matching—it has to be applied to that year. If not, it would increase your rent figure artificially and the effect of that would be to reduce your profit figure (and decrease your tax liability) for the previous financial year.

Accrued expenses

Accrued expenses are the opposite. An accrued expense is an amount relating to something in a financial period that remains *unpaid* at the end of that period. **19–30**

Let's say your telephone bill for the period from 6 March to 5 April is paid in the May, then that payment *should* be included in your P & L account to 5 April. Even though the money is paid in May, it relates to the *previous* tax year and—to apply the principle of matching—it has to be applied to that year. If not, it would decrease your telephone figure artificially and the effect of that would be to increase your profit figure (and increase your tax liability) for the previous financial year. Both are shown on your balance sheet (and more on balance sheets, later).

Work in progress (WIP)

WIP is the value of the work you carry out prior to a fee invoice being raised. Complex transactions can run for weeks, months or even years, with ever increasing WIP. Until you can convert this to cash (by rendering an invoice) it is your firm that has to bear the cost of the WIP (including the overheads referable to it). For the purposes of P & L accounts, where your firm has previously included a figure for WIP, then any increase experienced over a financial period is added to the fees section, with any reduction being deducted. **19–31**

Recording WIP within the P & L account looks like in Figure 5.

BALANCE SHEET

What is a balance sheet?

Your balance sheet shows you exactly what things of value a company controls (it's *assets*) and who owns those assets: is it someone else (*liabilities*) or does it belong to the business owners or partners (*owner's equity*)? Essentially, it summarises what your firm owns and what it owes. **19–32**

	2017		2018		2019	
Income	£	£	£	£	£	£
Fees Rendered	1,500,000		1,350,000		1,250,000	
Commission	125,000		95,000		68,000	
Bank Interest	8,125		7,225		6,950	
Add: Increase in WIP		100,000				40,000
Less: Decrease in WIP				-20,000		
		1,733,125		1,432,225		1,364,950
Less: Expenses						
Wages and salaries	725,000		805,000		875,000	
Office rent and rates	66,000		78,000		78,000	
Heating and lighting	35,250		38,925		41,135	
Telephone	9,995		11,995		12,495	
Post and stationery	20,475		18,775		16,985	
Insurance	5,205		8,875		11,750	
Professional subscriptions	3,750		4,425		4,995	
Travelling expenses	11,200		15,475		19,960	
Bank charges	22,195		24,295		25,295	
Motor car running costs	22,450		25,650		28,230	
Bad debts w/o	35,000		48,000		56,000	
Equipment repairs	1,500		1,750		1,680	
General expenses	4,800		3,760		5,245	
Depreciation charges:						
Motor car	2,500		1,875		1,406	
PCs	2,000		1,500			
Less: Sundry Expenses						
Loss on sale of PCs					2,500	
	967,320	-967,320	1,088,300	-1,088,300	1,180,676	-1,180,676
		765,805		343,925		184,274

Figure 5: Sim & Todd LLP—Summary Profit and Loss Accounts for the Periods from 2017 to 2019

Why is the balance sheet called a balance sheet?

The balance sheet is so named because the two sides of the balance sheet *always*   **19–33**
add up to the same amount. The balance sheet is separated with assets on one side
and liabilities and owner's capital on the other.

At first, this rule can be really confusing. But think of it this way. All the assets
owned by your firm fall into one of two categories: either a creditor owns them
(you had to take a loan to get them) or your firm owns them (your firm (i.e. the
partners) paid for them in full). That's pretty much all the rule says.

How does a balance sheet differ from a P & L account?

A balance sheet shows the financial position of your firm at a given date, for   **19–34**
example, 1 January 2019. This date could be monthly, quarterly and/or the end of
an accounting period such as the final day the tax year (5 April each year) or the
final day of your firm's financial year (Pinsent Masons and CMS both use 30
April as the final day of their financial year).

Think of a balance sheet as a snapshot, a frozen moment in time. It tells you
everything the firm owns and who owns it, but only for that specific moment.
This is different from a P & L account, which shows your financial position over
a set period of time (usually a year).

What does the balance sheet show?

A balance sheet explains, in relatively simple terms, what form all your assets,   **19–35**
liabilities and owner's equity take.

That means you can regularly check, for example on a monthly basis, four
crucial numbers:

1. how much cash you have in the bank;
2. the value of your WIP;
3. the value of all outstanding fees, and
4. how much your firm owes to other people.

What is an asset?

An asset is anything a business owns that has monetary value. These are divided   **19–36**
on a balance sheet into current assets and fixed assets.

A current asset is anything that can be easily converted into cash within one
calendar year. This includes cash, money held in current accounts, WIP (which
can be fee'd to clients) and invoices issued (albeit but not yet paid).

Fixed assets include land, buildings such as an office, any machinery or
equipment (such as IT systems or photocopiers), and vehicles that are used in
connection with the business.

What is a liability?

19–37   Liabilities are also divided into current and long-term liabilities. They include everything the firm owes, including, critically, the money originally invested to start the business.

For companies this may take the form of shares; for partnerships it could take the form of money invested by each of the partners (the owners' equity or, more commonly, *partners' capital* in law firm accounts).

Current liabilities include all bills that have not been paid and which are due to be paid within one calendar year. They also include any loan payments from a bank, for example, that are due to be paid back within a calendar year.

Long term liabilities are any debts or obligations owed by the business that are due more than one year out from the current date. For example, your firm may have paid off five years of a 20-year mortgage, of which the remaining 15 years, not counting the current year (which would be shown as a current liability), would be shown on the balance sheet as a long-term liability.

What is a balance sheet used for?

19–38   In simple terms, a balance sheet shows you how much money you have and how that's made up: cash, bank accounts, outstanding debts etc. You want to have as much money in the bank as possible (as we'll see in the next chapter on cash flow) and you want to collect outstanding fees as quickly as possible.

Additionally, you need to keep control of any money you owe so that you're always in a position to pay debts as they become due. If you know you have a large payment to make to the bank this year then you'll want to ensure you have as much cash as possible to pay it (or you've made alternative arrangements, such as another loan, in sufficient time to pay the debt).

Does the balance sheet have any other uses?

19–39   Yes. Along with helping you manage your cash and debts it also shows how your business is financed. The liabilities figure shows how much your partners have invested in the business (this is shown as partners' capital), how much (if any) your firm has borrowed from a bank (bank borrowing) and how much money is being reinvested each year from the profits your firm is making (retained profit).

What the balance sheet tells you is how your firm has approached its finance by how it has drawn from all three sources. It's important to get this mix right. If partners' capital is too high, there may be a problem with paying out to a retiring partner. If retained profits are too high, partners may have a problem financing their tax payments (as tax is paid on retained profits regardless of whether it is paid out to partners) and if bank borrowing is too high then interest payments are likely to be high too, and your firm will be required to make regular payments to the bank.

There is no right or wrong mix. It really depends on each firm, the work it does and how its partners approach the business. A cash rich business may be happy to pay regular high interest payments because it knows it will have the cash to pay it. A cash poor business may need to rely more on its partners who will cover costs while knowing they'll be paid back later.

Example of balance sheet

See Figure 6 for an example balance sheet.   **19–40**

Sim & Todd LLP
Balance Sheet - 05.04.19

Fixed Assets	(£)	(£)
Land and Buildings	200,000.00	
Motor Vehicles	30,000.00	
Computers	10,000.00	
Furniture	50,000.00	
Total Fixed Assets		290,000.00
Current assets		
Bank Account - Current	50,000.00	
Prepayments	2,500.00	
Debtors	80,000.00	
Total Current Assets		132,500.00
Less Current Liabilities		
Accounts Payable	120,000.00	
Loan	20,000.00	
Accruals	8,000.00	
Total Current Liabilities		148,000.00
Net Assets		**274,500.00**
Capital and Reserves		
Drawings	200,000.00	
Profit and loss account	74,500.00	
Total Equity		**274,500.00**

Figure 6: Sim & Todd LLP— Balance Sheet—05.04.19

A warning about P & L account and balance sheets

Though useful, there are disadvantages in relying solely on the P & L account and   **19–41**
balance sheets.

- They are historic documents reflecting the position of the firm 'as was';
- They are not forward looking (or predictive);
- They do not yield certain additional information that a modern firm needs.

MANAGEMENT ACCOUNTING

19–42   Earlier we said that accounts also give you some really useful management information, and it's to that we now turn our attention.

Fees

19–43   Your P & L account doesn't show you whether the fees you have rendered in the current year compare favourably (or not) with results from previous years. This can be resolved by taking the simple step of making a comparison with your previous figures.

Management accounting also enables more detailed information to be obtained, including:

1.   fees generated by each partner/fee earner;
2.   fees generated by each category of work that your firm undertakes; and
3.   fees generated by each department (or branch) of your firm.

Time

19–44   Another useful piece of information to have is your cost of time. Put simply, your firm's profit equates to its gross (total) fees less its total costs. It's possible to break the costs of time down for particular fee earners and/or types of work etc. By using this analysis your firm's management can work out the true cost of a particular piece of work, or a type of work.

To calculate the hourly cost of a fee earner, take the total cost of running the business and divide this by that fee earner's chargeable hours for the period.

Costs include staffing (salary, National Insurance contributions, pensions etc.) and property costs (rent, lighting, heating) etc. The resulting hourly cost rate varies from firm to firm and depends on a number of factors, including your firm's size and location etc. It also varies across different grades of fee earners; senior partners tend to have the highest hourly cost rate, whilst trainees usually have the lowest.

Here's the rub: if the rates you charge clients equal your firm's cost rates then, assuming all your fee earners meet their chargeable hour targets, the costs of running your firm will be recovered. Conversely, if targets are not met then your firm will operate at a loss—until either it makes money again or, worst case, it collapses.

What we've just talked about only gets you into the position of breaking even. But that's not good enough if you want to make money. We want profit (and to turn that profit into cash, as we explain in the next chapter).

For your firm to be profitable, the fees paid by your clients have to exceed the total costs of running the business. Working out your cost of time requires an appropriate time recording system to be in place. In smaller firms you might simply make a handwritten note on a file. In larger firms, however, usually sophisticated computer based systems are used (see Ch.11 (How to record time)).

The information from any time recording system helps a firm highlight areas of fee-earner inefficiency and also helps create accurate and reliable data on which to base your client fees.

WIP

The higher the level of WIP your firm carries, the greater the business risk should a client subsequently default. Your firm, therefore, should draft its terms of business to enable interim (e.g. monthly) fees. And, each fee earner should have his or her WIP reviewed on a regular (preferably weekly) basis (see Ch.12 (how to manage your time).

19–45

Control of expenses

Good control of your expenses is essential. It's good practice to collate expense analysis reports showing details of the different expenses your firm has incurred. Again, this can be tabulated with comparative data from previous years, to illustrate any trends in costs.

19–46

Client debtors

Clients defaulting on payments require a firm hand. Sadly, this is quite common and, if uncontrolled, impacts adversely on your firm. An analysis can be made of your debtor figures in the balance sheet, at the end of any financial year, to see if it's reasonable relative to your total fees rendered. Again, a comparison can be made with previous years to see if you're getting better (or worse) at controlling client default rates.

19–47

The aim is to minimise your debtor levels. If the situation is under constant review, cash flow is better protected and the risk of bad debts accumulating is reduced. A debtors aging schedule can be prepared, showing the length of time your clients' debts have remained unpaid, with reference to the fee earner/partner responsible.

Client outlays

The same guidance applies, here, as per WIP. Your firm should avoid accumulating a large balance of otherwise recoverable outlays. Outlays should be monitored and recovered regularly. Why subsidise your clients?

19–48

TREND ANALYSIS

Trend analysis is where your results from several periods are converted to a common statistical base, compared in terms of the changes that have occurred in each item from the current to the earliest year (the so-called 'base year'), and then expressed as a percentage.

19–49

Percentage changes show, at a glance, the levels of change in a really digestible way. The formula—which can be applied to anything, including fees, commission, expenses etc.—is:

$$[(\text{This year} - \text{Last year}) \div (\text{Last year})] \times (100 \div 1)$$

Ratios

19–50   Ratios are useful for summarising large amounts of financial information, particularly the results of different accounting periods. They emphasise changes that have occurred between financial periods. Trends become readily apparent, weaknesses can be identified easily and, in turn, appropriate future plans can be made. Ratios reduce the large number of accounting figures that can be produced into small sets of readily understood and meaningful indicators for financial planning. Let's look at the key ratios you need to be aware of. We'll use the numbers from our example P & L account.

Ratio one: Return on Capital Employed (ROCE)

19–51   This measures the return earned by the providers of long-term finance to a firm (i.e. your firm's partners). The formula is calculated by dividing your firm's net operating profit by its employed capital. Let's have a shot using Sim & Todd's 2019 figures. Let's assume Sim & Todd's total employed capital (i.e. all of its assets less all of its liabilities) stands at £80,000. The workings are:

$$\text{ROCE} = (\text{net operating profit} \div \text{capital employed})$$
$$\text{ROCE} = (£184,274 \div £80,000)$$
$$\text{ROCE} = 2.3{:}1$$

In other words, for every pound of Sim & Todd's capital, £2.30 is returned. When interpreting the results, the higher the ratio the better (2:1 is better than 1.5:1, and 4:1 is twice as good as 2:1).

Ratio two: Net Profit Percentage (NPP) (or profit margin)

19–52   This looks at net profit earned per £1 of fee (and other) income (i.e. your profit margin). Note that you can use an after-tax profit figure, if you wish. This is one of the best measures of your overall financial performance. Let's again use Sim & Todd's 2019 figures to illustrate it.

$$NPP = (\text{net profit/net sales}) \times 100$$
$$NPP = (£184,274 \div £1,364,950) \times 100$$
$$NPP = 13.5\%$$

Whether or not 13.5% is healthy, must be measured against industry averages.

Ratio three: Average Fees Per Partner (AFPP)

This simple ratio is worked out by dividing the total fees rendered by the number of partners. How is Sim & Todd LLP doing?

19–53

$$AFPP = (\text{total fees/partners})$$
$$AFPP = (£1,250,000 \div 2)$$
$$AFPP = £625,000$$

Ratio four: Average Fees Per Fee Earner (AFPF) (including partners)

This simple ratio is worked out by dividing the fees rendered figure by the number of fee earners. Sim & Todd clearly have staff; they spend £875,000 on wages after all! Let's assume (to keep it simple) that they have two salaried partners, three associates, four senior solicitors, five newly qualified solicitors (NQs) and four trainees (with the rest of the wages being spent on admin staff). Here's how the formula works:

19–54

$$AFPF = (\text{total fees/fee earners})$$
$$AFPF = (£1,250,000 \div 14)$$
$$AFPF = £89,286$$

Ratio five: expenses as % of turnover ratio

This considers your firm's expenses, per £1 of fees. This ratio can be applied to individual expenses (e.g. staffing costs, rent etc.) if more detail is needed. It's calculated by dividing a particular expense (or group of expenses) by your net fees. Let's dial-in Sim & Todd LLP's figures and see what we get. We've excluded both depreciation and the loss on the sale of the PCs, from our net expenses calculation (to give a slightly lower expenses figure of £1,176,770).

19–55

Expenses ratio = (Particular expense(s)/Fees) × 100
Expenses ratio = (£1,176,770 ÷ £1,250,000) × 100
Expenses ratio = 94%

The ratio shows what percentage of your fee income is used up by an individual expense (or a group of expenses). A lower ratio means more profitability; a higher ratio means less profitability. It's a helpful tool in controlling and estimating future expenses.

Ratio six: gross (turnover) and Net Profit per Employee (NPE)

19–56 These ratios measure staff productivity. They can be tweaked to show just fee earners or all staff (including partners). You can use either your firm's gross turnover, or you can use its net profit. In addition to having two salaried partners, three associates, four senior solicitors, five NQs and four trainees, let's assume that Sim & Todd LLP also has five admin staff. Let's have a look at a worked example, based on gross turnover (you can easily run the same calculation using the net figure, if you want to).

NPE = Gross/Net ÷ Number of employees
PPE = £1,364,950 ÷ 23
PPE = £59,345

Ratio seven: current ratio

19–57 This measures the ability of your firm to meet its short-term liabilities (e.g. creditors, bank overdrafts etc.) without having to resort to selling off its capital assets. Since current assets should become liquid within 12 months, this should correspond with the current liabilities, which will fall due for payment over the same period.

Let's assume that Sim & Todd LLP's cash in bank is its net profit (£184,274), it's owed £10,000 by its debtors (clients who haven't paid) and has £10,000 of WIP. It, in turn, owes £120,000 to its creditors.

Current ratio = current assets ÷ current liabilities
Current ratio = £204,274 ÷ £120,000
Current ratio = 1.7:1

A result greater than one implies that the firm is liquid; the higher the figure, the better the liquidity.

Ratio eight: liquid ratio (acid test ratio)

This removes WIP from the current ratio calculation, on the basis that it can't readily be turned into cash. Let's have a look at how that changes the scenario. In this case, we need to strip out £10,000 (being the WIP figure).

19–58

Liquid ratio = Current assets (less WIP) ÷ Current liabilities
Liquid ratio = £194,274 ÷ £120,000
Liquid ratio = 1.6:1

You can readily appreciate that the liquid ratio will always tend to give a more pessimistic (but perhaps realistic) view.

Ratio nine: debtor payment period (debtor days)

This measures the average amount of time taken by your firm to collect payment from its debtors. This is vitally important for your cash flow. The time taken to pay should equal (or be less than) the time given to pay.

19–59

The formula requires you to know the amount owed to your firm that is outstanding at the end of a financial year. Let's change our Sim & Todd LLP scenario and let's say that it is owed £250,000 at financial year-end.

Debtor days = (amount outstanding ÷ annual fees) × 365
Debtor days = (£250,000 ÷ £1,250,000) × 365
Debtor days = 73 days

In this scenario, the average time to pay is 73 days. If credit terms are 30 days, then clearly that is a significant issue for Sim & Todd LLP, because (on average) clients are taking twice as long as they should to pay. Sim & Todd LLP should revisit its credit control procedures.

Ratio 10: Longer Term Solvency (LTS) (cash cover)

Longer-term viability is analysed using this formula, which examines your firm's cash cover i.e. can its cash flow meet its short term and long term liabilities? Going back to Sim & Todd LLP, we earlier said that it owed £120,000 to its creditors. Let's add on, say, £50,000 of long-term debt, to make a grand total of £170,000. Remember, these are purely made-up figures, to illustrate how the formula works.

19–60

$$LTS = (\text{Net income} + \text{Depreciation}) \div (\text{Short} + \text{Long term liabilities})$$
$$LTS = (\pounds1,179,270 + \pounds1,406) \div (\pounds120,000 + \pounds50,000)$$
$$LTS = 6.9{:}1$$

This is a healthy enough ratio. However, the lower a firm's solvency ratio is, the greater the probability that it will default on its debt.

User considerations

19–61   Ratios come with a health warning. Firstly, you need to make sure that you choose appropriate ratios. Information needs to be collated regularly (and accurately). Be aware that ratios don't give the full picture; other information is needed and an in-depth knowledge of your business is required. A ratio relevant to one firm may be irrelevant to another.

You must compare like with like; figures and calculations must be consistent. Avoid information overload; it is best to select appropriate ratios for the purpose. Lastly, critically review the information i.e. what has caused the result; what has changed within your firm; what should your firm do? Ratios are pieces of a jigsaw and shouldn't be looked at in isolation. Comparative analysis with ratios from earlier periods, or indeed other competitors add value and perspective.

SUMMARY

19–62   Accounts can tell you a story and help you predict the future. The balance sheet and P & L account can show you how your business has spent its money and whether it'll be profitable. They don't however tell the whole story. Profits are not cash, and cash is the lifeblood of a business, as we'll see in the next chapter.

CHAPTER 20

How to manage cash

INTRODUCTION

Your partner looks worried at your monthly management meeting. You don't   **20-1**
know why. You've never been busier. You've had five new instructions this week.
You're working on good projects and your clients have all agreed to pay big fees.
Yet your partner is worried. "I don't know if we'll be able to pay salaries this
month—we just don't have any cash coming in." How can a successful business
be struggling so badly?

Even the biggest law firms can go out of business. You might wonder how an   **20-2**
otherwise seemingly lucrative business could ever go to the wall. In 2013, the law
firm Cobbetts, which had over 400 staff, collapsed. KPMG were appointed as
administrators and their report showed that between 2008 and 2010 the firm's
turnover dropped over £15m from nearly £60m to £44m. While profits were
stable, it had large costs it couldn't change. In 2006 and 2007 it had agreed
expensive new leases. And while it tried to sub-let space to reduce costs and to
renegotiate the rent with its landlords, it was unsuccessful with both. In 2013 it
collapsed owing £41m.[1]

Why do firms collapse? As with Cobbetts, there is usually a simple answer to
this question. It managed to get itself into the position whereby its cash (money
in) wasn't enough to cover its high fixed costs (money out). It was that basic: the
firm was spending more cash than it was receiving.

Often, people confuse profit with cash. Be under no illusion, cash is the money
available to your firm and includes coins, notes, money in bank accounts and any
unused overdraft facility. Profit, on the other hand, is what is left once all the
costs of running your firm are paid. Cash comes first. Profits later. And when
cash runs out, so will your business.

Outcomes

In the last chapter we looked at profit and loss statements and balance sheets, two   **20-3**
of the three main financial reports. In this chapter we'll examine the third—the
cash flow statement. You will learn how to read and understand a cash flow
statement and how to ask questions of it so that you get meaningful information.

---

[1] A detailed summary of Cobbett's collapse can be found in the Law Society Gazette: Paul Rogerson,
Jonathan Rayner, "Cobbetts' demise and resurrection–the full story", The Law Society Gazette,
lawgazette.co.uk, see *https://www.lawgazette.co.uk/news/cobbetts-demise-and-resurrection–the-full-
story/69546.article* [Accessed 12 February 2019].

A SIMPLE CASH FLOW STATEMENT

20–4   Let's start examining cash flow by examining a simple worked example. Sim & Todd is a boutique London based law firm. Its cash flow statement to 31 January 2019 looks something like this:

Sim & Todd: date—31.01.19

£	NOV *Actual*	DEC *Actual*	JAN *Actual*	FEB *Estimate*	MAR *Estimate*	APR *Estimate*
Fees	10,000	10,000	0	10,000	0	60,000
Other income	1,000	1,000	2,000	1,000	500	1,000
Subto-tal	**11,000**	**11,000**	**2,000**	**11,000**	500	**61,000**
Draw-ings	(–5,000)	(–9,000)	(–5,000)	(–5,000)	(–8,000)	(–5,000)
Rent	(–500)	(–500)	(–500)	(–500)	(–1000)	(–1000)
Heat and lighting	(–100)	(–100)	(–100)	(–100)	(–200)	(–200)
Travel	(–100)	(–100)	(–100)	(–100)	(–200)	(–200)
Subto-tal	**(5,700)**	**(9,700)**	**(5,700)**	**(5,700)**	**(9,400)**	**(6,400)**
Monthly total	+5,300	+1,300	–3,700	+5,300	–8,900	+54,600
Run-ning total	+5,300	+6,600	+2,900	+8,200	(700)	*+53,900*

Basics

20–5   What does this table show?

Horizontal

20–6   Firstly, look at the horizontal axis (i.e. left to right). This gives you the timeline. Notice that for November, December and January, Sim & Todd can record actual, known figures. That's because this statement is dated 31 January 2019 (the date at the top of the table). On 31 January 2019, Sim & Todd know what it has spent and what it has received. For February through to April, the firm can only record estimated figures (i.e. sensible best guesses) because, in January, the firm doesn't know what it'll actually receive or spend in February, March or April. It can only guess. That leads us to our first point; sometimes, when people prepare a cash flow statement, while actual, known numbers are included, poor estimates for the future are made.

That's why, cash flow statements are useful if you ask sensible questions about the data contained in it. If income is falling, month on month, should you predict a rise in fees. If there is a pattern of rising costs, should you keep your cost projections fixed at existing levels. By examining trends, you can ask sensible questions and, if necessary, update the cash flow statement to show more realistic figures.

Vertical

Next, look at the vertical axis (i.e. up and down). This shows what the firm spends money on—it's expenses and costs—and who (or what) it receives money from—it's income.

20–7

Monthly total

At the bottom of the table you find the total for each month, which is calculated by deducting the expenses from the income, leaving either a net surplus (good) or a net deficit (bad) figure.

20–8

Running total

Finally, you have the running total. Again, this is easily calculated, by adding the monthly total of the first month to that of the next month, and so on. Because Sim & Todd's cash flow statement starts in November, the running total figure for November is the same as its monthly total. However, skip to December, and you have a second month's data. You can add the running total from November to the monthly total for December, to create the running total for December (£6,600). Going forward, you add the running total for December with the monthly total for January, and so on.

20–9

Summary

Understanding the basic 'geography' of a cashflow statement is worth your time because all cash flow statements are similar in their layout and construction.

20–10

Before we move on, there are two general points to note. First, in our example, the column for January you may want to show as shaded light grey. This is to indicate that it's the current month under review. It's a good technique, when presenting any financial information to your team, to use colour shading to draw their attention to the month/period you need them to focus on. Secondly, the column for March you could also show as shaded dark grey, simply to draw your eye to this being the month in which it all goes wrong for Sim & Todd.

How to analyse a cash flow statement

20–11   Look at the figures. We've kept them low for simplicity—in reality your firm is more likely to be looking at hundreds of thousands if not millions each month. The point of our example is to demonstrate how an otherwise profitable firm can run out of cash. As we go through the figures we'll make some observations and ask some relevant questions about the data. For example, why is fee income low; why does the partner drawings vary from month to month; and why is the rent going up?

You also can practice, by thinking of additional questions that you might ask. Here are our general observations and questions:

- Fee income in November is healthy, at £10,000. If this were replicated each month, this firm would gross £120,000 per year.
- Estimated fee income in April shoots up to an astonishing £60,000. A question, here, could be why such a large fee has arisen? It may be that the firm has a large transaction which will complete in March. The fee has been agreed in advance and it expects to be paid in April. However, if, when questioned, the partners cannot justify the rise, you will want to make this figure more realistic.
- Other income will include things like interest received and commission (for referring business to another firm). Sim & Todd is earning at least something each month that can be classed as 'other income', which is a good bonus. A question you might ask is how this could be improved? For example, are all Sim & Todd's referrals yielding commission? If not, why not? You'd be surprised how many solicitors give their business leads away.
- Drawings are the sums of money that partners of a firm take out of the business as earnings. You'll see that Sim & Todd doesn't seem to have any control over its monthly drawings, with the figure changing all the time. Ominously, even though the firm is anticipating zero income in March, Sim & Todd still intend to take money out of the firm as drawings, and they plan to increase what they're taking. Is this sensible? Could the drawings be reduced or moved to another month when the firm has the cash to pay it?
- The firm's rent is due to double in March. In reality this would be almost impossible with a well-drafted commercial lease, but maybe Sim & Todd were not on the ball. A question you might ask is whether the firm could renegotiate a lower rent increase? Alternatively, could it give notice to quit and move to new, more cost effective premises?
- Heating and lighting costs are estimated to double, even though better spring and summer weather is coming. Perhaps the firm is being careless and leaving the lights on overnight? Perhaps it should consider energy efficiency measures?
- Travel costs are expected to increase substantially. Perhaps the partners are using first class travel, when standard class would suffice? Though don't be afraid to 'question your questions'. Perhaps standard class is inappropriate? Maybe Sim & Todd find they get more work done in first class as they have guaranteed access to a table for their laptops and a socket for power? Andrew used to work in London one week a month. His firm preferred staff

to catch the 6am flight to London as it was the cheapest flight. Andrew would always catch the 8am flight as getting up for a 6am flight meant he was no use to anyone by noon. There was no point flying to London if he wasn't able to work effectively when he got there.

Going back to the key point of the example, if you look at the projected figures for April, the firm hits the jackpot with estimated fees of £60,000. This, in turn, is projected to put Sim & Todd, that month, in a net cash position of +£54,600, and a cumulative cash position of £53,900.

When measured over the period covered by the statement, Sim & Todd is a profitable firm. However, it's only going to be profitable if it can trade until the end of April. Why might it not? Look at March, when fee and other income are projected to be low, with estimated costs and drawings projected to be high. Taken together, the firm is due to enter a financial deficit. That means it's going to spend more than it earns.

If this transpires, and if the firm's creditors are unwilling to renegotiate credit terms and instead demand immediate payment, Sim & Todd could be in big trouble. It just needs one client to default on fee, or one unexpected bill to crop up, and the firm will run out of cash and be unable to trade to April. You might well be wondering why Sim & Todd would even contemplate taking out cash as drawings, given the fee income projection. You'd be right. However, it assumes that Sim & Todd are preparing a regular cash flow forecast, on the one hand, and asking sensible questions about the data, on the other.

In reality, more complex variations on this simple theme have played out in the legal profession more often than you might think. There sadly are too many real-life examples where partners have failed to fee large jobs, have allowed costs to rise and yet have continued to take large drawings. Why do they do this? Partners are no different to anyone else. They need paid each month to pay for mortgages, rent, car loans, bills, food etc. Could you go a month without a salary?

Conclusion

For the moment, just lock into your minds that profit is not the same as cash. **20–12** Profit doesn't become cash until a fee note is rendered and paid by a client.

CASH FLOW FORECASTS

Get in the flow

Cash flow forecasts are the best tool to use to avoid ending up like Sim & Todd. **20–13** They let a firm predict the peaks and troughs in its cash balance. We showed you a simple forecast in the last example. You're well on your way to understanding, firstly, what a typical statement looks like and, secondly, the importance of asking good questions about the data it contains.

In order to make a profit, you have to deliver services to clients before they get paid (unless some money can be negotiated as a front-end payment). It's essential in legal business to control cash flow, so your firm always has enough cash to pay staff and suppliers before receiving payment from clients. What's more, regular cash outflows will be made on fixed dates (e.g. rent, wages, VAT). You must always be in a position to meet these payments in order to avoid fines, penalty interest or a disgruntled workforce. This is called aligning your *cash inflow* (that is, cash coming in from fees and other sources) with your *cash outflow* (money going out on wages, rent, utilities etc.).

Once you're able to see if (and when) problem months are going to occur, you can plan for them, whether you simply reduce partner drawings or, perhaps, arrange a bank loan (if that is your preferred way of bridging shortfalls). We look at other strategies a little later. It's worth noting at this point that many banks require forecasts before considering whether to lend.

Elements

20–14   A real-life cash flow forecast identifies all of the sources (and amounts) of cash coming into your firm, and the onward destinations (and amounts) of cash going out of your business, over a given period.

Cash inflows (i.e. the money coming in over the period) can include:

- fees from clients;
- receipt of a bank loan;
- bank interest on savings and investments; and
- commission (on referrals).

Cash outflows (the payments disbursed over the period) can include:

- staff wages and partner drawings;
- rent;
- gas and electrics;
- purchase of fixed assets (PCs, printers, furniture, cars etc.);
- loan repayments; and
- tax (income tax, corporation tax, VAT, National Insurance contributions for employees etc.).
- purchase of materials (stationery etc.);

In our earlier example, we kept it simple by using just one column. Often, however, you have two columns, one listing the forecast numbers and the other listing the actual numbers. A forecast is usually done for a year (or quarter) in advance and then updated monthly.

Note that your forecast figures should relate to sums that are due to be collected and sums that are due to be paid out, not invoices actually sent and payments actually received.

Commenting on a forecast

20–15   We've said this a lot. To reiterate, raw data is of no value unless it's subjected to sensible analysis. At a basic level, if a forecast shows a steady net outflow of cash then this is an indicator of problems that need to be addressed quickly. Another easy thing to spot is a misalignment of cash inflow and cash outflow. Be aware of divergences of your projected figures and actual figures. When commenting on your forecast, you should be trying to identify the reason (or reasons) for any variances, and then developing or revising your strategy to combat these issues, going forward.

Here are some examples of the sorts of things that you might ask.

1. Fee income has/is projected to come down.
   a. Has a competitor moved in?
   b. Is it affecting all types of work, or specific areas?
   c. Is it referable to the loss of a high profile partner (who has taken his or her clients away)?
   d. Is it symptomatic of an uncertain economy or is a result of changes in the market (e.g. a move to fixed fees from hourly rate)?
   e. Is there a seasonal variation?
   f. Is it worth improving your marketing?
   g. Can you undercut your competitors?
   h. Is it better to stop one type of work completely and consolidate in other areas?
   i. Can you implement any of the tips in chp 10 (how to fee) such as interim fees to reduce the risk of non-payment and increase cash coming into your firm while transactions are ongoing, rather than at the end of the transaction?
2. Commission income has/is projected to come down.
   a. Has the market shifted so that there is less commission work in general?
   b. Can the firm be appointed to other panels (e.g. for insurance work)?
3. Bank interest has/is projected to come down.
   a. Is it due to the base interest rate being fixed?
   b. Is there a more generous account from another funder?
   c. To get better interest will the firm need to tie up a chunk of its cash balance in notice accounts (e.g. 90-day notice accounts) and can it afford do this?
4. Gas and electricity costs have risen/are projected to rise.
   a. Is it part of a general market trend?
   b. Can the office switch off lights, appliances and heating on certain days (e.g. weekends)?
   c. Is it worth changing supplier?
5. Significant capital costs will push the firm into deficit.
   a. Can acquisitions or renewals be deferred?
   b. If they're necessary, can better payment terms be obtained?

Updates

Accurate forecasts are essential. This means you need to set aside time each **20–16** month to perform an update, by recording your actual (known) numbers. If you use a two-column model (one for projected figures and one for actual figures) you can easily tweak the following months' projections. For example, if fees are projected to be £10,000 a month and, over a three-month period you actually receive £8,000 a month, in the absence of any good reason that would tend to suggest an improvement in your fee income, it would be wise for you to reduce your projected future fees to £8,000 per month.

You have to also consider new factors such as the arrival of a new competitor on the market, and whether these changes need to be incorporated into the business plan or the forecast. When reviewing your forecast, you might choose to:

- keep your original forecast, but measure and understand any variances in the actual figures against the original budget; or
- use a rolling forecast; as each month's actual information is finalised, the forecast is updated to provide an additional month's data. This means that there is always a 12-month rolling projection.

DEALING WITH CASHFLOW ISSUES

20–17   What can you do if you spot problem months, when income doesn't cover expenditure?

Overdraft

20–18   One option is to negotiate an overdraft from your bank. Most business banking facilities offer an overdraft, but make you prove that you can trade in surplus for at least a year, and then charge you for the privilege of using it. In reality, an overdraft is not going to cover anything other than small shortfalls.

Borrow

20–19   The second option is to take a business loan. The issue here is that lenders nowadays require partners to have a good credit rating. Furthermore, the rate of interest usually is quite high (i.e. a high cost of borrowing). Finally, they often require the partners to give a personal guarantee of repayment. This means if the firm cannot pay, the bank can sue the partners direct.

Partner loan

20–20   This is probably the cheapest way to borrow money. Quite simply, you and your partners lend your firm the money it needs to cover any lean periods. That way, you can choose not to charge your firm interest (whereas a bank always will). There are no issues with credit worthiness and also there are fewer problems if you want to write-off your loans (i.e. not demand repayment).

Reduce drawings

20–21   If your firm routinely fails to hit its income target, it would be sensible to look at a new drawings policy. Are partners taking too much out?

Credit terms

It's sometimes possible to renegotiate terms with your creditors. However, it might come at an unexpected cost. Clearly, your creditors could just refuse. Alternatively, if they accept, they may wish to apply interest. It also can erode creditor confidence. Word can spread; a conversation with one creditor can lead to a loss of confidence across several suppliers. This, in turn, can cause a spiral effect, where your creditors all demand immediate payment. **20–22**

Other strategies

What else can you do to improve your cash flow, to try to avoid having to 'plug the gaps'? Ultimately, your aim has to be to speed up inflow and slow down outflow. This helps you build up a positive cash balance that, in turn, helps iron out any short-term problems, as well as funding the future growth of your firm. You can: **20–23**

- draft better invoicing terms to get clients to pay sooner, or on an interim basis;
- charge a front-end fee;
- implement proper and robust credit controls to chase debts;
- defer certain items of capital expenditure (e.g. firm car, PCs etc.);
- negotiate extended credit terms at the outset (this is much better than trying to re-negotiate after the event); and
- take steps to increase fees and profitability, generally (e.g. better marketing, reduced costs etc.).

PROBLEM CLIENTS

Before we examine a more complex cash flow forecast, let's look at some tips to detect problem clients. If your firm has only a few clients and one develops financial problems and can't pay his or her fees, it can have a serious impact. The first piece of advice is that you should avoid relying on a small number of clients if possible, and be vigilant for signs that existing (or indeed potential) clients are in financial trouble. There are several signs that a client might be struggling—for example: **20–24**

- a change for the worse in payment patterns;
- frequent mistakes on cheques (your client might be trying to buy time);
- your client refuses to talk to you;
- less frequent instructions; and
- your client unexpectedly seeks an extension to his or her credit.

It always pays to keep the ear to the ground and it's worth using a credit agency, like Experian or Equifax, to get access to databases with up-to-date financial information about individuals If your client is a company, or limited liability partnership (LLP), it's also worth accessing its accounts at Companies House.

Lastly, sometimes it's possible to help your problem clients by renegotiating their payment terms. This defers your firm's income, but it could also help you to retain that client in the future by supporting them during a difficult period.

EXAMPLE

20–25   Let's look at a more complex example. Sim & Todd has started again. This time better sense has prevailed and the partners have decided to prepare a cash flow forecast and keep it up to date.

This first table shows just the financial projections of Sim & Todd for April and May 2019. June 2019 has still to be completed.

Sim & Todd: forecast cash flow for the period from 1 April 2019 to 30 June 2019

	April Projected (£)	April Actual (£)	May Projected (£)	May Actual (£)	June Projected (£)	June Actual (£)
CASH INFLOW						
Fees recovered	45,000		45,000			
Commission	2,000		2,000			
Bank interest	160		160			
Total cash inflow	**47,160**	**0**	**47,160**	**0**	**0**	
Less: CASH OUTFLOWS						
Wages and salaries	3,750		3,750			
Rent	800		800			
Gas and electricity	420		420			
Telephone	180		180			
Other office costs	275		275			
Transport	150		150			
Capital outlays*	0		12,000			
Cash outflows Subtotal	**5,575**	**0**	**17,575**	**0**	**0**	

	April Projected (£)	April Actual (£)	May Projected (£)	May Actual (£)	June Projected (£)	June Actual (£)
TAXES						
Quarterly VAT	20,000		0			
National Insurance	450		500			
Cash outflows Subtotal	**26,025**	0	**18,075**	0	0	
NET CASH FLOW BEFORE	**21,135**		**29,085**			
DRAWINGS						
PARTNERS' DRAWINGS	10,000		10,000			
Less: partners' drawings						
NET CASH FLOW AFTER	**11,135**		**19,085**			
DRAWINGS						
CUMULATIVE CASH	5,000					
Opening bank/cash	11,135					
Net cash flow for month	16,135	0	0		0	
Closing bank/cash						

Below is the actual financial information recorded by Sim & Todd's accounts team.

APRIL	£	MAY	£
Fees received:	40,500	Fees received:	32,750
Commission:	875	Commission:	600
Bank interest:	114	Bank interest:	100
Wages and salaries:	3,750	Wages and salaries:	4,950
Rent:	800	Rent:	1,600
Gas and electricity:	580	Gas and electricity:	720
Telephone:	180	Telephone:	180
Other office costs:	415	Other office costs:	330
Transport costs:	180	Transport costs:	240
Capital outlays:	1,600	Capital outlays:	15.975
VAT:	20,000	VAT:	0
National Insurance:	450	National Insurance:	500
Drawings:	10,000	Drawings:	10,000

Instructions

Now you're going to do some work.   20–26

(1) Review the cash flow forecast for Sim & Todd.
(2) Note that the forecast covers the period from April until June 2019.
(3) Note that projected figures are provided for April and May.
(4) Complete the 'actual' columns for April and May, by plugging in the information provided above (you might want to photocopy the page first).
(5) Analyse the projected and actual figures and comment on them, on a sheet of blank A4
(6) Revise the projections for June and explain your revisions.
(7) Complete the cumulative cash position entries (at the foot of the forecast).

Once you've done that, read on as we've provided a suggested solution.

Sim & Todd: forecast cash flow for the period from 1 April 2019 to 30 June 2019

	April Projected (£)	April Actual (£)	May Projected (£)	May Actual (£)	June Projected (£)	June Actual (£)
CASH INFLOW						
Fees recovered	45,000	40,500	45,000	32,750	30,000	
Commission	2,000	875	2,000	600	500	
Bank interest	160	114	160	100	80	
Total cash Inflow	**47,160**	**41,489**	**47,160**	**33,450**	**30,580**	
Less: CASH OUTFLOWS						
Wages and salaries	3,750	3,750	3,750	4,950	4,950	
Rent	800	800	800	1,600	1,600	
Gas and electricity	420	580	420	720	720	
Telephone	180	180	180	180	180	
Other office costs	275	415	275	330	300	
Transport	150	180	150	240	240	
Capital outlays*	0	1,600	12,000	15,975	0	
Cash outflows Subtotal	**5,575**	**7,505**	**17,575**	**23,995**	**7,990**	

	April Projected (£)	April Actual (£)	May Projected (£)	May Actual (£)	June Projected (£)	June Actual (£)
TAXES						
Quarterly VAT	20,000	20,000	0	0	0	
National Insurance	450	450	500	500	500	
Cash outflows Subtotal	**26,025**	**27,955**	**18,075**	**24,495**	**8,490**	
NET CASH-FLOW BEFORE	**21,135**	**13,534**	**29,085**	**8,955**	**22,090**	
DRAWINGS						
PARTNERS' DRAWINGS	10,000	10,000	10,000	10,000	10,000	
Less: partners' drawings						
NET CASH-FLOW AFTER	**11,135**	**3,534**	**19,085**	**–1,045**	**12,090**	
DRAWINGS						
CUMULATIVE CASH	5,000	5,000	8,534	8,534	7,489	
Opening bank/cash						
Net cash flow for month	11,135	3,534	19,085	–1,045	12,090	
Closing bank/cash	16,135	8,534	27,619	7,489	19,579	

Analysis

20–27   Below are our observations, together with potential reasons (and/or issues to consider) and a range of possible solutions. This is not a full list. You should analyse the information and come up with your own observations, reasons, issues and solutions.

OBSERVATION	REASON(S)/ISSUES	SOLUTION(S)
Fee income projection is higher than actual fees.	• Has a competitor moved in? • Has a high profile partner left, taking clients? • Due to a sluggish post-recession economy? • Due to market shift (e.g. Alternative Business Structures (ABS)/removal of reserved status etc.)? • Due to a small client pool? • Seasonal variation? • Is it affecting all types of work or just some?	• Undercut competitors. • Improve marketing (targeted strategy and integrated social media). • Can the firm adopt new business models e.g. fixed fee conveyancing?
Commission income is below projected levels.	• Review the above (certain points apply, here). • Has there been a market shift such that there is less commission work generally?	• Can the firm seek out other panels (or similar) for insurance work? • Can the firm partner with other firms (including accountants) to cross-sell?
Bank interest is flat-lining.	• Is this due to a factor outwith the firm's control (e.g. the Bank of England has kept the base rate at 0.5%)?	• Can the firm change to a more generous account from the same/another provider? • To get better interest, can the firm tie up its cash in notice accounts (e.g. 30 days)?

OBSERVATION	REASON(S)/ISSUES	SOLUTION(S)
Wages and salaries are rising.	• Has the firm taken on new staff? • Are the increases in line with inflation? • Do the increases relate to bonuses?	• Review recruitment. • Consider redundancies. • Consider pay-freeze. • Consider moratorium on bonuses.
Rent is rising considerably.	• Why have the partners not taken avoiding action in good time? • Does the increase fall within the terms of the lease?	• Can the firm sub-let unused space? • Can the firm re-negotiate terms? • Is it viable to move premises?
Gas and electricity costs are rising significantly.	• Is this part of a market trend? • Is the office inefficient e.g. does it use too much electricity?	• Can the firm better use its power (e.g. switch-off appliances at night/ weekends)? • Does the firm have an energy policy? • Is it worth changing supplier?
Telephone costs showing no change.	• This is clearly good.	• Can the firm use online technologies for cheaper calls (e.g. Viber)? • Are there yet still more cost efficient providers?
Transport costs rising.	• Is this part of a market trend?	• Where possible any tickets should be booked in advance (e.g. through *train-line.com*) • Switch from first to standard class.
Other office costs fluctuating.	• What comprises the other costs? • Is the fluctuation within acceptable parameters?	• Can prices be fixed with suppliers?

OBSERVATION	REASON(S)/ISSUES	SOLUTION(S)
Capital outlays.	• What comprises the capital outlays? • Are the outlays necessary?	• Can the acquisitions or renewals be deferred? • If not, can better payment terms be negotiated? • Does the firm need such an expensive car? • Is it better to lease an asset as opposed to buying it?
VAT.	• Compliance issue. • Critical it is paid to avoid fines.	• Does the firm have a tax account, with a sensible reserve to meet VAT?
National Insurance (NI).	• Compliance issue.	• Does the firm have a tax account, with a sensible reserve to meet NI?
Partners' drawings steady, but high.	• Drawings are usually the single biggest drain on cash flow.	• Partners might consider reducing their take from the firm, for a period.

Projections

20–28 For your revised projections for June, you should slot in some sensible numbers. There is no right or wrong answer, but the following suggestions should keep you in the right ballpark.

ITEM	PROJECTION / REASON
Fees	Revise down to the actual fee figure for May.
Commission	Revise down to a more realistic level.
Bank interest	Revise down to reflect reduced fees and commission.
Wages and salaries	Use actual figure for May (pending staffing review).
Rent	Use actual figure for May (pending negotiation with landlord).
Gas/electricity	Use actual figure for May (pending change of supplier).
Telephone	Use actual figure for May (pending change of supplier).

ITEM	PROJECTION / REASON
Other office costs	Prudent to revise up slightly (as they're fluctuating).
Capital outlays	Zero—no outlays anticipated.
VAT	Zero—VAT is paid quarterly.
NI	Revise up—slight increase to reflect increased wages.
Drawings	Revise down—sensible to help ensure a return to surplus.

Other key questions

To conclude, we leave you with some more general questions. These are the sorts of 'big picture' questions you might ask in a financial analysis session.   **20–29**

- Has Sim & Todd been sensible, overall, in its financial projections?
    — Yes—it has actually created a cash flow forecast.
    — No—it has over-estimated key income figures significantly.
- Does the firm have a healthy cash balance?
    — No—in May it's in a cash negative position.
    — No—the margin in April was not significant, and a range of common occurrences was always likely to tip the firm in to a cash-negative situation e.g. loss of a major client; increase in overheads etc.
- Why are there heavier cash demands in certain months?
    — Some outlays (e.g. VAT) are incurred on a fixed, quarterly basis.
    — During the winter, gas and electricity costs, clearly, will be higher.
- What can Sim & Todd do to improve its cash flow and cash balance?
    — Draft better invoicing terms (interim fees).
    — Implement robust credit control.
    — Seek better credit terms.
    — Generally, seek to increase fees (increase hourly rates, widen the breadth of work the firm does, improve targeted marketing, maintain a current client database and cross-sell services to existing clients, improve social networking and firm branding, seek appointment to public authority and insurance panels etc.).
    — Generally, cut costs (review staffing, reallocate work so that partners do not undertake cost inefficient work more appropriately handled by an assistant, switch to using cheaper paralegals, more efficient use of office materials and utilities).
- What might the impact be of excessive partnership debts?
    — If not an LLP, Sim & Todd will have joint and several liability for the debts.
    — The partnership might be forced out of business, if creditors call in debts.

— Firm then reliant on: overdraft; a bridging loan; or partners injecting their own capital. These do not address underlying problems and the first two options are expensive ways to raise money.
— Partners might struggle to find a buyer (or complete a merger) on good terms.
— If the financial problems become known more widely, suppliers may impose more robust credit terms and clients may leave.

SUMMARY

20–30 Cash is the life-blood of any business. If you start losing cash then you won't be able to pay salaries, rent, suppliers and others. Without cash you can't run a business. The cash flow statement helps you track cash so that you can quickly and easily predict problems and deal with them.

PART 4

THE FUTURE

CHAPTER 21

Equality and diversity

"If we don't reflect the global nature of our business and our employees, how can we possibly hope to understand our customers? In the same way, we have to have a good balance of men and women. If we only have men building our products and services, how we going to appeal to half the world's population?"[1] Mark Palmer-Edgecumbe, Google's Head of Diversity and Inclusion

INTRODUCTION

How has modern diversity in the workplace developed? A number of factors can be identified, split across different types of diversity. One factor is generational. Not everyone who turns 60 wants to retire. Nowadays, many older employees want to remain working, because they both enjoy it and want to stay fit and active. Another factor is that the number of foreign workers coming into the UK has increased. For example, towards the end of 2018, some 2.25 million EU nationals and 1.24 million non-EU nationals were working in the UK.[2] While a third factor is the increase in female employees. While, according to the Law Society's Annual Statistics Report for 2017, the total number of women lawyers is now 50.1% of the profession, it's not all good new, the rate of female partnership is still lagging behind, improving to just over 30%.

    21–1

All these factors and more work together to ensure a multicultural and diverse workforce—despite cliched views of the profession. While many clients may have a traditional view of lawyers as old men with grey hair, the reality, as we can see, is that the legal profession has more female lawyers than male. While, in 2017, 16% of solicitors (over 19,000) were from BAME backgrounds—more than double the proportion in the previous decade. The profession is changing and this evolution presents a range of challenges to lawyers and law firms, who are required by the SRA's Code of Conduct to act "in a way that encourages equality, diversity and inclusion".

In this chapter we will look at how to tackle prejudice, stereotypes and discrimination within law firms because—if handled correctly—your firm can use diversity to improve the service it provides. Different people provide different perspectives and the same actions when viewed by someone with a different viewpoint may provide your client or your firm with ideas or action it may not

    21–2

---

[1] Richard Daft and Alan Benson, "*Managing Corporate Diversity*", in Sim, I. (ed.) *MG112: Managing in a Global Context*. [Andover: Cengage, 2016] p.456.

[2] Office of National Statistics (2018), *UK and Non-UK People in the Labour Market: November 2018,* [Accessed 25 January 2019] *https://www.ons.gov.uk/employmentandlabourmarket/ peopleinwork/employmentandemployeetypes/articles/ukandnonukpeopleinthelabourmarket/ november2018.*

have spotted. For example, Hogans Lovell was recognised in the Legal Diversity Awards 2017 for its approach to trans issues. Among other initiatives, it provided bespoke trans training on how to use appropriate language for trans clients. Such initiatives ensure that clients are dealt with in the way that is appropriate for them. And, as we explained in Ch.6 (Clients and you), it should be the aim of every lawyer to tailor their service to their client.

OUTCOMES

21-3   In this chapter we'll examine: the concept of diversity, working in a diverse team, creating a diversity plan and practical strategies. We also will review the main aspects of the Equality Act 2010 and the SRA Handbook.

WHAT IS DIVERSITY?

21-4   Diversity can be defined as all the ways in which people differ.[3] However it wasn't always defined this broadly. Traditionally, the concept was viewed more narrowly, focusing on race, gender, age, lifestyle and disability. We can see echoes of this in the Equality Act, which we'll examine later.

Whilst these definitions helped to develop awareness of diversity issues and to start to challenge prejudices, the concept was too narrow and so—over time—it was widened progressively.

In a sense, the old way of viewing diversity tended to focus on artefacts that are observable. It is easy to see the colour of a colleague's skin, their gender and their age. Today's more inclusive thinking encapsulates all of the ways in which employees differ, including those aspects that can be acquired or changed over time (such as competency, experience and personality).

WHAT ARE THE BENEFITS OF DIVERSITY?

21-5   The old adage is that great minds think alike. However, when it comes to diversity, you need to invert that formula; the greatest minds actually should not think alike.

The SRA reports that firms that are using their diversity data to promote diversity have said that—in turn—they are better able to:

- Identify barriers that prevent the development of all available talent;
- Win business by showing their commitment to diversity;
- Prevent costly discrimination claims by identifying problems early;
- Strengthen their reputation.[4]

---

[3] Wheeler, M (1995), *"Diversity: Business Rationale and Strategies"*, in *The Conference Board, Report No 1130-95-RR*, p. 25.
[4] *http://www.sra.org.uk/solicitors/resources/diversity-toolkit/benefits-diversity.page*, [Accessed 17 February 2019].

While pro-diversity commentators have coined the phrase 'diversity dividend'.[5] This captures a range of benefits:

Talent

Firms with the best talent are the ones that enjoy the most competitive advantage. However, attracting a diverse workforce is not enough and firms need to work to retain these employees so they can—in turn—maintain their competitive advantage.

21–6

Understanding of the market

A diverse workforce is better geared to anticipate (and respond to) changing client needs.

21–7

Enhanced leadership

Homogeneous management teams tend to be myopic in their perspectives.

21–8

Increased problem solving

Teams with diverse backgrounds bring different perspectives to a discussion, which results in creative ideas and solutions.

The director of flexibility and gender equity strategy at Ernst and Young has said:

21–9

> "You get better solutions when you put a diverse team at the table. People come from different backgrounds and they have different frames of reference. When you put these people together, you get the best solution for our clients."[6]

Reduced costs

Firms that have a diverse workforce reduce employee turnover and absenteeism. For example, firms that can offer flexible working clearly will appeal to men and women with young families.

21–10

WORKING IN A DIVERSE TEAM

To work successfully as part of a diverse team you need to understand what influences your own personal bias. Personal bias is acknowledged to include four things: prejudice, discriminatory behaviour, stereotyping and ethnocentrism. Let's look at each of these in turn.

21–11

---

[5] Daft and Benson, p.464.
[6] Daft and Benson, p.464.

Prejudice

21–12   Prejudice is a tendency to regard those who are different to you as being—in some way or other—deficient. If you act on your prejudice towards another team member, discrimination may have occurred.

Discrimination

21–13   Discrimination is pernicious, and it doesn't restrict itself to the obvious. In fact, it can arise in very subtle ways. For example, it may be that a partner in your firm continually fails to give one of your colleagues the best work, or perhaps a female colleague is routinely ignored during team meetings.

Stereotyping

21–14   The most significant aspect of prejudice is stereotyping. This is where you express exaggerated and irrational beliefs about a particular group of people.[7] If you are ever to achieve diversity in your firm, it is really important that you combat harmful stereotypes.

We are sure that you can think of a time when you might have witnessed stereotyping in action. To encourage your colleagues to reject stereotyping, remind them of three things:

- Stereotypes are based on myth, which then is exacerbated by media portrayals. Reality is different and the myths soon dissipate when subjected to robust analysis;
- Stereotypes are almost always negative. If your team members apply just a little thought to this, they will know that not all differences are inherently negative.
- Stereotypes assume that everyone within a group has the same characteristics. Clearly, not all members of a group share the same characteristics. The authors are always amused when overseas friends assume that Scotsmen play the bagpipes at dawn, eat haggis and wear kilts. This is not true. We play at dusk.

Stereotype threat

21–15   Be aware of the 'stereotype threat'. This describes the negative psychological experience of a person who is aware that he/she is being "labelled" and—moreover—that there is a perception that somehow he/she she will underperform.[8]

It goes without saying that the people most affected by this are those who might be considered at a disadvantage due to negative stereotypes (e.g. minorities, those from lower socioeconomic backgrounds, women etc.).[9] It is

---

[7] Norma Carr-Ruffino, *Managing Diversity*, (Pearson Learning Solutions, 2009) pp.98-99.
[8] Robertson, L and Kulik, C (2007), *"Stereotype Threat at Work"*, *Academy of Management Perspectives*, vol.21, no.2, p.26.
[9] Daft and Benson, p.468.

thought that the phenomenon is so impactful because those affected feel that they are being subjected to undue scrutiny and become worried that any failure (however slight) will reflect not only on themselves, but also on the wider group to which they belong.[10]

Ethnocentrism

Ethnocentrism is another issue you might have to contend with. This is the belief that your own group and culture are inherently superior to others.[11] It is a common problem but, in the interests of balance, it has to be said that commentators do not regard it as altogether unnatural. Everyone, after all, thinks that their country's capital city is the most beautiful in the world, or that their art is the best, and so on. You in fact see it manifesting across every culture in the world; in other words it is not a "Britain versus the World" issue. **21–16**

In business, however, an ethnocentric culture leads to the emergence of monoculture. A monoculture sees only one way of doing things. If this goes unchecked it inhibits the benefits that a diverse team can bring and the ability to think of alternative ideas or understand different viewpoints.

CREATING A DIVERSITY PLAN

The challenge that faces your firm (and indeed you) is to foster a culture that actually values diversity. A useful tool to strategically manage this is called a 'diversity plan'. **21–17**

A good diversity plan is one that enables your firm to demonstrate cultural competence, which is the ability to interact effectively with people of different cultures.[12] There are five steps to implementing a diversity plan:[13]

Diversity audit

You don't expect your doctor to make a diagnosis without first examining you. Similarly, your firm cannot assess its progress towards cultural competence without a cultural audit. An audit helps you to identify those areas that need to be improved; you undertake it by answering questions about the firm about a range of issues. **21–18**

Partnership commitment

Partner commitment to (and in support of) any diversity plan is essential to its success. This could involve your firm allocating resources to diversity activities and communicating a commitment to diversity, internally. **21–19**

---

[10] *ibid.*
[11] Daft and Benson, p.469.
[12] Mercedes Martin and Billy Vaughn, "Cultural Competence: The Nuts & Bolts of Diversity & Inclusion", (2010) *https://diversityofficermagazine.com/cultural-competence/cultural-competence-the-nuts-bolts-of-diversity-inclusion-2/.*
[13] Daft and Benson, p.473.

Choose balanced solutions

21–20   Perhaps the most appropriate solution to a diversity issue is one that tackles the most pressing problems uncovered by implementing the first step. However, in order to be effective, any solution should be balanced and should address three factors: education, enforcement and exposure. Education includes training to improve awareness and skills. Enforcement means incentivising employees who adhere to standards, with disciplinary action for those who violate them. Exposure involves mixing staff to help break down barriers.

Become goal driven

21–21   As with any goal, you must measure the output of your diversity strategy. Performance should be measured to ensure that the chosen solution is being implemented successfully.

For example, you might track the salaries of minority groups or their rates of promotion. Alternatively, you might ask employees to take part in a follow-up audit.[14]

Momentum

21–22   Success is a powerful motivator to continue your efforts. Firms should harness their successes to create the impetus to promote even greater diversity.

PRACTICAL STEPS

21–23   Let's turn our attention to some practical steps that you might wish to implement.

Structures and policies

21–24   Modern firms should put in place structures and policies that support diversity. For example, your firm should have a policy against racial and gender discrimination. To bolster that, there should be a published grievance procedure. To be really forward looking, you might elect to appoint a diversity partner, tasked with oversight, who would report to the executive board. Clifford Chance, for example, publishes all of its policies on its website. Its key policy is "Diversity, Dignity and Inclusiveness".[15] The statement (set out below) captures all of the headline policy points, which the firm refers to as its beliefs.[16]

---

[14] Daft and Benson, p.473.
[15] Clifford Chance, *Diversity Dignity and Inclusiveness (2019) https://www.cliffordchance.com/about_us/our-responsibilities/our-responsible-business-strategy/policies.html* [Accessed 21 February 2019].
[16] *ibid.*

High Level Statement

> *"We believe that being an equal opportunities firm means going beyond mere compliance with anti-discrimination legislation."*

Diversity

> *"We believe that promoting diversity means creating an inclusive work environment where everyone has the opportunity to succeed without obstacles based on their gender, gender identity and expression, marital and civil partnership status, race, colour, national or ethnic origin, social or economic background, disability, religious belief, sexual orientation, age or any other basis prohibited under applicable law."*

Backgrounds

> *"We recognise that people from varying backgrounds can bring a full range of worthwhile ideas and innovations to our working practices and business. Encouraging everyone at the Firm to respect the individuality of their colleagues and to feel comfortable in making their own contribution is a fundamental aspect of our values and critical to our business success."*

Scope of Equal Opportunities

> *"Our Equal Opportunities policy applies to recruitment and selection, terms and conditions of employment, including pay, promotion, training, transfers, and our approach to every other aspect of employment. The Firm aims to ensure that individuals are selected, promoted and treated on the basis of their individual abilities and merits and the needs of the Firm."*

Recruitment

Firms should reflect on their recruitment policies. How might they be changed to bolster inclusivity? Well, one example could be to offer work experience to students from less advantaged backgrounds and to reach out to minority groups. **21–25**

Clifford Chance, for example, actively seeks to improve its ethnic diversity through a partnership with diversity recruitment group, Rare. Rare was founded in 2005 to support minority candidates in securing graduate positions in top City firms. Clifford Chance reports that, since 2011, the firm has offered 169 training contracts through utilising this relationship.[17] At senior levels we have seen firms launch initiatives to promote more female candidates to partnerships. For example, Pinsents Masons launched Project Sky in 2014 with the aim of reaching 30% female partnership. Project Sky examined more transparent career development; greater accessibility to flexible or agile working; more structured support around parental leave and training to help identify and address subconscious bias. **21–26**

---

[17] Clifford Chance, Ethnic Diversity (2019), *https://www.cliffordchance.com/about_us/our-responsibilities/people-inclusion/inclusion-and-diversity/ethnic-diversity.html* [Accessed 21 February 2019].

21–27   The firm has adopted Rare's Contextual Recruitment System (CRS) to help it identify good quality candidates, by not only looking at their grades but also how these compare to a candidate's schooling and background. Since adopting the CRS, the firm reports that it now employs more candidates from disadvantaged backgrounds and, in recent years, its trainee intake of black, minority and ethnic candidates has averaged more than 40%.[18]

21–28   Clifford Chance has a further strategy in place to widen access to the profession viz. participation in a programme called PRIME. With PRIME, the firm provides up to 60 one-week work experience places to young people from less-privileged backgrounds. This is in order to give them an insight into the range of careers available. The placements are designed to allow participants to take part in a business challenge, meet with a barrister, join in skills development sessions and, finally, to network with trainees.[19]

Mentoring

21–29   One way to tackle that infamous glass ceiling is to have a mentoring structure in place, where a senior solicitor is tasked to provide support to a junior solicitor. One piece of research that examined the career progression of high potential minorities found that those who advanced the most all had a strong mentor to support them.[20]

Awareness

21–30   Firms should create awareness of harassment in the workplace. What does that mean, in 2019? One public sector organisation identified five types of harassment:

- General—remarks and actions directed towards a staff member based on their gender
- Inappropriate/offensive—behaviour that causes discomfort
- Solicitation—action which might be viewed as an attempt to purchase sex (with the potential of prosecution)
- Coercion—coercion of a staff member through the abuse of power (e.g. threats or the promise of promotion)
- Crime—behaviour that, if reported to the police, would be considered a criminal offence.[21]

---

[18] ibid.
[19] Social Mobility (2019) https://www.cliffordchance.com/about_us/our-responsibilities/people-inclusion/inclusion-and-diversity/social-mobility.html [Accessed 21 February 2019].
[20] Thomas, D (2001), "The Truth About Mentoring Minorities—Race Matters", Harvard Business Review , 79 (4) 98–107.
[21] Vanderbilt University (1993), Sexual Harassment: Vanderbilt University Policy.

Multicultural teams

Research has demonstrated that diverse teams tend to generate more (and better) solutions to corporate challenges than do homogeneous teams.[22] Quite simply a team comprising people with different perspectives and cultural values increases the mix of ideas, leading to greater creativity in decision-making.

21–31

Multicultural teams do come with challenges, especially around the potential for miscommunication and misunderstanding. However, with good training and management multicultural teams can learn to work well together.[23]

Affinity groups

Affinity groups are informal structures set up for groups who share social identities (such as gender or race). They are set-up by the employees themselves, in order to focus on any concerns they might have.

21–32

The groups arrange meetings, mentoring sessions, networking events and training, with the aim of developing social and professional ties. A recent study confirms that these are important tools that help firms retain high quality employees.[24] Clifford Chance operates a variation of this. As part of the firm's commitment to diversity and inclusivity, it supports its staff in establishing so-called diversity networks, which focus on the recruitment, retention and advancement of minority employees.[25] One example of a diversity network is Arcus.

Arcus is the firm's global LGBT+ community and it was launched in 2015. Around the world it has evolved so that there is now a Black and Latino Subcommittee and an Asian and Pacific Islanders Subcommittee. There are women's networks in the Americas, Asia, Amsterdam, France, Italy and London. Arcus runs events throughout the year and provides support and networking opportunities.

EQUALITY ACT 2010

We turn our attention now to the key provisions of the relevant legislation that applies in the UK, so you are clear about your legal rights and obligations. The applicable legislation is the Equality Act 2010. The Act sets out various "personal characteristics" that are protected by law and it also proscribes certain behaviours.

21–33

---

[22] Watson, W, Kumar, K and Michaelson, L (1993), "Cultural Diversity's Impact on Interaction Process and Performance: Comparing Homogeneous and Diverse Task Groups", *Academy of Management Journal*, vol.36, pp.590-602.

[23] Watson et al. (1993)

[24] Friedman, R and Holtom, B (2002), "The Effects of Network Groups on Minority Employee Turnover Intentions", *Human Resource Management*, vol.41, no. 4 pp. 405-421.

[25] Diversity Networks (2019), *https://www.cliffordchance.com/about_us/our-responsibilities/people-inclusion/diversity-networks.html* [Accessed 21 February 2019].

Who is responsible under the Act?

21–34   The Act casts the net of responsibility very widely, capturing:

- Government departments.
- Service providers.
- Employers.
- Education providers (including schools, further education colleges and Universities).
- Providers of public functions.
- Associations and membership bodies.
- Transport providers.

What are protected characteristics?

21–35   The protected characteristics set out in the Act are:

- Age.
- Disability.
- Gender Reassignment.
- Marriage and civil partnership.
- Pregnancy and maternity.
- Race.
- Religion and beliefs.
- Sex.

How does the Act define discrimination?

21–36   The Act handles discrimination in two ways. Firstly, if you treat one person worse than another because of a protected characteristic, this is classed as direct discrimination. Secondly, if you put in place a rule or policy which impacts negatively on someone with a protected characteristic relative to someone without, then unless this can be objectively justified then it is indirect discrimination.

How does the Act define harassment?

21–37   Harassment is viewed as any unwanted conduct relating to a protected characteristic, which has the purpose (or effect) of:

- violating someone's dignity, or;
- creating a hostile, degrading, humiliating or offensive environment for that person.

How does the Act define victimisation?

Victimisation is couched in terms of treating someone unfavourably because they **21–38** have taken (or might be taking) action under the Equality Act (or they are supporting somebody who is doing so).

Discrimination by association and perception

A colleague doesn't actually have to have a protected characteristic for **21–39** discrimination to arise. That's because the Act provides for two other forms of forms of discrimination called discrimination by association (or associative discrimination) and discrimination by perception (perceptive discrimination).

What is discrimination by association?

Associative discrimination arises if someone is treated unfavorably on the basis **21–40** of another person's protected characteristic. This may be hard to understand, so let's look at a simple example. Let's say your friend has been told she is joining your firm as a trainee. Suddenly, the offer is retracted after she tells your bosses that she has a disabled child with complicated care arrangements. The withdrawal of the job offer could constitute discrimination because of your friend's association with a disabled person (remember—disability is a protected characteristic).

Discrimination by association, however, doesn't apply to all protected characteristics. Marriage and civil partnership, pregnancy and maternity are not covered. Nor does the concept apply to indirect discrimination by association; in other words associative discrimination must be direct discrimination.

What is discrimination by perception?

Perceptive discrimination arises if someone is treated unfavorably because other **21–41** people believe he or she has a protected characteristic (even though in fact they do not). Once again you might be scratching your head, so let's look at another simple example. Let's say your friend is rejected for a job in a bar because he has an Arabic name. The owner of the bar assumes that he must be a Muslim and, accordingly, won't be able to handle alcohol. This could be considered discrimination by perception, whether or not your friend is a Muslim.

Perceptive discrimination does not apply to marriage and civil partnership, nor pregnancy and maternity, and—as with associative discrimination – must be direct.

THE LAW SOCIETY—DIVERSITY AND INCLUSION CHARTER

21-42 The Law Society established a Diversity and Inclusion Charter, in 2009. The Charter is designed to help firms achieve positive, practical outcomes for their staff and clients, as regards diversity. It is regarded as a public commitment by legal practices to promote the values of diversity and inclusion throughout their business.

Charter statement

21-43 As The Law Society states in its Charter Statement:

"Whether it's through recruitment, retention, career progression or training and development, all our signatories are committed to improving opportunities for people in the legal profession, regardless of their background or circumstances."[26]

21-44 The Charter sets out to achieve this by helping practices to record and measure their practices, policies and procedures against a set of diversity and inclusion standards. The Law Society then gives them opportunities to share best practice advice and guidance with peers. As of 2018, 490 firms and practices had signed up to the Charter, representing more than a third of the legal profession in England and Wales.[27]

Charter Signatories

21-45 Charter signatories subscribe the following set of principles:

"The signatories to this charter believe that a commitment to diversity and inclusion is essential to reflect the society we serve today. It makes business sense because it helps us to attract and retain the best talent, it enables us to understand and meet clients' needs more effectively and so provide a better quality service."[28]

Charter Commitments

21-46 The principles are then expanded into a set of commitments, with firms undertaking to:

- Strive to achieve best practice in recruitment, retention and career progression;
- Support the development of good diversity practice by collecting and sharing examples of practical activities that contribute to progress;
- Assign responsibility for meeting charter commitments to a named, senior level individual;

---

[26] Diversity and Inclusion Charter (2019), *https://www.lawsociety.org.uk/support-services/practice-management/diversity-inclusion/diversity-inclusion-charter/* [Accessed 23 February 2019].
[27] Ibid.
[28] Charter Signatories (2019), *https://www.lawsociety.org.uk/support-services/practice-management/diversity-inclusion/diversity-inclusion-charter/* [Accessed 23 February 2019].

- Work together to develop and adopt future protocols that support the practical implementation of the aims of the charter;
- Annually publish the diversity profile of employees;
- Publish a joint annual report on the basis of a monitoring exercise to measure the impact of the charter and its protocols.[29]

Charter protocols

The charter is accompanied by a set of protocols, which are designed to help signatories meet their commitments. A *reporting and monitoring protocol* helps firms collect diversity statistics. A *flexible working protocol* presents a business case for flexible working. A *legal procurement protocol* is a commitment by purchasers to consider diversity and inclusion as part of their normal tendering process.[30]   **21–47**

The Law Society—Statistics

The Law Society reports an improving picture, on diversity within the profession. According to its most recently available Diversity and Inclusion Biennial Report (2017):   **21–48**

- 82% of large firms report an aspiration to work with a diverse range of suppliers and are actively exploring opportunities to do so;
- Firms are more transparent and open around diversity, with 70% being members of inclusion networks;
- Firms publishing a diversity and inclusion report increased from 29% in 2015 to 40% in 2017;
- 62% of all solicitors working in signatory firms are women;
- Solicitors from non-white British backgrounds in signatory firms increased to 27% in 2017;
- 4% of people working in signatory firms identify as lesbian, gay, or bisexual.[31]

THE SRA HANDBOOK 2019

Updated SRA standards and regulations are due to come into force in 2019, as the new SRA Handbook. The final draft enshrines diversity and inclusion with its core principles. Principle 6 clearly states that you must act "in a way that encourages equality, diversity and inclusion".   **21–49**

The new Standards and Regulations will greatly simplify the provisions of the old Handbook. In particular, they contain two Codes of Conduct; one for

---

[29] Charter Signatories (2019),*https://www.lawsociety.org.uk/support-services/practice-management/diversity-inclusion/diversity-inclusion-charter/* [Accessed 23 February 2019].
[30] Diversity and Inclusion Charter Protocols (2019), *https://www.lawsociety.org.uk/support-services/practice-management/diversity-inclusion/diversity-inclusion-charter/diversity-and-inclusion-charter-protocols/* [Accessed 23 February 2019].
[31] Diversity and Inclusion Charter (2019), *https://www.lawsociety.org.uk/support-services/practice-management/diversity-inclusion/diversity-inclusion-charter/* [Accessed 23 February 2019].

solicitors and one for firms. Each contains a short requirement as regards diversity and inclusion. The new Code of Conduct for firms deals with it early on, under "Maintaining Trust and Acting Fairly". It states at Rule 1.5 that firms must "monitor, report and publish workforce diversity data, as prescribed."

The new Code of Conduct for solicitors states at Rule 1.1 (under the same heading) that you must not: "unfairly discriminate by allowing your personal views to affect your professional relationships and the way in which you provide your services".

The old 'outcomes' and 'indicative behaviours' have been replaced by the new 'requirements'. Iain Miller, of Kingsley Napley LLP, believes that the new system marks:

> "… a liberalisation of the current framework particularly around the ways in which solicitors can practise. It also seeks to enable a wider level of discretion or proportionality in the relationship between the regulator and the regulated."[32]

Miller argues that whilst fewer rules and wider discretion is in principle a good thing, in a sense the new Handbook does not provide all the answers and—instead— it requires solicitors and firms to *understand the policy, law and ethics which lie behind the rules to ensure that they are doing the right thing*.[33]

Practical Approach

21–50   Since the new system is not going to be defined or proscriptive about the actions required to promote diversity and inclusion, you should keep in mind the Law Society's charter as a good starting point to show actions which you and your firm should consider as best practice.

It seems reasonable to assume that the SRA (when assessing whether you have met the new 'requirements') will not opt for a lesser standard than that set by the current published 'outcomes' and 'indicative behaviours', and so it is worth re-stating them briefly. We suggest you continue to view them as "expected outcomes and behaviours". You should:

- not discriminate unlawfully, or victimise or harass anyone, in the course of your professional dealings;
- provide services to clients in a way that respects diversity;
- make reasonable adjustments to ensure that disabled clients, employees or managers are not placed at a substantial disadvantage compared to those who are not disabled;
- encourage equality of opportunity and respect for diversity in recruitment;
- deal with complaints promptly, fairly, openly, and effectively;
- have a written equality and diversity policy which is appropriate to the size and nature of the firm and which includes:
    - a commitment to the principles of equality and diversity and legislative requirements;

---

[32] SRH Handbook 2019–Time to Start Preparing (2019),*https://www.kingsleynapley.co.uk/insights/ blogs/regulatory-blog/sra-handbook-2019-time-to-start-preparing* [Accessed 25 February 2019].
[33] *ibid.*

- a requirement that all employees and managers comply with the outcomes;
- provisions to encompass your recruitment and interview processes;
- details of how the firm will implement, monitor, evaluate and update the policy;
- details of how the firm will ensure equality in relation to the treatment of employees, managers, clients and third parties instructed in connection with client matters;
- details of how complaints and disciplinary issues are to be dealt with;
- details of the firm's arrangements for workforce diversity monitoring; and
- details of how the firm will communicate the policy to employees, managers and clients.
- Provide employees and managers with training and information about complying with equality and diversity requirements;

SUMMARY

Your firm needs to consider diversity and equality when drafting its policies and procedures around: **21–51**

1. Recruitment.
2. Working hours, flexible working and time off.
3. Pay and benefits.
4. Training, development, promotion and transfer.
5. Managing workers.
6. Dismissal, redundancy, retirement and staff leaving.

As an employee of your firm, you are responsible for providing services to your clients in a manner consistent with the provision of the Act. This has the following implications:

1. You should know your firm's equality policy and ensure you participate in any training.
2. You should ensure that your service doesn't discriminate against clients based on protected characteristics. You also need to be aware of how perceptive and associative discrimination might arise.
3. You need to challenge or report instances of discrimination, victimisation and harassment.

More practically, you should think about how you might better structure your services to better assist a diverse client base. Some tips are:

Communication

21–52 What different communication needs might your clients have? How can you meet those needs whilst still ensuring that you are respecting the requirement to maintain client confidentiality?

Your practices

21–53 Consider how practices that you consider to be 'standard' might present problems or barriers for some clients. Some clients will need to do things differently in order to have a positive experience of your firm.

Adjustments

21–54 There may be obvious adjustments required, but you should not assume what these are. Intermediaries might be required e.g. a 'buddy' to attend meetings, or a translator.

Unconscious bias

21–55 Your background and personal experiences can have an impact on your actions. Unconscious bias happens when you make quick judgments about people. You may not be aware you are doing it, or be aware of the full impact it might have.

CHAPTER 22

Law and Technology (LegalTECH)

INTRODUCTION

It was a sunny Monday. It was our first day. We were nervous: we don't know **22–1**
what to expect as we walked into our new offices, in 2000. We were trainee
lawyers—but what did that mean? As savvy wannabe solicitors, we had all the
latest gadgets. Sim listened to his state of the art portable CD player; Todd made
calls on his Nokia 3310 mobile. Email had just been introduced to universities
and we'd used it to send out our traineeship applications (once we'd spent five
minutes dialling up to the web on 56k modems).

Yet, at the office, we had to research cases by working our way through library
shelves, we had to time record using paper slips, and we had to chase clients to
pay fees (which they then would settle by cheque rather than bank transfer). But
times change, technology has advanced, and law firms have modernised.
Technology has changed both how lawyers work and how clients expect services
to be delivered.

It's another sunny Monday. It's your first day. You're a trainee lawyer, you're
smart, you know the law and you're commercially aware. However, for a modern
career, do you also need to embrace technology?

What does new technology mean for the traditional solicitor—client **22–2**
relationship? According to Joanne Frears, a business-centric approach is needed:
"*As clients are better informed, having access to similar resources as lawyers and*
the infinite look-up possibilities of search engines, lawyers need to hone their
commercial skills. If free data and wide access to legal knowledge means lawyers
no longer need to be a memory bank of cases, then their experience of practical
application of the law to real life legal scenarios becomes crucial, as this can't be
Googled."[1]

Technology has affected consumer expectations. With instant access to
information, clients are more knowledgeable, more selective and more
demanding. They have come to expect more for their money, including
responsiveness and quick answers. This shift in expectations arguably has
increased competition in the legal services space and has had a real impact on the
delivery of legal services.[2] According to a study, less than 10% of people who call
a law firm get to speak to a solicitor and 42% of the time, potential clients have to

---

[1] How has Technology Changed the Legal Profession for Fee Earners, *https://www.bristows.com/*
news-and-publications/articles/how-has-technology-changed-the-legal-profession-for-fee-earners/
[Accessed 25 February 2019].
[2] How Can Law Firms Meet the Needs of 21st Century Legal Clients, *https://abovethelaw.com/2017/*
06/how-can-law-firms-meet-needs-of-21st-century-legal-clients/ [Accessed 25 February 2019].

wait for three days (or even more) to receive a reply to their enquiry. That's just not right, in our view. In this age of technology, clients aren't likely to wait terribly long to hear back from you.[3].

In many ways this neatly squares with what we said at the outset of this book; clients nowadays don't just want legal knowledge; they want you turn your theoretical knowledge into practical advice. In short, they want commercial awareness, and technology can help you show this.

In order to thrive in today's legal industry, you've got to stay ahead of the competition by delivering exceptional service. Kitty Rosser argues that there is a need for lawyers to establish their true value: *"As individual lawyers it is incumbent upon us to simply keep up with the ever increasing array of legal software that we use on a daily basis, whether that be automated document creation and review, e-filing systems or document and knowledge management systems. At a firm level, as technology develops (particularly in the area of artificial intelligence) we need to be constantly asking what it is that we as lawyers bring to the table, what is the unique input, output or insight we offer that a machine, no matter how sophisticated, cannot?"*[4]

OUTCOME

22–3   In this short chapter we explain the main legaltech themes—from AI and automation to new services and approached to risk—that affects law firms in 2019 and we examine how they are both changing firms and your role as a lawyer.

TECHNOLOGY AND COMMUNICATIONS

22–4   There has been a seismic shift in communications, over recent years. Email has become the default method of communication, with some 281 billion emails sent every day, around the world.[5] Most solicitors have a smart phone that gives them access to their work email. According to LifeWire, 86% of professionals name email as their favourite method of communication, with 66% of emails being read on mobile devices.[6] Modern smart phones also have better network coverage than at any time before.

22–5   On one analysis this technological evolution is fantastic. You can reach clients (and potential clients) anywhere in the world at any time; but they also can reach

---

[3] Alexa Lemzy, "3 ways to improve customer care at your law firm, The Law Society, see *https://www.lawsociety.org.uk/news/blog/3-ways-to-improve-customer-care-at-your-law-firm/* [Accessed 25 February 2019].

[4] LexisPLS, "How Has Technology Changed the Legal Profession for Fee Earners", see *https://blogs.lexisnexis.co.uk/content/future-of-law/how-has-technology-changed-the-legal-profession-for-fee-earners* [Accessed 25 February 2019].

[5] Heinz Tschabitscher, "The Number of Emails Sent Per Day in 2019" (9 May 2019), *https://www.lifewire.com/how-many-emails-are-sent-every-day-1171210* [Accessed 24 February 2019].

[6] The Number of Emails Sent Per Day in 2019, *https://www.lifewire.com/how-many-emails-are-sent-every-day-1171210* [Accessed 24 February 2019]

you. Whilst that certainly expands your horizons in terms of the projects that you can get involved with, it does mean that you are increasingly working in a 24/7 legal market, which has 24/7 expectations.

This presents a client care challenge; lawyers are reporting anecdotally that face-to-face meetings are increasingly being replaced by telephones calls (or video conferencing), and that clients now expect a degree of responsiveness around all contact they have with your firm. Joanne Frears, of Blandy and Blandy, explores some of the issues around client expectations. She notes: *"Client expectations that you can always be reached have definitely changed in the last five years, as has their expectation that you will be using the same level of technology as they do—both in terms of hardware and software. Clients expect digital archiving and immediate recall of documents, ideally from a secure source, be it extranet or private cloud, with data rooms for day-to-day documentation as well as deals. Our clients also quite rightly expect that their lawyers will have excellent security and be able to spot a scam! All of this means that the role of lawyers has moved from custodian of knowledge for clients to curators of it."*[7]

As a new lawyer, its important not to let technology dictate how you deal with clients. You need to ask questions, and to speak to clients and contacts, to understand what they want. You cannot have a conversation by email. Andrew tells all his lawyers that he would much rather they picked up the phone and called him to discuss any difficult legal points than to have them send him an email. He might ask for an email afterwards, to help review documents or clauses, but a phone call can quickly identify whether the 'difficult legal point' is difficult or not. While buying a company, Andrew was contacted by a lawyer to warn him that a potential site was landlocked. It would have no access from a main road. Andrew was able to tell the firm that the site was being valued at £1 so there was no need to spend any time considering potential solutions. A five-minute phone call saved the many hours that would have gone into the email setting out the problem and solutions.

TECHNOLOGY AND NETWORKING

In the same way, a lot of business development is moving towards being conducted online. While there remain a large number of face-to-face networking events that solicitors can attend, many solicitors have Linkedin, Facebook, Twitter and other social media accounts. Many law firms use social media for PR. We discuss this further in Ch.6 (Clients and You).

22–6

---

[7] How Has Technology Changed the Legal Profession for Fee Earners, *https://blogs.lexisnexis.co.uk/content/future-of-law/how-has-technology-changed-the-legal-profession-for-fee-earners* [Accessed 25 February 2019].

TECHNOLOGY AND PRODUCTIVITY

22–7   The most obvious benefit of technology in a law practice is the efficiencies that it can produce. Let's look at two quick examples of how technology has improved the way lawyers work. By using technology to automate processes that would have been done by hand, lawyers can reduce the time they need to work on it—and reduce the cost to either reduce fees to clients or increase profits for the firm (or both).

Family law

22–8   Divorces can take a long time, with drawn out negotiations between each party. With technology the process can be handled in a mere sixteen to twenty weeks. For example, online websites such as *DivorceOnline.co.uk* are able to offer clients a choice of a DIY divorce service, or a more expensive managed divorce service.[8]

22–9   The former is only an option in amicable divorce settlements i.e. if the divorcing parties are broadly in agreement. However it is technology that has made it possible, streamlining things to a four step process whereby clients paying online, papers being prepared (presumably automatically) and emailed out, all within 24 hours.[9]

Immigration law

22–10   In the wake of the Brexit process, tens of thousands of EEA citizens were left wondering what might happen when the Uk left the European Union. To remain in the country, the Government indicated that they would have to apply for so-called indefinite leave. However, with over 3.5 million people affected, the immigration system clearly would be under pressure. To solve this, the Home Office created an online application process. The process would replace the 85-page form that otherwise would have to be returned by post, for processing. While applicants would still have to fill out a form with the same level of detail, the time spent processing the form would decrease.[10]

Conveyancing

22–11   A number of law firms provide dedicated online portals to customers of banks who are remortgaging their homes. The on-line portal provides access to documents required to complete the remortgage without the customer requiring to

---

[8] How Long Does a Quick Divorce Take if we Both Agree, *https://www.divorce-online.co.uk/blog/how-long-does-a-divorce-take/* [Accessed 24 February 2019].

[9] DIY Divorce Service, *https://www.divorce-online.co.uk/divorce-services/diy-divorce-services/diy-divorce* [Accessed 24 February 2019].

[10] Apply for a permanent residence document or permanent residence card: form EEA (PR), *https://www.gov.uk/government/publications/apply-for-a-permanent-residence-document-or-permanent-residence-card-form-eea-pr* [Accessed 25 February 2019].

speak to a lawyer. By completing information themselves, the customer is providing the law firm with all the information it needs to complete the remortgage almost automatically.

TECHNOLOGY AND AUTOMATION

Technology has opened up a huge array of opportunities for firms to automate aspect of its services, from internal reporting to external client facing work. The parameters really are limitless, so some short, illustrative examples follow.

22–12

Automated contracts

A smart suite of documents can link information from one document into others so that if, for example, you enter a client's name and details once, they are reused in all documents. A good example is with shopping centres, where a new tenant may receive a lease, a license to undertake fit out works, a side letter and, if it's a new development, an agreement for lease. Rather than enter the same information in every document, a smart suite of documents only requires the information once. This system may also have alerts so that expiration, renewal and/or cancellation dates are not missed.

22–13

The next step is for law firms to set up documents via a client-facing portal that deploys document automation to enable clients to generate documents 24/7, without needing to contact their lawyers. We know of one FTSE100 company that paid for its lawyers to produce an automatic settlement agreement so that its HR team could issue the agreement knowing that it was always up to date, and all they needed to do was to provide the name of the departing employee, the settlement amount and whether any restrictions applied.

On a related point, software can now automatically check documents. For example, JP Morgan's COIN system automatically interprets commercial loan agreements, saving the firm some 360,000 hours of time each year.[11]

22–14

Automated research

Software can now undertake research automatically and—in turn—automatically update styles. If you have clients who operate within a heavily regulated industry with lots of contract work, this will both save time and reduce risk, if best practice contract forms are updated with the most current regulations on file.[12]

22–15

---

[11] Hugh Son, JPMorgan Software Does in Seconds What Took Lawyers 360,000 Hours, *https://www.independent.co.uk/news/business/news/jp-morgan-software-lawyers-coin-contract-intelligence-parsing-financial-deals-seconds-legal-working-a7603256.html* [Accessed 25 February 2019].
[12] Thomson Reuters, "Top Ten Ways Technology Can Help Lawyers in Small Legal Departments Save Time and Reduce Risk", *https://legalsolutions.thomsonreuters.co.uk/content/dam/openweb/documents/pdf/uki-legal-solutions/quick-reference-guide/legal-tracker-top-ten-technology-small-law-firms.pdf* [Accessed 25 February 2019].

Automated updates

22–16   Matter management software can send out updates regarding client matters on a regular basis. This sort of automation helps you to set interim fee invoices. As you know, regular feeling is excellent for cash flow. What's more, regular updates keep your clients happy, because they naturally want to know what it is going on with their transaction. Timely correspondence sates that desire and—in turn—reduces the likelihood of a client complaining to your boss, or worse the regulator.

Automated expenses

22–17   It is possible to control how your fee earners record their expenses. All you need to do is input expense guidelines (or parameters) into a software package and it will flag any infringements. These can then be automatically reduced to fall back within the guidelines you set.

Automated reports

22–18   A whole raft of useful reports can now be automated. At the click of a button you can download WIP reports, client debtor reports, client conversion rate reports; the categories are endless.

Automated billing

22–19   You can automate your billing process by using ebilling software. That saves you and your PA the laborious job of manually narrating and processing fee invoices.

Automated legal holds

22–20   A legal hold is a process that an organisation uses to preserve all relevant information when litigation is anticipated. Software can now log all audit trail information relating to a legal hold process. Doing this manually takes hours and hours of time, and also opens up the chance of mistakes being made. Clearly, therefore, this sort of automation is a major time saver and a great risk management tool, since it will eliminate the possibility of errors emerging.

Automation of low-value legal work

22–21   Technology has the potential to automate all of your low-value, repetitive work, which clearly is hugely beneficial. For example, Telstra has been testing an automated non-disclosure agreement.[13]

One of the consequences of this sort of evolution is that inevitably it will mean that firms require fewer legal staff. Instead, it will be possible to use a more cost

---

[13] Telstra, Our Contracts, *https://www.telstraglobal.com/uk/company/our-contracts* [Accessed 25 February 2019].

effective member of staff to undertake both the automation and monitoring. That person could be a paralegal or even a law student.

Whilst this will improve the margin of low-value work and will reduce costs for clients, it does mean that competition for legal jobs will increase even further.

TECHNOLOGY AND FLEXIBILITY IN WORKING

One of the benefits of technology in the legal workplace is the work-flexibility that it enables. For example, most legal research is now conducted online, and as such it can be undertaken remotely. In turn, this means that team members do not need to be at their desk, in the office, and could instead do this sort of work from home, and at a time to suit them.

22–22

TECHNOLOGY AND RISK

Technology not only drives efficiency, it also removes human beings from legal processes. This, of course, removes the variable of human error, which should help your firm better control its risk management.

22–23

The optimal use of technology has to be one of your main strategies in minimising your exposure to client complaints (and possible claims) because it introduces a degree of structure and standardisation to your workflow.

It also improves organisation across your firm. By way of example, with automatic alert technology, you should never miss a calendar deadline (e.g. a deadline for personal injury, or tax deadlines for private client estate work).

By using cloud software, everyone in your firm can access files. It also means that your team is always able to see upcoming deadlines and important tasks, so long as they have an internet connection. This will significantly improve your processes and help mitigate avoidable, but costly mistakes.[14]

22–24

TECHNOLOGY AND ARTIFICIAL INTELLIGENCE

The automation of tasks is one thing, but technology can do a lot more than form filling! Artificial intelligence is the next big evolution within legal technology. It's almost impossible to attend a conference today and not have someone mention it. Though still in its infancy, artificial intelligence-powered tools have developed to a point where they can add real value to a law firm.

22–25

Artificial intelligence (AI)

What is AI?

AI is the term used when machines are able to complete tasks that otherwise requires human input.

22–26

---

[14] Three Ways Technology Will Make Better Lawyers, *https://lexicata.com/blog/3-ways-technology-will-make-better-lawyer/* [Accessed 25 February 2019].

What is machine learning?

22–27   The term machine learning describes the process whereby computers use algorithms to analyse data, learn patterns from that data and, finally, provide useful insights and conclusions.[15] Machine learning is regarded as a subset of AI, where ultimately machines learn and, over time, become incrementally "smarter".

Robot lawyers

22–28   Current discussions about AI, in the legal context, sadly tend to be apocalyptic in tone, using terms like 'robot lawyers'. This is perhaps unfortunate. It generates a degree of suspicion among professionals that they may soon be at risk of being replaced by machines.

22–29   While machines may indeed one day perform some tedious, repetitive (and cost intensive) tasks, we are a long way away—if ever—from having them replace real solicitors, who are able to bring to bear skill and nuanced judgment to client matters. Accordingly, perhaps a better way of viewing AI is as 'augmented intelligence'. In other words, solicitors still make the key legal judgments, but now have powerful tools to offer new insights.

22–30   The hyperbole around AI also overshadows meaningful developments within the domain of machine learning. Machine learning is improving the interaction between humans and computers, helping solicitors to gain legal insights from ever-growing data sets. If handled in the correct way, solicitors should get better results, more quickly, and at a lower cost.[16]

Decision-making

22–31   In cases where the law is clear and the facts are uncontested, in theory it should be possible for more mundane matters to be 'adjudicated by software'. Think of situations where perhaps you simply want to contest a fine. The law is crystal clear; the facts are clear; the stakes are low. AI could resolve issued like these. By way of example, eBay has confirmed that, in some cases, automated computer systems settle disputes between buyers and sellers. Ebay has said: *"There are some cases with specific criteria that are handled by computer assistance. In these instances algorithms are set to the same decision-making process as if handled by a customer service agent. If the case was to be reviewed by a customer service agent the outcome would be same as the decision-making process is aligned. All information within the case flow is reviewed to make a decision. Outcomes are based on the merit of the individual case."*[17]

22–32   In cases where the law is less clear or the facts hotly contended, however, it clearly would be more difficult. It would be hard to imagine a scenario where

---

[15] Bernard Marr, "How AI And Machine Learning Are Transforming Law Firms And The Legal Sector" (23 May 2018), Forbes, see *https://www.forbes.com/sites/bernardmarr/2018/05/23/how-ai-and-machine-learning-are-transforming-law-firms-and-the-legal-sector/#2da285b932c3* [Accessed 25 February 2019].

[16] Jeff Pfeifer, "The Data Driven Lawyer and the Future of Legal Technology (15 January 2018), see , *https://www.lawtechnologytoday.org/2018/01/the-data-driven-lawyer/* [Accessed 25 February 2019].

[17] Quoted in *https://tamebay.com/2015/05/computers-rule-on-some-ebay-uk-disputes.html* [Accessed 26 February 2019].

people would be comfortable with contentious cases being decided by AI. Moreover, a key element of the judicial system is the trust that people have in the judgment of its officials; arguably the average person would be more comfortable trusting a person than a line of code.

Chatbots

Chatbots emerged in 2016 as the friendly face of artificial intelligence (AI) in business. Chatbots make customer services immediately scalable as they bring the ability to handle multiple interactions at the same time without the need to employ extra staff. As AI makes them more sophisticated, some chatbots are trained to identify more complex queries and refer them to a human operator. They are also relatively straightforward to build using a third-party AI platform.   **22–33**

DoNotPay is a chatbot based that asks questions about parking tickets in order   **22–34** to find grounds to appeal them.[18] These tasks typically would have been carried out by junior lawyers (as part of their traineeships). DoNotPay uses natural language processing, eliminating the need for lawyers to become acquainted with the technicalities of the system because the work is done in text.

Liability

There is a question around liability that you should be aware of. Coders need   **22–35** legal help in order to write the code that underpins adjudication software or chatbots. This brings into question interesting issues of liability: what if the code leads to incorrect legal advice being given? Are the coders at fault and thus liable?

Technology and legal analytics

An equally promising technology is data analytics. Data analytics is offering real   **22–36** value to legal practitioners. Legal analytics power better decision-making in a number of legal practice areas such as patent and trademark law, copyright, securities and commercial litigation.

Data analytics works by mining massive data sets e.g. docket data, legislation, case opinions and client contracts. By processing this data, lawyers can draw conclusions about contract drafts, opposing solicitors, judges and the litigants, unlocking insights that previously were not knowable.

Analytics are also being used to improve the ways firm approach the business   **22–37** of law. It does so by providing factual data from litigation records about the behavior and performance of law firms, and even individual solicitors, including information around win rates, cases with resolutions, time to injunction, etc.[19]

---

[18] Appeal a Parking Ticket, *https://www.donotpay.com/parking/* [Accessed 25 February 2019].
[19] DoNotPay, "Appeal a Parking Ticket", https://www.donotpay.com/parking/ [Accessed 13 June 2019]. Bernard Marr, "How AI and Machine Learning are Transforming Law Firms and the Legal Sector" (23 May 2018), Forbes, *https://www.forbes.com/sites/bernardmarr/2018/05/23/how-ai-and-machine-learning-are-transforming-law-firms-and-the-legal-sector/#2da285b932c3* [Accessed 25 February 2019].

Analytics can also be used to track industry trends around business development and marketing.[20]

TECHNOLOGY AND NEW SERVICES

22–38 Another benefit of technology is how it opens up new service offerings. As technology changes, so does the services lawyers provide. Again, two examples illustrate the point.

Probate: digital legacies

22–39 While probate once dealt with physical things like homes, land, cars, stocks, shares and other possessions, the rise of digital property has raised questions about who owns our digital legacy after we die.

22–40 Clients now need to understand how their music, books and films might (or not) form part of their digital estate and how that might be handled in their will. These assets also now require valuation. Many personal assets will be of sentimental value, only. However, financial digital assets (online bank accounts, online stocks etc.) will have a value (perhaps a considerable value). These can be valued in the usual way i.e. the balance as at date of death.

22–41 There are some interesting assets that might throw up issues with valuation. Digital music and film collections can contain thousands of pounds worth of content, and there maybe instances when a client owns collections outright. For example, access to a work email might be of great commercial value (particularly to an employer or business partner). How do you even start to value it, if indeed you need to?

22–42 A related point is a deceased client's domain name. Is a domain name an asset? You can't buy them outright; you pay a fee for a period of exclusive use (albeit you always have first refusal upon renewal). If a domain name is to be included as an asset, it will need to be valued as at date of death. Services like *sedo.com* can help with a valuation.

In recent years there has been an increase in 'virtual goods' that generate billions of pounds of revenue each year. Put simply, virtual goods are non-physical, abstract objects that are traded in online gaming communities but do not equate to physical wealth. However, there have been notable exceptions, which mean that virtual goods and their value may need to be considered in an individual's estate upon death. In 2010, a player of Entropia Universe set a world record for the most expensive virtual item purchased, buying an asset for the equivalent of $100,000.

---

[20] Jeff Pfeifer, "The Data Driven Lawyer and the Future of Legal Technology (15 January 2018), see *https://www.lawtechnologytoday.org/2018/01/the-data-driven-lawyer/* [Accessed 25 February 2019].

Conveyancing

Property search sites have disrupted the traditional property industry. The revolution has spread to conveyancing, with several new companies offering digital conveyancing services, as an alternative to a traditional solicitor lead service.

22–43

A good example is Move Home Faster, which covers off every aspect of conveyancing online and by email.[21] Rather than these tech startups taking your market, law firms could realign themselves to take advantage of this shift in market consumption trends.

TECHNOLOGY AND FINANCE

Blockchain

Blockchain is a network that allows computers to reach agreement (based on consensus) over shared data. It creates a record of digital transactions that is then open to, and updated by, the public.[22] It can only be updated by the consensus of a majority of the participants in the system. Once entered, information can never be erased.

22–44

Blockchains use distributed ledger technology (DLT), which means that copies of a digital ledger are kept and maintained by many people (or organisations) and no copy is the master (thus the ledger is said to be both distributed and decentralised). Blockchains can be publicly or privately distributed and publicly or privately owned. The technology works without compromising privacy; you can record the fact that an event has happened without ever revealing confidential information about who was involved.

22–45

Bitcoin

Blockchain is best known as the technology behind the digital currency bitcoin. When devising bitcoin, its inventor's aim was to create a stateless virtual currency, not controlled by any bank or government. The issue, however, is that with no third-party guarantor, how can cheats be prevented from spending coins more than once? The solution has been to entrust oversight to the whole network: all transactions are marked on the blockchain, and maintained by a peer-to-peer community of computers (or 'nodes').

22–46

When users spend their coins, nodes update the ledger. The decentralised structure ensures that it is nearly impossible to hack the network, forge transactions or freeze them, for you would need to change every single node. An almost impossible task. Its uses in financial services and the capital markets are

---

[21] Move Home Faster, "Making Your Home Move Easier", see *https://movehomefaster.co.uk* . [Accessed 25 February 2019].
[22] Trent Dykes, "Getting up to Speed on Blockchain" (7 June 2017), The Venture Alley, see, *https://www.theventurealley.com/2017/06/getting-up-to-speed-on-blockchain/* [Accessed 25 February 2019].

rapidly developing.[23] However, there are many sceptics as to whether bitcoin will become a credible and widely used currency, and cryptocurrency scams are common.

Why is it useful to lawyers?

22–47   The software behind blockchain brings with it opportunities for new services or even to change existing ways of working. For example, because blockchains provides an irrefutable record of transactions, they offer possible solutions for property lawyers who want to verify the chain of ownership of properties in minutes, rather than in days or weeks.

SUMMARY

22–48   Just as technology can provide solutions, it also can throw up problems. Arguably, the biggest problem created by technology is the actual growth of data. Electronic communications—emails, automatically recorded phone calls and online messaging systems—mean the amount of data stored has ballooned. This has swelled the scope of litigation and regulatory reviews to a size that is hard to comprehend. A document review that twenty years ago might have involved 20,000 documents might now hit two million documents. Trainees and new lawyers spends weeks, if not months, reviewing documents day after day to find the one sentence or word that might win or lose a case.

Automation, AI and data analysis can help, but the challenge for law firms is that technology is both the source of—and solution to—these problems. As technology changes there is now a constant need to modernise, otherwise law firms will get left behind and be unable to provide the sort of service clients need. Your goal as new lawyers is to use your commercial awareness to understand which technologies will benefit you, which will directly or indirectly benefit your clients, and make sure that you provide service that clients want.

22–49   Andrew was approached by one firm that proudly told him that they had technologists review every aspect of their plot sale service. They had case management software, online tracking, they'd automated documents and could offer a service unrivalled by any other firm. When Andrew asked them for a quote for the 700 homes sold annually, they quoted 25% more than the firm he currently uses who keep track of all homes with a black and a white board on the wall of their office. Always remember that technology is only the right solution if you know the right problem to solve. For Andrew, the problem was cost. Could he reduce his annual spend on plot sales? For the law firm, it was paperwork. They wanted to reduce the amount of paper used—and presumably to reduce their own costs. But when they didn't pass that saving on to their client, they missed out on a new instruction.

22–50   Alongside the growth in data is the question over who has access to this data. As recent scandals involving Facebook have shown, there is increased scrutiny

---

[23] Blockchain, *https://uk.practicallaw.thomsonreuters.com/w-005-9053?transitionType= Default&contextData=(sc.Default)&firstPage=true&comp=pluk&bhcp=1* [Accessed 25 February 2019].

around the world as to how our personal information is being used. The General Data Protection Regulations (GDPR) came into force on 25 May 2018 and was designed to modernise laws that protect individual's personal information. As lawyers, we understand confidentiality and ensuring clients information is protected but law firms are no more immune to hacking than any other organization as the 'Panama Papers' showed due to the unprecedented leak of 11.5m files from the database of the world's fourth biggest offshore law firm, Mossack Fonseca. GDPR has created not just new services for lawyers but also a renewed focus on understanding, controlling and protecting data.

TECHNOLOGY AND NEW ROLES

Within firms, technology has impacted on traditional, established roles: lawyers, business development, knowledge management and IT. For all of the reasons outlined in this chapter, everyone has to be better geared to harness the opportunities that technology can bring. **22–51**

It remains to be seen whether the use of increasingly sophisticated tech will lead to fewer solicitors being employed. At the lower value end of the spectrum, as we've seen, certainly it makes sense to use automation. But, does that mean that there will be fewer lawyers? **22–52**

It is arguable that in fact lawyers shouldn't be doing low-level tasks anyway, and that they instead should be tasked to higher value work, where they can unlock bigger margins for firms[24]. Having spare capacity at that pay-grade also opens up the opportunity for firms to redeploy these resources to new service areas, as part of a diversification strategy. However, the future law firms will have legal designers to transform how services are provided, pricing managers to ensure clients are charged a price that will help the firm return a profit, legal project managers who manage teams without managing the work itself. All these and other new roles will see new opportunities open up for new lawyers.

For example, Addleshaw Goddard's young lawyers can now qualify within the firm's innovation and legal technology team. The team is one of the first at the firm to have dedicated legal technologist trainees.[25] The firm is also establishing rolling six-month secondments for lawyers from each of its divisions to work within the legal technology team, in order that they can gain experience developing new technology platforms and solutions, as well as skills like coding, data capture and analytics. **22–53**

Kerry Westland, the firm's Head of Innovation and Legal Technology, says: *"With three trainees currently in the team, we have seen directly the benefits these roles bring. Their training contract gives them the unique ability to see how technology can help address internal or client challenges. Offering a seat within*

---

[24] We would recommend any textbook by Richard Susskind and, in particular, his seminal "The End of Lawyers", 2nd edn (USA: Oxford University Press, 2010). LawCareers.Net, "Addleshaw Goddard creates new role of legal technology associate" (3 April 2018), see *https://www.lawcareers.net/Information/News/Addleshaw-Goddard-creates-new-role-of-legal-technology-associate-03042018* [Accessed 13 June 2019].
[25] LawCareers.Net, Addleshaw Goddard Creates New Role of Legal Technology Associate, *https://www.lawcareers.net/Information/News/Addleshaw-Goddard-creates-new-role-of-legal-technology-associate-03042018* [Accessed 28 February 2019].

the team also ensures that our future lawyers will become equipped with additional skills that the lawyer of the future requires."[26]

Legal Engineering

22-54   One new role in particular has started to gain attention. Commentators believes that a distinction will emerge between firms that are prepared for the future and those that are not.[27] They suggest that this requires a mind-set change, and that firms need so-called 'legal engineers' who can identify opportunities to improve existing ways of working and deliver innovative solutions, all the while integrating legal knowledge and technological know-how.

22-55   Legal engineers use legal knowledge and tech know-how to optimise products, services and processes, and to create new solutions for clients. They could be a technologist who is familiar with legal processes, or a lawyer who is tech savvy. Technology itself is not the differentiator; it's how you use it. As Barr says: *"It's what you write in the Word document that differentiates you, not the fact that it's written in Word."*[28]

TECHNOLOGY AND COMMERCIAL AWARENESS

22-56   When you learn to drive you learn how to react in different circumstances. You learn how to reverse the car, to turn it in tight spots, to spot dangers and to drive safely in traffic. All of these different skills—and the knowledge you need to use them—combine to show people how you behave when you drive.

When you learn commercial awareness you're also demonstrating a variety of skills (and the knowledge underlying them) to show people how you behave. Take time management. It's not enough to say that you can delegate work to a trainee or your secretary because you know it saves time, you actually have to do it. You need to speak to them, pass over the file, and be responsible for what they do. Or take professionalism. If you want people to say that you're a good professional, then you need to know the code of conduct and principles so that you can spot professional issues (such as conflicts of interest) when they arise. Then you need to deal with them effectively, for example by speaking to clients and getting their consent to act or by refusing to act for one or more people. It's not enough to just spot a conflict, you need to act and deal with it to. You're using both your knowledge and your skill.

Technology is no different. It requires both the knowledge to use it along with the skill to put it into use. To take a simple example, it's not enough to know that your phone allows you to call people, you need call someone and talk.

When we started to think about commercial awareness we kept coming back to technology, because technology is always changing, just as is commercial awareness. When we discussed what topics to cover in this book we hesitated

---

[26] *ibid.*

[27] Stuart Barr, The Rise of the Legal Engineer, *https://blog.highq.com/enterprise-collaboration/the-rise-of-the-legal-engineer* [Accessed 28 February 2019].

[28] Stuart Barr, The Rise of the Legal Engineer, *https://blog.highq.com/enterprise-collaboration/the-rise-of-the-legal-engineer* [Accessed 28 February 2019].

before selecting them because any list runs the risk of being prescriptive and closed. Commerciality is a concept in flux. Just as fashions change, so does the knowledge and skills needed to show commercial awareness. The categories of what might be regarded as commercially aware continue to change in response to changes within the legal market, and also with technological advances. For example, fifteen years ago you wouldn't have thought of social media as a major part of your networking strategy to win new business. Equally, the idea that clients would obtain legal advice from a chatbot was science fiction. Today, some lawyers don't just write laws, they also code. If you were a lawyer during those fifteen years your knowledge would have to change to remain relevant, and—yes—commercially aware.

Jeff Bezos, the founder of Amazon, was once asked about predicting the future. This is what he said: *"I very frequently get the question: 'What's going to change in the next ten years?' And that is a very interesting question; it's a very common one. I almost never get the question: 'What's not going to change in the next ten years?' And I submit to you that that second question is actually the more important of the two—because you can build a business strategy around the things that are stable in time."*[29]

That's why the most important things you need to know as you start your career is not just what will change, but also what will stay the same. You will still be a lawyer. And you will still need to be commercially aware and know that:

- Commercial awareness means knowing what it means to be a lawyer.
- Commercial awareness means knowing the impact your advice has on your clients.
- Commercial awareness means knowing how to run a business and make money.

And that will remain true whether you start in the high street, in a rural town, in a big city, London or around the world in-house or in private practice. We want you to be a modern lawyer with commercial awareness.

---

[29] Jillian D'Onfro, "Jeff Bezos' brilliant advice for anyone running a business" (31 January 2015), *Business Insider*, see *https://www.businessinsider.com/jeff-bezos-brilliant-advice-for-anyone-running-a-business-2015-1?r=US&IR=T* [Accessed 29 February 2019].

APPENDIX 1

Goal setting form

WHAT IS YOUR GOAL:

Summary: A1–1
How is it SPECIFIC?
How will it be MEASURABLE?
Is it ATTAINABLE?
Is it RELEVANT?
What is your TIMELINE?

ACTION PLAN

Identify practical steps you need to take to achieve your goal.
1.
2.
3.

OBSTACLES

Identify any obstacles that might stand in the way of you achieving your goal. What is your strategy for dealing with them?
1.
2.
3.

ASSISTANCE

Identify any people who could help you achieve your goal.
1.
2.
3.

Identify any resources that you might use to help you achieve your goal.
1.
2.
3.

APPENDIX 2

Priority Matrix

A2–1

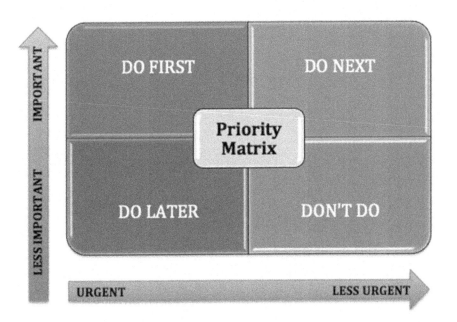

APPENDIX 3

Blueprints

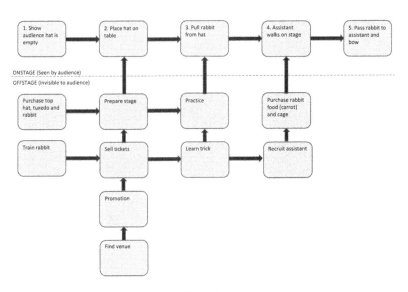

Figure 1

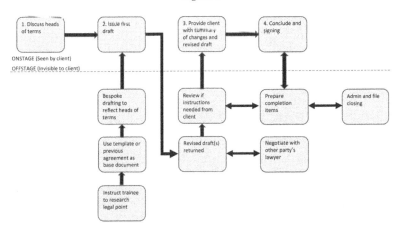

Figure 2

APPENDIX 4

Gantt Chart

Please see the Gantt chart on the next page.

A4–1

357

IMPORTANT CLIENT - NEW WILL & PoA
SIM & TODD LLP

Project Lead: Andy Todd
Project Start Date: 02-Sep-19
Display Week: 1

WBS	Task	Lead	Predecessor	Start	End	Cal. Days	% Done	Work Days
1	INSTRUCTIONS	AT						
1.1	Arrange meeting	A Todd		Mon 02/9/19	Mon 02/9/19	1	100%	1
1.2	Engagement letter / T.o.B	A Todd		Mon 02/9/19	Mon 02/9/19	1	100%	1
1.3	Practical: room/agenda etc	J Smith	1.2	Tue 03/9/19	Wed 04/9/19	2	50%	2
1.4	Meeting - take instructions	A Todd	1.1	Thu 05/9/19	Thu 05/9/19	1	0%	1
1.5	Dictate file note	A Todd	1.4	Thu 05/9/19	Thu 05/9/19	1	0%	1
1.6	Follow-up letter to client	A Todd	1.4	Fri 06/9/19	Fri 06/9/19	1	0%	1
2	DRAFTING	AT						
2.1	Team meeting - delegate work	A Todd	1.4	Mon 09/9/19	Mon 09/9/19	1	0%	1
2.2	Drafting Will	J Smith	2.1	Tue 10/9/19	Tue 10/9/19	1	0%	1
2.3	Drafting PoA	J Smith	2.2	Wed 11/9/19	Wed 11/9/19	1	0%	1
2.4	Checking drafts	A Todd	2.3	Thu 12/9/19	Fri 13/9/19	2	0%	2
3	CLIENT	AT						
3.1	Send drafts to client (inc review time)	J Smith	2.4	Mon 16/9/19	Fri 20/9/19	5	0%	5
3.2	Follow-up call for instructions	A Todd	3.1	Fri 20/9/19	Fri 20/9/19	1	0%	1
3.3	Revisals	J Smith	3.2	Fri 20/9/19	Fri 20/9/19	1	0%	1
4	SIGNING	AT						
4.1	Arrange meeting	J Smith	3.3	Mon 23/9/19	Mon 23/9/19	1	0%	1
4.2	Practical: room/agenda etc	J Smith	3.3	Mon 23/9/19	Mon 23/9/19	1	0%	1
4.3	Prepare principals	J Smith	4.2	Mon 23/9/19	Mon 23/9/19	1	0%	1
4.4	Meeting client - review docs and sign	A Todd	4.3	Tue 24/9/19	Tue 24/9/19	1	0%	1
5	POST-SIGNING	AT						
5.1	Register PoA with OPG	J Smith	4.4	Tue 24/9/19	Tue 24/9/19	1	0%	1
5.2	Send copies to client	J Smith	4.4	Tue 24/9/19	Tue 24/9/19	1	0%	1
5.3	Store principals in safe	J Smith	4.4	Tue 24/9/19	Tue 24/9/19	1	0%	1
5.4	Follow up letter to client	A Todd	5.2	Wed 25/9/19	Wed 25/9/19	1	0%	1
5.5	Fee note to client	J Smith	5.2	Wed 25/9/19	Wed 25/9/19	1	0%	1
5.6	De-brief	A Todd	5.5	Fri 27/9/19	Fri 27/9/19	1	0%	1

Week 1 — 02/09/2019
Week 2 — 09/09/2019
Week 3 — 16/09/2019
Week 4 — 23/09/2019

INDEX

LEGAL TAXONOMY
FROM SWEET & MAXWELL

This index has been prepared using Sweet & Maxwell's Legal Taxonomy. Main index entries conform to keywords provided by the Legal Taxonomy except where references to specific documents or non-standard terms (denoted by quotation marks) have been included. These keywords provide a means of identifying similar concepts in other Sweet & Maxwell publications and online services to which keywords from the Legal Taxonomy have been applied. Readers may find some minor differences between terms used in the text and those which appear in the index. Suggestions to *sweetandmaxwell.taxonomy@tr.com*.

All references are to paragraph number

risk, definition of, 16–4
risk identification
  common-risk checking, 16–25—16–26
  exercise, 16–28
  four Cs task, 16–29
  identifying outcome required, 16–21
  objectives-based risk identification, 16–22
  outcome, 16–20
  problem analysis, 16–19
  risk charting, 16–27
  scenario-based risk identification, 16–23
  selecting type of risk, 16–17
  source analysis, 16–18
  taxonomy-based risk identification, 16–24
risk management plans, 16–37
risk reduction, 16–34
risk sharing, 16–35
summary, 16–38
Rule of law
professional standards, 3–10
"Rural firms"
career options, 1–62
Savings
bank and building society accounts, 18–18
National Savings and Investments
  Children's Bonds, 18–31
  current accounts, 18–21
  generally, 18–20
  Income Bonds, 18–29
  Premium Bonds, 18–32
  savings accounts, 18–22
  Savings Certificates, 18–30
Scotland
career options, 1–60
Segmentation
see **Marketing**
Senior partners
generally, 1–22
Seven Ps
see **Marketing**
Shares
ordinary shares, 18–33
preference shares, 18–34
"Silver Circle"
career options, 1–57
SMART
see **"Goal setting"**
Snapchat
social media, 6–35
Social media
blogs, 6–34
Facebook, 6–30
generally, 6–29
LinkedIn, 6–32
Pinterest, Instagram, Snapchat and other photo
  sharing sites, 6–35
time management, 12–9
Twitter, 6–31

YouTube and other video sharing sites, 6–33
Sole traders
advantages, 4–38
business name, 4–33
business planning, 4–31
compliance, 4–35
disadvantages, 4–39
formation, 4–32
generally, 4–30
key features, 4–34
local authority licences, 4–37
tax and NICs, 4–36
VAT, 4–36
Speaking to clients
see **Meetings**
Stamp taxes
generally, 18–67
State pension
generally, 18–23—18–25
Stockbrokers
business clients, 2–30—2–31
Students
transition to trainee solicitor, 1–4—1–5
Success fees
generally, 10–24
Takeovers
generally, 4–17
Tax
business rates, 18–68
capital gains tax, 18–66
corporation tax, 18–64
direct taxes, 18–62
generally, 18–61
income tax, 18–63
indirect taxes, 18–69
limited companies, 4–79
limited liability partnerships, 4–64
national insurance contributions, 18–65
partnerships, 4–49
sole traders, 4–36
stamp taxes, 18–67
VAT
  definition, 18–70
  effect on businesses, 18–73
  exempt and zero-rated supplies, 18–72
  how VAT works, 18–71
  introduction, 18–69
"Teams"
choosing a team, 14–25
definition, 14–24
diversity
  discrimination, 21–13
  ethnocentrism, 21–16
  introduction, 21–11
  multicultural teams, 21–31
  prejudice, 21–12
  stereotyping, 21–14—21–15
introduction, 14–25

INDEX